Barbados

WORLD BIBLIOGRAPHICAL SERIES

General Editors:
Robert L. Collison (Editor-in-chief)
Sheila R. Herstein
Louis J. Reith
Hans H. Wellisch

VOLUMES IN THE SERIES

1 *Yugoslavia*, John J. Horton
2 *Lebanon*, Shereen Khairallah
3 *Lesotho*, Shelagh M. Willet and David Ambrose
4 *Rhodesia/Zimbabwe*, Oliver B. Pollack and Karen Pollack
5 *Saudi Arabia*, Frank A. Clements
6 *USSR*, Anthony Thompson
7 *South Africa*, Reuben Musiker
8 *Malawi*, Robert B. Boeder
9 *Guatemala*, Woodman B. Franklin
11 *Uganda*, Robert L. Collison
12 *Malaysia*, Ian Brown and Rajeswary Ampalavanar
13 *France*, Frances Chambers
14 *Panama*, Eleanor DeSelms Langstaff
15 *Hungary*, Thomas Kabdebo
16 *USA*, Sheila R. Herstein and Naomi Robbins
17 *Greece*, Richard Clogg and Mary Jo Clogg
18 *New Zealand*, R. F. Grover
19 *Algeria*, Richard I. Lawless
20 *Sri Lanka*, Vijaya Samaraweera
21 *Belize*, Ralph Lee Woodward, Jr.
23 *Luxembourg*, Carlo Hury and Jul Christophory
24 *Swaziland*, Balam Nyeko
25 *Kenya*, Robert L. Collison
26 *India*, Brijen K. Gupta and Datta S. Kharbas
27 *Turkey*, Meral Güçlü
28 *Cyprus*, P. M. Kitromilides and M. L. Evriviades
29 *Oman*, Frank A. Clements
31 *Finland*, J. E. O. Screen
32 *Poland*, Richard C. Lewański
33 *Tunisia*, Allan M. Findlay, Anne M. Findlay and Richard I. Lawless
34 *Scotland*, Eric G. Grant
35 *China*, Peter Cheng
36 *Qatar*, P. T. H. Unwin
37 *Iceland*, John J. Horton
39 *Haiti*, Frances Chambers
40 *Sudan*, M. W. Daly
41 *Vatican City State*, Michael J. Walsh
42 *Iraq*, A. J. Abdulrahman

43 *United Arab Emirates*, Frank A. Clements
44 *Nicaragua*, Ralph Lee Woodward, Jr.
45 *Jamaica*, K. E. Ingram
46 *Australia*, I. Kepars
47 *Morocco*, Anne M. Findlay, Allan M. Findlay and Richard I. Lawless
48 *Mexico*, Naomi Robbins
49 *Bahrain*, P. T. H. Unwin
50 *The Yemens*, G. Rex Smith
51 *Zambia*, Anne M. Bliss, J. A. Rigg
52 *Puerto Rico*, Elena E. Cevallos
53 *Namibia*, Stanley Schoeman and Elna Schoeman
54 *Tanzania*, Colin Darch
55 *Jordan*, Ian J. Seccombe
56 *Kuwait*, Frank A. Clements
57 *Brazil*, Solena V. Bryant
58 *Israel*, Esther M. Snyder (preliminary compilation E. Kreiner)
59 *Romania*, Andrea Deletant and Dennis Deletant
60 *Spain*, Graham J. Shields
61 *Atlantic Ocean*, H. G. R. King
63 *Cameroon*, Mark W. Delancey and Peter J. Schraeder
64 *Malta*, John Richard Thackrah
65 *Thailand*, Michael Watts
66 *Austria*, Denys Salt with the assistance of Arthur Farrand Radley
67 *Norway*, Leland B. Sather
68 *Czechoslovakia*, David Short
69 *Irish Republic*, Michael Owen Shannon
70 *Pacific Basin and Oceania*, Gerald W. Fry and Rufino Mauricio
71 *Portugal*, P. T. H. Unwin
73 *Syria*, Ian J. Seccombe
74 *Trinidad and Tobago*, Frances Chambers
76 *Barbados*, Robert B. Potter and Graham M. S. Dann
77 *East Germany*, Ian Wallace

VOLUME 76

Barbados

Robert B. Potter
Graham M. S. Dann
Compilers

CLIO PRESS

OXFORD, ENGLAND · SANTA BARBARA, CALIFORNIA
DENVER, COLORADO

British Library Cataloguing in Publication Data

Potter, Robert B.
Barbados.——(World bibliographical series; no. 76)
1. Barbados——Bibliography
I. Title   II. Dann, Graham   III. Series
016.97298'1   Z1561.B3

ISBN 1-85109-022-3

Clio Press Ltd.,
55 St. Thomas' Street.
Oxford OX1 1JG, England.

ABC-Clio Information Services.
Riviera Campus, 2040 Alameda Padre Serra.
Santa Barbara, Ca. 93103, USA.

Designed by Bernard Crossland
Typeset by Columns Design and Production Services, Reading, England
Printed and bound in Great Britain by
Billing and Sons Ltd., Worcester

THE WORLD BIBLIOGRAPHICAL SERIES

This series will eventually cover every country in the world, each in a separate volume comprising annotated entries on works dealing with its history, geography, economy and politics: and with its people, their culture, customs, religion and social organization. Attention will also be paid to current living conditions – housing, education, newspapers, clothing, etc. – that are all too often ignored in standard bibliographies; and to those particular aspects relevant to individual countries. Each volume seeks to achieve, by use of careful selectivity and critical assessment of the literature, an expression of the country and an appreciation of its nature and national aspirations, to guide the reader towards an understanding of its importance. The keynote of the series is to provide, in a uniform format, an interpretation of each country that will express its culture, its place in the world, and the qualities and background that make it unique.

SERIES EDITORS

Robert L. Collison (Editor-in-chief) is Professor Emeritus, Library and Information Studies, University of California, Los Angeles, and is currently the President of the Society of Indexers. Following the war, he served as Reference Librarian for the City of Westminster and later became Librarian to the BBC. During his fifty years as a professional librarian in England and the USA, he has written more than twenty works on bibliography, librarianship, indexing and related subjects.

Sheila R. Herstein is Reference Librarian and Library Instruction Co-ordinator at the City College of the City University of New York. She has extensive bibliographic experience and has described her innovations in the field of bibliographic instruction in 'Team teaching and bibliographic instruction'. *The Bookmark*, Autumn 1979. In addition, Doctor Herstein co-authored a basic annotated bibliography in history for Funk & Wagnalls *New encyclopedia*, and for several years reviewed books for *Library Journal*.

Louis J. Reith is librarian with the Franciscan Institute, St. Bonaventure University, New York. He received his PhD from Stanford University, California, and later studied at Eberhard-Karls-Universität, Tübingen. In addition to his activities as a librarian, Dr. Reith is a specialist on 16th-century German history and the Reformation and has published many articles and papers in both German and English. He was also editor of the *American Society for Reformation Research Newsletter*.

Hans H. Wellisch is a Professor at the College of Library and Information Services, University of Maryland, and a member of the American Society of Indexers and the International Federation for Documentation. He is the author of numerous articles and several books on indexing and abstracting, and has also published *Indexing and abstracting: an international bibliography*. He also contributes frequently to *Journal of the American Society for Information Science, Library Quarterly*, and *The Indexer*.

76702

For
Virginia and Elizabeth

Contents

Contents

Contents

Introduction

The most easterly of the Caribbean chain of islands, Barbados is located at approximately 13° N and 59° W, measuring some thirty-two by twenty-three km, and with a total surface area of 430 square km. At the last census conducted in 1980, this small island was home to 248,983 people, with an overall population density of 578 persons per square km, making it one of the most densely populated territories in the world. Unlike its neighbouring islands, Barbados is non-volcanic in origin and its present-day surface has resulted from the uplift of coral limestone rock which was deposited under marine conditions in geologically recent times. This coral cap, which covers eighty-five per cent of the surface of the island, was formed upon sticky white clay-like rocks known as the Oceanic beds, which in turn cover the basement rocks of Barbados, referred to as the Scotland series. These latter beds consist of thick layers of sedimentary rocks, mainly shales, sands, clays and conglomerates. Today, it is only in the north-eastern section of the island, known as the Scotland District on account of its hilly topography, that erosion has exposed these basal rocks. The remainder of Barbados is relatively flat and undulating, consisting of a series of coral terraces, the edges of which represent fossil cliffs cut by the sea as the land surface was being uplifted. The highest point on the island is Mount Hillaby, which reaches an altitude of 335 metres above sea level.

Barbados experienced continuous British rule from 1627 to 1966, when it gained full independence. Soon after initial colonization, plantation-type sugar cultivation had been established and for the next three centuries continued to dominate the island's agriculture. Although there have been recent attempts at agricultural diversification, Barbados has continued to concentrate almost exclusively on the production of sugar, with little emphasis being placed on alternative fruit and vegetable crops.

Introduction

Thus, in spite of the sporadic cultivation of bananas, guava, citrus, soursop (a local high-vitamin cherry), breadfruit, avocado, yam, sweet potato and cassava, and comparatively small cotton, livestock and fishing industries, Barbados continues to face an annual food import bill in the region of seventy-five million US dollars. However, since 1960, change has been quite substantial, particularly with regard to the economy. For example, during this period, Barbados moved from being what the United Nations describes as a 'non-industrial' country to an 'industrializing' one, and both tourism and manufacturing currently contribute significantly more to gross domestic product than sugar. Equally saliently, perhaps, marked social changes have occurred during the period since the 1960s.

History

When Portuguese navigators first sighted the island in 1536, they allegedly named it after the bearded fig trees they discovered growing there. Although they found Barbados uninhabited, archaeological evidence points to permanent settlement of the island by Barrancoid Indians from around the time of Christ, and to a four- or five-hundred-year Arawak presence from about 1,000 AD onwards. It was not until 1627, however, that Barbados was colonized by eighty English settlers under William Courteen. They landed in Jamestown, now Holetown, the same spot which had been claimed for king and country some two years earlier by a group of compatriots sailing in the good ship *Olive Blossom*. From there Courteen's men quickly established their headquarters, and appointed a governor, William Dean.

Although these early years were characterized by inter-group rivalry and disputes over proprietorship, nevertheless a pattern of administration was soon established with the division of the island into parishes between 1629 and 1645, and the establishment of a parliament in 1639. Lack of agricultural produce and expertise was remedied by a mission to present-day Guyana. This resulted in the importation of crops and forty Arawaks, and, with the help of Irish and Scottish indentured labour, the subsequent cultivation of indigo and tobacco. When these commodities ceased to be economically viable, the planters turned their attention to sugar, news of which had been supplied by the Dutch trading from Pernambuco in Brazil. The changeover from tobacco to sugar was coterminous with the commencement of imported slave labour from Africa, with the realization that the latter offered far greater profitability than mere reliance on the sickly efforts of social outcasts from the mother country. The decision to cultivate sugar also resulted in a transformation of the agricultural sector from a collection of small-holdings to a plantation economy. Without the prospect of a secure livelihood, many white labourers consequently emigrated, only to have their places in the sun taken by black slaves.

Despite initial difficulties, and the occasional ravages of hurricane, drought and disease, sugar cultivation rapidly became big business and formed a solid basis for the island's import-export trade. As a result, more and more Englishmen, particularly those opposed to Cromwell's rule, turned to Barbados as an opportunity to redeem their fortunes. With a swelling of the ranks of those in favour of the Royalist cause, it is no small wonder that the Cavaliers of Barbados strongly resisted Roundhead attempts to diminish their independence. Even when a task force headed by Ayscue in 1652 forced their eventual surrender, they still managed to negotiate very favourable terms of agreement in what was to form the basis for the constitution of the island, with its firm guarantees of civil and religious rights. Not surprisingly, there are several commentators who view this episode as characteristic of a Barbadian spirit of autonomy, one which resurfaced time and again in disputes between governors and assemblymen, in local opposition to the hated stamp duty of 1663, in the confederation crisis of 1876, and indeed, many would argue, one which is still evident today.

The iniquitous system of slavery lasted almost two hundred years in Barbados, for emancipation was not proclaimed until 1834, some twenty-seven years after the abolition of the slave trade, with its associated auctions of human cargoes which had managed to survive the notorious Middle Passage. Notwithstanding non-conformist protest to the contrary, and the religious instruction received on the Codrington estates, slaves were generally regarded as little more than beasts of burden, without redeemable souls, and without languages and cultures of their own. Instead they were simply viewed as objects of labour whose stock could be replenished by successful breeding management. Not surprisingly, today there is little remaining of their rich cultural heritage, and men continue to be marginal to a family life characterized by a seventy-eight per cent illegitimacy rate.

Even after a four-year system of apprenticeship, the former slaves in 1838 could still hardly regard themselves as completely free men. The fact that there was virtually no alternative employment, that agricultural land was almost entirely devoted to sugar, and that there was little absentee ownership, meant in practice that they were still tied to plantation tenantries, exchanging labour for a small house spot which did not belong to them. Furthermore, in spite of recent legislation to the contrary, remnants of this situation continue in contemporary Barbados, where many own small wooden chattel houses on plantation land. Indeed, fifty-seven per cent of the present housing stock is built entirely of timber, and virtually fifty per cent has exceeded its twenty-year life expectancy.

The contemporary situation and patterns of progress

In other respects, however, Barbados has come a long way since the days of slavery. In education, for example, whereas schooling was reserved exclusively for whites until the opening of St. Mary's School for coloured boys in 1818, today, thanks to the reforms of men such as Mitchinson and Rawle, and with certain reservations as to the relevance of the curriculum and the quality of teaching, Barbadians now enjoy free education from the primary to tertiary level. Additionally, they have access to a community college, a polytechnic, a local campus of the University of the West Indies, and several evening institutes. There are also facilities for the training of teachers, ministers of religion, policemen, doctors and lawyers, and specialized programmes are offered for the acquisition of technical and managerial skills.

Politically, too, Barbados has moved from a situation of total disenfranchisement of the black majority to one in which there is a theoretical, if not practical, thriving independent parliamentary democracy and mass participation in the electoral process. Yet such a state of affairs is only comparatively recent, given that full adult franchise was not attained until 1950, and a ministerial system of government was not established until 1954. Prior to these reforms, executive powers lay with the governor and his committee, acting with various degrees of willingness in accordance with the wishes of the Colonial Office.

Progress has also been made in the domain of health. From a situation in which the population was routinely exposed to epidemics of cholera, typhoid, dysentery, smallpox and yellow fever, today Barbados boasts a 600-bed teaching hospital, an institution for the mentally sick, a series of welfare agencies and district polyclinics, and a not unreasonable patient/doctor ratio among its well-trained corps of private medical practitioners. Additionally, there is a satisfactory and regular sanitation service, and an excellent supply of pure water available to practically every household most of the time. Consequently, life expectancy has risen from approximately twenty-eight years at the turn of the century to a current average figure in excess of seventy years. Since the advent of family planning in 1955, and with the combined effect of emigration, the birth rate has also been halved from roughly thirty-three per thousand to just under seventeen per thousand today.

Employment opportunities have correspondingly increased. Whereas in former years the means of livelihood were traditionally restricted to agriculture and the female occupations of seamstress and hawker, now tourism and light manufacturing have overtaken the sugar-dominated economy to the extent that they jointly provide numerous private sector opportunities. When these are combined with the retail trade, construction, banking and insurance, together with openings in the civil service, Barbadians, in spite of sometimes disappointing levels of employment, can consider themselves fortunate when compared to their counterparts in the rest of the developing world. At the same time, a responsible and cohesive trade union movement has overridden criticism in its attempts to safeguard the rights of workers and the preservation of a living wage. Going hand in hand with employment, there has also been a relatively successful management of the economy, to the extent that the country is not excessively overburdened with foreign debt, and inflation, running at single digits, is well under control. Development loans are forthcoming from international agencies, and the island has never come under persistent pressure to devalue its currency.

Transport and communication are other areas in which substantial progress has been achieved. From the days of the camel and horse, when an internal network of cart tracks existed principally to link plantations with a number of small ports, and eventually with Bridgetown, Barbados now has an efficient deep water harbour suitable for container vessels, a modern international airport, and both public and private bus transportation systems which convey thousands about their business along 1360 km of paved roads of varying quality. Additionally, there is a good, though expensive, digital telephone system reaching every continent, a fair to moderate international postal service, and advanced satellite and inter-computer communication. Both the local and available overseas press offers unrestricted coverage of, and commentary on, national, regional and international news, as to a lesser extent do the less sophisticated electronic media. Consequently, and with few limitations, Barbados understandably sees itself as a more developed country on the threshold of the post-industrial era, ready to take advantage of the technological progress that it has made.

Needless to say, there are inevitable problems associated with such rapid social change. Possibly the greatest of these is a growing secularization and the concomitant quest for a good life of material comfort, aided and abetted by the demonstration effect of tourism: today the annual number of visitors outstrips the local population by a ratio of three to two. Another dilemma relates to the island's Caribbean identity. Precisely as a result of the developed facilities offered by Barbados, several regional and international organizations have chosen the island as their headquarters. Barbados thus tends to view itself as somehow different from its neighbours, and, in many ways, a cut above the rest. At the same time, it recognizes that it is expected to cooperate with such regional institutions as CARICOM, the CXC Examinations Council and the Caribbean Development Bank.

Ironically, while insiders tend to emphasize the idiosyncratic features of the island, outsiders often stress West Indian territorial similarities. There is thus a prevailing dichotomy between individual insularity and regional collectivity, the familiar philosophical problem of one and many. The tension is further aggravated when Barbados' links with the former colonial power become highlighted to the point where its principle of individuation is interpreted as residing in a microcosmic anglophilism, a topic worthy of separate consideration, and one to which we now turn.

Little England

For one reason or another, Barbados over the years has come to be described as 'Little England'. Travel accounts, both early and contemporary, have underlined the comparison between the island and the mother country by pointing to such similarities as the pastel-shaded rolling landscape, driving on the left, the Westminster-style parliament, the law courts with their bewigged judges, the educational system with its élite colleges of Harrison and Queen's resembling those of Eton and Roedean, and even the emulation of the eleven-plus examination and comprehensive schools as a reflection of Britain a decade or so ago. Then there is the police force with its resplendent uniform and observation of Scotland Yard ranking and procedure, the Anglican Church with its choir boys, ritual, vestments, hymns, psalms and Canterbury intonation, and the exclusive Bridgetown and Royal Barbados Yacht clubs modelled on the segregationist policies of their City of London professional counterparts. If that is not enough, then place names such as Worthing, Hastings and Trafalgar Square, with its statue of Lord Nelson, are sufficient to conjure up the idea of a tropical Tewkesbury-on-Sea. Even the local football teams carry such names as Everton, United and Spurs.

However, it is in the game of cricket that the greatest resemblance lies, for herein can be learned all the gentlemanly virtues of honour, team spirit, respect for authority, grit, endurance, stiff upper lip in times of adversity, being a good loser, and doing one's best for monarch and country. No small wonder that the description stuck when, at the threat of some European war, Whitehall reportedly received the message 'Go ahead England, Barbados is behind you'. Whether it was George III, George IV or George V who accepted the encouragement is unclear, but one thing is certain – such undying allegiance had indeed come from 'Little England', Britain's jewel in the tropics, at one time valued more than all its other Atlantic possessions put together.

Yet, in spite of this stereotypical image, today there are several indications that Barbados has turned its eyes northwards in the direction of the United States, and that 'Little America' might be a more appropriate description of the former colony. While it is true that local radio stations still broadcast thrice-daily news from the BBC World Service, complete with Oxford accent and careful understatement, nevertheless local announcers can be more easily identified with the twang of Uncle Sam and chewing gum. Simultaneous events from the States are relayed by CNN satellite and attention has become riveted on the trivial pursuits of *Dallas* and *Dynasty*.

The influence of mass tourism, and the operations of Hilton Hotels, Marriott's, Best Western Hotels and Kentucky Fried Chicken, have ensured that each passing North American fad is meticulously mimicked as the population becomes caught up in a whirlwind of jogging, break dancing, beauty pageants, discos, health clubs and aerobics. The imitative lifestyle is further reinforced by the frequent exodus of thousands of Barbadians in search of relatives and US dollars, courtesy of Eastern, American or Pan Am.

That the mentality and language have changed can be seen from a perusal of the yellow pages of the latest Barbados telephone directory. There one finds that cars are no longer hired. Instead automobiles are rented or leased. Barber shops, and beauty salons with trained cosmetologists, have replaced hairdressers, and one has entered the world of attorneys, gas stations, variety stores, funeral homes, apartments, trucks, mufflers, elevators, realtors, condos, checking accounts, garbage collection, janitor services, aluminum, cookies and crackers. Even in the time of sickness, one need only take a cab to a pharmacy, or call a Miami-based jet ambulance with in-flight medical care. Whether or not the local political directorate is enamoured of the land of cowboys, the population has decidedly voted with its feet and head.

Anomalies of culture clash

The clash of American and British cultures, along with sporadic attempts at Africanization and a rather half-hearted quest for roots, has undoubtedly produced a series of anomalies within the Barbadian psyche. The outcome has been a strange mixture of myth and aspiration, a struggle to come to terms with the national motto of 'Pride and Industry', resulting possibly in an emphasis on the former attribute at the expense of the latter. Indeed, more than one visitor to the island has echoed Trollope's observation that no group of people has ever praised itself so incessantly with so little basis in reality. For example, until quite recently it was a commonly held belief that Barbados had a literacy rate of over ninety-eight per cent, some three points higher than the United States, and generally acknowledged as having the highest level in the world. In the cold light of day, however, and with the advent of more rigorous research, it transpires that, in spite of a well-ordered educational system, more than twenty-five per cent of children aged between seven and ten can scarcely read or write and are in urgent need of remedial teaching.

Again, until a few years ago, a sign at the former Seawell airport announced to arriving passengers that Barbados had no illegal drugs problem. When the new Grantley Adams terminal was completed in 1979, however, the notice had either disappeared or been removed, perhaps with the uncomfortable realization that the island had become something of a transhipment centre and that many of the inhabitants had either already succumbed, or would soon, to the 'delights' of marijuana, cocaine, crack and rock.

Another odd myth which continues to be perpetuated is that Barbadians are deeply religious people. Yet the truth of the matter is that approximately four in ten of the population have no declared affiliation whatsoever and of the remainder, less than twenty-five per cent attend church on a regular basis. Furthermore, less than ten per cent of those presented for baptism receive traditional Christian names, but instead become labelled for life with the designation of a film star, Indian prince or Middle Eastern sheikh. Admittedly religious practice is only one dimension of religiosity, but inspection of another – ethical consequences of religious belief – reveals the anomaly that, notwithstanding scriptural injunction to the contrary, over three-quarters of the consenting adult population are technically living in sin. Moreover, of the minority who do embrace holy wedlock, roughly a quarter do so without the blessing of the church, and over a third see their marriages terminate in divorce.

From the above examples it can be seen how a misplaced sense of pride can lead to exaggeration. This is often manifested by describing Barbados in superlative terms, as having achieved the global optimum. One might hear for instance that it is the most highly educated, most democratic, or freest black nation in the world. While closer scrutiny usually gives the lie to such claims, to the extent that the particular vaunted characteristic or achievement is at best only mediocre in comparison with other countries, paradoxically, those areas in which the island's population really does excel are often played down to an equal point of embarrassment.

In the field of sport, for example, any reading of the record books clearly demonstrates that over the last three or four decades Barbados has consistently produced more outstanding top class cricketers than any other community in the world. As a result, the seemingly invincible West Indies eleven regularly includes five or six Barbadians. Moreover, national teams beginning their tour of the region in Barbados often commence by losing their opening match to an island side which selects from a population no larger than that of many large towns in their own country. Yet to listen to critical members of the home crowd at Kensington Oval, one would imagine that they were supporting a second- or third-rate village squad. Even when performances

Introduction

almost reach perfection, a local radio commentator may grudgingly agree that this is 'quite good', or when Barbados is poised for a ten-wicket victory over its opponents, he may begin to speak of cricket as a game of glorious uncertainties. Body building is the other sport in which Barbados excels internationally. Yet it receives comparatively little press coverage, and, to the best of our knowledge, there has not been a single book published highlighting the achievements of the local muscle men.

Then there is the issue of Barbadian rum, which has managed to capture several prestigious awards in international competition, and which is of very high quality by any reckoning. Yet its share of the world market is minimal, when compared with inferior products from elsewhere in the Caribbean. Additionally, many residents, far from buying local, instead support alternative brands, or even an entirely different alcoholic beverage.

In the realms of literature too, some Barbadian authors have attained international recognition. Yet their works are rarely read by the population which raised and nourished them, and sadly they have left the island for a life of self-imposed exile.

Possible explanations for cultural anomalies

In trying to explain the foregoing paradox, in which excellence is denigrated and the mediocre is exalted, some observers refer to the legacy of slavery, under which African culture was systematically destroyed and black persons treated as little more than hewers of wood and carriers of water. As a result, they could arguably gain no self-confidence, and their overriding attitude was one of instilled inferiority. Whatever their achievements, they were all subordinated to those of white 'massa'. Furthermore, this caste-like system of stratification, with one notable exception, was reinforced by the established Anglican Church, with its denial of membership through catechesis and baptism to those it considered to be without souls and beyond redemption. Not surprisingly, well after emancipation, and possibly right up to the present day, black aspirations and values have been so entrenched as third rate that they have become thus regarded by many black Barbadians themselves.

In this connection, the traditional agents of socialization have played no small part in reinforcing the status quo. The typical matriarchal family, with its absent father figure, is looked upon as something less than the Western nuclear arrangement, and both visiting and common law relationships are often viewed as inferior to the ideal of marriage. No small wonder that children brought up in such an environment are led to believe that they are second-class citizens.

Thus disadvantaged, they are sent to school in order to better themselves. However, the educational institution, with its emphasis on academic subjects and certification, only serves to perpetuate social divisions based on racial considerations, as is quite evident at the all-important point of transfer to the secondary school. Here examination results clearly indicate that the more privileged, coming from two-parent homes, with smaller families and greater access to educational material in the form of toys and books, are themselves far more successful than the socially deprived. With inequality of educational opportunity normatively established, in turn the better endowed go on to prepare themselves adequately for a world of work and relative affluence, while their counterpart failures face the possibilities of a menial job, unemployment or a life of poverty. The wheel turns full circle when the latter come to raise their own families and find avenues of social mobility blocked to their children.

Possibly the foregoing scenario is a trifle forced, when used as an explanation for feelings of racial inferiority, since in post-independence Barbados one can point to numbers of successful coloured lawyers, doctors and other professionals, and to the undeniable reality of black political power. At the same time, it is necessary to appreciate that such progress has only been achieved comparatively recently, that is in the last three or four decades in a 350-year history of exploitation. Moreover, the present state of affairs has only come about as a result of struggle and rebellion, principally highlighted in slave uprisings, the workers' riots of 1937, and the establishment of a vibrant trade union movement. Even in areas where the black majority has been successful, such as cricket, today few seem to recognize the original difficulties encountered by those seeking selection in the face of the impenetrable, respectable white-dominated clubs of the time.

Additionally, it is necessary to realize that the enjoyment of political power is only possible to the extent that there is equality of access to economic power. Here the picture is far less promising for the black Barbadian. After years of plantation slavery, control of land, and a merging of interests with the merchant community, the white agro-mercantile bourgeoisie continues to have a stranglehold on the vital import trade. This it achieves through a series of major corporations which effectively control the private sector, and which impact significantly on the public sector's involvement in the three main pillars of the economy – agriculture, manufacturing and tourism. Consequently, successful black businessmen are few and far between, and the degree to which ninety-three per cent of the population materially benefits from the profits of the minority is quite minimal. The legacy of slavery argument is therefore not quite so sweeping or groundless as it might at first appear.

Considerations of structural inequality

However, as a provision of understanding for the oscillation between pride and negative feelings of self-worth, we feel that the previous line of reasoning may not be entirely adequate, if only because a genetic explanation may inform us how a phenomenon arises, without necessarily helping us appreciate the mechanism for its continuance and preservation.

In order to satisfy the latter condition, we believe that the argument should be supplemented by reference to existing social structures. More specifically, we wish to speak about social divisions and the polarization of Barbadian society from a number of perspectives, since we consider that the presence of patterns of inequality can and does contribute to pride and lack of self-esteem, depending on whether status is described in terms of superordination and subordination. In particular, we feel the need to refer to divisions based on considerations of race, politics, area of residence and gender.

The racial factor has already been touched upon in reference to the legacy of slavery. Here it need simply be stated that, time and again, historians and travel writers have referred to the pronounced racial stratification of Barbados, some describing it as the most caste-like system in the Caribbean, with the possible exception of Martinique and its division into *békés* and *noirs*. Not that these authors personally experienced racial hostility. As a matter of fact, very few did, since many gravitated towards the planter or expatriate communities, thereby effectively isolating themselves from the majority population. Moreover, in their comments, some merely reinforced an ideology of racial superiority by speaking of blacks in derogatory terms. Yet, in spite of this unfortunate tendency, they still underlined social division based on phenotypical characteristics and skin colour.

Although contemporary accounts and information guides are less emphatic, one still detects allusions to a twofold world based on colour, and the following examples tend to reinforce the point. For instance, in the primary cornerstone of the economy – tourism – the glossy brochures continue to portray the native in the roles of bellboy, waiter or taximan, while management is distinctly Caucasian in appearance. The pattern also extends to the retail and banking sectors, with senior positions held by expatriates and white Barbadians, and those of salespersons, clerks, hawkers and beach vendors reserved for those of darker complexion. Furthermore, as places of accommodation and entertainment become more exclusive, some even reverting to the former title of club, so too is there an accompanying lightening of skin of associated personnel. On the other hand, those places and events which visitors rarely frequent, such as local rum shops and popular weekend dances, are predominantly patronized by the resident black population. Only the beachboy, it would seem, stands at the boundary of both worlds, and he is generally marginal to host and guest alike. That such a tacit allocation of space exists perhaps explains why there is so little overt racial tension between the two groups, but it nevertheless reinforces the existing structures in a society predicated on colour, and should help us understand feelings of subservience.

Since the advent of adult franchise and the emergence of popular party politics in Barbados, several commentators have referred to political polarization in the island, a phenomenon said by many to be on the increase. Excessive in-group identification with one of the two major groupings has led to charges of victimization, 'yard fowlism' and political patronage. The run-up to, and aftermath of, general elections is furthermore a period of hostility and bitterness marked by vitriolic attacks on personalities in the press and in radio phone-in programmes. Throughout the exercise the accent is placed on the transfer of power, rather than a possible change of stewardship. As a result, a chasm appears between the victor and the vanquished, one which ultimately leads to asymmetry in relationships and to respective feelings of superiority or loss of self-worth. Since the former usually pervades most areas of national life, commencing with the vital domain of employment, the power enjoyed by the political majority is often interpreted by the opposition as arrogance, and a call for change via the ballot box is made. If and when there is a changing of the guard, with a corresponding switch of allegiance by some former faithful of the defeated party, the familiar pattern repeats itself in what is literally a vicious circle.

Although some observers consider Barbados to be a homogeneous society, with few noteworthy differences between urban and rural areas, we maintain by contrast that such variation is highly pronounced and is intimately associated with social inequality between the two sets of residents. However, we believe that the distinction lies not so much between those living in Bridgetown and the rest of the island, but rather between the North, Central and Eastern parishes of St. Lucy, St. Andrew, St. Thomas, St. Joseph and St. John and the more desirable residential areas of St. Peter, St. James and Christ Church and, to a lesser extent, those of St. Philip, St. George and St. Michael. While the full development of our position has been treated by us both separately and independently elsewhere, here we can briefly summarize the major points of the argument. First, whether one analyses subjective evaluation of spatial preferences or objective internal migration statistics, there has been a steady exodus from the villages of the North and East and a movement towards suburbia. Second, this population transfer has to do with an imbalance in the supply of basic utilities such as electricity, water, natural gas and telephone. Third, the migration may be predicated on the provision of, or relative lack of, such institutional necessities as educational facilities, job opportunities and medical care. The problem of access may be further compounded by comparatively poor transportation. Whereas formerly both areas were equally locally administered by means of the vestry system, today they fall under the aegis of central government. The fact of the matter is that now the centralized bureaucracy, through its various development plans, has largely ignored the rural areas in favour of the tourist commercial belt of the West and South coasts. In spite of the fact that both sets of residents pay taxes, one receives a recognizable return for its money, while the other experiences abandonment. The result is a *de facto* socio-geographical polarization of society, with accompanying feelings of superiority and inferiority.

Finally, there is the question of discrimination by gender in Barbados. In a nutshell, Barbados, in common with most other West Indian territories, is a sex-typed society, which exists under a prevailing ethic of machismo and a two-tiered morality. The superordination of men and the subordination of women is perpetuated in all cultural institutions, ranging from the family, education, religion, work, leisure, politics and economics, to even the law itself. Society thus becomes divided into two worlds. The first belongs to women and their daughters, and contains the home, the primary school, church and nearest relative. The second, for the male of the species, comprises the workplace, commerce, professional contacts, higher education, and the sphere of leisure, which also includes the rum shop. The distinction between the two worlds is also spatial – the first covers a maximum radius of about two miles from the home, the second extends beyond this area to any distance permitted by the physical confines of the island. The life of the former is thus limited to an inner world in which the woman is expected to stay inside the prescribed territory. The latter world is one in which men can 'step outside', 'go out' for an evening, and have 'outside' affairs. Needless to say, the effect of such a spatial dichotomy is also felt in terms of feelings of inferiority and superiority.

We thus find contemporary Barbados facing a series of anomalies, many of which are derived from the past. Of all these, perhaps the greatest is its problem of national identity. On the one hand, it is fiercely independent, quite naturally wishing to stress its many achievements, even to the point of nationalist fervour. On the other, it seems prepared to sink its autonomy and individualism to the lowest common denominator of cultural diffusion, thereby earning the titles of 'Little England' or 'Little America'. It is this overriding dualism which one encounters time and again, either implicitly or explicitly, in the literature, and indeed in many of the works featured in this bibliography.

The bibliography

To assemble a bibliography about a tropical island the size of Barbados might at first glance appear to be a relatively simple task, a matter of no more than a few months' work. Yet the realization that Barbados has played no insignificant part in British and American history, and that it continues to have an importance quite disproportionate to its size, alerts one to the likelihood that there may well be a great deal of writing about the island by both residents and visitors alike. That this is indeed the case came as no real surprise, since one of us has been teaching and researching in Barbados for the past eleven years, while the other has made several extensive trips for the purpose of field-work. Rather than trying desperately to assemble a handful of bibliographical entries, we were faced with the problem of which items to omit from a select bibliography and how to establish criteria for inclusion or exclusion.

Fortunately we had at our disposal such well-established bibliographies as those compiled by Comitas, Cundall, Handler and Ragatz, and a very useful source book produced by Chandler. Additionally, we had ready access to our own university libraries, together with those located in Bridgetown, the Institute of Social and Economic Research, Bellairs Research Institute, the Commonwealth Institute and Institute of Commonwealth Studies in London. Several colleagues were also able to point us in the correct direction whenever we looked like going astray. However, as the amount of material generated from these various sources ran into several thousand possible titles, we decided at the outset that only those works would be included which: (a) offered relative ease of access; (b) had been inspected in detail by us; (c) were deemed to be key works; (d) were considered useful to the interested reader; and (e) were non-technical in nature.

In practice (a) and (b) tended to coincide, since availability usually resulted in perusal. Moreover, if (c), (d) and (e) were satisfied, this led to closer inspection, if not a complete reading. Obvious exceptions to the latter were, for example, the Blue Books or the Laws of Barbados. Naturally restriction of access ruled out consideration of manuscripts in private hands, and those cases where only one copy existed in a single collection. For this reason, it was not necessary to identify the location of source material, a practice followed in some bibliographies.

At the same time, the criterion of availability had the opposite effect of opening up our search to theses, journal papers, and magazine articles which were sufficiently academic in outlook. Consequently we relied quite heavily on microfilmed texts, and articles found in such local publications as *The Bajan*, *Social and Economic Studies*, *The Bulletin of Eastern Caribbean Affairs*, and *The Journal of the Barbados Museum and Historical Society*, all of which are readily available overseas on a subscription basis, and via specialist libraries or inter-library loans. However, undergraduate work from the University of the West Indies, which featured as a coursework requirement for Caribbean Studies, Methods of Social Investigation or Law in Society, although an extremely rich source of information about Barbados, was generally omitted unless it had been published in some form or other. Similarly, with a very few exceptions, which were well known to us, we did not consider forthcoming titles. Yet we were aware of at least a dozen books in progress or awaiting publication, including two on the life of former premier Tom Adams and a couple on the history of cricket in Barbados.

Whether or not a work was deemed significant or useful was

largely a matter of interpretation, and one on which we tended to rely on the help of others the further we strayed from the boundaries of our own disciplines and interests. Nevertheless, undoubtedly a number of items eluded us in the exercise of this subjective evaluation, and a few may have slipped in which could strike some as being rather mundane or uninspired.

However, the axe came down hardest in the application of criterion (e), since there were many esoteric works, particularly in the fields of education, economics, geology, marine biology and medicine, which in our view were of little relevance to all but experts and aficionados. Similarly in the case of cartography, we omitted a plethora of 'tourist maps', many of them highly stylized and pictorial, preferring instead to include only recognized topographical maps and atlases. Yet for those interested in the foregoing subject areas, we can assure them that there are literally hundreds of articles and monographs featuring Barbados.

Furthermore, ever conscious of editorial guidelines and limitations of space, we also decided to extend criterion (e) to encompass a veritable multitude of official government publications, particularly those appearing serially as reports of statutory boards, ministries, or sub-sections of the same. Yet there can be no denying that they contain an abundance of factual data about the functioning of the island on a day to day basis. Occasionally, however, we have included the findings of specially appointed commissions, or items related to national development, particularly where these related to a key subject category, such as local government, constitutional reform, economic or physical development planning or salient infrastructural projects.

Due to the foregoing restrictions, the resulting collection of titles should therefore be seen as selective, rather than comprehensive or exhaustive. Additionally, some subject areas (eg. geography, environment, tourism and travel) may appear to have received undue emphasis when compared to the relative neglect of others. If this is the case, it simply reflects our own spheres of competence, rather than any deliberate policy, since our essential aim was to introduce readers to an overall cross-section of available, useful, informative and non-technical material on Barbados. Those wishing to further their knowledge about specific aspects of island life are invited to consult the lists of references contained in many of the featured publications.

The classification scheme followed is broadly that found in other volumes of Clio Press's *World Bibliographical Series*. Adoption of the scheme in practice also means that the collection offers considerable scope for comparative research.

However, we were given a certain latitude in deciding whether to merge or expand categories, or indeed whether to include others which were of particular relevance to Barbados. We found it necessary to include a sub-section entitled 'Contemporary Caribbean context', in order to feature regional material incorporating Barbados, and to add a special sub-section on plantocracy, peasantry and slavery. Reflecting the importance of the industry to Barbados, tourism was also expanded, under the sub-headings 'Guides and information', and 'Social and economic impact'. In turn, these were distinguished from early and 20th-century travel accounts. Population, geography and the environment were subdivided in analogous fashion. A separate section of women's studies was also added to reflect the growing significance of this field. Among the principal amalgamated categories were: finance, banking and trade; education, science and technology; employment, labour and trade unions; and directories, yearbooks and handbooks. The main reason for reclassification was not so much a dearth of material, but rather its technical or official nature.

At the same time, in a number of categories we found that there was an imbalance between the importance of particular prevailing conditions and the number of works published about them. Under religion, for instance, apart from a few sporadic articles, we encountered relatively few works charting the pluriformity of religious commitment in Barbados, and none devoted to a description of disenchantment with institutionalized religion. Yet both these features are salient aspects of the contemporary situation. Consequently, in the absence of such material, we were obliged to limit ourselves to the presentation of a few titles covering the major religious denominations. Again, since there has, to the best of our knowledge, been no book-length publication describing the history and role of the mass media in Barbados, our entries simply embraced the principal newspapers and their origin, together with a couple of general items on broadcasting.

In the field of sports and recreation, we found that practically nothing has been written on patterns of leisure in Barbados. Furthermore, and perhaps understandably, the little that exists has been almost entirely dominated by King Cricket. Thus, in spite of our awareness of the real situation, our titles reflect this disparity in the literature, and are mainly restricted to a selection of works featuring the island's better-known cricketers. Similar asymmetry exists in the realms of the arts and literature, where the novels, poetry, short stories and literary criticism of a few internationally acclaimed practitioners have virtually swamped contributions from the worlds of sculpture, painting, song, dance and theatre.

Finally, we felt that, since some categories were insufficiently or ambiguously defined, it became necessary to clarify the scope of various topics as our search progressed. Social conditions constituted one such case. There is sometimes confusion in the literature between standard of living and quality of life, or between so-called 'objective' indicators of physical well-being and their subjective evaluation. Barbados appears to be no exception to this general rule, since per capita income, longevity statistics, numbers of inhabitants per doctor and per hospital bed, etc. are often employed by the press and United Nations' agencies as surrogate measures of prevailing social conditions. That these are simply quantitative, and often distorted by abuse of parametric statistics, is regrettable enough, but that they fail to show how members of a given population view their daily lives is even more deplorable. For this reason, under social conditions we attempted to emphasize questions of social structure, stratification and perceived life quality, and tended to omit such details as the number of houses with electricity or running water. Instead we tried to include references to culture, social problems, vignettes of everyday life, family organization and patterns of discrimination based on race and class. Needless to say, present social conditions develop from the past, and several entries reflect such development.

Another example of an unclear category was that of professional periodicals, for, if one includes professional newsletters, in-house magazines and annual reports, there are over 150 current publications of this nature in Barbados. Consequently, we decided to limit our attention to journals with an academic content. In so doing, ironically, we broadened our scope to include a number of regional publications which featured Barbados on a regular basis. Similar working definitions were constructed for other categories, and in most instances it is relatively easy for the reader to see how these were shaped. These points are raised here, however, to alert people to the operation of value judgements in the compilation of any bibliography.

Introduction

Acknowledgements

One major constraint on this joint compilation was that of geographical distance, given that we were located some 6,500 km apart. This raised difficulties of consultation, and, on occasion, resulted in duplication of effort. Nevertheless, we were able to manage a couple of visits in each direction, and the remainder of our communications were conducted through correspondence and telephone calls. The problem only raised its ugly head again at the stages of editing, proof reading and the writing of this introduction, and in these instances the publishers became directly involved. For their assistance and patience, we are most grateful to Robert Neville and Sarah Stubbings. In this connection it should also be mentioned that our wives suffered the rigours of the operation over a two-year period.

We also wish to acknowledge the assistance of Sir Alexander Hoyos and Cecilia Karch in Barbados, and the help provided by the following colleagues drawn from the three campuses of the University of the West Indies: Christine Barrow, George Belle, Selwyn Carrington, Andrew Downes, Neville Duncan, Elaine Fido, Michael Gilkes, Michael Howard, John Mayo, George Roberts and Eric St. Cyr. In particular, we should like to pay tribute to Neville Hall, who was most helpful in his characteristically cheerful way and whose untimely and tragic death is a source of deep sadness and regret.

Library staffs were most cooperative and useful in the advice they gave. If we may single out individuals for special mention, we should like especially to thank Jenipher Carnegie and Deighton Alleyne of the University of the West Indies, Cave Hill, Audine Wilkinson of the Institute of Social and Economic Research (Eastern Caribbean), and Edwin Ifill of the Barbados Public Library. All of these unlocked the treasures of their West Indies collections to us, and were also able to propose and locate volumes for our perusal.

On the other side of the Atlantic, although not awarded specifically to finance this work, a series of grants received by Robert Potter enabled him to carry out field-work projects in Barbados during the period 1980-86, and these indirectly both led to and facilitated this volume. The Central Research Fund of the University of London awarded grants in 1980, 1982 and 1984 in support of work on various aspects of urban development, planning and environmental perception in Barbados. In both 1980 and 1982, the 20th International Congress Fund admin-

Introduction

istered by the Royal Society provided small contributions towards these field-work visits. The British Academy funded comparative work along these lines set in Barbados, St. Lucia and Trinidad and Tobago in the summer of 1984. In early 1986, the Nuffield Foundation made available a generous grant in connection with a project analysing the provision of low-income housing in Barbados. We are grateful to these institutions for support received.

We also wish to express our gratitude to Ann Jarrett of the library of Royal Holloway and Bedford New College for suggesting a number of past and current titles, and to Val Allport of the inter-library loans section for dealing promptly with a constant stream of request cards. Kathy Roberts, secretary in the Department of Geography, should also be thanked for her efficient typing of parts of the manuscript. We are perhaps a trifle more circumspect in thanking Tim Unwin for suggesting that we should attempt the bibliography in the first place, although we are definitely grateful to him for illustrating points of procedure in the works he has compiled in the same series.

Glossary

Backra, buckra
As in 'poor backra' or 'backra johny' to designate a poor white or redleg. Backra may be a corruption of 'back row', the place in church to which the lowest stratum of society was relegated.

Bajan
Used as a noun or adjective to describe an inhabitant of Barbados. A contraction of 'Barbadian' and the title of a monthly magazine.

Big Six
The group of six main companies controlling the commercial interests of the island.

Bim
Possibly a corruption of Major Byam who defended the Royalist cause from 1650-1652. His followers apparently became known as 'Bims'. Gradually the term was extended to all Barbadians and even to the island itself. Some writers, however, reserve the expression for local whites. 'Bim' has been used as a malapropism for 'bin' or 'dustbin', the title of a literary magazine, and a brand name for a soft drink.

Bimshire
An extension of 'Bim' by which the country Barbados is sometimes nostalgically represented. The suffix has Little England connotations.

Careenage
Literally the place where boats were careened, that is, cleaned and caulked. A narrow waterway extending from the sea into the heart of Bridgetown where,

until recently, ships would undergo repair and inter-island vessels would ply a trade of fruit and vegetables. Today it is a berthing spot for yachts visiting the island.

CARICOM The Caribbean Community and Common Market, established in July 1973 by the Treaty of Chaguaramas. It was designed to give a common market, increase functional cooperation in transport, education and health, and provide for the coordination of foreign policy.

CARIFTA The Caribbean Free Trade Association, which came into being in August 1968, with the specific aim of eliminating most tariff barriers between Commonwealth Caribbean countries.

Chattel house A rectangular wooden house, generally set on a pile of rocks. Such vernacular houses are movable, reflecting the fact that they are owned by the occupant, whilst the land is rented, often from plantations, at peppercorn rents. The standard gable-roofed chattel house may measure little more than 5.4 m by 2.7 m.

Cou-cou A mixture of stirred corn meal and okras, often served with flying fish as the national dish.

CXC The Caribbean Examinations Council, the body responsible for setting and administering school examinations.

Falernum A sweet liquor made by maturing white rum, lime and almond. When combined with additional dark rum, the result is known locally as 'corn'n oil'.

Hawkers Less frequently 'hucksters' or 'higglers'. Women street vendors of fruit and vegetables from the rural areas.

Johny A descendant of the Irish and Scottish indentured servants.

Jug-jug A thick purée made from guinea corn flour, peas, and a minced mixture of

Landship

meat, onions and herbs. Often served at Christmas time with slices of ham.

Started by Moses Ward, a Barbadian seaman who had lived in Cardiff and Southampton. It is a friendly society which serves as a form of lower-class insurance against unemployment, sickness and death. Members are assigned to a ship under the command of an admiral and undertake nautical exercises and duties. The movement, now over one hundred years old, is often in evidence at festivals, such as Crop Over, and at funerals. Although 'the ships' are metaphorical, the naval imagery and attire remain.

Leeward

The protected western or Caribbean Sea side of the island.

Little England

A term sometimes used interchangeably with Barbados to connote native love of the mother country. In particular, overseas travel writers often make the comparison between England and Barbados.

Mauby

A frothy bitter-sweet drink made from dried mauby bark, mace, cinnamon, cloves, orange peel, sugar and water. The mauby seller, once a familiar sight, has long since disappeared from the streets of Bridgetown.

MDCs

More developed countries within the Third World, having a higher standard of living than less developed countries (LDCs). In the Caribbean, Trinidad and Tobago, Barbados, Jamaica and Guyana (in that order) are reckoned to belong to the former group. The normal criterion for classification is per capita income, which in Barbados is currently estimated at just under 9,000 Barbados dollars (2 Bds = 1 US dollar approximately, at fixed parity).

Meeting turn

An informal mutual savings arrange-

Glossary

Mr. Harding

ment, whereby members of a group agree to place a small fixed sum of money into a common fund on a regular basis. At 'meetings', the person whose 'turn' it is receives the content of the kitty. Today this institution has been largely displaced by the cooperative.

A representation of the typical cruel gang driver made by the slaves from sugar cane trash, and dressed in an old black coat and top hat. At Crop Over, Mr. Harding's effigy would be burnt to the song of 'Hold fast Old Ned at the door', signifying that, with the crop harvested, hard times lay ahead.

Obeah

A form of sorcery based on imitative magic and African in origin. Among the slave population of Barbados, obeah was used principally for curative purposes, to bewitch enemies and to remove curses. In 1806, legislation was enacted making obeah a felony punishable by death. Although the equivalent of obeah can be found in several Afro and Amerindian cults, including Haitian voodoo, remnants of the practice in contemporary Barbados are limited to private consultation and superstitious beliefs.

Redlegs

Alternatively 'backras', 'buckras', 'poor backras', 'backra johnies', 'spawgees', 'poor whites', 'white niggers' or 'ecky bekkies'. The term refers to the effect of the sun on the pale blotched skin of the thousand or so inter-married descendants of Irish and Scottish indentured servants still to be found in parts of the parishes of St. John, St. Joseph and St. Andrew.

Rum shop

An establishment for the sale of alcoholic drinks, but which also frequently acts as a rural grocery store and a social meeting place.

Glossary

Scotland District
The hilly and eroded area in the north-east of the country, approximately coterminous with the parishes of St. Andrew, St. Joseph and the northern part of St. John.

Seawell Airport
Now Grantley Adams International Airport. The former name came from that of the original plantation land on which the airport is located in Christ Church.

Tea meeting
A social occasion for the working class to meet at a neighbourhood house and engage in light refreshment, songs and gossip. Sometimes speeches would be given, liberally interspersed with (often faulty) Latin phrases, as a form of ego-enhancement for the orator. An institution which had virtually disappeared by the end of the 1920s.

Tenantry
A group of two or more rented chattel house spots on plantation land. In 1980, a programme was put into operation to enable the residents of tenantries to purchase the freehold of their lots.

Tuk band
A group of strolling musicians, playing a lively calypso-type music on a variety of home-made instruments, and often joined by spontaneous dancers. Tuk bands can still be seen today at various island festivals, such as those held annually at Holetown and Oistins.

USAID
United States Agency for International Development.

Vestry system
The former system of local government based on administration by parish.

West Indies Federation
The first attempt at regional integration within the Caribbean which ran from 1958–1962.

Windward
The exposed eastern or Atlantic Ocean side of the island.

The Country and Its People

General

1 **Barbados, outsider of the Antilles.**
Charles Allmon. *National Geographical Magazine*, vol. 111, no. 3 (1952), p. 363-92.
Including twenty-eight photographs taken by the author, this lengthy article ranges widely over the land and population of Barbados, providing comments on diverse topics such as its discovery, sugar production, housing, oil prospecting, cricket and flying fish.

2 **Barbados: Commonwealth fact sheet.**
London: Commonwealth Institute, 1976. 9p. map. bibliog.
This periodically updated fact sheet provides background information on the land, people, history, constitution, government, economy and social development of Barbados. It contains a number of useful data tabulations on economic conditions, and can be freely used and cited without acknowledgement.

3 **Barbados: a special survey for businessmen.**
Barbados Development Board. Bridgetown: Barbados Development Board [n.d.]. 1,229p. (pagination non-sequential). maps.
Intended as a general compilation of information concerning Barbados, this report was published as part of 'Operation Beehive – design for industry in Barbados', the country's industrial development programme. It contains basic maps, along with information on the geography of Barbados, its history, economy, industrial development, constitution, transport, communications and utilities. A detailed but now rather dated account, of limited circulation.

1

4 **Barbados: a profile.**
Barbados Industrial Development Corporation. Bridgetown:
Barbados Industrial Development Corporation, 1979. 35p.
Designed for prospective business investors, this brief guide has sections on the
country's geography, living in Barbados, accommodation, recreational activities,
associations, immigration requirements, taxation, dividends and duties, the
history of Barbados, the sugar industry, and ties with the USA and Canada. Each
of these sections is further sub-divided.

5 **Barbados: an independent nation.**
Barbados Ministry of Education. Nassau: Island Graphics, 1966.
[not paginated]. map.
Consisting of over sixty pages, this is the official Barbados independence
magazine, produced in November 1966. It sets out to describe, in both words and
pictures, the people and their country. Illustrated with numerous colour and
black-and-white photographs, there are sections on virtually every aspect of
Barbadian national life. Although now dated, this publication does give a good
general impression of the nation at the time of independence.

6 **And what am I bid?**
Céline Barnard. *Bajan & South Caribbean*, (March 1978), p. 4-7.
An interview with Barbados' most colourful and witty auctioneer. In the late
1970s, Harold Bowen's saleroom at Skagway had become a veritable institution.
It was also an outstanding place for free entertainment, since descriptions of items
were spiced with humorous commentary on the island's social life. The sales were
run by the entire Bowen family, and included the help of an old lady known as
E. P., who used to kiss Harold for luck at the beginning of each auction.

7 **Barbados.**
John Malcolm Brinnin. *Atlantic*, vol. 209, no. 2 (1962), p. 104-07.
After somewhat protracted descriptions of the ship on which he travelled to
Barbados and his hotel on the island, referred to as the 'Ocean Grand', the
author discusses Bridgetown, Barbados and the Barbadian people in this very
journalistic account. The author not only sees Barbados as 'Little England', but
goes on to compare Bridgetown with Plymouth. Other localities are also evoked;
the sugar cane fields are said to look like Iowa cornfields, whilst it is posited that
the 'Older native houses are often inexplicably Scandinavian in feeling'. However,
the author returns to the English influence, claiming that 'The English signature,
strongly marked in architecture and general prospect, is even more clearly
apparent in the bearing of the citizens. They have the same sort of politeness in
the street that one encounters in London and, by and large, the same sense of
propriety in dress and public appearance.'

8 **Images of Barbados, an island and its people.**
Roger La Brucherie.   Hong Kong printed: the author, 1979. 112p.
2 maps.

A pictorial essay containing over eighty photographs, most of which are in colour.
A brief commentary accompanies the illustrations. The volume focuses on people
rather than scenes, and thus it vividly captures various facets of Barbadian
everyday life and culture, ranging from housing, education, the workplace and
religion to leisure and of course cricket.

9 **A Barbados journey.**
Roger La Brucherie.   Santo Domingo: Imágenes Press, 1982. 114p.
3 maps.

In the companion volume to his *Images of Barbados* (q.v.), the author seeks to
complement his earlier account by providing a greater historical perspective. Over
one hundred colour photographs focus more on institutions than people, and
there is an emphasis on buildings and the industries of sugar and tourism.
La Brucherie maintains that the enthusiasm of a stranger can awaken a fresh
interest in an otherwise familiar world, and this beautifully presented book more
than substantiates such a claim.

10 **Caribbean and Central American databook.**
Caribbean and Central American Action.   Washington, DC:
Caribbean and Central American Action, 1984. 378p. 34 maps.

Aims to provide information on the Caribbean basin, principally for potential
American investors. The entries on each territory are accompanied by a map. In
the case of Barbados (p. 33-42), the map contains so many place-name errors that
it serves little practical use. Other information includes summaries on geography,
population, history, government, transportation, US non-profit-making private
organizations, US business firms with operations in Barbados, and a selection of
key economic indicators. However, some of these details are either out of date or
factually incorrect.

11 **Everyday life in Barbados: a sociological perspective.**
Edited by Graham M. S. Dann.   Leiden, The Netherlands:
Department of Caribbean Studies of the Royal Institute of
Linguistics and Anthropology, 1979. 190p. map. bibliog

This volume comprises seven chapters by eight contributors. The aim is to focus
on aspects of daily life in Barbados that seem obvious and are taken for granted.
The essays originated as student projects. Graham Dann˙provides a strongly
methodological overview in chapter one, and the substantive chapters then
follow: 'Barbadian village games of yesterday' by Ernestine Jackman; 'The Bajan
Sunday school' by Annette Woodroffe; 'Picnics in Barbados' by Barbara Corbin;
'The nutseller' by Winston Crichlow; 'The rural rum shop: a comparative case
study' by Janet Stoute and Kenneth Ifill; and 'The elderly' by Glennis Nurse. The
volume provides some fascinating insights for those interested in the life and
people of Barbados as seen from a strongly sociological perspective.

12   **The quality of life in Barbados.**
Graham M. S. Dann.   London; Basingstoke, England: Macmillan,
1984. 290p. 2 maps. bibliog.
Provides a detailed overview of the contemporary social structure of Barbados.
The volume is based primarily on a survey of people's social satisfactions with
regard to seven broad aspects of life. The main chapters report on these topics:
housing, district, education, employment, leisure, health and religion. Overall
patterns of life satisfaction are evaluated in chapter ten and broad themes
pervading future aspirations such as moral decay, loss of freedom, the
politicization of Barbadian life and fear of the future are reviewed in chapter
eleven. A principal strength of the book is that each of the substantive chapters
provides a well-rounded review of the life domain under study before the results
of the field survey are presented. In short, a very useful introduction to the island.

13   **Barbados 1900-1950. The olden days in pictures and verse.**
Kathleen Hawkins.   Wildey, St. Michael, Barbados: Letchworth
Press, 1986. 23p.
A nostalgic series of handwritten poems illustrated by the author. Topics include
crop time, the cane field, the blacksmith, bringing in fodder, donkeys, the
cottage, the policeman, a mule tram, buggies and racehorses.

14   **Barbados our island home.**
F. A. Hoyos.   London: Macmillan Caribbean, 1979. 3rd ed. 212p.
maps. bibliog.
Written primarily as a secondary school text, this book, which was first published
in 1960, provides perhaps the best general introduction to the country. It covers
the flora and fauna, geology, prehistory, history, government and education
system of the island. The text is accompanied by over sixty black-and-white
photographs and line diagrams. Suggestions for further reading appear at the end
of each chapter.

15   **Barbados yesterday and today.**
Edited by Patrick Hoyos.   Marine Gardens, Christ Church,
Barbados: Barbadian Heritage Productions Trust, [n.d.]. 56p.
A collection of photographs of old Barbados, mainly taken between 1880 and
1920; many of them are presented on a 'then' and 'now' comparative basis. The
four principal sections cover Bridgetown, the people, suburbs, and rural areas.
The photographs are accompanied by short historical notes compiled by Edward
A. Stoute. This is a useful pictorial introduction to aspects of Barbados and its
people.

16   **The West Indian islands.**
George Hunte.   London: Batsford, 1972. Reprinted, 1973. 246p.
9 maps. bibliog.
Written by a former resident of Barbados and editor of the *Bajan* magazine from
1953 to 1970, this informative volume is divided into two sections: background
and foreground. The former traces the prehistory and history of the islands up to

4

the era of independence. It also briefly examines the impact of tourism, arts, crafts and folklore, and the problem of Caribbean identity. Although references to the Barbadian way of life are liberally included throughout the book, and are often accompanied by the author's own evaluations, specific treatment of the island occurs only on p. 179-93 and p. 196-201. Rather than describe places of interest, Hunte prefers to reflect on the Bajan character and on social change.

17 **Barbados.**
George Hunte. London: Batsford, 1974. 219p. 4 maps. bibliog.
Provides an historical background of Barbados, before examining the principal contemporary sights of Bridgetown and the various parishes. Sections are also devoted to general information, people, language, flora and fauna, food and drink, and even pirates, treasure, legends and the supernatural. Several photographs accompany the text, which is aimed at a general audience.

18 **Exploring historic Barbados.**
Maurice Bateman Hutt. Bedford, Nova Scotia, Canada: Layne, 1981. 128p. maps.
A series of routes within Barbados are described together with the features of interest that are to be seen along them. However, the detail and illustrations make this volume more than a tourist guide and it provides an effective introduction to the human and physical landscape of Barbados. The major chapters are as follows: 'Exploring St. Peter and St. Lucy'; 'From Bridgetown through St. Joseph to the East Coast and Codrington College'; 'From Bridgetown through Christ Church to the Crane and Sam Lord's Castle'; 'Cross country route via Holetown to Welchman Hall Gully, Harrison's Cave and Bathsheba to Cherry Tree Hill and Pie Corner'; 'Holetown via Vaucluse and Castle Grant to Villa Nova, St. John, Martin's Bay and Ragged Point'; 'Exploring St. George's Parish'; 'Speightstown via Rock Hall to Belleplaine, Turner's Hall Woods and Mt. Hillaby'; 'Bridgetown cross country to Belleplaine, Bissex Hill, Castle Grant and St. John's Church'; 'Through Christ Church and St. Philip's Parishes (sic)', and 'Walking and driving the St. Lucy coast'.

19 **Barbados and tomorrow.**
John Kirwan. *Canadian Geographical Journal*, vol. 65, no. 5 (1962), p. 162-65.
This short paper, which is accompanied by seven photographs, affords a brief overview of the land and people of Barbados in the early 1960s. It ranges over topics such as the settling of the island, its geology, population, economy and government. The paper finishes by anticipating the likely ascendancy of tourism and light industry over sugar production in the economic life of the island.

20 **Barbados.**
Ingrid Kowlen. In: *What you should know about the Caribbean.*
Compiled by Ingrid Kowlen. Leiden, The Netherlands: Department
of Caribbean Studies of the Royal Institute of Linguistics and
Anthropology, 1980, p. 61-69.
Compiled to provide participants in the fourth inter-university course on the
Caribbean, held at Leiden, with basic background information on the region. As
for the other countries, the sections included on Barbados are reproduced from
newspaper and journal articles and books. They cover its history, economy,
economic progress, agriculture, manufacturing, tourism, employment and
development planning activities.

21 **Barbados.**
Albert Leeman. *Geographica Helvetica*, vol. 25 (1970), p. 130-35.
Written in German, this concise account provides a brief introduction covering
the country's population and politics, its predominantly English way of life,
economy, healthy climate, educational system, town planning and the capital city.

22 **Barbados: island in the sun.**
Arbon Jack Lowe. *Américas (Organization of American States),*
vol. 27, no. 10 (1975), p. 1-24.
Opening with the statement that Barbados is 'small in size only', and that it 'has
all the attributes of a great country', this article provides a detailed overview of
Barbadian history and political organization, cities and landscapes, the people and
their culture, and social and economic development. The text is enhanced by
approximately eighty photographs. This clearly written and well-organized
introduction to the country and its people takes a strongly pro-Bajan view,
suggesting that 'Chief among the island's attractions are the Barbadians
themselves.'

23 **Windward of the Caribbean.**
S. W. C. Pack. London: Alvin Redman, 1964. 226p. map. bibliog.
The author, who has been familiar with Barbados since the 1920s when he spent
three years working in the oil industry of Trinidad, rejects the 'Little England'
view of Barbados. He argues instead that 'It is itself. There is nothing like it. It is
windward of everything in the Caribbean. It is quite different from all the other
islands in the West Indies.' The book aims to answer many of the questions that
are stimulated by a visit to the island. Although now somewhat dated, and with a
highly anecdotal style, this is still an interesting guide to Barbadians, the history
of the country and its landscape. Well illustrated with black-and-white
photographs.

24 **Mental maps of Barbados, part I: how Barbadians perceive their environment.**
Robert B. Potter. *Bajan and South Caribbean*, no. 357 (Aug. 1983), p. 40-41.

This short article in a popular journal considers the findings of a social survey which examined Barbadian nationals' liking for the different parishes of the island. Some interesting variations in perception are shown to exist between residents from Bridgetown, Oistins, Speightstown, Belleplaine and Six Cross Roads. When, however, the patterns are taken as a whole, a consensus mental map is derived which stresses the perceived desirability of the parishes comprising the south-western urban linear corridor. The high standing of Christ Church, St. James and St. Philip is particularly evident.

25 **The bridge Barbados.**
Patrick Roach. Wildey, St. Michael, Barbados: Coles Printery, [n.d.]. 146p. 2 maps.

A combination of historical, anecdotal and autobiographical material. Published at the time of the bicentenary of American Independence, the book begins with chapters on George Washington and residents of the former colonies, particularly those of South Carolina. There are also sections dealing with Barbados' involvement in the Second World War, the arrival of Ra II, obeah and redlegs. A rather mixed collection of stories and events, which nevertheless fills many gaps left by other social historians. The title is taken from the first designation of the modern capital Bridgetown.

26 **Barbados the singular island.**
David Smithers. *Geographical Magazine*, vol. 40, no. 5 (1967), p. 407-22.

Written just after independence in 1966, this article uses the then current slogan of the tourist board, 'Barbados is a singular island', to stress its locational, geographical and cultural individuality. It documents in an interesting way the emergence of tourism, light manufacturing and agricultural diversification to supplement sugar production. The dependence of Barbados on other countries is emphasized.

27 **Barbados as a sovereign state.**
Hugh W. Springer. *Journal of the Royal Society of Arts*, vol. 115 (1967), p. 627-41.

The text of the Henry Morley lecture, delivered to the Commonwealth Section of the Royal Society of Arts on 23 February, 1967. Following Barbados' emergence as a sovereign state the previous year, Springer begins with the assertion that 'all independence is relative independence' and ranges adroitly over questions of territorial size, emigration, history, development policy and political economy. It is concluded that 'quality is the real answer to smallness'. An excellent account, despite its age.

28   **The thing about Barbados.**
John Wickham. *Journal of the Barbados Museum and Historical Society*, vol. 35, no. 3 (1977), p. 223-30.
An attempt to evaluate Barbados and Barbadians by 'a son of the soil'. In an attempt to 'see ourselves as others see us', Wickham quotes some outsiders (such as Gordon Lewis, Bruce Hamilton and Anthony Trollope), some insiders (George Bernard, Frank Collymore and George Lamming) and one person who falls between the two (Austin Clarke), to try to understand the pride, industry, conservatism, insularity, chauvinism and friendliness of the Barbadian at home or overseas.

The Caribbean islands.
See item no. 178.

West Indian Eden: the book of Barbados.
See item no. 191.

The Barbados book.
See item no. 192.

The population of Barbados.
See item no. 397.

Wayside sketches: pen pictures of Barbadian life.
See item no. 476.

Barbados Independence Issue.
See item no. 830.

Caribbean essays: an anthology.
See item no. 858.

Barbados in the contemporary Caribbean context

29   **Insularity and identity in the Caribbean.**
Colin G. Clarke. *Geography*, vol. 61, no. 1 (1976), p. 8-16.
Argues that rejection of the Caribbean and yearning for Europe permeate West Indian life. Allegiances at their broadest may be described as insular, and such insularity was at the root of the break-up of the West Indies Federation. 'Only when abroad does the Jamaican, Barbadian or Montserratian speak of himself as a West Indian.' Barbados and Barbadians feature heavily in this useful account.

The Country and Its People. Barbados in the contemporary Caribbean context.

30   **The social structure of the British Caribbean (excluding Jamaica).**
George Cumper.   Millwood, New York: Kraus Reprint, 1978.
41p. + 47p. + 43p.
A series of republished pamphlets originally intended for extramural study groups. The essays are in three sections. Part one deals with demography, part two with the family, housing, racial composition and urban-rural differences, and part three with employment and income. Most of the material is quite dated, since it is based on the 1946 census and earlier sources. Nevertheless, it is interesting to look at such factors as overcrowding, literacy and race in Barbados, and to compare them with other Caribbean territories in different periods over the last hundred years.

31   **The Caribbean community in the 1980s: report by a group of Caribbean experts.**
Chaired by William Demas.   Georgetown: Caribbean Community Secretariat, 1981. 157p.
An analysis of the situation and problems faced by CARICOM at the beginning of the 1980s with a number of recommendations for the future. The two major proposals relate to joint regional production and coordination of external economic relations. In a number of appended tables it is possible to compare Barbados' relative success as an MDC with the less than rosy economic positions of its partners. Barbados is also commended for taking bilateral initiatives, such as the Arawak Cement Plant with Trinidad and Tobago, and for enacting legislation which enables the swift implementation of CARICOM decisions.

32   **The Caribbean: the English-speaking islands in pictures.**
Lancelot Evans, Philip Davis, David Lewis.   New York: Sterling; London: Oak Tree Press, 1969. 2nd ed. 64p. 5 maps.
One of a popular geography series providing worldwide coverage. The treatment of Barbados, (p. 35-42), is necessarily superficial. It includes a brief history, plus a few comments on the nature of government and Federation prior to independence. A lopsided map of the island is also provided.

33   **The Caribbean in the twentieth century.**
John Griffiths.   London: Batsford, 1984. 72p.
A school text highlighting the Caribbean as a region in crisis, with declining living standards and subject to growing American influence. In this respect, Barbados is no exception to its island neighbours; in fact only Jamaica under Edward Seaga is reckoned to be more pro-United States in outlook. A 1927 photograph of Broad Street, Bridgetown, emphasizes that the process of Americanization was in full swing almost sixty years ago. This consciousness-raising account questions the conventional wisdom of current political and economic models and encourages further attempts at regional integration.

The Country and Its People. Barbados in the contemporary Caribbean context

34 **West Indian people.**
Jack Harewood. In: *Caribbean economy: dependence and backwardness.* Edited by George L. Beckford. Mona, Jamaica: Institute of Social and Economic Research, 1975, p. 1-33.
An interesting introduction to the peopling of the Caribbean region. Although the chapter focuses primarily on historical periods of demographic change, its scope is wide and covers race, family organization, migration, human resources, family planning and economic development. Although the account is primarily pan-Caribbean, it should be of broad interest to those wishing to consider in particular the people and land of Barbados.

35 **The West Indies.**
Carter Harman, the Editors of Life. Amsterdam: Time-Life International, 1965. 160p. 3 maps. bibliog.
A comprehensive account of the region, with pictures and a commentary. Emphasis is, however, on the larger territories. In the flat outpost of Barbados, similarities are found to the byways and manors of England. However, the island's apparently smooth history is said to be deceptive, since inwardly it is restless: 'Its people, polite to the point of subservience, have a bitter readiness to rise and riot'. The island's first settlers seemingly spent so much time bickering over boundaries that they neglected their crops and came close to starvation.

36 **The changing face of the Caribbean.**
Irene Hawkins. Bridgetown: Cedar Press, 1976. 271p. 2 maps. bibliog.
Written after two years' residence in Barbados by a German-born economic journalist who had also visited the Greater and Lesser Antilles and the Guyanas. As an outsider, the author feels that she can in a detached way point to the political, economic and socio-structural problems faced by small territories, hampered as they are by external foreign domination and poor communication links. After examining various development initiatives, she endorses regional integration as the only viable strategy. Although this sometimes provocative account is not a country-by-country analysis, there are several references to Barbados. These include commentaries on racial stratification, tourism, agriculture, population, banking and political freedom. More than a decade after the publication of this book, the author's plea to enhance the quality of rural life by making farming a financially and psychologically rewarding occupation, thereby also halting the drift to suburbia, seems still to be falling on deaf ears.

37 **The Caribbean: the genesis of fragmented nationalism.**
Franklin Knight. New York: Oxford University Press, 1978. 251p. 3 maps. bibliog.
Studies the economic and political realities of the Caribbean from the inside out, rather than simply regarding the region as a by-product of metropolitan interests. There is a particular emphasis on the emergence of nationalism and the problems such 'patriachiquismo' pose for regional unity. The shared experience of the Caribbean is one of dependency, and this can only be overcome by revolutionary change. Barbados, with its close ties to Britain and the United States, is no

exception. The account is accompanied by a political chronology and a selected guide to the literature.

38   **Black power in the Caribbean context.**
David Lowenthal. *Economic Geography*, vol. 48 (1972),
p. 116-34.

Argues that 'The Black Power movement seeks to eradicate the effects of colonial emulation, in part by engendering pride in African heritage'. The paper essentially provides an overview of economic and social dependence in the Caribbean. Barbados is discussed in several sections, and this paper provides an excellent introduction for all those studying Caribbean societies.

39   **The stability of the Caribbean.**
Edited by Robert Moss.   London: Institute for the Study of
Conflict; Washington, DC: Center for Strategic and International
Studies, Georgetown University, 1973. 137p. 2 maps.

The proceedings of a conference hosted by the publishers to examine the problems of Caribbean small states exposed to political unrest and both economic and social tension. While Barbados manages to avoid the excesses associated with the Black Power movement, nevertheless some of the conditions favouring that reaction still exist on the island. Apart from the negative effects of tourism, the problems of high unemployment and of matching improvements in education with the job market are also covered. This last factor is analysed in detail by Malcolm Cross, in a thoughtful essay entitled 'Education and job opportunities' (p. 51-76).

40   **Documents on international relations in the Caribbean.**
Edited by Roy Preiswerk.   Rio Piédras, Puerto Rico: Institute of
Caribbean Studies, University of Puerto Rico, 1970. 853p. bibliog.

The documents are assembled under six categories: foreign policy, extra-regional economic relations, regional cooperation, status of dependent territories, defence, conflicts and disputes. Among the more interesting items featuring Barbados are the addresses of Errol Barrow to the United Nations in 1966 and to the Organization of American States in 1968, an extract from a White Paper on the federal negotiatons (1962-65), and a report by Sir Arthur Lewis on the views of Eastern Caribbean islands about the future of the West Indies Federation in 1961.

41   **Caribbean citizen.**
Philip Sherlock.   London: Longmans, 1957. 2nd ed. 1963. 120p.

A text on civics for schools aimed at creating a sense of Caribbean identity and pride among young West Indians. By describing the history, government, resources, people and multi-racial communities of the region, the author provides the necessary background to explain the eventual desire for independence. Examples from Barbados include the pioneer work of Parris, Harrison and Bovell in developing new breeds of sugar cane, the achievements of Garfield Sobers in cricket, George Lamming and Hilton Vaughan in literature, and Grantley Adams and the labour movement.

42   **The United States and the Caribbean.**
Edited by Tad Szulc.   Englewood Cliffs, New Jersey: Prentice
Hall, 1971. 212p. map.

A collection of essays prepared for the 38th American Assembly of Columbia University, a non-partisan educational organization considering the social, political and economic post-war relationship between the United States and the Caribbean. References to Barbados are not particularly complimentary, and include mention of divisions based on politics and social class similar to those found in Jamaica. However, tensions can be overcome in Barbados on account of its deeper sense of national identity. At the same time, the society is thought to be the most rigidly stratified in the Caribbean (with the possible exception of Martinique) with its caste-like structures separating whites from blacks. Reinforcing these barriers are institutions such as the Anglican Church, the Savannah Club, Codrington College, and the harbour police in their 18th-century uniforms which were admired so much by Queen Victoria. It is not surprising, therefore, that in spite of the Protestant ethic, there is little mass participation in economic life, and a virtual absence of popular folklore in Barbados. Ironically, while faced with an unemployment problem, Barbados has been known to import cane cutters from St. Vincent and St. Lucia, while its own nationals travel to Florida to do the same work.

Sovereignty, dependency and social change in the Caribbean.
See item no 478.

Contemporary Caribbean: a sociological reader.
See item no. 480.

West Indian societies.
See item no. 489.

The Commonwealth Caribbean: the integration experience . . .
See item no. 600.

The Cambridge encyclopedia of Latin America and the Caribbean.
See item no. 927.

A Year Book of the Commonwealth.
See item no. 928.

Geography

General

43   **Geopolitics of the Caribbean: ministates in a wider world.**
Thomas D. Anderson.   New York: Praeger; Stanford, California:
Hoover Institution Press, 1984. 175p. 8 maps. bibliog.

Focus in this work is primarily on the small Eastern Caribbean islands, along with
Jamaica, the Bahamas and Trinidad and Tobago. Thus, Barbados features quite
frequently, especially in the several useful data tabulations. The work provides an
overview of the contemporary environment and political geography of the region.
Following an introductory chapter, the geographical setting is covered, including
political entities, the physical setting and the economic base. The section on
historical background outlines early history, the early colonial period, the
plantation era, the early role of the United States and the development of modern
Caribbean politics. Chapter four deals with contemporary geopolitical issues such
as marine boundaries, the role of Cuba, and recent US policies towards the
Caribbean, whilst foreign policy options are considered in chapter five. A useful
introductory account.

44   **Geography for C.X.C.**
Wilma Bailey, Patricia H. Pemberton.   Walton-on-Thames,
Surrey, England: Nelson, 1983. 154p. maps.

Aimed at fourth- and fifth-year pupils at secondary schools who are preparing for
the Caribbean Examinations Council (CXC) geography examinations. The book
follows a thematic approach, dealing with topics such as the physical setting of the
Caribbean, sugar, industrialization, transport, communications, CARICOM and
migration. A sound introduction to the general geography of the Caribbean in
which Barbados is mentioned in several sections.

45 **A modern secondary geography of the West Indies.**
R. M. Bent. Kingston: Jamaica Publishing House, 1971. 220p.
maps.
The author, formerly Chief Education Officer at the Ministry of Education in
Jamaica, provides a traditional geography, following an almost exclusively island-
by-island approach, with only a very brief introduction to the region as a whole.
Chapter thirteen is devoted to the geography of Barbados and covers its
formation and scenery, water supplies, overpopulation, the importance of sugar
and other types of farming, manufacturing and processing industries and the
country's prospects.

46 **The Caribbean islands.**
Helmut Blume, translated from the German by Johannes
Maczewski, Ann Norton. London: Longman, 1974. 464p. 89
maps. bibliog.
Although by now urgently in need of revision, this remains the standard work on
the geography of the Caribbean. The first part presents a general survey of the
topography, oceanography, landforms, climate, flora and fauna, history, peopling
and economic disposition of the Caribbean islands. In part two, Blume presents
an island-by-island survey. Although readers may find the account of Barbados
(p. 353-58) somewhat compressed, it is still worth reading from the point of view
of the island's physical and historical geography. In other respects, it is less
adequate. Barbados is, of course, mentioned frequently in the systematic
discussions included in part one.

47 **Latin America: a regional geography.**
Gilbert J. Butland. London: Longman, 1960. 373p. 61 maps.
bibliog.
A general textbook aiming to describe the regional geography of Latin America,
and containing a chapter on the West Indies (p. 96-132). The treatment is country-
by-country and Barbados is dealt with on p. 121-23, although the treatment is
highly generalized, covering physical geography, occupations, agriculture and
other economic activities.

48 **A new geography of the Caribbean.**
Alan Eyre. London: George Philip & Son, 1979. 5th ed. 162p.
maps. bibliog.
The author, who at the time of publication was Senior Lecturer in Geography at
the University of the West Indies, provides a secondary school text on the
region's basic geography. A short overview prefaces a country-by-country
account, in which Barbados is treated on p. 42-50. There are short sections on the
island's situation and structure, soils, climate, settlement history, sugar cane and
land use, food imports, fishing, tourist industry, its deep-water port, Bridgetown,
overseas trade, population problems and Barbados as a one-product economy. A
basic, but nevertheless sound introduction to the geography of Barbados.

49 **Barbados: a geographical study of the densely populated island in tropical America.**
    Alice Foster. *Journal of Geography*, vol. 22, no. 6 (1923), p. 205-16.

Written during the first quarter of the 20th century, this paper is by now mainly of historical interest. For example, it records that in 1912, 4,000 first-class passengers landed on the island. The article discusses the geographical bases of agriculture, houses and living conditions, the shipping and economic activities of Bridgetown and the island's then declining population. Given the changes which have occurred since publication, some of the views and ideas expressed now seem erroneous or questionable.

50 **Principles of Caribbean geography: a CXC approach.**
    Norrell A. London.   Port of Spain, Kingston, London: Longman, 1983. 236p. maps.

Aims to provide an overview of both physical and human geography on a topical basis. A general introduction to the subject is provided in part one. The lithosphere, rivers, deserts, underground water, the work of ice, weather, climate, oceans, vegetation and soils are covered in part two. In part three, the focus is on socioeconomic conditions including resources, agriculture, population, settlement, industry, trade, transport and tourism. The examples are not exclusively drawn from the Caribbean, but are generally so, and Barbados is featured in many of the sections.

51 **Caribbean lands.**
    John Macpherson.   Port of Spain, Kingston: Longman Caribbean; London: Longman, 1980. 4th ed. 200p. maps.

This book, first published in 1963, provides the general reader with an excellent introduction to the geography of the Caribbean. The book is designed for use in the upper sections of secondary schools. It is clearly written and very well illustrated both with black-and-white photographs and line diagrams and maps. After four introductory chapters which set the human and physical scene, the islands are considered individually. The section on Barbados (p. 82-92) covers development, landforms, rainfall, soils, land use and tenure, agriculture, livestock and fishing, occupations, tourism, population, communication and trade. This work is highly recommended as a non-technical overview of the country's geography.

52 **The Caribbean.**
    David L. Niddrie.   In: *Latin America: geographical perspectives*. Edited by Harold Blakemore, Clifford T. Smith.   London: Methuen, 1983, 2nd ed., p. 77-132.

A broad overview of the geography of the Caribbean, including the physical setting, environmental influences and hazards, pre-Columbian occupation of the islands and slavery. Recent aspects such as urbanization and economic development are also covered, and Barbados is mentioned in a number of the sections. Provides useful background reading.

53 **Modern Caribbean geography: for certificate examinations.**
John Niles.   London; Basingstoke, England: Macmillan Caribbean, 1986. 154p. maps.

A secondary school geography text written to cover the requirements of the CXC syllabus, taking into account its revision in 1985. After an introductory account which considers the nature of resources, the remaining chapters are arranged into five sections which deal with: 'Agriculture', 'Other primary industries', 'Extractive and manufacturing industry', 'Tertiary industry', and 'Population and settlement studies'. The text includes numerous photographs, diagrams and maps. Barbados is referred to in relation to urban development in particular. At the time of writing, the author was Head of Geography at Fatima College, Port of Spain, Trinidad.

54 **Notes on the geography of Barbados.**
Edward T. Price.   *Journal of the Barbados Museum and Historical Society*, vol. 29 (1962), p. 119-54.

This long article provides a detailed introduction principally to the physical geography of the island, although a short section discusses human aspects of early settlement and demography and contemporary agriculture (p. 122–27). Following this, there are lengthy sections on past and present shorelines, sea cliffs, soils, terraces, earth movements and erosion in the Scotland District. The article is well illustrated with maps, line diagrams and photographs and represents essential reading for those requiring an overview of the physical landscape of Barbados.

55 **Latin America.**
Harry Robinson.   London: Macdonald & Evans, 1970. 3rd ed. 509p. maps. bibliog.

Contains a quite detailed chapter on the West Indies (p. 184-222), and Barbados is considered on p. 213-14. This short account covers the island's location, structure, population and agriculture.

56 **Barbados: our environment.**
Ivan L. Waterman.   London: Macmillan Caribbean, 1979. 90p. maps.

This account is intended as an introduction to the physical and social environment of Barbados for the upper levels of primary schools and lower levels of secondary schools. However, as the foreword stresses, the book should also prove of use to parents and other adults, including tour guides and visitors, who are seeking a basic introductory guide to the country. The book is split into four main units dealing with the physical environment, communities, employment, communications and transport.

57 **Middle America: its land and peoples.**
Robert C. West, John P. Augelli.   Englewood Cliffs, New Jersey: Prentice-Hall, 1976. 2nd ed. 494p. maps. bibliog.

A very detailed text on the geography of Middle America, which places a strong emphasis on cultural and historical geographical matters. Barbados is described in chapter seven. The account covers the land, economic patterns, population and settlement in a short but very effective manner. Maps of major soil types and annual rainfall are included. Chapters three to five, which deal with the West Indies as a whole, are also of interest as Barbados is frequently discussed. These chapters cover geographical aspects of West Indian history, present-day economic geography and contemporary population and political geography.

58 **Nelson's West Indian geography: a new study of the Commonwealth Caribbean and Guyana.**
    W. Williams-Bailey, P. H. Pemberton.   Walton-on-Thames, Surrey, England: Nelson, 1979. 2nd ed. 164p. maps.

Presents a thematic study of West Indian geography, with each major theme illustrated by a detailed case study chosen from a specific territory. The chapters cover: 'The physical setting', 'The background to a problem', 'Sugar today', 'The contribution of the small farmers', 'Extractive industries in the West Indies', 'Forest and sea: two under-used resources', 'Industrialisation', 'Animal husbandry and tourism: areas of development in our economics', 'Transport, communications, and inter-island migration', 'Rural-urban migration and the growth of towns' and 'Conclusion: the problems of the West Indies'. Barbados features in several of the chapters, its history being dealt with on p. 36-37 as a microcosm of the Caribbean.

Barbados and tomorrow.
See item no. 19.

The history of Barbados.
See item no. 356.

Caribbean Geography.
See item no. 907.

Human geography

59 **Geographic notes on the Barbados malaria epidemic.**
    L. Schuyler Fonaroff.   *Professional Geographer*, vol. 18 (1966), p. 155-63.

During the autumn of 1927, Barbados experienced its first, sudden and violent epidemic of malaria fever. This paper follows a strongly geographical approach in mapping the first and second epidemic waves, the former focusing on coastal St. James, the latter on Christ Church. These events are examined in relation to factors such as the physical geography of the island and it is concluded that a series of almost unrelated geographical situations came together to make disease transmission possible at the time of the epidemic.

60 **Landscape as resource for national development: a Caribbean view.**
Brian J. Hudson. *Geography*, vol. 71, no. 2 (1986), p. 116-21.
Presents the case for regarding landscape as a cultural and economic resource, and maintains that in many Third World areas such as the West Indies, the importance of landscape is all too frequently overlooked. The need for careful physical planning to ensure that landscape is a renewable resource is the theme taken up in the second half of the paper. Barbados is mentioned several times in this pan-Caribbean view.

61 **Centres, peripheries, tourism and socio-spatial development.**
Winston C. Husbands. *Ontario Geographer*, vol. 17 (1981), p. 37-59.
The geographical or spatial aspects of development resulting from tourism are examined in this article by a Barbadian national. It is argued that without a radical and critical restructuring, such developments frequently increase spatial inequalities on a centre and periphery basis. Although examples are drawn from around the world, Barbados is cited in table three (p. 47) and many of the general arguments are highly germane.

62 **Caribbean views of Caribbean land.**
David Lowenthal. *Canadian Geographer*, vol. 5, no. 2 (1961), p. 1-9.
Focusing mainly on the British West Indies, the author examines why it is that economic perspectives have always dominated views of people-land relationships in the Caribbean region. This is a distractingly wide and interesting essay, covering agriculture, housing and urbanization. The main argument is that 'whether resident or absentee, proprietors thought of land principally as a machine for making money'.

63 **A West Indies geographic pathology survey: causes of death in some English-speaking Caribbean countries.**
N. D. McGlashan. Hobart, Tasmania: University of Tasmania, Department of Geography, 1982. 67p. maps. bibliog. (Occasional Paper no. 12).
This careful study in medical geography analyses a number of causes of death in ten English-speaking Caribbean countries, including Barbados. The incidence of deaths from various cancers, heart disease, diabetes, motor vehicle accidents, and their ecological relations are investigated. Barbados is shown to have a relatively high crude mortality rate for males, but a relatively low one for all deaths among the female population.

64 **An epidemiological spectrum in the Caribbean.**
Neil D. McGlashan. *Caribbean Geography*, vol. 1, no. 4 (1984), p. 234-46.
Examines patterns of mortality in ten Commonwealth Caribbean islands, Barbados among them. Aspects of mortality are correlated with several measures

18

of economic development, showing for instance a strong association between heart disease and motor vehicle density in the ten countries.

65 Migration and rural development in the Caribbean.
Janet D. Momsen. *Tijdschrift voor Economische en Sociale Geografie*, vol. 77, no. 1 (1986), p. 50-58.

Starting from the observation that 'migration is an institutionalised aspect of Caribbean societies', this geographical account briefly reviews the migration destinations of West Indians both within the Caribbean and in Europe and North America, before assessing the impact of such movements on rural areas and agriculture. It is argued that rather than providing capital for investment in agriculture, migration generally encourages decline in agricultural activity and productivity.

66 Mapping educational disparities in the Caribbean.
Mike Morrissey. *Teaching Geography*, vol. 10, no. 2 (1985), p. 56-60.

Presents basic data on secondary and tertiary educational attainment in the political entities of the Caribbean archipelago as the basis for a mapping exercise in social geography.

67 Congruence between space preferences and socio-demographic structure in Barbados, West Indies: the use of cognitive studies in Third World urban planning and development.
Robert B. Potter. *Geoforum*, vol. 14, no. 3 (1983), p. 249-65.

This paper seeks to examine the similarity existing between patterns of social, economic and demographic change over time in Barbados on the one hand, and the perceptions of a sample of residents on the other. As such, the paper examines the sociodemographic change that has occurred in Barbados since its first settlement. The increasing spatial concentration of people and activities in the metropolitan Bridgetown area is emphasized. An index of present-day socioeconomic study is developed at the parish level.

68 Spatial inequalities in Barbados, West Indies.
Robert B. Potter. *Transactions of the Institute of British Geographers*, new series, vol. 11, no. 2 (1986), p. 183-98.

After an introduction concerning spatial development theory, this paper presents a suggested method for the identification, analysis and monitoring of spatial inequalities, based on personal construct theory. The method is illustrated by field research carried out in Barbados, providing indices of socioeconomic development, agricultural standing and population change. Subsequently, the evolution and present-day nature of spatial inequalities in Barbados are discussed using conventional socioeconomic indicators. By such means, the acuity of the semantic grid approach is demonstrated.

69   **Slavery to freedom in the British Caribbean: ecological considerations.**
      Bonham C. Richardson.   *Caribbean Geography*, vol. 1, no. 3 (1984), p. 164-75.

Suggests that differing environments were important variables in the British Caribbean at emancipation. The paper looks at three different ecologically-oriented adaptations – 'highland', 'lowland' and 'migration'. Barbados is placed in the latter category, for ex-slaves were given access only to rented tenantry ground. Thus, thousands of freedmen emigrated in response.

70   **The economic geography of Barbados: a study of the relationships between environmental variations and economic development.**
      Otis Paul Starkey.   New York: Columbia University Press, 1939. 228p. maps. bibliog.

Despite its age, this book, which was originally submitted as a PhD thesis at Columbia University, still affords a useful introduction to the economic geography of Barbados. Chapter one 'Introduction' and chapter two 'The Barbadian environment' offer a good overview of the island's basic geography. The latter covers its position, climate, ocean currents, structure and relief, water supply, soils, flora, fauna and minerals, and finishes with a regional survey. The remaining chapters deal with: 'The beginnings of the sugar and slave economy, 1625-51; 'The development of the sugar and slave economy, 1652-1748'; 'Barbados under the planter aristocracy, 1748-1833': 'Barbados since emancipation'; 'The recent Barbadian economy: production'; 'The recent Barbadian economy: consumption'; and 'Conclusions'.

71   **Land use change in Western Barbados.**
      P. Wilson.   MSc. dissertation, McGill University, Montreal, 1984. 291p. maps. bibliog.

Researched during the late 1970s and early 1980s, this dissertation seeks to examine recent land use changes on the populated leeward side of the island, using aerial photographs and other available evidence.

Barbados: outsider of the Antilles.
See item no. 1.

Barbados.
See item no. 21.

Mental maps of Barbados, part 1: how Barbadians perceive their environment.
See item no. 24.

Barbados the singular island.
See item no. 26.

Insularity and identity in the Caribbean.
See item no. 29.

20

The genesis of tourism in Barbados: further notes on the welcoming society.
See item no. 208.

Tourism and development: the case of Barbados, West Indies.
See item no. 214.

The presugar era of European settlement in Barbados.
See item no. 348.

The population of Barbados.
See item no. 397.

Metropolitan dominance and family planning in Barbados.
See item no. 404.

Migration as an agent of change in Caribbean island ecosystems.
See item no. 419.

West Indian migration to Britain: a social geography.
See item no. 439.

West Indian societies.
See item no. 489.

The dissolution of the West Indies Federation, a study in political geography.
See item no. 583.

The sugar industry in Barbados during the seventeenth century.
See item no. 677.

The spatial structure of Barbadian peasant agriculture.
See item no. 689.

Recent developments in planning the settlement hierarchy of Barbados: implications concerning the debate on urban primacy.
See item no. 748.

The hand analysis of repertory grids: an appropriate method for Third World environmental studies.
See item no. 750.

Spatial perceptions and public involvement in Third World urban planning: the example of Barbados.
See item no. 751.

Mental maps and spatial variations in residential desirability: a Barbados case study.
See item no. 794.

Age differences in the content and style of cognitive maps of Barbadian schoolchildren.
See item no. 824.

Physical geography

72 **Beach changes and recreational planning on the west coast of Barbados, West Indies.**
J. Brian Bird. *Geographica Polonica*, vol. 36 (1977), p. 31-41.
This paper takes a broad look at changes in beach morphology and sediments along the west coast. These include changes resulting from both human activities and natural causes such as hurricanes. It is argued that although beach changes are generally not great, small changes may lead to disproportionately large effects. Includes rather less on the topic of recreational planning than the title implies.

73 **Coastal subsystems of Western Barbados, West Indies.**
J. Brian Bird, A. Richards, P. P. Wong. *Geografiska Annaler*,
vol. 61A (1979), p. 221-36.
Extended analysis shows that the main features of the west coast are inherited from events associated with complex sea-level fluctuations and the extension of coral terraces in the Quaternary period. Nineteen beach cells were identified along the west coast and intensive studies of wave and current processes leading to changes in beach planform and profile were made at two of them, Gibbes and Sandy Lane Bays.

74 **The Lesser Antilles.**
William Morris Davis.   New York: American Geographical Society, 1926. 207p. maps. bibliog. (American Geographical Society Map of Hispanic America Publication, no. 2).
Illustrated with sixty-six line diagrams and sixteen black-and-white plates. The author, the doyen of American geomorphologists, provides a basic introduction to the structural history and present-day physical form of the islands of the Lesser Antilles arc. Most of these have been formed by volcanic processes, so Barbados is described as an 'aberrant island' which does not 'fit into the scheme that accounts so well for the other islands'.

75 **Doline morphology and development in Barbados.**
Michael Day.   *Annals of the Association of American Geographers*,
vol. 73, no. 2 (1983) p. 206-19.
The doline, or small enclosed depression, is a characteristic of the eighty-five per cent of Barbados that is composed of coralline limestone, although such features occupy only one per cent of the total surface area. A sample of 360 dolines were surveyed in the field and their salient attributes analysed. Perhaps most significantly, doline densities increase up to an altitude of around 150 metres and decline thereafter.

76 **The dry valleys of Barbados: a critical review of their pattern and origin.**

J. Fermor. *Transactions of the Institute of British Geographers*, no. 57 (1972), p. 153-65.

Analyses a major erosional feature of the Barbados landscape, namely the valleys which radiate from the high ground of the Scotland District. Most of these valleys reach the sea and are dry, save for short stretches near to their mouths, and infrequent ephemeral flows after heavy storms. It is posited that such surface run-off after heavy storms is the causal mechanism, with climatic change and karstification acting as contributory factors.

77 **Our water supply.**

W. H. E. Garrod. *Journal of the Barbados Museum and Historical Society*, vol. 19, no. 3 (1952), p. 107-11.

Reproduces the text of a talk given to members of the Barbados Museum and Historical Society on 9 June 1952. The author first summarizes the geology of the island along with its hydrology, before turning in some detail to its water collection and distribution system.

78 **Physical changes in Barbados since 1627.**

E. G. B. Gooding. *Journal of the Barbados Museum and Historical Society*, vol. 35, no. 3 (1977), p. 178-88.

Considers the main physiographic, landscape and other changes that have occurred in Barbados since its settlement by the British in 1627. Comments on forest clearance, soil erosion and landslips in the Scotland District are provided.

79 **The coastal soils of Barbados.**

Roland E. Randall. *Journal of the Barbados Museum and Historical Society*, vol. 33, no. 1 (1969), p. 25-27.

Fifty soil samples were taken at various distances from the sea along profile transects. These were then analysed for calcium carbonate, carbon, moisture, pH and salt; and grain size analyses were also carried out. The results are presented in a comprehensive table (to be found on p. 90 of the same issue), and are discussed in the short text of the paper.

80 **A comparative study of some soil nutrients in the coralline sugarcane soils of Barbados.**

J. B. D. Robinson. *Journal of Soil Science*, vol. 3 (1952), p. 182-89.

Reports the results of field-to-field sampling of soils in 1947 in comparison with a comparable sampling between the years 1929 and 1932. The two sets of data obtained are compared in the light of agricultural advancement, particularly change in manurial policy which occurred at around the time of the first field sampling. The results show there had been a mean increase in soil organic carbon of forty-one per cent during the fifteen to eighteen year period.

81 **Plant introduction and landscape change in Barbados, 1625 to 1830.**
David Watts. PhD thesis, McGill University, Montreal, 1963.
383p. maps. bibliog.

A detailed study of the introduction of plants into Barbados, stressing that the effects of this have been such that the present-day landscape of Barbados bears little or no resemblance to that before European settlement in 1627, with the exception of the small area of Turner's Hall Wood in the Scotland District.

82 **Man's influence on the vegetation of Barbados 1627-1800.**
David Watts. Hull, England: University of Hull, 1966. 96p. maps.
bibliog. (Occasional Papers in Geography, no. 4).

This is essentially an abridged and more readily available version of the same author's PhD thesis, *Plant introduction and landscape change in Barbados, 1625 to 1830* (q.v.). The chapters are as follows: 'The physical influences'; 'The pre-European vegetation'; 'Forest clearance 1627 to 1665'; 'Plant introduction 1627 to 1800'; 'Conclusion'.

83 **Persistence and change in the vegetation of oceanic islands: an example from Barbados, West Indies.**
David Watts. *Canadian Geographer*, vol. 14, no. 2 (1970),
p. 91-109.

A biogeographical account of the vegetation of Barbados, stressing that apart from Turner's Hall Wood and the mangrove forest, all present-day plant associations have been greatly influenced and modified by humans and by grazing animals, if not actually owing their very existence to them. The paper includes a summary of the present-day vegetation of Barbados, a briefer account of the vegetation before 1627 and details of 'plant aliens' brought into Barbados.

84 **Caribbean soils: a soil study for agricultural science.**
Collin C. Weir. Kingston, London: Heinemann Educational, 1980.
125p. maps. bibliog.

The purpose of the book is to provide an introduction to the study of soils in the Caribbean, and it is aimed at those studying agriculture, forestry and geology. The text is divided into five parts: 'Soil formation and properties'; 'The soil and the plant'; 'Soil examination, management and improvement'; 'Soils of the Commonwealth Caribbean'; and 'Experiments in soil science'. The soils of Barbados are considered on p. 90-92 and there is a clear summary map of soil types in the country.

The economic geography of Barbados: a study of the relationships between environmental variations and economic development.
See item no. 70.

The formation of the Lesser Antilles.
See item no. 114.

The geology of Barbados, part 1: the coral rocks of Barbados and other West-Indian islands.
See item no. 123.

Geological background to soil conservation and land rehabilitation measures in Barbados, W.I.
See item no. 131.

Vegetation and environment on the Barbados coast.
See item no. 275.

The availability of soil water: with reference to studies with sugarcane growing in clay soils in Barbados.
See item no. 696.

Plantation and peasant farm – Barbados 1627-1960.
See item no. 697.

Evapotranspiration and sugar cane yields in Barbados.
See item no. 703.

The problems relative to soil conservation in the Scotland District.
See item no. 801.

The land conservation conundrum of Eastern Barbados.
See item no. 802.

Mechanisms and spatial patterns of erosion and instability in the Joe's River basin, Barbados.
See item no. 810.

Causes of environmental deterioration in Eastern Barbados since colonization.
See item no. 811.

Weather and climate

85 **The killer of 1780.**
  Warren Alleyne. *Bajan and South Caribbean*, no. 321 (Aug. 1980), p. 14-17.
A hurricane on 10 October 1780 killed over 4,000 people and caused widespread destruction, especially in Bridgetown where reportedly only 30 houses out of 1,200 escaped considerable damage.

86 **Barbados storm swell.**
William L. Donn, William T. McGuiness. *Journal of Geophysical Research*, vol. 64, no. 12 (1959), p. 2,341-49.

High and damaging sea waves often strike Barbados, although they do not appear to be associated with any local or known Caribbean storms. From the study, it appears that distant storms to the north, off the eastern coast of the United States, generate swell which affects both sides of Barbados.

87 **Hurricane 'Janet' at Barbados.**
Journal of the Barbados Museum and Historical Society, vol. 23, no. 4 (1956), p. 153-65.

A memorandum prepared by the Barbados Weather Observers Association on the conditions experienced during Hurricane Janet which hit Barbados on 22 September 1955. After a short introduction, the weather of the two preceding days is described, along with that experienced during the approach and passage of the hurricane.

88 **The great hurricane.**
David M. Ludlum. *Journal of the Barbados Museum and Historical Society*, vol. 31, no. 3 (1965), p. 127-31.

Describes the storm of October 1780, the severity of which results in its still being referred to as the 'Great Hurricane'. The loss of life in Barbados alone was estimated at 4,326, and the estimate for the entire West Indies was a staggering 22,000, whilst the loss of property is believed to have amounted to 1.3 million pounds.

89 **The hurricane of August 1831.**
George C. McAllister. *Journal of the Barbados Museum and Historical Society*, vol. 31, no. 4 (1966), p. 180-89.

George C. McAllister, an American sea captain, happened to be calling at Barbados when it was hit by a hurricane. This paper presents extracts from his journal, 10-18 August 1831, which describe the passage of the hurricane.

90 **Effects of Hurricane Allen on the Bellairs fringing reef.**
A. J. Mah. MSc dissertation, McGill University, Montreal, 1984. 258p. bibliog.

Following Hurricane Allen in the summer of 1980, this thesis looks at the effects that the storm system had on part of the western coast of Barbados. The Bellairs reef fronts the Bellairs Research Station of McGill University, which is situated on the St. James coast, just to the north of Holetown.

91 **The astronomical theory of climatic change: Barbados data.**
K. J. Mesolella, R. K. Matthews, W. S. Broecker, D. L. Thurber. *Journal of Geology*, vol. 77 (1968), p. 250-74.

The paper shows that periods of relatively high sea levels and associated reef development some 82,000, 105,000 and 125,000 years before the present correspond closely with periods of maximum summer solar insolation in the Northern Hemisphere. Such evidence tends to support strongly the astronomical theory of climatic change.

92 **The world weather guide.**
E. A. Pearce, C. G. Smith. London: Hutchinson, 1984. 480p. bibliog.

Aims to provide a description of the weather that can be expected in any part of the world at any given time during the year. The Caribbean islands are dealt with on p. 315-29, and Barbados specifically on p. 328. A table is given for the Bridgetown weather station, and for each month of the year details of temperature, relative humidity and precipitation are provided.

93 **Weather observations and records in Barbados, 1924-33.**
C. C. Skeete. *Journal of the Barbados Museum and Historical Society*, vol. 1, no. 3 (1934), p. 115-36.

Using records of the author's personal observations and various other meteorological data, a summary is provided of the weather in Barbados during the ten year period in question. Rainfall, wind direction and velocity, temperature, sunshine hours, thunderstorms and cyclonic weather are all considered in detail.

94 **Hurricanes.**
C. C. Skeete. *Journal of the Barbados Museum and Historical Society*, vol. 18, nos. 1-2 (1951), p. 39-43.

A résumé of a talk given by Skeete, then the Director of Agriculture, to members of the Museum and Historical Society on 21 August 1950. He explains the evolution of hurricanes, notes that the first fortnight in September appears to be the most likely time for their occurrence in Barbados, and lists the signs of an approaching hurricane.

95 **An historical description of the weather of the island of Barbados, West Indies during the period 1901 to 1960.**
C. C. Skeete. St. Michael, Barbados: Barbados Government Printing Office, [ca. 1968]. 364p. 2 maps.

This long and closely printed volume contains detailed descriptive accounts of the weather in Barbados during the first sixty years of the 20th century. The records are compiled from the author's personal weather diaries, supplemented by those of his relatives. A strong emphasis is placed on rainfall records. Chapter one presents a summary of the weather of Barbados, with a month-by-month guide. Chapter two provides a chronological listing of incidents of special interest, such as heavy rains, whilst tropical disturbances, storms and hurricanes are listed in chapter three. Chapters four and onwards describe the weather for each month of the years from 1901 to 1960.

96 **The weather in Barbados 1961-1970: supplement to an historical description of the weather of the island of Barbados, West Indies during the period, 1901-1960.**
C. C. Skeete, St. Michael, Barbados: Barbados Government Printing Office, [ca. 1972]. 98p.

This supplement to *An historical description of the weather of the island of Barbados, West Indies during the period 1901 to 1960* (q.v.) follows the same overall format, and documents weather conditions, particularly rainfall, from 1961 to 1970. Details of the island's records of atmospheric pressure, wind velocity, temperature, sunshine and rainfall taken at Codrington Agricultural Station, St. Michael are reproduced.

97 **Hurricanes: their nature and history particularly those of the West Indies and the southern coasts of the United States.**
Ivan Ray Tannehill. Princeton, New Jersey: Princeton University Press, 1938. Reprinted, New York: Greenwood Press, 1969. 257p. maps. bibliog.

The author, who at the time of writing was the Chief of the Marine Division, US Weather Bureau, Department of Agriculture, Washington, sets out to establish the essential facts and theories regarding tropical cyclones. As a part of the account, the author records the known history of hurricanes in the West Indies, the United States and adjacent waters of the Atlantic Ocean, the Gulf of Mexico and the Caribbean Sea. The effects of the 1780 and 1831 hurricanes on Barbados are quite extensively covered.

98 **An analysis of the 1964 solar radiation record at the Brace Experimental Station, St. James, Barbados.**
D. G. Trout. *Climatological Bulletin*, vol. 2 (1967), p. 29-44.

The author worked at the Brace Experimental Station of McGill University in 1964, undertaking the task of hand-scaling the solar radiation charts to obtain hourly values for both total solar radiation and diffuse sky radiation received on a horizontal surface. This paper, which is for the expert rather than the lay reader, presents a detailed analysis of this material.

99 **The climate of Barbados**
D. G. Trout. *Climatological Bulletin*, vol. 3 (1968), p. 1-17.

A useful paper providing a detailed overview of the island's climate. After introductory matters have been addressed, including the influence of the Inter-tropical Convergence Zone, separate sections present concise statements concerning temperatures, rainfall, cloudiness and sunshine, wind, solar radiation, hurricanes and sea surges. The text is supported by three maps, a photograph and three tables.

The economic geography of Barbados: a study of the relationships between environmental variations and economic development.
See item no. 70.

An early Wisconsin reef terrace at Barbados, West Indies and its climatic implications.
See item no. 121.

Climatic control of distribution and cultivation of sugar cane.
See item no. 708.

The Bellairs Research Institute.
See item no. 819.

Publications and theses from the Bellairs Research Institute and the Brace Research Institute of McGill University in Barbados, 1956-1984.
See item no. 951.

Maps and atlases

100   **Atlas for Barbados, Windwards and Leewards.**
London; Basingstoke, England: Macmillan Caribbean, 1974. 33p.
maps.

Intended as a junior school atlas for the Southern Caribbean, maps (on p. 4-5) are provided on the physical features, population densities, products, land uses, annual rainfall and winds, and soils of Barbados. The colour reproduction and graphics are somewhat basic.

101   **Barbados.**
London: Published by the Directorate of Colonial Surveys, 1956.
18 sheets. (DCS 18).

Based on aerial photography conducted during 1950-51, this 1:10,000 map covers the entire island. It is now over thirty years old and in desperate need of revision, a project that is currently under way.

102   **Barbados.**
London: Published for Barbados by the British Government's
Overseas Development Administration (Directorate of Overseas
Surveys), 1974. (DOS 418).

General topographical map of the island in one sheet at the scale of 1:50,000. This is effectively the second edition of the map, compiled from aerial photography undertaken in 1972. The first edition appeared in 1959.

103 **Bridgetown and environs, Barbados.**
London: Published for Barbados by the British Government's
Ministry of Overseas Development (Directorate of Overseas
Surveys), 1975. (DOS 118).
Provides a useful street plan of Bridgetown at the scale of 1:5,000. The map is
colour printed and shows the location of major public buildings, including
churches, educational institutions, government offices, hotels, public markets,
post offices, sports facilities, cinemas and recreational centres.

104 **Caribbean social studies atlas.**
Kingston, London: Heinemann Educational Books (Caribbean),
George Philip & Son, 1986. 56p. maps.
Intended specifically for the secondary school audience, this is an excellent
production. It presents thematic maps on the Caribbean region's history, people,
agriculture, industry, commerce and physical environment. The early sections
contain photographs, tables and graphs as well as atlas-type maps. A more
traditional world atlas section is included in the second half. The coverage of
Barbados is good and the atlas is also to be recommended for the general reader.

105 **Macmillan Caribbean certificate atlas.**
London: Macmillan, 1978. 2nd ed. 104p. maps.
This atlas includes pan-Caribbean maps of the region's physical and political
geography and tropical disturbances. Barbados is mapped on p. 22–23, although
rather poor colour reproduction reduces the effectiveness of this presentation.

106 **Philip's certificate atlas for the Caribbean.**
London: George Philip & Son, 1982. 137p. maps.
This atlas is aimed at secondary school students and accordingly it seeks to
provide a basic introduction to the field of geography as well as a comprehensive
atlas. Barbados is mapped on p. 56, a useful presentation highlighting relief and
settlements, land use, annual rainfall, soil types and population densities. A series
of Caribbean regional maps (p. 30-41) should also prove of interest. These depict
facets of history, physical and political geography, climate, geology, population,
agriculture and economic geography. An excellent atlas.

107 **A descriptive list of maps of Barbados.**
E. M. Shilstone. *Journal of the Barbados Museum and Historical
Society*, vol. 5, no. 2 (1938), p. 57-84.
A chronological listing of some sixty-four maps of Barbados and parts of the
island, mainly the city of Bridgetown, between 1657 and 1936. A descriptive
annotation is provided for each item included. The paper represents an essential
source for all those interested in historical aspects of cartography.

108 **Wallmap of Barbados.**
Basingstoke, England: Macmillan Caribbean, [n.d.].
This wallmap, reproduced at the scale 1:35,000 and measuring 1,150 × 875 mm, shows in one large map the principal physical and administrative features of the country, along with an inset street plan of Bridgetown. Three inset maps cover products, soils and rainfall.

109 **Wallmap of the Caribbean.**
Basingstoke, England: Macmillan Caribbean, [n.d.].
Measuring 850 × 1,220 mm, and at the scale of 1:3,500,000, this display map, which was produced in association with the West Indies Committee, covers basic aspects of the region's geography, including ports and transport routes, settlements and CARICOM membership. Barbados is included as a large-scale inset, as also are Trinidad, Jamaica, Belize, the Virgin Isles and the Leewards.

110 **West Indies and the Caribbean: Cosmopolitan Map Series.**
Chicago: Rand McNally, [n.d.].
A wallmap of the entire Caribbean region at the scale of 1:3,500,000, or 1cm on the map to 35km on the ground. A simple inset map of Barbados is provided along with the other major islands in the Caribbean chain.

Caribbean history in maps.
See item no. 295.

Geology

111 The geology and mineral resource assessment of the island of Barbados.
Leslie H. Barker, Einar G. Poole.   Bridgetown: Government Printing Office, [n.d.]. 109p. maps. bibliog.

This basic guide to the geology of Barbados was compiled as part of a programme of field mapping and mineral resource evaluation that was carried out for the Government of Barbados during 1979 and 1980. Strangely perhaps, the report starts with an account of the geology of the Scotland District, with its 40 km^2 of rugged badland relief. The geological history of the island is then covered on p. 23-26. The second part of the volume examines the mineral resource potential of the island (p. 31-52), while part three focuses on soil erosion in the Scotland District (p. 53-59).

112 Fossil birds from Barbados, West Indies.
Pierce Brodkorb.   *Journal of the Barbados Museum and Historical Society*, vol. 31, no. 1 (1964), p. 3-10.

Decribes fossil finds collected during the period 22-27 February 1963 from post-coral rock deposits, apparently of late Pleistocene age, from Ragged Point, St. Philip. Six species of bird are recognized, only two of which still occur in Barbados today, the Audubon's shearwater and the black-bellied tree-duck. Two others do not extend as far south today. The remaining two, a small goose and a coot are extinct and represent indigenous species new to science.

113   **Underthrusting of the eastern margin of the Antilles by the floor of the western North Atlantic Ocean and the origin of the Barbados ridge.**
       R. L. Chase, E. T. Bunce. *Journal of Geophysical Research*, vol. 74 (1969), p. 1,413-20.

Elucidates how the land mass of Barbados emerged from the sea when Tertiary sediments were compressed and then elevated along the junction of the Atlantic and Caribbean tectonic plates.

114   **The formation of the Lesser Antilles.**
       William Morris Davis. *Proceedings of the National Academy of Sciences*, vol. 10, no. 6 (1924), p. 205-11.

Inferences concerning the geological history of the islands of the Lesser Antilles from Puerto Rico to Trinidad and Tobago are presented, based primarily on observations made during a voyage in October and November 1923. Although Barbados receives only passing attention, the introduction highlights the fact that Barbados has different origins from most of the other islands. The article is of interest in that it places Barbadian geology within that of the Caribbean region.

115   **The Globigerina marls (and basal reef rocks) of Barbados with an appendix on the Foraminifera by F. Chapman.**
       G. F. Franks, J. B. Harrison. *Quarterly Journal of the Geological Society*, vol. 54 (1898), p. 540-55.

An early paper which deals with the formation and the structural characteristics of the basal layers of the island. Brief descriptive comments on the coral cap of the island are also to be found at the beginning of the paper.

116   **A note on diatoms in general.**
       Dingley P. Fuge. *Journal of the Barbados Museum and Historical Society*, vol. 1, no. 2 (1934), p. 84-89.

Diatoms are unicellular algae, the remains of which are found fossilized in the basement rocks of the island. The aim of this brief article is to describe such diatoms. Illustrations of some typical diatoms are included on p. 84.

117   **The geology of Barbados.**
       J. B. Harrison, A. J. Jukes-Browne. *Geological Magazine*, vol. 4 (1902), p. 550-54.

Following the publication of Joseph Spencer's paper, 'On the geological and physical development of Barbados: with notes on Trinidad' (q.v.) in the *Quarterly Journal of the Geological Society* earlier in 1902, Harrison and Jukes-Browne raise a series of objections to the geological constructions placed on evidence presented in that paper.

118 **The coral rocks of Barbados.**
J. B. Harrison. *Quarterly Journal of the Geological Society*,
vol. 63 (1907), p. 318-37.

Harrison visited the island for three weeks during August 1906 and devoted as much of that time as possible to examining the areas described by Joseph Spencer in his paper 'On the geological and physical development of Barbados: with notes on Trinidad' (q.v.) published in the *Quarterly Journal of the Geological Society* in 1902. In this article, Harrison provides critical comments on the stratigraphical details included in Spencer's paper. The work is based on a series of traverses made from the middle of the island to the Crane on the south-eastern coast. The article is accompanied by an extract from the geological map of Barbados prepared by J. B. Harrison and A. J. Jukes-Browne.

119 **Notes on the extraneous minerals in the coral limestones of Barbados.**
J. B. Harrison with the assistance of C. B. W. Anderson.
Quarterly Journal of the Geological Society, vol. 75 (1919),
p. 158-72.

Fragments of limestone were dissolved in dilute hydrochloric acid in order to test for extraneous minerals. The fragments of minerals and splinters of glass found contained in the corals are regarded as being pieces of wind-borne volcanic debris which have been protected from weathering by their enclosure in limestone.

120 **Near-surface subaerial diagenesis of Pleistocene carbonates, Barbados, West Indies.**
Randolph S. Harrison. PhD thesis, Brown University,
Providence, Rhode Island, 1974. 332p. bibliog.

Argues that Barbados represents a unique natural laboratory for the examination of problems of near-surface subaerial diagenesis. The aim is to examine the nature and distribution of caliche profiles developed on a succession of tectonically uplifted, subaerially exposed Pleistocene reef tracts. Concludes that the evolution of caliche is governed by the four factors of climate, soil cover, substrate and time.

121 **An early Wisconsin reef terrace at Barbados, West Indies and its climatic implications.**
Noel P. James, E. Mountjoy, A. Ohmura. *Bulletin of the Geological Society of America*, vol. 82 (1971), p. 2,011-18.

The discovery of a reef terrace between 0 and 4.5 metres above sea level and located along the north-western coast of Barbados is reported in this paper. The reef is dated at approximately 60,000 years before the present, and appears to have been formed during the last warm period.

122   **Late Pleistocene reef limestones, Northern Barbados, West Indies.**
      Noel P. James.   PhD thesis, McGill University, Montreal, 1972.
      242p.

Separate reef complexes were formed on either side of the northern Barbados pre-Pleistocene structural arch during marine transgressions some 83,000 and 104,000 years ago. Late Pleistocene uplift has exposed both of these reefs and also a narrow fringing reef deposited some 60,000 years ago. The dissertation analyses the geological characteristics of these exposed reefs.

123   **The geology of Barbados, part I: the coral rocks of Barbados and**
      other West Indian islands.
      A. J. Jukes-Browne, J. B. Harrison.   *Quarterly Journal of the*
      Geological Society, vol. 47 (1891), p. 197-250.

A 19th-century classic which starts by stressing that although Barbados had always been a station for British forces, and the first port of call for Royal Mail steamers, at the time of writing there was no adequate account concerning the geology of the island. The paper includes sections covering contemporary coral reefs, the raised reefs or coral rocks, analyses of coral rocks, comparison of the raised reefs of Barbados with similar formations in other West Indian islands and the physical geography of the Caribbean region during the formation of the reefs. A short note by William Hill, 'On the minute structure of some coral limestones from Barbados' is included as appendix one.

124   **The geology of Barbados, part II: the oceanic deposits.**
      A. J. Jukes-Browne, J. B. Harrison.   *Quarterly Journal of the*
      Geological Society, vol. 48 (1892), p. 170-226.

A detailed study of the oceanic rocks of Barbados.

125   **The tertiary of Barbados, W.I.**
      H. G. Kugler.   *Geological Magazine*, vol. 98, no. 4 (1961),
      p. 348-50.

Published as correspondence to the editor, this short piece discusses the utility of a range of stratigraphic terms proposed in a paper published by another author in 1960. In so doing, attention is turned to the Scotland Formation, Joe's River Formation, Oceanic Formation and Bissex Hill Formation.

126   **Recent sediments off the west coast of Barbados, West Indies.**
      I. G. Macintyre.   PhD dissertation, McGill University, Montreal,
      1967. 169p. maps. bibliog.

Provides an examination of the sediments and morphology of the sea floor off the west coast of Barbados to an outer limit of 1,300 feet.

127 **Submerged coral reefs, west coast of Barbados, West Indies.**
I. G. Macintyre. *Canadian Journal of Earth Science*, vol. 4 (1967), p. 461-74.

Evidence from sonar profiles indicates that two submerged barrier reefs parallel the west coast at depths of around 70 feet and 230 feet.

128 **Preliminary mapping of the insular shelf off the west coast of Barbados, West Indies.**
I. G. Macintyre. *Caribbean Journal of Science*, vol. 8 (1968), p. 95-100.

Presents the results of a rapid reconnaissance survey of the insular shelf noting its division into fringe reefs, sand belt, dead coral rubble and active coral growth.

129 **Sediments off the west coast of Barbados: diversity of origins.**
I. G. Macintyre. *Marine Geology*, vol. 9 (1970), p. 5-23.

Summarizes the diverse sources of the sediments found off the west coast of Barbados to an outer depth of 1,300 feet.

130 **Mechanical and biological erosion of beachrock in Barbados, West Indies.**
Roger F. McLean. PhD dissertation, McGill University, Montreal, 1964. 266p.

Provides a regionally-based study of the distribution, forms, processes and rates of mechanical and biological erosion of carbonate clastic rocks in the littoral zone.

131 **Geological background to soil conservation and land rehabilitation measures in Barbados, W.I.**
P. Martin-Kaye, J. Badcock. *Journal of the Barbados Museum and Historical Society*, vol. 30, no. 1 (1962), p. 3-13.

This revised version of a paper read at the Third Caribbean Geological Conference held in Jamaica in April 1962 examines the geological causes of land movement in the twenty-two square mile Scotland District. This useful and straightforward account considers the area's stratigraphy, groundwater conditions, conservation practices, block movements, surface stabilization, land shaping, earth dams and roads.

132 **The old basement of Barbados with some remarks on Barbadian geology.**
C. A. Matley. *Geological Magazine*, vol. 69 (1932), p. 366-73.

Starting with the observation that 'the island of Barbados occupies a position of exceptional geographical and geological interest in the West Indian region', Matley summarizes some additions to knowledge of the island's stratigraphy resulting from the search for oil, before describing the nature and form of the basement rocks of Barbados, evidence being drawn from samples taken from the Chalky Mount area in November 1929.

133 Zonation of uplifted Pleistocene coral reefs on Barbados, West Indies.

Kenneth J. Mesolella. *Science*, vol. 156 (1967), p. 638-40.

The species composition and physical zonation of the uplifted coral reefs of Barbados are reported in this short paper. The most frequently represented coral species are shown to be *Acropora palmata*, *Acropora cervicornis*, and *Montastrea annularis*. These Pleistocene reefs are demonstrated to be similar in composition to recent reef formations in the Caribbean basin.

134 The uplifted reefs of Barbados: physical stratigraphy, facies relationships and absolute chronology.

Kenneth J. Mesolella.   PhD thesis, Brown University, Providence, Rhode Island, 1968. 736p. maps. bibliog.

Barbados has undergone tectonic uplift during the Pleistocene at an average rate of 1 foot per 1,000 years. During this uplift, reef tracts formed periodically around the island. These have been exposed in the form of a 'terraced coral cap' to the island. Each terrace represents an uplifted reef tract and, therefore, is essentially constructional in origin, rather than erosional. This lengthy and highly detailed thesis considers the geological attributes of these uplifted reefs.

135 A small assemblage of vertebrate fossils from Spring Bay, Barbados.

Clayton E. Ray. *Journal of the Barbados Museum and Historical Society*, vol. 31, no. 1 (1964), p. 11-22.

A period of nine days was spent in Barbados during the latter half of February 1963, the primary purpose being to search for fossil vertebrates, but the opportunity to collect modern vertebrates and terrestrial gastropods was also taken. The finds are summarized and discussed in this paper.

136 Paleogene of Barbados and its bearing on history and structure of Antillean-Caribbean region.

A. Senn. *Bulletin of the American Association of Petroleum Geologists*, vol. 24, no. 9 (1940), p. 1,548-610.

A useful paper which examines in detail the stratigraphic sequence of Barbados, with particular reference to the Scotland Beds, Joe's River Formation, Oceanic Formation, Bissex Hill marl and the coral rock. Examines the ages of these formations in relation to the geological history of the wider Antillean-Caribbean region.

137 On the geological and physical development of Barbados: with notes on Trinidad.

Joseph William Winthrop Spencer. *Quarterly Journal of the Geological Society*, vol. 57 (1902), p. 354-67.

Noting that there was already by 1902 a quite extensive literature on the geology of Barbados and Trinidad, the author aims to record some newly observed features. The sections in the paper on Barbados deal with the island's hydrographical relationships, physical characteristics and erosion features, its older geological formations (Scotland Beds and Oceanic Series), the White Limestone Formation, the Ragged Point Series and the Bath-Reef Series.

138   The uplifted reef tracts of Barbados, West Indies: detailed mapping and radiometric dating of selected areas.

Frederick Wiley Taylor.   MSc dissertation, Brown University, Providence, Rhode Island, 1974. 235p. maps. bibliog.

Detailed fieldwork and mapping of the reef tracts in a number of parts of the island are presented. The style makes this more suited to the specialist rather than the layperson.

139   The Scotland Beds of Barbados.

C. T. Trenchmann.   *Geological Magazine*, vol. 62 (1925), p. 481-504.

A frequently cited paper arguing that Barbados 'deserves special attention from geologists'. At the outset, the division of its rocks into three series, the coral rock, Oceanic Series and the Scotland Beds is explained. The paper is then concerned to determine the age of the Scotland Beds which form the basement of the island, underlying the coral rock and the Oceanics everywhere. In previous investigations, J. B. Harrison and A. J. Jukes-Browne had tentatively expressed the view that the Scotland Beds are Miocene in age. The present paper, via a detailed review of fossil finds, concludes that they are of a High Eocene aspect. The paper contains six photographs and one map.

140   The uplift of Barbados.

C. T. Trenchmann.   *Geological Magazine*, vol. 70 (1933), p. 19-47.

Essentially, the present-day surface of Barbados has been formed by the uplift of coral limestone rock laid under marine conditions on top of the Oceanic and Scotland Beds. The coral rock has been raised to a maximum height of 1,100 feet, and is approximately 240 feet thick. This paper discusses the process of uplift and the erosion of the coral cap in the north-east of the island to form the Scotland District. It is argued that the coral rock was formed almost entirely before the process of uplift commenced. This important article contains a much reproduced cross-section of the geology of the island, drawn from the west to east coasts.

141   The base and top of the coral rock in Barbados.

C. T. Trenchmann.   *Geological Magazine*, vol. 74 (1937), p. 337-59.

The coral limestone rock which caps approximately eighty-five per cent of the island of Barbados is considered in detail in this early paper. Different theories concerning the development of the terraces found on the coral cap are discussed, relating primarily to the processes of either marine erosion or fault scarping.

Barbados our island home.
See item no. 14.

The Lesser Antilles.
See item no. 74.

Our water supply.
See item no. 77.

The astronomical theory of climatic change: Barbados data.
See item no. 91.

The natural history of Barbados.
See item no. 250.

Calcareous encrusting organisms of the recent and Pleistocene reefs of Barbados, West Indies.
See item no. 266.

Quantitative analysis of community pattern and structure on a coral reef bank in Barbados, West Indies.
See item no. 270.

The history of Barbados.
See item no. 356.

The problems relative to soil conservation in the Scotland District.
See item no. 801.

An annotated bibliography of research on contemporary fossil reefs in Barbados, West Indies.
See item no. 945.

Travellers' Accounts

Pre-20th century

142 **Barbados' first hotelier.** ·
Warren Alleyne. *Bajan & South Caribbean*, no. 291 (Feb. 1978),
p. 4-7.

Although not strictly a traveller's account, this provides interesting information
on early tourism and hotels in Barbados. Using extracts from his own *Historic
Bridgetown* (q.v.), Alleyne traces the story of the corpulent Rachel Pringle
Polgreen. She was the daughter of an African slave woman and a lascivious
Scottish absentee schoolmaster, William Lauder, who arrived in Barbados around
1750. Through devious means, and a few dubious Royal Navy visiting
connections, Rachel managed to escape the incestuous advances of her father,
and by 1781 had established the island's first hotel in Canary Street (the present
St. George Street) in Bridgetown. Through the indiscretions and riotous conduct
of Prince William Henry, later William IV, Rachel was able to bill royalty for
£700, and thereby extend her hostelries tenfold. Other 'unmarried' female
hoteliers are also chronicled, including the well-known Caroline Lee. In the same
issue of the *Bajan* there is an interesting article on Barbados' hotels today.

143 **A voyage to Guinea, Brazil and the West Indies.**
John Atkins. London: Cass, 1970. 265p.

The account of a voyage undertaken from 1721 to 1723 by a surgeon in the Royal
Navy. After traversing the West African coast for several months, the ship finally
arrived in Barbados on 3 August 1722, where it stopped for six days to take on
board rum and provisions. There are descriptions of sugar manufacturing, trade
and the government of the island. The high life of the gay and handsome planters
is said to have degenerated into drinking and gaming, while their womenfolk,
though homely, are described as great swearers. A charity sermon preached by

command of the governor in 1734, and outlining the duty of the rich towards the poor, is also included. This account was first published in 1735.

144 **Four years residence in the West Indies.**
F. Bayley. London: William Kidd; Dublin: W. F. Wakeman; Glasgow: R. J. Finlay; Edinburgh: Adam Black, 1833. 3rd ed. 742p.

The account of the son of a military officer who was asked to accompany his father to the West Indies at the tender age of eighteen years. The Barbados section (p. 24-151) begins with a landing by night and changing 'hotels' from Betsy Austin's to Sabina Brade's. There is a description of Bridgetown – its houses, shops (though no booksellers!), public buildings and military barracks. In spite of a series of expatriate invitations to dine out, the author managed to find time to visit a plantation, Codrington College and Speightstown. He reflects on the system of education, the apparent distrust Barbadians have for 'redcoats', the dishonesty of domestic slaves, negro parties and entertainment and the general dislike of Methodists. The style is a little precious at times, with Bayley making remarks in French and Latin and quoting pieces of poetry. However, his advice to begin the day at 5 am in order to see Barbados at its best is something which can be recommended for any visitor to the island.

145 **An account of Barbados two hundred years ago.**
Introduced by Henry Cadbury. *Journal of the Barbados Museum and Historical Society*, vol. 9, no. 2 (Feb. 1942), p. 81-83.

Describes the fourteen-week stay of a Quaker, John Smith of Burlington, New Jersey, in 1742. The account refers to visits to the synagogue (including mention of its garrulous congregation), various churches belonging to the Anglicans, and meeting centres of the Society of Friends. There are also references to the island's main towns and fortifications, and to the necessity for the inhabitants to drink water filtered through large stones due to the poor quality of the supply.

146 **A Quaker account of Barbados in 1718.**
Introduced by Henry Cadbury. *Journal of the Barbados Museum and Historical Society*, vol. 10, no. 3 (May 1943), p. 118-24.

An extract from the journal of Thomas Chalkley (1675-1741), an English businessman and Quaker who had emigrated to Philadelphia. The account is of a three-month visit to Barbados in 1718. Chalkley is very critical of the morals and particularly the drunkenness of most of the population, a vice which often led to premature death (Chalkley attended several funerals during his stay). His natural sympathy for the plight of the slaves is epitomized in the gruesome description of a mastiff devouring the carcase of a negro. There are references to some of the island's natural attractions, such as 'the Spout' and Oliver's Cave, and to natural disasters in the form of hurricane and earthquake.

147 **Six months in the West Indies.**
Henry Nelson Coleridge. London: John Murray, 1825.
Reprinted, New York: Negro Universities Press, 1970. 332p.

The account of a traveller seeking a cure for rheumatism. It is liberally interspersed with a 'vagabond humour' said to be inherited from his mother, and several impressive lapses into French, Spanish, Portuguese and Latin. Coleridge arrived in Barbados in January 1825 with his distinguished relative William H. Coleridge (the first bishop of the island), and describes the wild delight of the negro inhabitants who were believed to live better than those in any other colony. There are references to Bridgetown clubs, the prison housed in the Parliament buildings, the Central School, the education of the free coloureds, and the general lack of sophistication and foul language of the local whites. However, most criticism is reserved for matters religious. Insufficient churches, their poor design, and the inadequacy of Codrington College as a tertiary institution, are given as typical examples calling for improvement.

148 **Hotel keepers and hotels in Barbados.**
Neville Connell. *Journal of the Barbados Museum and Historical Society*, vol. 33, no. 4 (Nov. 1970), p. 162-85.

An entertaining history of various inns, taverns and hotels in Barbados from those of the 17th century to the early 20th-century precursors of today's tourist industry. Most of the early references are taken from the accounts of travellers (including Dr. George Pinckard in 1796, H. N Bailey in 1826 and C. W. Day in 1852), together with their descriptions of the hostelries and their keepers. Connell provides details of the establishments and persons of Mary Bella Green, Rachel Pringle Polgreen, Sabina Brade, Betsy Lemon, Nancy Clark, Betsy Austin, Caroline Lee and Hannah Lewis. There are also references to the Ice House, other Bridgetown hotels, and the Marine under George Pomeroy.

149 **The West Indies before and since slave emancipation.**
John Davy. London: W. Cash; Dublin: J. Glashan & J. Gilpin;
Bridgetown: J. Bowen, 1854. Reprinted, London: Cass, 1971. rev.
ed. 551p. map. bibliog.

The observations of an inspector general of army hospitals who had resided mainly in Barbados from 1845 to 1848. Information is also provided by friends and the official returns found in the 'Blue Books'. After a general introduction to the Windwards and Leewards, the author devotes three out of seventeen chapters to Barbados. In these, he discusses the island's relative importance, its geology, rainfall, climate, racial and occupational composition, agricultural production before and after emancipation, and a few rather unusual, if not somewhat inaccessible, places of interest. There is also an interesting and quite detailed subsection on redlegs, in which their health, anatomy, education and behaviour are compared with those of other whites, together with the coloured and negro members of the population.

150 **The memoirs of Père Labat 1693-1705.**
Translated and abridged by John Eaden. London: Cass, 1931.
Reprinted, 1970. rev. ed. 263p.

A summary of the posthumous *Nouveau voyage aux isles de l'Amérique*, which omits much of the botanical and historical narrative and concentrates on the personal adventures of this French missionary priest of the Jacobin order. Labat was thirty-seven when he came to Barbados in September 1700 for a ten-day visit, during which he only saw the leeward side of the island. As an architect, he offers some impressions of the island's housing. There are also careful observations on the strength of the militia and fortifications, and reflections on the cruel treatment of slaves, both black and white. The account is injected with a great deal of humour. While dining with the governor, for instance, he pretends to puff at a proffered post-prandial pipe out of politeness, even though he is a confessed non-smoker.

151 **Desultory sketches and tales of Barbados.**
Theodore Easel. London: Stewart & Murray, 1840. 264p.

Written by an Englishman, possibly under a pen-name, as he 'whiled away the tedium of a long voyage' towards home. Easel originally arrived in Barbados on board a fever-ridden ship from Sierra Leone and was promptly invited to recuperate at a friend's bay house on the west coast. This rather strange book, replete with imitations of the local negro accent, is full of anecdotes and odd descriptions ranging from pirates to obeah, most of which are probably more amusing to the author than to his readers. However, there are more sober references to the Animal Flower Cave, Nicholas Abbey, Cherry Tree Hill, the Boiling Spring, Turner's Hall Wood, the east coast, Cole's Cave and Codrington College.

152 **Roaming through the West Indies.**
Harry Franck. London: Harper & Brothers, [ca. 1920]. 486p.

Based on an eight months' tour of the Greater and Lesser Antilles by an American voyager who had previously travelled the world on foot. The book is intended more 'for the entertainment of the armchair traveller than for the information of the traveller in the flesh'. Franck's arrival in Barbados (p. 360-82) coincides with the first visit by royalty to the colony. A wall sign announces a welcome to the 'Prints of Whales', and the author's impression of 'Little England' becomes established. No wonder that his observations serve to reinforce the description of place-names and mannerisms, or that among his several disparaging criticisms of the island's negroes one finds that 'the Briton, even when his skin is black, is first cousin to Mrs Grundy'. References are also made to overcrowding, bustling Bridgetown, friendly societies, undertakers, beggars, the railway, mule trams, lifeless Sundays, redlegs and sugar production.

153   **The English in the West Indies; or, the bow of Ulysses.**
James Anthony Froude.   New York: Charles Scribner, 1888.
Reprinted, New York: Negro Universities Press, 1969. rev. ed.
373p.

The arrogant impressions of a visit to the West Indies by a well-known English
historian in 1887. His arrival in Barbados coincided with a time of financial ruin
for the sugar planters. In spite of this (and possibly due to the fact that he stayed
at the governor's residence and was escorted by gentlemen in high positions),
Froude did not see any manifest signs of poverty or malnutrition. The roads were
said to be in a good state of repair; only some of the houses were in poor
condition. His sole lament seems to have been Barbados' increasing connections
with America, and the number of shoddily produced goods from that country in
the Bridgetown shops. As an unashamed imperialist, half of his account is given
over to reflections on the benefits of colonial rule, the subordinate position of the
negro, and the tragedy which would befall the island if ever the English gave it
up.

154   **Father Antoine Biet's visit to Barbados in 1654.**
Jerome Handler.   *Journal of the Barbados Museum and Historical
Society*, vol. 32, no. 2 (May 1967), p. 56-76.

Brings to a wider readership the three-month visit of a French priest to Barbados
in 1654 by translating certain sections of his account *Voyage de la France
Equinoxiale en l'isle de Cayenne entrepris par les François en l'année MDCLII.*
These are more than a traveller's impressions, since they describe, for instance,
the situation of the 2,000 Catholics at the time, the maltreatment of slaves and the
lifestyle of the rich.

155   **Memoirs of an old army officer.**
Edited by Jerome Handler.   *Journal of the Barbados Museum and
Historical Society*, vol. 35, no. 1 (March 1975), p. 21-30.

Taken from a 420-page unpublished manuscript of the same title, this account
concerns Englishman Richard Wyvill's two visits to Barbados in 1796 and 1806-07,
one for three days, the other for sixteen months. In the first, he is appalled at the
physical condition of the negroes and the run-down appearance of Bridgetown.
During his second visit, Wyvill again concentrates his observations on the plight
of the negro slave and contrasts it with the luxurious lifestyle of whites and freed
mulattos. As a titbit of information one learns that the poisonous manchineel has
the advantage of preserving clothes from cockroaches.

156   **Down the islands: a voyage to the Caribbees.**
William Paton.   New York: Scribners, 1887. Reprinted, New
York: Negro Universities Press, 1969. 301p. map.

The account of a five-week Caribbean trip taken by steamship through the
Windwards, Leewards and Guyana. Paton, a New Yorker accompanied by his
doctor, feels that the expression 'Bimshire' is derived from the vim and energy of
the bustling Barbadians, who have turned over all but 7,000 out of 106,000 acres
to cultivation. However, the author's arrival unfortunately coincided with the

collapse of the price of sugar due to competition from European beet, and he reflects on the misfortune of the inhabitants. There is a vivid description of Bridgetown's hospitable Ice House, with its bulletin board, and unlimited quantities of pepperpot, swizzles (recipes provided), and of course ice, and a reference to the island's railway. The touting and teeming 'darkies' are apparently prepared to take the visitor anywhere for a small fee.

157 Notes on the West Indies . . .

George Pinckard.   London: Longman, Hurst, Rees & Orme, 1806. 3 vols.

Written by a physician attached to General Abercromby's military expedition and 'including observations on the island of Barbadoes' (most of which are in volume one and the first half of volume two). After several false starts, the author eventually arrives in Carlisle Bay and begins recording his impressions in a series of letters. There are descriptions of harbour scenes, taverns, fighting slaves, the selling of meat, negro music and funerals, sugar plantations, rum production, the Scotland District and windward coast, the House of Assembly, the practice of medicine, the health of the troops and even the local method of carrying children.

158 The ordeal of free labor in the British West Indies.

William Sewell.   New York: Harper & Bros.; London: Sampson Low, 1861. Reprinted, London: Cass, 1968. 325p.

The impressions of an American traveller arriving by horse boat from New York. There are many comparisons between Barbados and seedier locations in the writer's home country, and the account (originally appearing as correspondence in the *New York Times*) contains several derogatory descriptions of the indolence and moral turpitude of the negroes. The pre- and post-emancipation situations are judged from a commercial standpoint. Consequently, Sewell concludes that sugar production is less expensive, and Barbados' prosperity is greater, after slavery, due to the high price of land and concomitant low cost of 'free' labour. Such relative affluence in turn has led to increases in commercial activity and foreign trade. In spite of these improvements and the ascendancy of the mulatto, the major problem to be overcome in the island is the caste-like system of racial stratification.

159 The West Indies in 1837.

Joseph Sturge, Thomas Harvey.   London: Hamilton, Adams & Company, 1837. Reprinted, 1838. 476p. maps.

Subtitled 'the journal of a visit to Antigua, Montserrat, Dominica, St. Lucia, Barbadoes and Jamaica undertaken for the purpose of ascertaining the actual condition of the negro population of those islands'. The authors are English Quakers and are intent on seeing the situation of freedom from slavery and the system of apprenticeship for themselves. Impressions of Barbados are limited to a couple of observations on the Wesleyan and Moravian churches, education and work conditions in the fields. Companions Lloyd and Scoble, however, visited the Bridgetown jail and witnessed stone breaking, the infamous treadmill, and the flogging of those men and women who could not keep up with their punishment.

160 **Froudacity.**
J. Thomas, introductions by Donald Wood, C. L. R. James.
London: T. F. Unwin, 1889. London, Port of Spain: New Beacon
Books, 1969. 2nd ed. 195p.

A reaction to James Anthony Froude's *The English in the West Indies; or the bow of Ulysses* (q.v.) by a self-made Trinidadian school teacher and author, originally published in the *St. George's Chronicle* and *Grenada Gazette* as a series of articles. Thomas finds Froude to be frankly racist, and the latter's thought of passing over self-government to negroes becomes an obsessional phobia haunting all his descriptions. In reference to Barbados, Thomas objects to Froude's paternalistic observations of 'pure blacks . . . as thick as bees at swarming time', their happy-go-lucky attitudes and their inability to pronounce English words correctly.

161 **The West Indies and the Spanish main.**
Anthony Trollope. London: Chapman & Hall, 1859. Reprinted,
London: Cass, 1968. 2nd ed. 395p. map.

The vivid and witty reflections of a semi-official visit to the Caribbean and Central America in 1858 by the celebrated English novelist. Frankly, Trollope is not impressed with Barbados. He finds it ugly and overcrowded. Though doubting an informant who tells him that there are more inhabitants than in China, he still wonders 'whether there is even room for a picnic'. As a guest at Miss Caroline Lee's hotel and a frequent patron of the Ice House, he reflects on conversations held with planters, who, in their nasal twang, claim to know everything, think so much of their own achievements and praise themselves constantly. The negroes, whom Trollope did not meet, are reckoned to be more intelligent than those of other islands, but more insolent and lacking in humour.

162 **Narrative of a visit to the West Indies in 1840 and 1841.**
George Truman, John Jackson, Thomas
Longstreth. Philadelphia: Merrihew & Thompson, 1844.
Reprinted, New York: Books for Libraries Press, 1972. 2nd ed.
130p.

A visit of three Quakers to the West Indies and their impressions of the islands some six years after emancipation. In Barbados they met Samuel Prescod, and stayed with two Moravian missionaries who were able to tell them about the religious composition of the island and their battle against slavery. They express reservations about the threat of eviction for tenants who are unwilling to accept the planters' low wages and high rental charges. They also have their doubts about the instruction of former slaves by priests of the Church of England. The opportunity is taken to hold several meetings, and there are reflections on the tolerance now displayed towards the Society of Friends in comparison with the antipathy shown to George Fox and his followers in 1681.

163 **A voyage in the West Indies containing various observations made during a residence in Barbadoes and several of the Leeward Islands; with some notices and illustrations relative to the city of Paramaribo in Surinam.**

John Augustine Waller. London: printed for Sir Richard Phillips & Company, Bride Court, Bridge St., 1820. 106p. map.

The account of a surgeon in the Royal Navy written after a stay in Barbados. There are several descriptions of windmills, plantation houses, slave huts, overpriced taverns, stores with merchandise in its original wrapping, food and drink, varieties of currency, flora and fauna and the climate. These observations are accompanied by medical reflections on the diet, prevailing tropical diseases and various insect bites. The doctor also believes that the white population is unnecessarily indolent and that the morals of its menfolk leave much to be desired.

20th century

164 **Intimate glimpses of the West Indies.**

Frank Coutant. New York: Vantage Press, 1957. 119p.

Supposedly based on twenty-five years' travel experience in the Caribbean by an American writer. The brief Barbados section (p. 25-32) is a mixture of fact and fallacy. The Victorian-English island is said to be lacking in excitement. The reader is (incorrectly) told of extremes in wealth and education, that fathers universally love and support their children, that there is no divorce, no government low-cost housing policy, and no worthwhile leadership or willingness to work hard among Bajuns (*sic*). A few travel tips are appended as are some entries on local dialect taken from Frank Collymore's *Notes for a glossary of words and phrases of Barbadian dialect* (q.v.).

165 **Orchids on the calabash tree.**

George Eggleston. London: Frederick Muller, 1962. 254p.

Written just before the tourist boom of the 1960s by an American businessman recuperating from a slipped disc, and urged to rest in the Caribbean by his doctor. As a yachtsman, his comments about Barbados often concern nautical matters, such as references to the island schooners in the Careenage, the contribution of the deep-water harbour to the economy, details of its construction, the escapades of Sam Lord, the difficulties of navigating coral reefs, and the problems of attacking the island by sea owing to the direction of the prevailing winds.

166 **The traveller's tree: a journey through the Caribbean islands.**

Patrick Leigh Fermor. London: John Murray, 1950. Reprinted, 1955. 403p. map.

Contains impressions of an autumn and winter Caribbean trip in the late 1940s. The emphasis is on the life of the French- and English-speaking islands as it 'impinges on the interested stranger'. The Barbados chapter (p. 131-53) plays up the 'Little England' image more than most comparable accounts, since Fermor portrays the island as a tropical shire reflecting 'the social and intellectual values and prejudices of a golf club in outer London'. Consequently, plantation houses and parish churches feature prominently, although there are also interesting diversions on redlegs, treasure divining, the House of Assembly, and the Palaeologus tomb in St. John's churchyard. A disparaging reference is made to the existence of exclusive clubs and their role in perpetuating racism in a hypocritical society. With such a conclusion, it is not surprising that the author leaves the island 'without a pang'.

167 **Islands in the sun.**
Rosita Forbes. London: Evans Brothers, 1949. 167p. 2 maps.
The chapter on Barbadoes (*sic*) (p. 112-25) is entitled 'Victorian interlude'. It emphasizes the inherent conservatism of island life, despite the socialist leanings of Grantley Adams, the black leader of one of the two major political parties. Conditions in the late 1940s are described, with the conclusion that Barbados is ready for a tourist boom. A brief history of the island is also provided.

168 **Fourteen islands in the sun.**
Charles Graves. London: Leslie Frewin, 1965. 220p. 15 maps. bibliog.
The Barbados section (p. 95-124) of this Englishman's Caribbean tour oscillates between anecdote and travelogue. After a description of the hotels and the nightlife of the island, including a titillating visit to the notorious Harry's Nitery, the names, houses and timetables of the expatriate and jet set are supplied, along with those of several exclusive white clubs. A few trade secrets are given away: membership of the 'Big 6' companies, how to dance on cut glass, and the contents of a bush bath. The introduction and the chapter on Barbados provide additional information on the redlegs. Whatever the biases, the account is interesting, since it supplies details of many places of accommodation and entertainment at the beginning of the tourist boom which are now defunct.

169 **The Caribbean islands.**
Hans Hannau. Miami, Florida: Argos, [n.d., post-1966]. 144p. 30 maps.
This pictorial guide to the Greater and Lesser Antilles gives a brief history of the region before providing a country-by-country vignette. The Barbados entry contains six well-produced photographs with explanatory notes. The commentary highlights a few touristic points of interest, plays on the 'Little England' image, and reminds readers that George Washington once slept on the island.

170 **Caribbean circuit.**
Harry Luke. London: Nicholson & Watson, 1950. 262p. 8 maps.
Written by a former experienced member of the Colonial Service with considerable contacts among various island governors. Barbados is described as a 'colony of traditions', with references to uninterrupted British rule, its House of Assembly, race, old plantation houses, the sangaree served at the Bridgetown

Club and the redlegs, who are reckoned to be the only real peasants of English stock in the world. In an epilogue, Luke discusses future prospects for the West Indies, and provides details of various conferences tackling the question of federation and of a recommendation of the Moyne Commission for improving the economic and social conditions of the islands.

171 **With a Carib eye.**
Edgar Mittelholzer. London: Secker & Warburg, 1958. 192p.

Attempts to balance the typical metropolitan travel account, with its penchant for the exotic and primitive, with the views of a Caribbean man, who in this case is a Guyanese writer of some renown. Mittelholzer's observations on Barbados are based on three years' residence. His vivid impressions oscillate from the childlike and spontaneous to the reflective and analytical. Among the former there is an emphasis on smell – the magnificent reek of the Careenage, for instance, with its whiffs of oakum, tar, sugar bags, rotting potatoes, molasses and petrol. A predilection for trees, particularly the casuarina, is also evident. The latter type of impression includes analyses of race and class (including four types of white and the occupational factionalism of the middle class), and the poor state of literature, literary criticism and the arts.

172 **Behold the West Indies.**
Amy Oakley. New York, London: Appleton Century, 1941. 540p.

An account of three winter seasons' travel in the islands and countries bordering the Caribbean Sea by an American writer and her husband, the latter providing illustrations for the text. The inevitable comparison is made between England and Barbados, and there are the usual descriptions of activity at the harbour, sugar factories, redlegs at Bethsheba (sic), and St. John's parish church. A passing reference is made to 'divorce houses', which are dwellings sawn in half as a result of a broken relationship. The Barbados section is on p. 359-78.

173 **White elephants in the Caribbean.**
Henry Phillips. New York: Robert McBride, 1936. 301p. map.

This aims to be more than a guidebook for the tourist. Its American author spent two years in the West Indies and Central America trying to come to terms with the Caribbean peoples, their problems and mental attitudes, in order to present their way of life to his readers. After visiting several other islands, Phillips expresses disappointment with the flat and overcrowded landscape of Barbados, but his enthusiasm picks up with descriptions of the bustling harbour and market of Bridgetown. However, the mixture of popular history and traveller's impressions does succumb to occasional error – that Columbus discovered the island, for instance, or that it was settled in 1605. There are also incorrect references to Harrington (Harrison) College and to the bawbee (mauby) woman.

174 **Souvenirs de voyage aux Antilles et Guyanes.** (Memories of travel in the Eastern Caribbean and Guyanas.)
André Questel. Paris: Imprimerie Pradier, 1919. 156p. bibliog.
A voyage undertaken from Guadeloupe to Dominica, Martinique, St. Lucia, Barbados, British and Dutch Guyana, and Trinidad, from 10 November 1917 to 15 January 1918. Questel describes the account as historical, geographical and touristic. Four days were spent in Barbados (14-17 November 1917) at the house of his nephew in Barbarees Hill. The passage contains a brief history and a number of impressions of the island. Among the latter are included the severity of customs officials, the relative dearth of Catholics, the presence of masonic lodges, and the efficiency of the fire brigade and the parish police force. Questel is occasionally mistaken; for instance, he believes that the Ursuline sisters are Protestant, and that Harrison College is a seminary.

175 **The Caribbean.**
Selden Rodman. New York: Hawthorn Books, 1968; 1969. 320p.
Recounts the travels of an American writer and his accompanying artist in 1966. The Barbadian section is necessarily superficial since it is based on a visit of just a few days. There are reflections on Sam Lord's Castle, redlegs, and an evening with Frank Collymore, plus snippets of conversations with an hotelier and a taxi driver.

176 **If crab no walk: a traveller in the West Indies.**
Owen Rutter. London: Hutchinson, 1933. 288p. 3 maps. bibliog.
The title is taken from a negro proverb 'if crab no walk he no see notting' in order to explain the author's own wanderlust and his decision to leave England and travel to the West Indies on a banana boat. Rutter appears well prepared for the trip since he quotes extensively from Père Labat and Froude. He later extends his experiences in conversations with Louis Gale, editor of the *Barbados Advocate*. While there is much reflection on such questions as the system of government, overpopulation and the sugar industry, there is surprisingly little description of the 'museum piece of the Caribbean'. The author's only criticism of Barbados is reserved for the touts who seem to pursue the tourist everywhere.

177 **Barbados, British West Indies.**
Raymond Savage. London: Arthur Barker, 1936. 105p. map.
A brief travelogue of the late 1930s, describing a three-week round-trip by sea from England to Barbados and recording impressions of the island. This rather unsystematic and rambling account has a distinctly imperial bias. At times it is also unnecessarily critical of the majority black population, referring to its inherent laziness, immorality, lack of humour and 'mañana mentality'. While some of the major sights are highlighted, a predilection for the exclusively white Aquatic Club, Bridgetown Club and Yacht Club is evident.

178 **The Caribbean islands.**
Mary Slater. London: Batsford, 1968. 244p. 7 maps. bibliog.
More than a travelogue or visitor's impressions, the account of this English writer is founded on a mixture of residential experience and research. The style is

pedagogic and attempts to answer questions posed by fellow countrymen about life in the West Indies. Each chapter concludes with a useful summary. The Barbados section (p. 200-13), which seeks to describe this 'frustrating, heavenly island', where 'every slave was set free with a bottle of rum and a Bible and people have clung to both since', is strong on local architecture and dialect. However, there are a number of inaccuracies.

179   **The cradle of the deep: an account of a visit to the West Indies.**
Frederick Treves.   London: Smith, Elder & Company, 1913.
378p. 4 maps.

A very readable account of a trip to the West Indies by mail boat from England by a former surgeon to British royalty. The work is extremely vivid, sometimes racist, and occasionally quite witty. The first port of call, Barbados, is treated on p.7-55. There are some interesting observations of the island's majority black population, their mode of dress and living quarters, and descriptions of the leprosarium, lunatic asylum and Codrington College. History is injected with a fair measure of anecdote and humour when the author elaborates on Major Stede Bonnet's conversion to piracy, the Beefsteak and Tripe Club, the prices paid for slaves, the life of the plantocracy, poor whites, the day the sun never rose, and the saga of the brigand Bartholomew Sharp.

180   **The sunlit Caribbean.**
Alec Waugh.   London: Evans Brothers, 1948. 127p. map. bibliog.

Written for the tourist by an itinerant English novelist. Barbados is seen as something of a disappointment due to its flat uninspiring scenery, overcrowding and lack of history. However, for the longer-stay visitor with appropriate letters of introduction (to one or more old-established families) there is an attractiveness about the 'slightly starched atmosphere . . . that is very welcome after the general informality of the tropics.' The author nevertheless warns that Barbados is 'almost the only island where the colour line is still strictly drawn'.

Tourism

Guides and information

181 The pocket guide to the West Indies.
Algernon Aspinall.   London: Sifton, Praed & Company, 1907.
Reprinted, 1935. 6th rev. ed. 527p. 18 maps. bibliog.

One of the most widely used guides prior to the advent of mass tourism. There are two chapters of general information providing a background to the West Indies and supplying the traveller with hints on health, food and drink, and dress. The Barbados section (p. 72-111) includes a brief history before outlining the various sights of the island. Liberal historical and social comments are scattered throughout the text. Several pages are devoted to the mystery of the moving coffins in the Chase Vault of Christ Church. There are also details about the clubs of the period and the railway. This handbook will still be useful to those interested in obtaining a fuller picture of Barbadian life in the 1930s.

182 Baedeker's Caribbean including Bermuda.
Edited by Baedeker (Stuttgart), translated from the German by James Hogarth.   Englewood Cliffs, New Jersey: Prentice Hall, 1982. 344p. 69 maps.

The impressive academic editorial board is headed by Professor Helmut Blume, who is responsible for an introduction to the Caribbean, ranging from climate and rainfall to music, literature and painting. The work attempts to maintain Karl Baedeker's tradition of writing a guidebook in the field rather than at an office desk. The Barbados section (p. 71-78), although generally well researched, surprisingly contains a number of factual errors (such as details of the population, number of parishes, the location of the observatory, and classification of the indigenous monkey). Three tours from Bridgetown are featured. The guide concludes with practical information, including dire warnings relating to crime against visitors.

183   **Barbados: unlike any other island.**
Barbados Board of Tourism.   Bridgetown: Barbados Board of
Tourism, [n.d.]. 43p. map.

Probably published in 1985 as a companion to the 1985/6 official guide. Contains a
geographical and historical background as well as an alphabetically arranged facts
and figures section. The latter includes information on airlines, antique dealers,
art galleries, banking, cinemas, currency, diplomatic representatives, driving,
duty free shopping, entertainment, entry regulations, festivals, flora and fauna,
government, hospitals, markets, periodicals, parks, postal services, public
holidays, service clubs, shopping hours, sightseeing and sporting activities,
telecommunication, and transportation. Unfortunately religion and restaurants
become intertwined and no details are provided on accommodation.

184   **Fodor's budget travel: Caribbean 1986.**
Edited by Andrew Beresky.   New York: Fodor's Travel Guides;
London: Hodder & Stoughton, 1985. 244p. 6 maps.

Prepared in order to rebut the stereotype of the Caribbean as simply a playground
for the wealthy, this guide seeks out hotels and restaurants towards the lower end
of the market. The writers do not hesitate to make value-laden recommendations
based on personal touristic experience of the islands. In the case of Barbados
(p. 20-32), for which they allow 'a full day to swing around the island's perimeter
and explore the interior', practical information includes names of tour operators,
currency, transportation, food and drink, nightlife, shopping, sports and other
activities, and accommodation ranked from 'quality reasonable' to 'rock bottom'.

185   **Berlitz travel guide: Southern Caribbean.**
Edited by staff of Editions Berlitz.   Lausanne, Switzerland:
Editions Berlitz, 1981. 128p. 8 maps.

A pocket-size guide for the jet age, covering the Southern Caribbean islands of
Barbados, St. Lucia, St. Vincent and the Grenadines, Grenada and Trinidad and
Tobago. General sections deal with the islands and their people, present a brief
history, outline details of what to do, dining and drinks, how to get there, when to
go, budget planning and an A-Z summary of practical information. The Barbados
entry (p. 17-30) reads like any travelogue, with a mixture of cliché epithets and
occasional historical inaccuracies. Strangely, only the Barbados Museum merits
the Berlitz traveller symbol as a place to visit.

186   **Tourism reference guide to the Caribbean.**
Caribbean Tourism Association.   New York: Caribbean Tourism
Association, 1984. 200p.

Twenty-eight member territories, including Barbados, are treated separately with
respect to size, geographical location, language, history, airlines, hotel information, beaches, sightseeing, climate, suggested dress, travel documents, medical
facilities, religious services, currency and other basic information of use to visitors
and travel agents.

187 **The Caribbean and El Dorado.**
John Crocker. Fontwell, Sussex, England: Centaur Press, 1968.
416p. 20 maps. bibliog.

A guide book whose underpinning hypothesis is that the Caribbean islands are more European- than American-oriented. Barbados is no exception to this observation, with centuries of unbroken British rule, clubs, stately homes, mastery at cricket and the English university training of its élites. The author allows a day in and around Bridgetown for shopping, and on another devotes the morning to the four southern parishes and the afternoon to the remainder of the island. As with most guides, there are errors. In this case the incorrect references are to Errol Barrow's Barbados Labour Party, to Trent Bay in St. John and to Chimboraza. However, what will swell the deserved pride of most Barbadians is the description of their famous Kensington Oval as the headquarters of cricket in the Western hemisphere.

188 **Barbados.**
Barbara Currie. In: *Fodor's Caribbean and the Bahamas 1985*.
New York: Fodor's Travel Guides, 1984, p. 189-209. map.

After a brief historical introduction to the island, the chapter describes the major tourist attractions of Barbados. Facts on such matters as airlines, climate and currency are provided. There is also a classification of hotels into de luxe, expensive, moderate and inexpensive, and examples within each category are supplied. Additional information includes transportation, special events, tours, parks and gardens, beaches, sports, historic sites, music and dance, shopping and restaurants. Although fairly comprehensive, the chapter does contain a number of errors.

189 **Cook's pocket travel guide to the West Indies.**
Sheridan Garth, William Kaufman. New York; Montreal: Pocket Books, 1963. 484p. 16 maps.

Written for the North American visitor at a time when the island was poised for the tourist boom. The Barbados section (p. 136-47) speaks rather condescendingly of the natives as 'negroes of a happy and bustling nature, thoroughly Anglicized with a rich English intonation to their talk', and plays heavily on the 'Little England' quaint stereotype of 'bobbies', cricket and driving on the left. Two half-day tours are recommended, highlighting a few places of interest, while at the same time implying that Barbados has little to offer to the sightseeing tourist. An accompanying topsy-turvy map serves to emphasize the point. Information on hotels, restaurants, shops and public holidays is summarized on p. 431-35. An introductory chapter spells out the mechanics of choosing a Caribbean destination and the role of Thomas Cook in planning the trip.

190 **Barbados: the visitor's guide.**
F. A. Hoyos. London: Macmillan Caribbean, 1982. 160p.
9 maps.

The most popular of the author's many works on Barbados, since it is targeted primarily at the tourist. After a brief introduction to the constitution, government, economy and people of Barbados, chapters take visitors on a series of tours. Commencing with Bridgetown, the tours are arranged for a number of daily outings, which go farther and farther afield and take in all the major landmarks. There is also a section dealing with nightlife. Hoyos draws on extensive historical and local knowledge to highlight points of interest in an appealing style. About fifty colour photographs illustrate the text.

191 **West Indian Eden: the book of Barbados.**
Louis Lynch. Glasgow: Robert Maclehose, 1959. 312p.

The forerunner of *The Barbados book* (q.v.), this volume contains an introduction to the history and flora and fauna of the island and a conclusion providing now-dated tourist information. There are about 200 pages in the middle covering the whole gamut of Barbadian cultural institutions and folklore, ranging from the Landship to tea meetings. The commentary is laced with numerous amusing anecdotes, many of which are written in local dialect. The late Louis Lynch certainly possessed the rare ability to laugh at his fellow countrymen, and was prepared to share these lighter moments of life with his readers.

192 **The Barbados book.**
Louis Lynch. London: André Deutsch, 1972. 2nd rev. ed. by E. L. Cozier, 262p. map.

Written by a former mayor of Bridgetown, this book falls into three sections. The first provides a brief history of the island, and introduces the reader to flora and fauna, education, industries and religious institutions. The second part is principally written for the visitor, though much of this information is now somewhat out of date. The final section is the most original and entertaining. It comprises some twenty-two essays, which capture traditional and contemporary life in Barbados. They cover such topics as dialect, place-names, cricket, crabbing and kite flying, and include several amusing and nostalgic anecdotes.

193 **The ins and outs of Barbados: the 1986 guide.**
Keith Miller, Sally Miller. Wildey, St. Michael, Barbados: Letchworth Press, 1986. 64p. maps. bibliog.

This travel guide contains information on Barbadian daily life, rum, food, sightseeing, shopping and restaurants and their prices. There is also a glossary of some Barbadian expressions and a reading list.

194 **Stark's history and guide to Barbados and the Caribbee islands.**
James Stark. Boston, Massachusetts: the author; London: Sampson Low, Marston & Company, 1903. 197p. 4 maps.

Designed as an early tourist guide for those unacquainted with the Caribbean. The Barbados section is by far the longest and contains details of the island's history, inhabitants, east coast attractions, caves and ravines, agriculture, religion, education, geology and the visit of George Washington. However, Stark seems unable to refrain from racist comment and his pessimistic remarks on the black Barbadian population are far from flattering.

195 **Barbados 1985/1986 official guide.**
Edited by Angela Zephirin, Céline Barnard, the Barbados Board
of Tourism. Bridgetown: Barbados Board of Tourism, 1985. 96p.
map.

A guide providing information about Barbados and stylistically targeted at the
North American tourist. There are entries on such topics as the history,
geography, government and economy of the island, plus details of hotels,
restaurants, sightseeing and places of entertainment. Specifically Barbadian items
include the manufacture of sugar and rum, and some notes on Bajan dialect.
Unfortunately, accommodation prices are omitted and there are a number of
spelling mistakes. As in much material promoting tourist destinations, there is
also an overabundance of superlatives.

Exploring historic Barbados.
See item no. 18.

Barbados' first hotelier.
See item no. 142.

Social and economic impact

196 **Caribbean tourist trade: a regional approach.**
Anglo-American Caribbean Commission. Washington, DC:
Kaufmann Press, 1945. 171p. map. bibliog.

Examines the potential of post-war tourism development in the region based on
the premise (which is of contemporary relevance) that regional collaboration and
promotion are more desirable than single territory initiatives. The various
economic and social advantages are explored in reference to the experience of
traditional holiday destinations and a number of factors which were considered
likely to attract tourists are discussed. A report of a 1943 island-by-island
feasibility survey undertaken by one of the commissioners is also reproduced.
Here Barbados is said already to be capable of accommodating 800 visitors in a
pleasant climate and amid considerable social life. Tourist recreational facilities
are established. Just a few more and larger hotels are required, including
development on the picturesque east coast! Barbados is described as a place
where 'living is cheap, servants are plentiful, and there are drives over an
excellent system of motor roads'!

197 **Effects of the tourist industry in Barbados, West Indies.**
Ewart Archer. PhD thesis, University of Texas at Austin, 1980.
180p. bibliog. (Available from University Microfilms, Ann Arbor,
Michigan, order no. GAX80-21394).

Measures the effects of tourism on the economy and environment since the 1950s.
Respective benefits accrue in the areas of development and improvements in the

landscape. Social costs occur in the spheres of multinational domination and coastal water pollution.

198   **A structural analysis of the Barbados economy, 1968, with an application to the tourist industry.**
W. Armstrong, S. Daniel, A. Francis.   *Social and Economic Studies*, vol. 23, no. 4 (Dec. 1974), p. 493-520.
A technical paper employing input-output analysis for thirteen principal industrial sectors of the economy. The impact of tourist expenditure (excluding cruise ship passengers) on the economy is similarly evaluated. Here it is estimated that every dollar spent generates either directly or indirectly another forty-one cents of output over all industrial sectors taken together. Hotels account for some fifty per cent and manufacturing about one-third of the total output generated.

199   **An analysis of the determinants of demand for tourism in Barbados.**
Carl Denzil Clarke.   PhD dissertation, Fordham University, Bronx, New York, 1978. 159p. bibliog. (Available from University Microfilms, Ann Arbor, Michigan, order no. GAX79-10683).
The purpose of this dissertation is to develop a series of thirty-two equations to explain and predict the demand for bednights in Barbados at various categories of hotel and at different times of the year. It is generally found that demand is inelastic to promotional expenditure and room rates, but elastic to air fares and the per capita income of tourist-generating countries.

200   **Prices, incomes and the growth of tourism in Barbados, 1956-83.**
Carl Denzil Clarke, Celeste Wood, De Lisle Worrell.   *Central Bank of Barbados Economic Review*, vol. 13, no. 1 (1986), p. 10-45.
Seeks to analyse the effects on tourist arrivals in Barbados of variables such as per capita incomes in the visitors' countries of origin, Barbados hotel rates, hotel rates in the competing island of Antigua, air fares to Barbados and the promotional expenditures of the Barbados Board of Tourism. Although the results and ensuing conclusions are somewhat predictable, the paper provides a mass of data in the form of appendixes.

201   **The economic and social impact of international tourism on developing countries.**
Robert Clevesdon.   London: Economist Intelligence Unit, 1979.
A technical, though comprehensible, report geared towards those in the industry. From the comparative data supplied, it is possible to contextualize Barbados' worldwide position in the late 1970s, with respect to such indicators as visitor arrivals, bednights, tourist density, and tourism revenue as a percentage both of Gross Domestic Product and visible exports. The evaluation examines the positive and negative effects of tourism. Additionally, it is a useful introduction explaining the otherwise mysterious and jargonized world of multipliers, leakages and cost/benefit analysis so often employed in tourism research.

202 **Organisation of the tourist industry in Commonwealth countries as at December 1971.**

London: Commonwealth Secretariat, 1972. 192p.

Examines the value and extent of the tourist industry, official tourism organizations, internal and infrastructural organization, government participation, current activities and future plans, for all member countries grouped by continent. Figures for Barbados show that, by the end of the 1960s, with an average annual growth rate of fifteen per cent, tourism accounted for thirty-five per cent of all foreign exchange earnings, the highest proportion for any Commonwealth country for which statistics were available. Direct employment was provided for 10,000 and indirect employment for a further 13,000 persons. Analysis of visitor arrivals shows a predominance of North American points of origin, but there was a growth in the European market. The activities and projections of the Barbados Tourist Board are also examined, along with governmental involvement in the industry. The problem of seasonality is also highlighted. Although the data refer to an earlier era, they nevertheless provide evidence of Barbados' success at that stage of its development.

203 **The holiday was simply fantastic.**

Graham Dann. *Revue de Tourisme*, no. 3 (1976), p. 19-23.

A qualitative content analysis of 522 interviews conducted between December 1975 and April 1976 among visitors to Barbados. The study seeks to ascertain the extent to which fantasy plays an important part in motivating respondents to travel to a tropical island and indulge in behaviour otherwise subject to cultural constraints in their home environment. Several types of fantasy are unearthed, including those associated with naming, colour, noise, sex, politics, religion, education, family, sports and economics. It emerges that the way tourists define situations at the pre-trip stage of a holiday is the all-important factor for operators and hosts to appreciate. Many clients and guests are far more romantically inclined than they might be prepared to imagine.

204 **Anomie, ego-enhancement and tourism.**

Graham Dann. *Annals of Tourism Research*, vol. 4, no. 4 (March-April 1977), p. 184-94.

Based on a survey of 422 visitors to Barbados in the winter season of 1976, the study seeks to unearth the various push factors underpinning tourist motivation (i.e. what makes them want to travel in the first place). More specifically, the two variables of anomie and ego-enhancement are investigated by means of multi-item scales, and visitor profiles for each are established. The results have clear implications for the marketing of Barbados as a destination, hitherto conducted almost entirely in pull factor (i.e. resort attractions) terms.

205 **An ideal summer resort.**

Graham Dann. *Bajan and South Caribbean*, no. 294 (May 1978), p. 4-14.

Outlines some of the advantages for tourists holidaying during Barbados' (slack) summer season. These include fifty per cent reductions in hotel room rates, a greater choice of accommodation due to lower levels of occupancy, and participation with members of the host community at cultural events such as Crop Over Festival. However, if such bonuses are to be maximized, there is a greater need for motivational research, more extensive marketing in non-traditional areas, and educational programmes designed for visitors.

206   **The tourist industry in Barbados: a socio-economic assessment.**
George Doxey and associates.   Kitchener, Ontario, Canada:
Dusco Graphics, [n.d.]. 171p. map.

Based on surveys of visitors, employees, residents and accommodation establishments, conducted between 1969 and 1970. After discussing the nature of tourism in general, and in specific relation to Barbados, the report analyses the survey data in detail. Among areas examined in the tourist investigation are the establishment of visitor profiles and facility evaluations. The labour force study is also attitudinal and focuses both on job motivation and satisfaction. Two appendixes look at the relationship between tourism, food production and the construction industry.

207   **The impact of tourism in the Caribbean: a methodological study.**
Theo Hills, Jan Lundgren.   *Annals of Tourism Research,* vol. 4,
no. 5 (May-Sept. 1977), p. 248-67.

Examines the impact of mass tourism in a number of Caribbean destinations, including Barbados. With recourse to official statistics, the study demonstrates the metropolitan dominance of international tourism predicated on a philosophy of unrestrained growth and maximization of profit. It is maintained that multinational corporations of the industry pay little regard to social cost or to the economic, cultural and ecological problems they pose to the host community. The authors argue that saturation points should be more carefully monitored, and propose an irritation index under a selection of density conditions.

208   **The genesis of tourism in Barbados: further notes on the welcoming society.**
Winston C. Husbands.   *Caribbean Geography,* vol. 1, no. 2
(1983), p. 107-20.

A geographical paper which argues that the development of tourism in Barbados does not represent a new phenomenon, but rather an established predisposition to 'welcome', which has long since had an important social and political function. Presents some useful ideas, although the written style is difficult to follow in some places.

209   **Periphery resort tourism and tourist-resident stress: an example from Barbados.**
Winston C. Husbands.   *Leisure Studies,* vol. 5 (1986), p. 175-88.

This article examines, with reference to Barbados, the rival hypotheses that either tourism creates international understanding or introduces tension between hosts and guests in small developing countries dependent on that industry. Husbands argues that both positions are too simplistic. Instead, the level of resort maturity should be considered, along with the patterns of behaviour of visitors and residents as they compete for space. After statistically analysing responses to a questionnaire conducted during the winter season of 1982 among ninety-nine residents and ninety-six tourists, the author finds that there is relatively little interaction between the two groups, since the former gravitate towards the towns for their daily activities, while the latter visit attractions. Consequently, the report concludes, there is little tourism stress in Barbados.

210 **Close encounters of the Third World.**
C. Karch, G. Dann. *Human Relations*, vol. 34, no. 4 (1981), p. 249-68.

A symbolic interactionist analysis of the beachboy phenomenon in Barbados. This is a form of male prostitution in which usually black marginal members of the host society offer sexual services in return for money, gifts, or promises of a future overseas. On the basis of non-participant observation, the authors highlight the problems inherent in asymmetrical encounters predicated on differences in class, sex and race, differences which are said to characterize the society at large.

211 **Assessing the environmental effects of tourism development on the carrying capacity of small island systems: the case for Barbados.**
Clement Lewsey. PhD dissertation, Cornell University, Ithaca, New York, 1978. 235p. bibliog. (Available from University Microfilms, Ann Arbor, Michigan, order no. GAX78-178).

Stresses the negative impact of the rapid growth of mass tourism with its over-concentration on the south and west coasts of the island. As consumption of electricity and water by tourists surpasses that of residents, deleterious effects are bound to be felt in industry and agriculture. Coastal erosion and water pollution are also attributable to uncontrolled expansion in tourism.

212 **Perceived effects of international inflation and recession on tourism in Barbados.**
Dawn Marshall, Andy Taitt. *Bulletin of Eastern Caribbean Affairs*, vol. 1, no. 4 (June 1975), p. 4-9; vol. 1, no. 8 (Oct. 1975), p. 1-5.

This two-part article examines the effects of recession on tourism in Barbados from 1964 to 1974, and compares such objective data with the perceptions of local managers/owners/operators of 106 accommodation establishments. Surprisingly, up to 40 per cent of the interviewees were apparently not affected by recession, and none of those who mentioned the topic referred to the recession of 1969-70. Among those who did speak of recession, reference was made to the specific adverse effects of cost, the decline in the numbers of tourists, and a shortfall in luxury visitors. Generally, hoteliers were found to be suspicious of outsiders. Furthermore, some did not even keep records, although they are required to do so by the Department of Statistics. The authors conclude that there is a need for greater dialogue and professionalism in Barbados' hospitality industry.

213 **International tourism in Barbados.**
Robert C. Mings. *Caribbean Geography*, vol. 2, no. 1 (1985),
p. 69-72.

This short research note describes a current project which is seeking to test the
hypothesis that international tourism contributes to international understanding,
using questionnaire methods among tourist-sector employed and non-tourist-
employed Barbadian nationals. Despite the controversial nature of the thesis,
some signs of a positive relationship are claimed.

214 **Tourism and development: the case of Barbados, West Indies.**
Robert B. Potter. *Geography*, vol. 68, no. 3 (1983), p. 46-50.

Describes the development of the tourist industry and its associated legislation
before examining some of the economic and social issues that are associated with
it. Includes a summary map showing the spatial distribution of tourist facilities
and development zones in 1980.

215 **Tourism in the Caribbean.**
Edited by H. J. Prakke, H. M. Prakke. Assen, The Netherlands:
Royal Vangorcum, 1964. 141p.

A curious collection of non-academic essays dealing with promotional problems in
the early days of mass tourism to the Caribbean. Topics include: tourism as
industry?; types of tourists; the expectations, desires and behaviour of tourists;
the tourist and the law; publicity's role in tourism; historical monuments in the
Caribbean; and problems of tourism in Jamaica. Among difficulties experienced
in Barbados are the need to educate the public about the tourist and the benefits
of tourism, more professional marketing, and more diversified itineraries for
visitors so that they can encounter aspects of everyday life, such as poverty, as
well as such historical sights as Codrington College, the Chase Vault and the
Holetown monument.

216 **Caribbean tourism: profits and performance through 1980.**
Timothy Prime. Port of Spain: Key Caribbean Publications, 1976.
121p. map. bibliog.

Essentially a marketing study which examines the state of tourism in the English-
speaking member countries of the Caribbean Tourism Research Centre. Tourist
flows, air transport, the supply of and demand for accommodation, hotel
construction planning, investments and profits are all treated, as well as prospects
for the future. In the case of Barbados, a reduction in hotel building is
recommended, together with a doubling of current occupancy levels in the
existing plant.

217 **Caribbean cruise industry study.**
Gerhard von Hauenschild, Esmond Devas. Hastings, Christ
Church, Barbados: Caribbean Tourism Research and
Development Centre, 1983. 2 vols. 5 maps. bibliog.

Provides detailed information on cruise ship operations in the Caribbean,
embarkation points, routings, trends in passenger travel and destination facilities.

Pre- and post-trip surveys were undertaken as well as individual after-visit port surveys. From this information respondent profiles and patterns of expenditure were generated, together with evaluations of satisfaction and motivation. The data show that, while Barbados accounted for a mere 3.1 per cent of all Caribbean cruise passenger landings, many of these mainly American and elderly clients nevertheless expressed either a desire to return to the island or to have spent longer ashore. Among negative comments were the high price of duty free goods and tours, lack of prior information about the island, and the fact that some guides and taxi drivers apparently did not speak English!

218 **Caribbean tourism markets: structures and strategies.**
Edited by Cynthia Wilson. Hastings, Christ Church, Barbados: Caribbean Tourism Research and Development Centre, 1980. 231p. map.

The proceedings of a Caribbean marketing seminar with concentration on European and North American generating countries, in the light of the prevailing growth of all-inclusive group travel and low dollar exchange rates. There are also contributions from small hoteliers and the problem of seasonality is examined. The latter is said by local hotelier Budge O'Hara to be particularly acute in Barbados, due to lack of airline seats and their occupancy by resident travellers, and also to the phenomenon of traditional repeat winter season business. Solutions are seen in market diversification with a concentration on Europe, a limitation on hotel construction, a reinforcement of the 'sunlust' image, and the introduction of shoulder rates. Underpinning all the presentations is the desire for a regional approach to marketing the Caribbean 'tourism product'.

219 **The future of tourism in the Eastern Caribbean.**
H. Zinder and associates. Washington, DC: Zinder & Associates, 1969. 288p. 10 maps. bibliog.

A report under contract with USAID, and sponsored by the Regional Development Agency. The investigation, which is primarily economic, evaluates the current situation and examines prospects for the future. Hotel and infrastructural requirements, together with their financing, are looked at, and a number of short- and long-term recommendations are made. The report concludes with an island-by-island analysis. Here Barbados is commended for its marketing and communication. However, it is criticized for simply promoting itself without any tourism development programme (which includes financial and physical planning, training, host education and research). Barbados is also asked to consider regional collaboration in promotion, developing convention business, swifter handling of tourists at strategic points, and more organized island tours.

Centres, peripheries, tourism and socio-spatial development.
See item no. 61.

The economy of Barbados 1946-1980.
See item no. 631.

A vital industry battles the recession.
See item no. 660.

Tourism and employment in Barbados.
See item no. 730.

Emerging environmental problems in a tourist zone: the case of Barbados.
See item no. 800.

Guarding our health, enhancing our beauty: a look at the Ministry of Tourism and Environment.
See item no. 803.

Flora and Fauna

220 **Caribbean flora.**

C. Dennis Adams. Sunbury-on-Thames, Middlesex, England; Kingston: Nelson Caribbean, 1976. 61p.

A basic overview of Caribbean plants which contains some excellent colour photographs. The book starts with an account of the clearance of the forest cover of Barbados. It notes that the 'Barbados Pride' certainly did not come from Barbados, although plant geographers have been unable to decide on its exact origins (p. 34-35).

221 **The development of the whistling frog *Eleutherodactylus martinicensis* of Barbados.**

L. Adamson, R. G. Harrison, Iris Bayley. *Proceedings of the Zoological Society of London*, vol. 133, no. 3 (1960), p. 453-69.

Locally known as the whistling frog due to the shrill piping noise it makes during the evening, *Eleutherodactylus martinicensis* is an inhabitant of Barbados and other West Indian islands. The frog was introduced to Barbados some time after 1850 and is common all over the island. This paper explains the animal's biological growth and temporal development.

222 **The grasses of Barbados.**

James Andrew Allan. London: HM Stationery Office, 1957. 114p. (Colonial Office, Colonial Research Publications, no. 23).

Allan, who started collecting the local grasses of Barbados as early as 1937, here provides descriptions of some eighty species that occur in Barbados, fifty-six of these being illustrated by line drawings (p. 59-114). The work also includes a glossary of botancial terms. A very interesting reference source.

223 **Some observations on the birds of Barbados.**
F. C. K. Anderson. *Journal of the Barbados Museum and Historical Society*, vol. 2, no 2 (1934), p. 53–60; vol. 2, no. 3 (1934), p. 135-42.

The author considers birds of Barbados in the widest sense of residents and visitors, both regular and irregular. In the first article, the migration of birds is discussed before a description of resident birds of Barbados, such as the sparrow, blackbird, sugar bird and yellow bird, is provided. The account is continued in the second article with an inventory of birds of passage.

224 **Vegetation in the Caribbean area.**
G. F. Asprey. *Caribbean Quarterly*, vol. 5 (1959), p. 245-63.

A useful paper summarizing the main plant associations found within the Caribbean area as a whole. The plant associations are viewed in terms of their specific ecological conditions.

225 **The whistling frogs of Barbados.**
Iris Bayley. *Journal of the Barbados Museum and Historical Society*, vol. 17, no. 4 (1950), p. 161-70.

The whistling frog (*Eleutherodactylus martinicensis*) first attracts attention by the noise it makes at night, the volume of which is quite out of proportion to its size. It is generally believed that the frog was introduced into Barbados in the second half of the 19th century. One story maintains that this was effected by a man who wished to annoy his neighbour! The habitat of adult whistling frogs and their development are both considered in detail in this account which is accompanied by two photographic plates.

226 **The natural vegetation of the Windward and Leeward Islands.**
J. S. Beard. London: Oxford University Press, 1949. 192p. bibliog.

After a general review of environmental factors, plant geography and the classification of plants, plant communities are described on an island-by-island basis. Barbados is considered in section L of chapter five (p. 166-67), which makes the point that practically every vestige of the original vegetation has disappeared, save for Turner's Hall Wood and some patches of scrub woodland under Hackleton's Cliff and in ravines.

227 **Birds of the West Indies.**
James Bond. London: Collins, 1983. 5th ed. 256p.

Covers the avifauna of the entire West Indies, excluding Trinidad and Tobago which has a South American or neotropical fauna. Every known species of bird from these islands is included. For each, there are sections on local names, habitat, nidification and range. Includes 186 line drawings and eight colour plates.

228 **Some observations on the snappers of Barbados.**
Robert S. Butsch. *Journal of the Barbados Museum and Historical Society*, vol. 6, no. 2 (1939), p. 67-73.

The family *Lutianidae*, known almost universally as 'snappers', represent a valuable food resource. In Barbados, snappers are second only to the flying fish in terms of economic importance. The account provides descriptions of some thirteen specimens secured in Barbadian fish markets, including the red snapper and the snaggle-toothed snapper.

229 **The reef builders at Barbados.**
Robert S. Butsch. *Journal of the Barbados Museum and Historical Society*, vol. 6, no. 3 (1939), p. 129-38.

Endeavours to explain the most important features of the tiny animals which have played such an important role in the island's formation. The paper includes a listing of the more common and conspicuous species of coral, and a number of useful black-and-white plates.

230 **A list of Barbadian fishes.**
Robert S. Butsch. *Journal of the Barbados Museum and Historical Society*, vol. 7, no. 1 (1939), p. 17-31.

Compiled from notes taken during the period 1938-39 and stressing the varied and colourful fish of Barbados, this article presents an annotated list of the most commonly observed species.

231 **Ferns of Barbados.**
Daisy Coulter. *Journal of the Barbados Museum and Historical Society*, vol. 32, no. 3 (1968), p. 152-54.

Observes initially that Richard Ligon makes no mention of ferns in his *A true and exact history of the island of Barbadoes* (q.v.), and that Griffith Hughes lists only four in his *Natural history of Barbados* (q.v.). However, although it is true that owing to a lack of moisture and shade, Barbados does not have as many ferns as other West Indian islands, Richard Proctor of the Institute of Jamaica has identified thirty-seven different varieties of fern. These are listed and described by Daisy Coulter.

232 **Observations on some Barbadian birds.**
Stuart T. Danforth. *Journal of the Barbados Museum and Historical Society*, vol. 5, no. 3 (1938), p. 119-29.

The author, who at the time of writing was Professor of Zoology and Entomology at the University of Puerto Rico, made several short visits to Barbados between 1922 and 1937. Although making no claim to comprehensive coverage, this article presents an annotated list of some twenty-eight important specimens.

233   **History of green monkeys in the West Indies: part I – migration from Africa.**
Woodrow W. Denham.   *Journal of the Barbados Museum and Historical Society*, vol. 36, no. 3 (1981), p. 210-28.

This paper summarizes what is known about the history of the West Indian green monkeys, focusing in particular on their migration from Africa to Barbados, St. Kitts and Nevis. The account relies on documentary evidence from the 17th to the 20th century.

234   **History of green monkeys in the West Indies: part II – population dynamics of Barbadian monkeys.**
Woodrow W. Denham.   *Journal of the Barbados Museum and Historical Society*, vol. 36, no. 4 (1982), p. 353-71.

Based on field investigations conducted in 1977-78, this article studies the mechanics of demographic change among the population of monkeys in Barbados.

235   **Normal stages of the early development of the Barbados flying fish *Hirundichthys affinis* (Gunther).**
John W. Evans.   MA dissertation, McGill University, Montreal, 1959. 132p. bibliog.

Rather patchy in respect of the standard of presentation of the short written text, but describes in detail the development of the flying fish from the newly fertilized egg to the young fish, ten days old and 15 mm long.

236   **Shark!**
Norma Faria.   *Bajan* (March 1985), p. 16-17.

Identifies the main types of shark found in Barbadian coastal waters, and stresses that there have been very few attacks on persons.

237   **FAO species identification sheets for fishery purposes: Western Central Atlantic (fishing area 31).**
Edited by W. Fischer.   Rome: Food and Agriculture Organisation of the United Nations, 1978. 7 vols.

The series of which these volumes form a part is aimed at establishing a world-wide annotated and illustrated inventory of aquatic species of interest to fisheries, which should also provide a tool for the correct identification of species. Each entry describes a single species and provides its name (both scientific and vernacular), a drawing, diagnostic field characteristics, distinction from other similar species, range of habitats and data on its fishery and use. Volumes one to four cover bony fishes; volume five studies bony fishes, sharks and batoid fishes; and volume six lobsters, shrimps, prawns, true crabs, stomatopods, bivalves, gastropods, chitons, cephalopods and sea turtles. Volume seven provides an index of both scientific and vernacular names.

238 **Flowers of the Caribbean.**
Jeanne Garrard, photography and design by Hans W.
Hannau. Miami, Florida: Argos, 1972. 63p.

This volume is useful because of the thirty-two pages of full colour photographs of various Caribbean flowers, and the accompanying descriptions. However, the text is too clichéd to be of great assistance to those wanting a detailed understanding of flowers.

239 **Facts and beliefs about Barbadian plants.**
Evelyn Graham Beaujon Gooding. *Journal of the Barbados Museum and Historical Society*, vol. 7 (1940) p. 170-74; vol. 8 (1940) p. 32-35; p. 70-73; p. 103-06; p. 194-97; vol. 9 (1941) p. 17-19; p. 84-88, p. 126-29, p. 192-94; vol. 10 (1942) p. 3-6.

This series of articles aims to provide an account of some of the more interesting plants of Barbados. It is emphasized that even in so small an island as Barbados, beliefs and customs vary considerably in different parts and it is entirely conceivable that a given plant may be used for quite different purposes.

240 **Turner's Hall Wood, Barbados.**
Evelyn Graham Beaujon Gooding. *Caribbean Forester*, vol. 5, no. 4 (1944), p. 153-68.

Turner's Hall Wood, some fifty acres in extent, is the only remaining forested area in Barbados. This paper summarizes the general characteristics of the wood, the details of its climate and soils and the structure of the forest (tree layer, shrub layer, herb layer, climbers, epiphytes and introduced plants). Diagrammatic sections through parts of the wood and species lists are also included.

241 **Observations on the sand dunes of Barbados.**
Evelyn Graham Beaujon Gooding. *Journal of Ecology*, vol. 34, (1947), p. 111-25.

Reports Gooding's tentative conclusions concerning the plant life of the sand dunes of the island. Three areas on the windward coast were selected for intensive study: Belleplaine, Chancery Lane and Silver Sands. Two other beaches, one near to Enterprise and the other at Maxwell, also provided some relevant data. It is noted that distinct vegetation zones running parallel to the sea margin can be traced in such areas.

242 **Flora of Barbados.**
Evelyn Graham Beaujon Gooding, A. R. Loveless, G. R. Proctor. London: HM Stationery Office, 1965. 486p. map. bibliog. (Ministry of Overseas Development, Overseas Research Publication, no. 7).

The definitive work on the flora of Barbados, aimed at teachers, agriculturalists and amateur botanists. 'Its primary objective is to enable anybody with only a slight knowledge of botany to identify any wild flowering plant he or she may come across.' Basically, the volume aims to bring up to date Professor F. Hardy's

Some aspects of the flora of Barbados (q.v.). Gooding's work provides an overall key to the families, genera and species of flowering plants in Barbados, splitting them into Monocotyledons and Dicotyledons. A list of common names and their botanical equivalents is also included. Despite its length, this is a manual for identification and not a prose text.

243 **Historic relics in the flora of Barbados.**
Evelyn Graham Beaujon Gooding. *Journal of the Barbados Museum and Historical Society*, vol. 33, no. 3 (1970), p. 101-10.

The text of a talk given at the annual meeting of the Museum and Historical Society held on 29 October 1969. Gooding briefly reviews the extensive literature on the flora of the island, before reconstructing a picture of what the strongly forested vegetation was like at the time of its discovery, thereby serving to identify some relics of the original flora of the country.

244 **Wayside trees and shrubs of Barbados.**
Evelyn Graham Beaujon Gooding. London: Macmillan (for Wayfarer Bookstore Limited), 1973. 96p. bibliog.

Presents a selection of the more common and beautiful species of trees and shrubs that grow in Barbados today and which can be seen without leaving the main highways. Some forty-eight trees and shrubs are described and illustrated by full-colour photographs taken by Eric A. Gomez. A very useful introductory guide, especially for overseas visitors and tourists.

245 **The plant communities of Barbados.**
Evelyn Graham Beaujon Gooding. Bridgetown: Government Printing Office, 1974. 243p. maps. bibliog.

This basic reference source is essential reading for all those interested in the flora of Barbados. The volume is divided into six main sections. The first two general ones look at the factors which govern the distribution of plants in Barbados, and their classification into ecological groups. The next four sections describe and explain the wild plants of Barbados: the natural plant communities (part three), man-made habitats (part four), the origin of the flora of Barbados (part five) and descriptions of common wild plants of Barbados (part six). The book covers some 300 of the total of over 600 wild plants of Barbados. Despite the typescript format, this is a well-written and extremely well illustrated volume.

246 **Caribbean zooplankton: part I –** *Siphonophora, Heteropoda, Copepoda, Euphausiacea, Chaetognatha* **and** *Salpidae***; part II –** *Thecosomata.*
H. B. Michel, Maria Foyo, D. A. Haagensen. Washington, D.C.: Office of Naval Research, Department of the Navy, 1976. 711p. maps. bibliog.

Reports on the results of an extensive programme of zooplankton sampling in the Caribbean Sea, carried out from 1966 to 1969. The original purpose and aim of the research was to provide basic information on the relative abundance and distribution of known species of important holoplanktonic groups. Describes the findings from 801 samples taken on eight cruises.

247 **Some aspects of the flora of Barbados.**
F. Hardy. Bridgetown: Advocate Company Limited, 1917. 185p. map. bibliog.

An early and important contribution to the study of the plant life of Barbados, primarily intended as a handbook to serve the needs of students of botany at Harrison College and other Barbadian secondary schools. Includes sections on factors governing the distribution of plants in Barbados, descriptive identifications of the vegetation, and the origin of the flora of Barbados (with particular reference to the agents of ocean currents, birds, winds and man). The lack of diagrams for identification reduces the volume's utility for non-specialists, however. Although it was written in 1917, this work was not generally available until 1934.

248 **A leatherback turtle from Barbados waters.**
Christopher M. Hawkins, Gary Borstad. *Journal of the Barbados Museum and Historical Society*, vol. 35, no. 4 (1978), p. 267-70.

In 1974, researchers from the Bellairs Research Institute examined a relatively uncommon sea turtle, the leatherback (*Dermochelys coriacea*) caught approximately eight kilometres off the north-east coast of the island. The specimen is described in detail in this paper.

249 **Manchineel trees and tumors in mice.**
Bruce M. Howard. *Bajan* (Feb. 1985), p. 24-26.

The author, who was working at the Cave Hill Campus of the University of the West Indies during the academic year 1984-85, describes some of his work on the natural history, chemical constituents and poisonous-irritant effects of the manchineel tree.

250 **The natural history of Barbados.**
Griffith Hughes. London: the author, 1750. Reprinted, New York: Arno Press, 1972. 314p. map.

Written by a former rector of St. Lucy's parish church and dedicated to the Archbishop of Canterbury, this much cited work is as much a social as a natural history. It comprises ten 'books' or chapters. Among the many topics covered in the first four are the discovery of the island, the origins of place names, previous and present inhabitants, their beliefs and superstitions, the climate, hurricanes, quality of the water supply, diseases and their remedies, fossils, minerals, caves, birds and insects. While books five to eight are taken up with detailed descriptions of trees and plants, the last two concentrate on the coastline and marine life. There are several accompanying illustrations, numerous explanatory notes and liberal quotations from the classics.

251 **Sea shells of the West Indies: a guide to the marine molluscs of the Caribbean.**
Michael Humfrey. London: Collins, 1975. 351p. 3 maps. bibliog.

The principal aim of this work is to provide a general illustrated guide to West Indian marine shells. In all, some 497 shells are described and illustrated, and at least one locality is given where each species is known to occur. The author writes principally from Jamaican experiences, and so most of the habitats described are Jamaican. However, this information generally has overall Caribbean relevance and should be of interest to the student of Barbados. The text is accompanied by full-colour photographs of shells. A general introduction to molluscs is provided in part one.

252 **Marine life of the Caribbean.**
A. Jones, N. Sefton. London; Basingstoke, England: Macmillan, 1979. 90p. map. bibliog.

The volume opens with a call for environmental conservation in what is described as this 'gem of the seas'. All aspects of the marine life of mangroves, sandy shores, sea-grass beds, rocky shores, coral reefs and open seas are then examined. Chapters on turtles and ecology and conservation conclude the book.

253 **Preliminary studies on the Brachyuran Crustacea of Barbados, I and II.**
H. C. Jones. *Journal of the Barbados Museum and Historical Society*, vol. 32 (1968), p. 154-60; 187-89.

In these two papers, twelve species of crab previously not recorded for Barbados are listed and details of them provided.

254 **Three additions to the flora of Barbados.**
H. C. Jones. *Journal of the Barbados Museum and Historical Society*, vol. 34, no. 3 (1973), p. 113-16.

Describes in detail the features of three new plant finds in Barbados, two of which are orchids, and the other a newly discovered mushroom.

255 **Caribbean biology: an integrated approach.**
W. K. King, R. Soper, S. Tyrell Smith. London: Macmillan Caribbean, 1983. 2nd ed. 313p.

Although designed to meet the general requirements of Caribbean schools teaching Ordinary Level biology, much of the material included relates to the Caribbean. For example, the chapters on ecology and marine biology are largely devoted to specific Caribbean habitats.

256 **Flowers of the Caribbean.**
G. W. Lennox, S. A. Seddon. London: Macmillan Caribbean, 1978. 72p.

Illustrates and describes some of the more common flowering plants of the Caribbean. The book is designed to be used by individuals with little or no botanical training. In fact, it is aimed squarely at the tourist, as witnessed by the inclusion of a visitor's 'I spy' check list on p. 70-71. Covers herbs and shrubs, trees and orchids and includes excellent full-colour photographs. An accessible and reliable introduction.

257   The biology of the tropical sea urchin, *Tripneustes esculentus Leske*, in Barbados, West Indies.

John B. Lewis. *Canadian Journal of Zoology*, vol. 16 (1958), p. 608-21.

Discusses the growth, reproduction, development, reactions and feeding methods of the large white-spined sea urchin which is common in Barbadian coastal waters.

258   The coral reefs and coral communities of Barbados, West Indies.

John B. Lewis. *Canadian Journal of Zoology*, vol. 38 (1960), p. 1,133-45.

This paper presents an overview of the structure of the fringing reefs of Barbados, together with an account of associated reef fauna.

259   The fauna of rocky shores of Barbados, West Indies.

John B. Lewis. *Canadian Journal of Zoology*, vol. 38 (1960), p. 391-435.

A long and detailed account describing the biology of the common species found in the intertidal zone of Barbados. General environmental factors, such as tides, temperatures and wave action are considered. The data observation stations were at River Bay, Bathsheba, Conset Bay, Silver Sands, Oistins, Paynes Bay and Six Men's Bay.

260   List of the Echinoidea of Barbados.

John B. Lewis. *Journal of the Barbados Museum and Historical Society*, vol. 28, no. 2 (1961), p. 52-53.

Following investigations of deep-water communities by the Bellairs Research Institute of McGill University, this paper provides an up-to-date list of seventeen types of urchins found in the seas around Barbados.

261   Notes on the Barbados 'sea egg'.

John B. Lewis. *Journal of the Barbados Museum and Historical Society*, vol. 29, no. 3 (1962), p. 79-81.

A summary of the results of previous research on the edible sea urchin of Barbados, covering topics such as breeding, growth, reaction to light, food and feeding patterns.

262   Community structure of ophiuroids (*echinodermata*) from three different habitats on a coral reef in Barbados, West Indies.

John B. Lewis, R. D. Bray. *Marine Biology*, vol. 73 (1983), p. 171-76.

Populations of ophiuroids were sampled from three different habitats, living coral, dead coral and coral rubble on a coral reef in Barbados. The differential population levels, species diversity and mean size of the ophiuroids in the three habitats are observed in this paper.

263   The *Acropora* inheritance: a reinterpretation of the development of fringing reefs in Barbados, West Indies.
      John B. Lewis.   *Coral Reefs*, vol. 3 (1984), p. 117-22.

Although earlier accounts have stressed the importance of *Montastrea annularis* as the main living component of contemporary reefs, the widespread occurrence of the reef coral *Acropora palmata* on the fringing reefs of the west coast of Barbados calls for a new interpretation of their Holocene development. Radiocarbon dating suggests that reef construction by this species began as early as 2,300 years ago. *Acropora palmata* probably flourished into the present century, but has now declined.

264   Non-flowering plants of Barbados.
      Marilyn H. S. Light.   Bridgetown: Ministry of Education, 1976.
      48p. bibliog.

In the foreword, E. G. B. Gooding notes that although the botanical literature of Barbados is rich, this material generally deals with 'higher' or flowering plants, and that the mosses, liverworts, lichens, fungi and ferns have generally remained neglected. Only the more common genera of plants representative of each group have been included in this guide. In total, just over seventy plant species are described and there are numerous line diagrams. A short glossary of botanical terms is also included.

265   Evidence does not support the existence of a Bajan mouse.
      Rex E. Marsh.   *Journal of the Barbados Museum and Historical Society*, vol. 37, no. 2 (1984), p. 159-60.

Robert Schomburgk in his classic volume *The history of Barbados* (q.v.) suggested that a native mouse species was present in Barbados at the time of the first settlement. From a zoogeographic perspective, it is argued here that the probability of this is extremely remote.

266   Calcareous encrusting organisms of the recent and Pleistocene reefs of Barbados, West Indies.
      William Martindale.   PhD thesis, University of Edinburgh,
      Edinburgh, 1976. 141p.

The research relates the anatomy, morphology and distribution of various calcareous encrusting organisms, such as corals, to their physical and biotic environments. On the basis of such observations, in the second part of the thesis, a model of encruster ecology is produced. This is then used in the interpretation of the growth of uplifted Pleistocene reefs on the island. Includes copious illustrations of the organisms.

267   Some notes on the fishes of Barbados.
      C. C. Nutting.   *Journal of the Barbados Museum and Historical Society*, vol. 2, no. 4 (1935), p. 187-90.

The author, after an expedition to Barbados and Antigua, comments on some of the more common fish to be found in Barbados waters, including the flying fish, dolphin, horse-eye and various reef fishes.

268 **Some notes on the Crustacea of Barbados.**
C. C. Nutting. *Journal of the Barbados Museum and Historical Society*, vol. 3, no. 2 (1936), p. 81-86.

A detailed but somewhat tedious account of the specimens collected during an expedition to Barbados completed in the early part of the 20th century, describing, for instance, crayfish, land crabs and hermit crabs. From the text it is not entirely clear whether Nutting was more interested in collecting and documenting or cooking and eating such specimens.

269 **Some notes on the echinoderms (starfish, sea eggs) of Barbados.**
C. C. Nutting. *Journal of the Barbados Museum and Historical Society*, vol. 4, no. 2 (1937), p. 68-71.

A further paper describing the specimens found on an expedition to Barbados, particularly the 'white' and 'black' sea eggs or urchins. Once again, Nutting shows a clear interest in the culinary potential of such animals, observing that the local people 'feel no impulse to restrict themselves and apparently suffer no ill effects'.

270 **Quantitative analysis of community pattern and structure on a coral reef bank in Barbados, West Indies.**
Bruce Ott. PhD dissertation, McGill University, Montreal, 1975. 185p. maps. bibliog.

This thesis presents the findings of an examination of community dispersion and complexity patterns on a bank reef off the west coast of Barbados. The results show that corals are responding in a complex manner to an extremely heterogeneous physical and biological environment. Species diversity and biomass patterns indicate that optimum growth occurs at about twenty metres on either side of the bank on the sloping faces. Corals cover thirty per cent of the bottom with live tissues.

271 **Fishes of the Western North Atlantic.**
Edited by Albert E. Parr. New Haven, Connecticut: Sears Foundation for Marine Research, Yale University, 1948-66. 5 vols.

Intended for use by lay persons as well as by ichthyologists and marine biologists. Under each species will be found both the distinctive characteristics which set it apart from its nearest relatives, and a detailed description, as well as discussions of its colour, size, general habitat, range, economic importance, danger to man, sporting qualities and occurrence in the Western Atlantic. Volume one covers lancelets, cyclostomes and sharks; volume two sawfishes, guitarfishes, skates, rays and chimaeroids; volumes three to five deal with soft-rayed bony fishes.

272 **A note on the mosses of Barbados.**
E. J. Pearce. *Journal of the Barbados Museum and Historical Society*, vol. 31, no. 2 (1963), p. 59-60.

It is noted that mosses have received little attention in the literature, due mainly to climatic restriction of their overall abundance on the island. From 1961 to 1963, the author collected specimens of mosses from Welchman Hall Gully and Jack-in-the-Box Gully. Four species were found to be represented, all previously unrecorded for the island.

273 **An attempted re-appraisal of the butterflies of Barbados with reference to certain weather phenomena.**

E. J. Pearce. *Journal of the Barbados Museum and Historical Society*, vol. 33, no. 2 (1969), p. 76-84.

This article, containing three full-colour plates, discusses the butterflies of Barbados, noting that only about a dozen truly and regularly endemic species can be claimed, along with a few which put in an occasional appearance. The total is therefore much smaller than for any other West Indian island of similar area. Detailed notes are presented on the main species found in, and visiting, Barbados.

274 **Caribbean reef fishes.**

John E. Randall. Hong Kong: T. F. H. Publications, 1968. 318p.

Provides for the ready identification of about 300 of the most common fishes that are to be observed whilst swimming on the reefs of the Caribbean Sea or over adjacent sand flat or sea-grass environments. Each of the species is illustrated by a photograph, which is in many cases in full colour. A useful glossary of ichthyological terms is given on p. 297-302.

275 **Vegetation and environment on the Barbados coast.**

Roland E. Randall. *Journal of Ecology*, vol. 58 (1970), p. 155-72.

The relationship between vegetation type and environmental conditions at fifteen selected coastal locations around the island is described and explained. It is recorded that a maximum of four vegetation zones occurs in coastal cliff ecosystems, five on leeward beaches and seven on windward beaches and dune systems.

276 **A field guide to the butterflies of the West Indies.**

Norman D. Riley. London: Collins, 1975. 224p. map.

Described by the publishers as the first-ever comprehensive guide to the identification of West Indian butterflies, in which every known species is included. An overview is provided on p. 15-28. In the main part of the book, each butterfly species is described individually, with details of local and scientific names, plate reference in the book, notes on size, colour, special characteristics, distribution, habitat, variation and early stages, if known. There are 338 fine colour illustrations, and a further twenty-eight species are illustrated by line drawings.

277 **The cattle egrets and mangroves of Graeme Hall Swamp.**

Deborah River-Ramsey. *Bajan and South Caribbean*, no. 327 (Feb. 1981), p. 8-15.

Considers the general biology, behaviour and ecology of cattle egrets. Over 3,000 of these birds inhabit the Graeme Hall Swamp, the only area in Barbados where mangroves are still to be found in appreciable numbers.

278 **Botany for the Caribbean.**
Edith Thom Robertson, Evelyn Graham Beaujon
Gooding. London: Collins, 1970. 2nd ed. 246p. bibliog.

Intended to cover the upper secondary school syllabus in botany. Based on
E. G. B. Gooding's teaching notes at Lodge School, Barbados and rewritten by
Robertson to include examples of West Indian plants and communities other than
those occurring in Barbados. Although written for a school audience, the book
contains useful basic information on the morphology of flowering plants (part
one), the anatomy and physiology of flowering plants (part two), ecology (part
three), further study of the flower and fruit (part four), and the classification of
flowering plants (part five).

279 **The complete collector's guide to shells and shelling.**
Sandra Romashko. Miami, Florida: Windward Publishing, 1984.
112p.

Describes in detail the sea shells found in the waters of the North American
Atlantic and Pacific Oceans, Gulf of Mexico, Gulf of California, the Caribbean,
the Bahamas and Hawaii. Contains full-colour illustrations of shells and a very
useful glossary of technical terms.

280 **Fishes of the Caribbean reefs.**
Ian F. Took. London: Macmillan Caribbean, 1978. 92p.

After a brief general introduction and a practical guide to 'fish-watching', this
short book deals with the coral reef (p. 9-15) and conservation matters (p. 16-18).
The text then considers the fishes of the Caribbean, documenting some eighty-five
species (p. 20-83). There follows a short section on underwater photography and
an index. The excellent colour photographs make this essential for the visitor to
Barbados who wishes to know about fish life.

281 **Insects in houses in Barbados: how to recognise and control them.**
R. W. E. Tucker. *Journal of the Barbados Museum and
Historical Society*, vol. 1, no. 2 (1934), p. 73-79.

At the time of publication Tucker was an entomologist with the Department of
Agriculture in Barbados. The paper provides non-technical information on some
of the insects which are seen at various times in houses in Barbados: 'It can safely
be said that cockroaches rank first as universal household pests; followed by
"worms" in books and furniture, and, at certain times by mosquitoes'. There are
sections on cockroaches, flies and mosquitoes, bookworms, ants and termites,
crickets, spiders, centipedes, millipedes and scorpions.

282 **Insects of Barbados.**
R. W. E. Tucker. *Journal of the Barbados Museum and
Historical Society*, vol. 20, no. 4 (1953), p. 155-81.

A brief introduction to insects in general is followed by a record of the insect life
of Barbados.

283 **West Indian reptiles.**
Garth Underwood. *Caribbean Quarterly*, vol. 3 (1953),
p. 174-80.

Examines the distribution of snakes and lizards from a temporal and ecological viewpoint. The effects of the introduction of the mongoose are given particular emphasis.

284 **The interstitial fauna of selected beaches in Barbados.**
Bjorn Urhammer. MSc dissertation, McGill University,
Montreal, 1969. 157p. bibliog.

Presents the results of a quantitative study of seven tropical marine tidal beaches in Barbados. Faunal distribution is then related to tide, wave action, beach slope, grain size, chemical composition, porosity and saturation, temperature, salinity, dissolved oxygen, pH, free carbon dioxide and nutritional sources. Of the abiotic factors, wave action appeared to have the greatest influence on faunal distribution.

285 **Caribbean seashells: a guide to the marine mollusks of Puerto Rico and other West Indian islands, Bermuda and the Lower Florida Keys.**
Germaine L. Warmke, R. Tuker Abbott. Narberth,
Pennsylvania: Livingston Publishing Company, 1961. 346p. maps.

The emphasis is on Puerto Rico and according to the index Barbados is only directly referred to on p. 13. However, this handbook aims to assist the ready identification of all West Indian shells: 'Because Puerto Rico stands at the zoological crossroads of the West Indies, its fauna is a mixture of most of the elements of the tropical Western Atlantic – hence, this is as much a book about Caribbean shells as it is a near-complete census of the marine molluscs of Puerto Rico'. Contains excellent photographs, including some colour plates.

Barbados our island home.
See item no. 14.

The economic geography of Barbados: a study of the relationships between environmental variations and economic development.
See item no. 70.

Physical changes in Barbados since 1627.
See item no. 78.

Plant introduction and landscape change in Barbados, 1625 to 1830.
See item no. 81.

Man's influence on the vegetation of Barbados 1627-1800.
See item no. 82.

Persistence and change in the vegetation of oceanic islands: an example from Barbados, West Indies.
See item no. 83.

Flora and Fauna

Fossil birds from Barbados, West Indies.
See item no. 112.

A note on diatoms in general.
See item no. 116.

A small assemblage of vertebrate fossils from Spring Bay, Barbados.
See item no. 135.

The history of Barbados.
See item no. 356.

The bush teas of Barbados.
See item no. 500.

Save the Graeme Hall swamp.
See item no. 799.

An annotated bibliography of research on contemporary fossil reefs in Barbados, West Indies.
See item no. 945.

Prehistory and Archaeology

286 **The prehistory of Barbados.**
G. T. Barton. Bridgetown: Advocate Company Limited, 1953.
88p. 2 maps. bibliog.

Despite the rather amateurishly drawn illustrations, this book represented for a long period the basic guide to issues surrounding the prehistory and archaeological relics of Barbados. The evidence of the plentiful pottery remains and the abundant shell tools reviewed in the book indicates quite clearly that European settlers were not the first humans to set foot in Barbados. It is stressed that well before the first European settlement, Arawak Indians of the Ignerian cultural group occupied the island either as permanent inhabitants or seasonal visitors. Of course, it is now generally believed that pre-Arawak peoples inhabited Barbados, as reported by Professor Ripley P. Bullen in his paper 'Barbados and the archaeology of the Caribbean' (q.v.) which was published in the *Journal of the Barbados Museum and Historical Society* in 1966, following the discovery of new finds earlier that year.

287 **Barbados and the archaeology of the Caribbean.**
Ripley P. Bullen. *Journal of the Barbados Museum and Historical Society*, vol. 30, no. 2 (1966), p. 16-19.

The résumé of a talk given to members of the society on 25 April 1966, following the discovery some three days previously at a site near the South Point lighthouse of Saladoid-Barrancoid pottery, evidence that pre-Arawak people inhabited Barbados. The paper suggests that Barbados was first inhabited ca. AD 400 by a pre-Arawak people and that an interval occurred somewhere between then and AD 800 during which the island was not occupied. It is envisaged that Arawaks reached Barbados around AD 800 and lived there until the Caribs conquered them, probably about AD 1200.

288 The first Barbadians.
     C. Cooksey. *Timehri*, vol. 2 (1912), p. 142-44.
This is an early account seeking to resolve the mystery of the first inhabitants of the island, based on the finds of stone and shell implements and pottery available at that time. It is thereby ventured that 'the first Barbadians were Indians, few in number, wanting in many of the implements and arts of their continental brethren, and unable to defend themselves from the guile or force of the small ships' companies which visited the island at long intervals during the hundreds of years which preceded the English settlement'.

289 'In search of Bim': the Barbados Museum's new permanent
     exhibition.
     Alissandra Cummins, Steve Hackenberger. *Bajan*, (Feb.-March 1986), p. 4-5.
Describes the establishment of a new permanent exhibition, which in 30 cases and over 200 feet of panels seeks to tell the story of Barbados. The exhibition emphasizes the island's initial settlement by the Amerindians, and also covers English colonization, the development of the slave system and the achievement of emancipation.

290 Barbados and the archaeology of the Caribbean.
     M. Diksic, j. L. Galinier, L. Yaffe. *Journal of the Barbados Museum and Historical Society*, vol. 36, no. 3 (1981), p. 229-35.
The discovery of several fragments of pottery, which Professor Bullen stylistically attributed as Saladoid-Barrancoid, raised the question whether pre-Arawak people had inhabited Barbados. This paper reports the findings of X-ray fluorescence analysis of elementary micro-constituents of fragments of the pottery found by Bullen. The same analysis was carried out for a variety of Arawak and Carib potsherds as well as for a large number of clay samples found in Barbados. These were all subjected to multivariate analysis to see if their composition was similar. The results show that the sample stylistically assigned as pre-Arawak did not belong to the other samples at the ninety-five per cent confidence level. 'Thus the sample may well originate elsewhere and probably could have been brought to Barbados.'

291 An archaeological investigation of the domestic life of plantation
     slaves in Barbados.
     Jerome S. Handler. *Journal of the Barbados Museum and Historical Society*, vol. 34, no. 2 (1972), p. 64-72.
A modified version of a talk given at the Centre for Multi-Racial Studies at the Cave Hill Campus of the University of the West Indies on 21 January 1972, in which the author describes the overall context of a research project on Barbados slaves and goes on to detail the archaeological component of this work.

292 **Plantation slavery in Barbados: an archaeological and historical investigation.**
Jerome S. Handler, Frederick W. Lange, with the assistance of Robert V. Riordan. Cambridge, Massachusetts: Harvard University Press, 1978. 368p. 3 maps. bibliog.

A carefully researched volume, excellently presented and with numerous fine line drawings. It is based on archaeological field work in Barbados which spanned two seasons in 1971-72. In all, fourteen plantations were examined, with particularly extensive excavations being undertaken at the large Newton plantation in Christ Church. A detailed archaeological record of skeletons and associated artefacts such as buttons, tacks, china, beads and metal objects is provided.

293 **Old Barbados.**
C. N. C. Roach. *Journal of the Barbados Museum and Historical Society*, vol. 3, no. 3 (1936), p. 137-48; vol. 3, no. 4 (1936), p. 211-22; vol. 4, no. 1 (1936), p. 12-21; vol. 4, no. 2 (1937), p. 53-67; vol. 4, no. 3 (1937), p. 109-22; vol. 4, no. 4 (1937), p. 167-79; vol. 5, no. 1 (1937), p. 3-11; vol. 5, no. 2 (1938), p. 85-100; vol. 5, no. 3 (1938), p. 130–43; vol. 6, no. 1 (1938). p. 26-40; vol. 6, no. 2 (1939), p. 74-86; vol. 6, no. 3 (1939), p. 139-51; vol. 6, no. 4 (1939), p. 191-97.

This series of thirteen articles considers various aspects of the Amerindian prehistory of Barbados. The account is presented in seven chapters and represents a mine of information, although it is written in a somewhat 'old world' style. Chapter one (vol. 3, no. 3) introduces the shell implements and clay pots found at Golders Green and Indian Mount, both in the parish of St. Lucy, in order to build up a picture of the Amerindian inhabitants of Barbados. The antipathy between Arawaks and Caribs is discussed, as well as the resemblances between them in chapter two (vol. 3, no. 4, and vol. 4, no. 1). Chapter three (vol. 4, nos. 2, 3 and 4) chronicles in detail conch shell implements such as hatchets, gouges, axes, adzes, augers, spear-heads, toys, scrapers, knives, spoons, cups and pounders, along with notes on how they were made. Chapter four (vol. 5, no. 1) is devoted to aboriginal stone tools and weapons, which although never abundant, must have existed in greater numbers prior to European settlement. Stone axes, hammerstones, whetstones, grindstones, awls and other boring implements are also described, as are some bone tools. Pottery finds are detailed in chapter five which appears in three parts (vol. 5, no. 2; vol. 5, no. 3; vol. 6, no. 1). In the last three pieces, chapters six (vol. 6, no. 2) and chapter seven (vol. 6, no. 3; vol. 6, no. 4), pottery handles, and finds relating to the activities of fishing, canoe building and hunting are reviewed and explained respectively.

Barbados our island home.
See item no. 14.

The West Indian islands.
See item no. 16.

Prehistory and Archaeology

A short history of Barbados.
See item no. 334.

Barbados: a history from the Amerindians to independence.
See item no. 347.

History

History of the Caribbean region

294 Caribbean pirates.
Warren Alleyne.   London: Macmillan Caribbean, 1982. 113p. map. bibliog.

Written by one of Barbados' leading historians. After a general introduction, the lives of individual pirates are featured. Those having a connection with Barbados include the notorious Henry Morgan, Edward Teach (alias Blackbeard), Bartholomew Roberts, George Lowther and Francis Spriggs. However, only (Major) Stede Bonnet was Barbados-born. Alleyne, who today lives only a short distance from Bonnet's residence, dubs him the 'gentleman pirate'.

295 Caribbean history in maps.
Peter Ashdown.   Port of Spain, Kingston, London: Longman Caribbean, 1979. 84p. maps.

Divided into 15 sections, this series of over 175 excellent maps and diagrams seeks to present a visual depiction of Caribbean history. The chapters are 'General'; 'The Amerindian peoples'; 'European exploration and settlement'; 'Slavery and the plantation society'; 'European rivalry'; 'Revolt and revolution'; 'Emancipation'; 'The decline of sugar'; 'Problems 1834-1900'; 'The U.S.A. in the Caribbean'; 'Economic distress and the rise of nationalism'; 'Regional co-operation: failure and success'; 'The West Indies in the 1970s'; 'West Indian heroes'; 'The history of individual states'. This pan-Caribbean volume is of direct relevance to those interested in Barbadian social and economic circumstances.

296 **The making of the West Indies.**
F. Augier, S. Gordon, D. Hall, M. Reckord. London: Longman,
1960. 310p. 10 maps. bibliog.

One of the first GCE textbooks charting the history of the region. The book is
divided into three parts: importing the society; establishing the society; and
establishing freedom. After each chapter there are suggestions for further reading
and questions for discussion. It is recommended that students follow up the
references for their own territories, and, in this way, familiarize themselves with
their own histories. In the case of Barbados there are references to settlement,
tobacco and sugar cultivation, servants, slaves, trade, government, taxes,
buccaneers, religion, the Middle Passage, wars, emigration, emancipation,
apprenticeship, social conditions, education, trade unions, the 1937 disturbances
and their effects, federation and relations with the United States.

297 **Sources of West Indian history.**
Compiled by F. Augier, S. Gordon. London: Longman, 1962.
Reprinted, 1969. 308p.

A collection of excerpts from primary sources, classified under seven headings:
people of the Caribbean; economic life; religion and education before emancipation; slavery and its abolition; emancipation and apprenticeship; social
conditions since emancipation; and government and politics. There are several
entries on Barbados, including references to plantation life, sugar and tobacco
cultivation, trading, slavery, education, religion, juvenile crime, federation,
independence and regional cooperation. The book is compiled with the advanced
secondary school student in mind.

298 **No peace beyond the line: the English in the Caribbean 1624-1690.**
Carl Bridenbaugh, Roberta Bridenbaugh. New York: Oxford
University Press, 1972. 440p. 4 maps. bibliog.

The 'line' in the title refers to the vast area west of the Azores and south of the
Tropic of Cancer, beyond which people took their chances against friend, foe and
nature, in seeking to improve their fortunes. The settlement of Barbados was no
exception, and the account focuses on the extreme hardships endured in the battle
against nature – the rudimentary huts or tents the colonizers lived in, and the
hammocks in which they slept fearful of cockroaches and rats. Fear also
characterized human relationships between slaves, servants and planters, and
among themselves, just as there was a phobia about foreigners, pirates and trade
competitors. So dim were the prospects for many smallholders that they seized
any opportunity to escape or to join an (ill-fated) expedition against another
territory. Apart from the usual references to sugar cultivation and slavery, there is
an interesting description of the construction details of the Glebe House in
St. John in 1679, and also included is Samuel Copen's prospect of Bridgetown in
1695.

299 **The British West Indies.**
W. Burn. London: Hutchinson, 1951. 196p. bibliog.

A brief treatment of the history of the British West Indies from the time of
settlement to the mid-20th century, which includes an appendix on the Falklands!

The author, a former governor of Jamaica, tends to concentrate on 'macro' phenomena such as trade, war and legislation, which he sees as bound up with events in the 'mother country'. References to Barbados include mentions of early conditions, the fluctuations in sugar prices, reactions to the Acts of Trade, an attempted attack by the Dutch in 1665, the slave rising of 1816, and the confederation riots of 1876.

300   **History of the British West Indies.**
Alan Burns.   London: Allen & Unwin, 1954. 2nd rev. ed., 1965.
849p. 29 maps. bibliog.

An even more comprehensive account than the title suggests, since the work also includes detailed descriptions of non-English-speaking territories. For this reason the settlement of Barbados does not occur until p. 196. Burns draws on a wealth of primary and secondary sources to enhance his *magnum opus*, which is all the more readable because the author, by his own admission, is not a historian. There are many extra pieces of interesting information in the narrative which are usually glossed over or omitted by others. All the key turning points in the development of Barbados from settlement to just before independence are chronicled and placed in the wider context of world events.

301   **Caribbeana – containing letters and dissertations together with poetical essays on various subjects and occasions; chiefly wrote by several hands in the West Indies and some of them to gentlemen residing there.**
London: printed for T. Osborne, J. Clarke, S. Austin,
G. Hawkins, R. Dodsley, W. Lewis, 1741. Reprinted, Millwood,
New York: Kraus Reprint, 1978. 2 vols.

There is a definite focus on Barbados in this miscellany of poems, addresses to grand juries, speeches in the House of Assembly, and letters to the printer of the *Barbados Gazette*, etc. This work is only of limited interest to the general reader.

302   **Caribbean story.**
William Claypole, John Robottom.   London: Longman
Caribbean, 1980-81. 2 vols. 45 maps. bibliog.

This textbook comprehensively covers the Caribbean Examinations Council's history syllabus. Book one, 'Foundations', deals with the period from the Amerindians to emancipation, while book two, 'The inheritors', extends the account to the contemporary post-independence era. Entries on Barbados include references to Carib artefacts, the island's position *vis-à-vis* prevailing winds, problems of settlement, bondservants and their mutinies, the advent of sugar, trading with the Dutch, land prices, the slave trade and slave rebellions, apprenticeship, Moravians, Methodists and Quakers, the short-lived joint governorship with the Leewards, the federation riots of 1876, the West Indies Federation and independence.

303 **Readings in Caribbean history and economics: an introduction to the region. Volume 1.**
Edited and introduced by Roberta Marx Delson. New York: Gordon & Breach, 1981. 336p. bibliog.

An anthology of previously published excerpts intended for students of the West Indian diaspora and others with an interest in Caribbean studies. For academic, analytic and ideological reasons, the region is treated as a whole, since it has a shared history and political economy. There are forty-two contributions ranging from original discovery and conquest to independence. Two relate directly to Barbados: 'Freedom in Barbados' by Jerome Handler, and 'Poor whites in Barbados' by Jill Sheppard. A Barbadian contributor, Woodville Marshall, writes on 'West Indian peasantry'.

304 **The history civil and commercial of the British colonies in the West Indies.**
Bryan Edwards. London: John Stockdale, 1801. 3rd ed. 3 vols. 9 maps.

An extensive work comprising some 1,670 pages. Barbados is treated in volumes one and three. Volume one contains a detailed map of the island prepared by Edwards in 1794. There is an account of the first landing of the English in 1605, when they found the place 'uninhabited and overgrown with woods . . .', yet containing 'pigs, pigeons and parrots'. Also chronicled are the disputes between Carlisle and Courteen, Tufton and Hawley. By 1650, during the Civil War in England, Edwards estimates that there were 20,000 whites in Barbados, most of them Royalists. Additional references are to territorial disputes among the planters, Ayscue's blockade of the island, general descriptions, and patterns of trade. The latter are reinforced with details of ships and their cargoes from 1786 to 1792. Volume three includes a tour through several islands by Sir William Young and the day he spent in Bridgetown on 6 December 1791.

305 **History of the West Indies.**
A. Garcia. London: George Harrap, 1965. 296p. 4 maps.

A GCE O-level textbook written by a teacher for students and teachers of history. The account traces developments from discovery to Federation, and includes references to Barbados. The emphasis is on trade and warfare, rather than living conditions under slavery or in the post-emancipation era.

306 **A source book of West Indian history for use in secondary schools.**
Introduced by Shirley Gordon. Spaldings, Jamaica: Knox Educational Services, 1956. 212p. map. bibliog.

The forerunner to the author's *Caribbean generations* (q.v.), this source book arose out of a conference for history teachers held at the University College of the West Indies in 1956. The participants saw the need to familiarize themselves and their students with their own history, as distinct from that of colonial powers, and the present work seeks to fill the void. There are eight sections including: the origins and traditions of the peoples of the Caribbean; the development of political institutions; agriculture and trade; the slave system and its abolition; emancipation and its effects; the growth of the community and the part played by religion and education; social services and developing ideas of public responsibility; and the background to federation. There are approximately twenty texts which refer to Barbados, and these relate mainly to sugar production, government and federation.

307 Caribbean generations.

Shirley Gordon. London: Longman Caribbean, 1983. 338p. map. bibliog.

A textbook prepared for the Caribbean Examinations Council. The work is divided into the following sections: the firstcomers; sugar and slavery; slave resistance; revolt and freedom; adjustments to the problems of emancipation; the 20th century; the United States of America in the Caribbean; and movements towards independence. By a careful selection of material and by asking appropriate questions, the author guides the students towards a critical evaluation of sources. There are several references to Barbados, which cover the escape of some slaves to St. Vincent, trading with the Dutch, sugar production, indentured servants, the purchase of slaves, religion, emigration to Trinidad, child labour, government, the 1937 riots, patterns of employment, work in Panama, labour movements, independence and regional integration.

308 The British in the Caribbean.

Cyril Hamshere. London: Weidenfeld & Nicolson, 1972. 240p. 13 maps. bibliog.

Since this work forms part of a series entitled 'A social history of the British overseas', it is only natural that the emphasis is placed on events, and their relative success and failure, as seen from the point of view of Britain. This account begins at least one hundred years before many comparable narratives. Consequently, the two early chapters on 'Tudor seamen' and 'Pioneers of English colonization' contextualize to a greater extent than most the settlement and conquest of the West Indies. The style is easy-going and the author has a welcome capacity for presenting interesting detail. References to Barbados are no exception. The reader is told, for instance, that during the Civil War in England, if anyone on the island uttered the words 'Roundhead' or 'Cavalier', he had to offer to all who heard him the forfeit meal of a young pig and turkey. Trade with the Dutch is also extensively described, as are the exploits of Barbadian planters in Surinam.

309 The buccaneers in the West Indies in the XVIIth century.

C. Haring. New York: Methuen, 1910. Reprinted, Hamden, Connecticut: Archon Books, 1966. 298p. 6 maps. bibliog.

An amended Oxford University BLitt thesis, this account seeks to reconcile traditional narratives with neglected historical documents. Captain William Jackson seems to have been the first to mobilize a buccaneer crew from Barbados and St. Kitts in 1642 when he plundered the towns of Maracaibo and Truxillo. The following year he ransomed St. Jago de la Vega (Jamaica) from the Spaniards. There is also the saga of Barbados' involvement in the 1655 Penn-Venables abortive (piratical?) attack on Santo Domingo and subsequent capture of Jamaica. Quakers from Barbados, along with vagabonds and criminals from England, were sent to the new colony to swell the white population, and

Modyford, a planter in Barbados, assumed the governorship in 1664. The final reference is from Père Labat, who, in 1694, spoke of a mass 'celebrating' the capture of two English vessels near Barbados. Although the author claims originality and fidelity to historical sources, there are nevertheless some inaccuracies, inconsistencies and significant omissions.

310 **Colonising expeditions to the West Indies and Guiana 1623-1667.**
Edited by Vincent Harlow. London: Hakluyt Society, 1925.
Reprinted, Nendeln, Liechtenstein: Kraus Reprint, 1967. 262p.
6 maps. bibliog.

Brings together early accounts and personal narratives of pioneer settlers in order to throw light on British overseas expansion. Excerpts relating to Barbados include manuscripts housed in the Bodleian, Trinity College Dublin and Cambridge University libraries. They refer to the Courteen versus Carlisle dispute, descriptions of the island around 1650 and the impressions of Sir Henry Colt. The narratives contain details of flora, fauna, dietary habits, the inhabitants' over-indulgence in liquor, heated arguments and their consequent idleness. Harlow provides a useful eighty-two-page historical introduction.

311 **Distinction, death and disgrace: governorship of the Leeward Islands in the early eighteenth century.**
William Laws. Kingston: Jamaica Historical Society, 1976. 100p.
map. bibliog.

Although not specifically about Barbados, this book nevertheless provides several insights into that island's relationship with its neighbours. It also highlights the many responsibilities of governors of the period as they played the role of mediator between sugar interests and the British government. However, the main connection between Barbados and the Leewards group was in the person of Barbadian-born Christopher Codrington (the younger) who became governor of those islands. Yet even his appeals for help during wars with the French went largely unheeded by Barbados. Laws claims that Barbados' isolationist policy was due in the main to exploiting the price of sugar. If a small island producer/competitor were routed by the enemy, this would have the beneficial effect of raising the market value of that commodity.

312 **Nelson's West Indian history.**
R. N. Murray. London: Nelson, 1971. 190p. 7 maps. bibliog.

A secondary school text written to respond to the demands of the GCE O-level syllabus. The problem of condensing the vast period from discovery to independence is tackled by bearing the West Indian reader in mind, and by including only those events which highlight the similarities of Caribbean culture and experience. Barbados is thus seen as sharing a history of slavery, sugar production, emancipation, missionary education and colonial rule. However, it differs with respect to uninterrupted British domination, patterns of indentureship and constitutional development. Although there is an attempt to keep the account simple, at the same time there is a tendency to hop from topic to topic, thereby exposing the student to chronological confusion.

313 **British Empire in America.**
J. Oldmixon. London: printed for J. Brotherton, J. Clarke [et
al.], 1741. 2nd ed. Reprinted, New York: Augustus Kelley, 1969.
2 vols. maps. bibliog.

A mercantilist account of the colonies with an emphasis on trade with Britain.
The Barbados section occurs in volume two (p. 1-171), and comprises nine
chapters. Chapter one is an historical account of the discovery, settlement and
progress of Barbados. Chapter two features a geographical description of the
island, including towns, forts, ports, harbours, public and private buildings.
Chapters three and four deal with the climate, agricultural production and fauna.
Chapter six treats the government of Barbados, together with laws, revenues and
church affairs, while chapter seven looks at the sugar industry and the production
of rum and molasses. The last two chapters describe patterns of trade and the
perceived advantages to England. Probably the most interesting subsection is
chapter five, which examines the lives of the masters and slaves, including details
of diet and recreational activities.

314 **Caribbeana: being miscellaneous papers relating to the history,
genealogy, topography and antiquities of the British West Indies.**
Edited by Vere Langford Oliver. London: Mitchell Hughes &
Clarke, 1912. 6 vols.

Amidst the organized chaos of a plethora of West Indian material, there are
Barbadian items on births, deaths, marriages, lists of wills, early settlers and notes
on various families. Most of the Barbadian entries were submitted by Darnell
Davis and E. Sinckler, to whom the compiler expresses deep gratitude.

315 **War and trade in the West Indies 1739-1763.**
Richard Pares. Oxford: Clarendon Press, 1936. 631p. map.
bibliog.

Covers two major wars, against Spain (1739-48) and France (1756-62), and the
implications these had for life and trade in the West Indies. The case of Barbados
is interesting in that it was never attacked and rarely did it send men to relieve a
nearby island. The exception was in 1761-62 when volunteers were raised from
the debtors' prison. Barbados' reluctance to take the military initiative was only
matched by its unwillingness to subsidize a British regiment. Although wars
inevitably affected the sugar trade, again Barbados did not appear to suffer
unduly, as prices, insurance rates, shipping and tonnage of the period
demonstrate. As a matter of fact, the island gained in its sale of rum. The main
inconvenience seems to have been sharing a convoy with the Leewards. This had
the effect of delaying the shipment of partially refined sugar, since by the time the
claying process was complete, it was often necessary to await the sailing of the
next convoy.

316 **A short history of the West Indies.**
  J. Parry, P. Sherlock. London: Macmillan, 1956. Reprinted,
  1978. 3rd ed. 337p. bibliog.

A history which examines the region as a whole from the standpoint of insiders, as well as analysing the linkages with former colonial powers. The account traces the major events from discovery to independence with greater emphasis on the English-speaking Caribbean. Apart from the customary textbook references to Barbadian sugar production and slavery, the authors here tend to highlight the part played by Barbadians elsewhere in the West Indies. They deal with early patterns of emigration brought about by the forced evacuation of smallholders during the transition from tobacco to sugar cultivaton. They also refer to Barbadian involvement in the expedition against Hispaniola and the conquest of Jamaica, the recapture of Antigua and Montserrat, and the accompaniment by many Barbadians to Jamaica of the new governor, Modyford.

317 **The colonial agents of the British West Indies: a study in colonial administration mainly in the eighteenth century.**
  Lillian Penson. London: Cass, 1924. Reprinted, 1971. 2nd ed.
  318p. map. bibliog.

A history of that group of individuals who acted as liaison officers between the colony and the mother country, and who initially represented the interests of governors, but later those of the islands themselves. The account also examines the difficulties experienced by governors in conflict with the alternative aspirations of assemblymen, planters and merchants. Barbados had twenty-five of these agents from 1671 to 1848. The book describes their origin, the factionalism between Royalist and Roundhead supporters, how the island assumed the leading position of importance from St. Christopher, independent attitudes of assemblymen, problems faced by early governors and difficulties surrounding the appointment of agents. There are also references to the gentlemen planters of London and the formation of the Committee for the Concern of Barbados.

318 **The development of the British West Indies 1700-1763.**
  Frank Pitman. New Haven, Connecticut: Yale University Press,
  1917. Reprinted, London: Cass, 1967. 495p. map. bibliog.

A revision of the author's doctoral dissertation. The published version attempts an investigation of the industrial and social conditions which led to the growth and dissolution of the British Empire. Based on manuscripts housed in the Public Record Office and the British Museum, the account examines patterns of trade between the West Indian islands and both Europe and North America. The antipathy of the big planters and merchants to the latter's commercial interests, and the protectionist measures taken to safeguard their own, ironically brought about the destruction of the West Indian islands' trade. There are several descriptions of Barbados taken from local histories, official correspondence and travellers' tales, mentioning the depraved opulence of the plantocracy, poor whites, the slave trade and small planters.

319 **Harry Morgan's way: the biography of Sir Henry Morgan, 1635-1684.**
Dudley Pope. London: Secker & Warburg, 1977. 379p. 3 maps. bibliog.

An eminently readable account of the exploits of this famous Welsh buccaneer who ended up as governor of Jamaica. Morgan's contact with Barbados stemmed from his involvement as a young officer in the Western Design of Cromwell, and subsequently his friendship with Modyford, who later, as governor of Jamaica, was to encourage his raids on the Spanish Main. Indeed, so successful was Morgan's plundering that his attack on Portobelo realized more than three times the amount of Barbados' annual trade at the peak of that island's commercial prosperity. Apart from references to early travellers' accounts of Barbados, there is also a description of Newport's attack on Caguaya (Jamaica) in 1603. Having beaten off the Spaniards, however, his motley crew, many of them said to have been recruited in Barbados, succumbed to the contents of a warehouse full of liquor. This is strange to say the least, since Barbados was not settled for another quarter of a century.

320 **The Caribbean: the story of our sea of destiny.**
W. Adolphe Roberts. New York: Negro Universities Press, 1969. Reprint of 1940 ed. 361p. 13 maps. bibliog.

A history from the time of Columbus to the Second World War with a focus on the Caribbean as another Mediterranean of extreme strategic significance. Consequently, the emphasis is on the exploits of seafarers, navies and buccaneers. The treatment of Barbados is no exception. Among featured personalities are the notorious Henry Morgan and Bartholomew Roberts. The latter, having once been repulsed from the island, flew a flag with the letters BH and MH, signifying a head from Barbados and Martinique whenever captives were taken from those shores. There are also references to Barbados' role in the attack on Hispaniola, rum, sugar production and the treatment of slaves. Details of settlement given in this work are largely inaccurate.

321 **The Caribbean confederation.**
C. S. Salmon. London: Cassell, 1888. Reprinted, London: Cass, 1971. 175p. map.

A plea for equal treatment of black British subjects, and for self-government in the form of a confederacy uniting the whole British West Indies. In maintaining such a position, Salmon seeks to rebut the popular racist views of Froude and Trollope by examining West Indian African origins, and by showing that lack of opportunity, rather than inferiority, explains the dilemma of the black man. Regarding Barbados, the Froudian position is demolished with reference to the appointment of a black attorney general, the limitation of the franchise to property owners of independent means, the method of implementing the Encumbered States Court Act, known as the 'consignees lien', and the unfounded opinion that the island's prosperity, standard of living and system of education ended with emancipation. There are also sections dealing with balance of trade figures, the intelligence and industry of Barbadians, the taxes paid on various consumer items, education and school attendance rates, emigration and external communication and the system of government as a model for future confederation.

322 **The golden Antilles.**
Timothy Severin. London: Hamish Hamilton, 1970. 336p. map.
bibliog.

Recounts three English and one Scottish attempts at capturing Spanish possessions in the Caribbean. The third of these, under Cromwell, and jointly commanded by Admiral Penn and General Venables, concerns Barbados. The Western Design, as it was known, was targeted at Santo Domingo, and, in 1655, Barbados became the launching, recruiting and training stage of the operation. Unfortunately, the conscripts, being mainly ex-convicts, runaway smallholders and drunkards, were of such poor quality that the attack on Hispaniola was transformed into a military disaster. Profiteering by Barbadian merchants, and the consequent necessity to turn to alternative stocks of dumped food, also led to sickness and death from food poisoning. The capture of Jamaica was more successful, but that island was so detested by the Barbadian contingent, that they preferred to be shipped back home to face punishment rather than remain there.

323 **West Indian nations.**
Philip Sherlock. Kingston: Jamaica Publishing House; London: Macmillan, 1973. 362p. 14 maps. bibliog.

Written as a sequel to *A short history of the West Indies* (q.v.), which was jointly written by Sherlock and J. Parry, in order to emphasize the cumulative experience and aspirations of the islands' black and brown majorities. Consequently, a large proportion of the book is devoted to slave origins, the slave trade, plantation life, resistance and rebellion against white hegemony, emancipation, and the quest for independence and self-sufficiency. The Barbados entries follow this general pattern from discovery to the premiership of Errol Barrow.

324 **The rise and growth of the West-India colonies.**
Dalby Thomas. London: printed for Jo Hindmarth, 1690.
Reprinted, New York: Arno Press, 1972. 53p.

This mercantilist treatise seeks to demonstrate the usefulness of the colonies for bilateral trade with the mother country. There are details on the arrangement of a plantation, the processes of sugar, molasses and rum production and cane planting. Also mentioned are tropical hazards associated with agriculture and the various costs involved, some of which necessitate imports from England. In a similar vein there are also references to the cultivation of cotton, ginger, indigo, cocoa and tobacco. Thomas takes up the planter cause against the imposition of the infamous $4\frac{1}{2}$ per cent duty on sugar and proposes a number of suggestions for the amelioration of their lot. The latter include the establishment of a council of trade, a credit bank and a common factory.

325 **The West Indian heritage: a history of the West Indies.**
Jack Watson. London: John Murray, 1979. 210p. 20 maps.
bibliog.

A textbook aimed at West Indian readers, enabling them to appreciate their rich heritage and encouraging them to study it further. The main events from settlement to the formation of CARICOM are treated at the 'macro' level in the widest Caribbean context. The commentary is enhanced with some early prints,

Punch cartoons, photographs and commemorative issues of stamps of the region. There is an accompanying glossary and suggestions for additional reading. References to Barbados are fairly sparse since the author's perspective is predominantly international.

326 Documents of West Indian history. Vol. 1: 1492-1655.
Eric Williams.   Port of Spain: PNM, 1963. 310p. bibliog.

Intended as the first of five volumes to bring together various sources for scholarship and research on the West Indies. The work is subtitled 'From the Spanish discovery to the British conquest of Jamaica'. Entries are classified as follows: the discovery of the West Indies; the economic organization of the Spanish Caribbean; the white population problem; the problem of aboriginal Indian labour; negro slavery and the slave trade; the Spanish colonial system; the international struggle for the Caribbean; and the early organization of the non-Spanish colonies. Barbadian items include references to Richelieu's interest in the island, the granting of the territory to Carlisle, tobacco and sugar production, the sending of convicts there, the matters of democracy and self-government and Whistler's description of Barbados as Britain's dunghill.

327 From Columbus to Castro: the history of the Caribbean 1492-1969.
Eric Williams.   London: André Deutsch, 1970. Reprinted, 1976. 576p. 2 maps. bibliog.

A work which took eighteen years to complete and which, for the first time, attempts to bring together fragmented accounts into a common whole, so as to embrace the whole Caribbean, whether French, Spanish, Dutch, British, American or Danish. There are several references to Barbados. The most interesting include accounts of French and English indentured labour, the establishment of a society to encourage spinning and weaving for unemployed poor whites, comparisons of sugar production methods in Barbados, Hispaniola and Jamaica, and statistics of slave importation and mortality. However, Williams seems to take more delight in underlining the provincial and isolationist outlook of Barbadians, who, as far back as 1683 stated that they would not spend twenty shillings to save either the Leeward Islands or Jamaica from the ravages of piracy. The spirit of 'independence' is also manifested in the island's request for self-government during the struggle between Cavaliers and Roundheads, its subsequent repudiation of Cromwell, negative attitudes towards federation, demand to elect members to the British Parliament, and refusal to abide by enactments of the latter since Barbadians were not represented there. The author argues that the same mentality is evident today.

328 The Caribbee islands under the proprietary patents.
James Williamson.   Oxford: Oxford University Press, 1926. 229p. map. bibliog.

Examines the motives for and traffic in proprietary patents within the context of the political and social life of the islands. Barbados plays no small part in the account, since even in the early days of settlement, there was the infamous proprietary dispute between the factions of Carlisle and Courteen. In an appendix Williamson includes hitherto unused Chancery documents which throw additional light on the formative years of the island.

329 **A short history of the British West Indies.**
H. Wiseman. London: University of London Press, 1950. 159p.
map. bibliog.

Based on the premise that the history of the British West Indies forms part of a wider Caribbean history, and that the latter in turn is linked with the fortunes of colonial powers. The main events from settlement to the late 1940s are traced: patterns of trade, wars, slavery and its abolition, constitutional development, social conditions and hopes for the future. Studies are recommended which focus on West Indian attitudes to work and the problem of imitation through culture contact. References to Barbados tend to stress its unique characteristics: uninterrupted colonial rule, freedom from attack and a model constitution.

The church in the West Indies.
See item no. 450.

A history of the West Indies.
See item no. 452.

Caribbean Quakers.
See item no. 454.

Church and society in Barbados in the eighteenth century.
See item no. 458.

A history of the Moravian Church, Eastern West Indies province.
See item no. 461.

Treasure in the Caribbean: a first study of Georgian buildings in the British West Indies.
See item no. 774.

Historic architecture of the Caribbean.
See item no. 777.

The evolution of vernacular architecture in the Western Caribbean.
See item no. 783.

A study on the historiography of the British West Indies to the end of the nineteenth century.
See item no. 939.

History of Barbados

330 **Historic Bridgetown.**
Warren Alleyne. Bridgetown: Barbados National Trust, 1978.
117p. map. bibliog.

Traces the history of Bridgetown from its inception in 1628, when it was known as the Indian Bridge or Bridge, through the period 1660 to the 19th century (when it was called St. Michael's Town or Doncaster), to the present day. The development of early streets, neighbourhoods, schools, churches, docks, wharves, hotels, fountains and government buildings is outlined. There are also references to the introduction of public utilities and to a number of serious city fires. The descriptions are well researched and there is a useful accompanying list of source materials.

331 **Genealogies of Barbados families.**
Compiled by James Brandow. Baltimore, Maryland:
Genealogical Publishing Company, 1983. 753p.

Contains details of Barbadian families originally published in Oliver's *Caribbeana* . . . (q.v.) and early numbers of the *Journal of the Barbados Museum and Historical Society*, the latter featuring (anonymous) work by Shilstone. About 100 well-known names, from Alleyne to Walrond, are thoroughly researched with copious notes, and there are appendixes dealing with burial inscriptions in St. Michael's Cathedral and lists of Quakers. There is even a separate entry on Sam Lord and his castle and various readers' queries are answered. The appeal to the many Americans who have Barbadian roots possibly explains the place of publication.

332 **West Indian opposition to British policy: Barbadian politics 1774-82.**
Selwyn Carrington. *Journal of Caribbean History* vol. 17 (1982), p. 26-49.

Examines Barbadian politics during the American War of Independence and the conflict between the planter-dominated Assembly and the governor and his Council. While the former hardly sought separation from Britain, it nevertheless jealously attempted to preserve and augment its power as an entity independent from Parliament in the mother country. The author cites several instances of such conflict including: the riots of 1775 protesting about official attempts to curb smuggling with America, opposition to securing supplies for British troops fighting in America, the running battles between Henry Duke the Solicitor General and Governor Hay, the refusal of the Assembly to pass any tax bills or to renew the Militia Act under the administration of Governor Cuninghame (but instead a decision to reduce his salary). Carrington concludes that 'the repeated conflicts between the assemblymen and the royal governors brought important constitutional changes which confirmed the House's control over most local matters and its power over the executive branch'.

333 **A true and faithful account of four of the chiefest plantations of the English in America, to wit of Virginia, New England, Bermudus, Barbados.**
Samuel Clarke. London: privately printed, 1670. 85p.
The Barbados section (p. 57-85) deals with the discovery of the island by the Portuguese, its towns, bays, animals, fish, climate, diseases, baking of bread, food and drink, servants and slaves, birds, snakes, insects, trees, plants, fruit and the planting of sugar cane. Among various herbal remedies, a cure for 'stones' is supplied. This involves the grinding of the pizzle of a green turtle to powder and mixing it with beer, ale or white wine.

334 **A short history of Barbados.**
Neville Connell. *Journal of the Barbados Museum and Historical Society*, vol. 27, no. 1 (Nov. 1959), p. 7-30.
A revised version of an article first published in the *Advocate Year Book* for 1951. It is essentially a popular, partially documented account, which, after a brief introduction to the geology, prehistory and discovery of Barbados, traces the main events from settlement to the West Indies Federation. There is also a description of the former vestry system, and of local government by district and the mayor and corporation of Bridgetown. A list of the island's governors is appended. Interestingly, Connell raises doubts about the derivation of the name Barbados from the bearded fig tree (*ficus laurifolia*), since this grows inland, and would scarcely have been sighted by the early Portuguese navigators.

335 **Cavaliers and roundheads of Barbados 1650-1652, with some account of the early history of Barbados.**
N. Darnell Davis. Georgetown: Argosy Press, 1887. 259p.
Describes how the Civil War in England affected life in Little England and the factionalism between the local Royalist majority and Roundhead minority. Events are traced from the time of settlement up to the point of capitulation to the forces of Ayscue and the signing of the famous Articles of Agreement, reckoned to form the background to the American Declaration of Independence. The volume uses sources such as Nicholas Foster's *A briefe relation of the late horrid rebellion acted in the Island Barbadas in the West Indies wherein it is contained* (q.v.) and Richard Ligon's *A true and exact history of the island of Barbadoes* (q.v.) and reproduces facsimiles of their title pages.

336 **The Barbados census of 1680: profile of the richest colony in English America.**
Richard Dunn. *William & Mary Quarterly*, 3rd series, vol. 26, no. 1 (Jan. 1969), p. 3-30. bibliog.
An analysis of the contents of Governor Atkins' box of census data returned at the request of the Plantation Office in Whitehall. This is probably the most comprehensive surviving census of any English colony in the 17th century. There is a wealth of information on judges, councillors, assemblymen, the militia, shipping, the importation of slaves and baptismal and burial records. In addition, there are alphabetical lists by parish of the land holders with the extent of their

holdings and number of slaves owned, an enumeration of householders in Bridgetown indicating marital status and number of children, and a list of those leaving the island complete with details of their intended destination. After putting all his information together and checking with other accounts of the period, Dunn argues that in the boom sugar years Barbados was a highly stratified society, with the minority of large planters exerting a virtual monopoly in all positions of power. At the same time, among the rest of the population, he points to conditions of overcrowding and horrific infant mortality rates.

337 **About Barbados.**
J. Y. Edghill. London: Tallis & Company, 1890. 141p.

A collection of articles, most of which had been previously published. Topics treated include the development of the island's roads (from sheep and goat tracks), Codrington College, the Moravians, the hurricane of 1831, various governors and the Savings Bank. There are also extracts from the notebooks of a physician and a reporter, and reminiscences of 1854, the year of a cholera epidemic. The style is lively and anecdotal, and vivid accounts of social conditions in the island are presented.

338 **A briefe relation of the late horrid rebellion acted in the Island Barbadas in the West Indies wherein it is contained.**
Nicholas Foster. London: I.G., 1650. Reprinted, London: Spottiswoode & Ballantyne, 1927. 86p.

An early account of the power politics of the island, featuring the clash between the Walrond and Drax families, and written by a Roundhead sympathizer of the latter. Particular reference is made to the (obnoxious) requirement for citizens to take an oath of allegiance to the government under pain of fines and banishment. Objections, in the form of letters and petitions, are raised against this harsh measure, further aggravated by the absence of stipulated annual elections, and its use as a tactic to preserve positions of power.

339 **A short history of Barbados from its first discovery and settlement to the end of year 1767.**
H. Frere. London: printed for J. Dodsley, 1768. 121p.

Written to demonstrate Barbados' unbroken loyalty to the mother country, in the hope that it will receive more than simply the returns from the much-hated stamp duty. Rapidly outlines the early years of settlement, governors, members of council, various disputes, etc. There are also sections on the constitution, trade, soil and climate, and a list of commanders-in-chief of Barbados from 1629 to 1767.

340 **Governors and generals: the relationship of civil and military commands in Barbados 1783-1815.**
Neville Hall. *Caribbean Studies*, vol. 10, no. 4 (1971), p. 93-112.

Examines the strategic significance of Barbados, particularly during a period of conflict with France, and the clash of power between various commanders-in-chief and island governors and presidents, among whom were Parry, Bishop, Ricketts and Seaforth. The diminution of gubernatorial authority was also evident in running battles with the Assembly and Legislative Council, and the questions of control over prisoners of war and the monthly packet boats. Only with the appointment of Beckwith and Leith as both civil and military chiefs were such conflicts resolved.

341 **Law and society in Barbados at the turn of the nineeteenth century.**
Neville Hall. *Journal of Caribbean History*, vol. 5 (1972),
p. 20-45.

Highlights the coincidence of justice with political and economic privilege in Barbados. More specifically, the article examines the power of the plantocracy in protecting its vested interests, and the relative legal deprivation of the remainder of the population. Since governors were both chancellors and law makers, problems were bound to arise due to their lack of legal training (the first qualified judge did not appear until 1841), or, as in the case of Seaforth, where there were impediments of speech and hearing. Inadequacies were further reflected in the unqualified precinct judiciary, magistracy, courts of grand and quarter sessions, courts of appeal, and the composition of juries. Only in 1825 were the full defects of the system pointed out by an investigative commission.

342 **A general account of the first settlement and of the trade and constitution of the island of Barbados.**
Richard Hall. Barbados: the author, 1755. Reprinted,
Bridgetown: C. P. Bowen in *The Herald*, 1895; Bridgetown:
E. M. Shilstone, 1924. 65p.

Shilstone's introduction to the latest edition of this early work provides the pedigree of the Hall family and the roles the author played as an assemblyman and acting magistrate in St. Michael. The account itself deals with settlement, the advent of sugar cane, the distribution of slaves and whites, principal towns, imports and exports, governmental expenditure and administration, parish taxes, the judiciary and Governors General.

343 **Barbados and the confederation question, 1871-1885.**
Bruce Hamilton. London: Eyre & Spottiswoode, 1956. 149p.
bibliog.

Based on a PhD thesis for the University of London. After a brief description of Barbados in the 1950s (and particularly its constitution), the account examines the triumph of the fiercely independent local Assembly over the British Colonial Office, forcing the latter to abandon its policy of federation in the Eastern Caribbean. The social and political situation of Victorian Barbados is briefly sketched, together with the administrations of various Governors General of the period, the successes they enjoyed and the hostilities they generated. In particular, the verbal battles in parliament and in the press, and the corresponding riots in the streets, are carefully described.

344 **A history of Barbados 1625-1685.**
Vincent Harlow. Oxford: Clarendon Press, 1926. Reprinted,
New York: Negro Universities Press, 1969. 347p. 2 maps. bibliog.

Based on research into early manuscripts, documents and narratives, most of which were in Britain, the account elaborates Harlow's Oxford University BLitt thesis. The first years from the time of settlement are traced, together with the Carlisle-Courteen factionalism and the Cavalier-Roundhead divisions of allegiance. The administrations of various governors of the period are also examined. A chapter on trade relations between Barbados and New England is said by the author's thesis supervisor to be 'careful and well documented'. There is also a section devoted to white indentured servants and black slaves, and two appendixes feature local government and population respectively.

345 **Our common heritage.**
F. A. Hoyos. Bridgetown: Advocate Press, 1953. 147p.

Originally intended as a school text which would rekindle interest in local history among Barbadians by providing thirty biographical sketches of prominent persons who have contributed to the foundations of Barbadian society. The emphasis is on the often neglected post-emancipation period. Those selected comprise governors, churchmen, politicians, statesmen, agriculturalists, educationalists and journalists. Linkages to the outside world are established by the inclusion of a number of Englishmen who played a major role in shaping the island community.

346 **Builders of Barbados.**
F. A. Hoyos. London: Macmillan, 1972. 146p. bibliog.

Intended as a school text, this is a sequel to *Our common heritage* (q.v.). There are eighteen biographical sketches spanning three centuries of Barbadian history from Christopher Codrington to Errol Barrow. Among the persons selected are leading churchmen, judges, educationalists, journalists and parliamentarians. Each chapter concludes with a short list of further recommended readings.

347 **Barbados: a history from the Amerindians to independence.**
F. A. Hoyos. London: Macmillan, 1976. 293p. 3 maps. bibliog.

Perhaps the most comprehensive contemporary account of the island's history since Schomburgk's *The history of Barbados* (q.v.). While this well-documented work was intended primarily as an advanced secondary school text, its lucid style is nevertheless appealing to a wider public. The endnotes and references contain a wealth of primary and secondary source material.

348 **The presugar era of European settlement in Barbados.**
F. Innes. *Journal of Caribbean History*, vol. 1 (Nov. 1970),
p. 1-22.

Provides details of the early land grants and patterns of settlement from 1627 to 1640. An island completely covered by forest was transformed into an allotment cultivating tobacco, cotton and indigo. Important and useful references for this period are also supplied in a series of footnotes.

349   **The transformation and consolidation of the corporate plantation economy in Barbados 1860-1977.**
Cecilia Karch.   PhD dissertation, Rutgers University, New Brunswick, New Jersey, 1979. 482p. bibliog. (Available from University Microfilms, Ann Arbor, Michigan, order no. GAX79-16145).

An analysis of the social formation of Barbados from an historical materialist perspective. The thesis examines the unique responses of the dominant classes to changes wrought by industrial capitalism and the collapse of the sugar preferential system. The internal economic transformation of the island during the period is said to influence greatly not only past, but also contemporary conflicts based jointly on race and class. The work is useful for providing a rare glimpse of the emergence of the agro-commercial bourgeoisie and its subsequent impact on social relationships in Barbados.

350   **The role of the Barbados Mutual Life Assurance Society during the international sugar crisis of the late nineteenth century.**
Cecilia Karch.   In: *Proceedings of the twelfth conference of the Association of Caribbean Historians*. Edited by K. Laurence. n.p.: Association of Caribbean Historians, 1980, p. 95-133.

Explores the role of a significant local financial institution in providing virtually the sole line of credit to an otherwise almost bankrupt plantation economy, thereby also facilitating the emergence of an agro-commercial bourgeoisie. The research examines the records and minute books of the Barbados Mutual Life Assurance Society from its inception in 1840 to show its increasing involvement in the plantation mortgage business at a time when alternative sources of funding were unavailable. The society's close association with the Chancery Court, involvement in the land evaluation process, artificial maintenance of high values, preservation of estates from subdivision, and lending policies assured the controlling interests of the white oligarchy. It also played no small part in the corporatization process and in providing the capital formation and investment for the emergence of the 'Big Six' group of companies.

351   **A true and exact history of the island of Barbadoes.**
Richard Ligon.   London: Cass, 1970. 2nd rev. ed. 122p. map.

The earliest complete set of impressions of an English visitor to the island, written from the debtors' prison at Newgate and first published in 1657. Deals with a transatlantic voyage and stay from 15 June 1647 to 15 April 1650. Details are supplied of plantation life and the first days of slavery. The process and profitability of sugar production are also outlined. Sometimes amusing comparisons are made between Barbados and the mother country with respect to climate, flora and fauna, food and drink. The latter receives extensive treatment with a number of gastronomic accounts of plantocratic prandial delights. An interesting map is provided, featuring the early patterns of settlement and camels. A work heavily plagiarized by others.

352 Memoirs of the first settlement of the island of Barbados and the other Caribbee islands with the succession of the governors and commanders in chief of Barbados to the year 1742.

London: printed for E. Owen and W. Meadows, 1743. Reprinted, Bridgetown: Evans Walcott, 1891. 73p.

Independent evidence shows that there was probably an earlier edition of this work published in Barbados in 1741. A further subtitle indicates that the contents were 'extracted from the ancient records, papers and accounts taken from Mr William Arnold, Mr Samuel Bulkly and Mr John Summers, some of the first settlers, the last of whom was alive in 1688, aged 82'. The account of the first settlement, early legislation, various governors and their lamentable disputes, is written in diary format with key dates as entries. An alphabetical list of the inhabitants in 1638 is also provided. In a separate appendix there are details of the government and administration of the island. This was almost certainly the first book to be published in Barbados.

353 Creoleana, or social and domestic scenes and incidents in Barbados in the days of yore.

J. W. Orderson. Bridgetown: no publisher given, 1841. 246p.

Describes conditions in Barbados after the Bridgetown fire of 1776, with high prices, poor crop yields and smallpox. The account is presented through the eyes of the daughter of a certain Mr Fairfield, a businessman who retired to St. George after his premises had been lost in the fire. Amid the saga of Caroline's love life, most of the references to people, places and events of the period are provided in a number of anecdotal asides.

354 The history of Barbados from the first discovery of the island, 1605, till the accession of Lord Seaforth, 1801.

John Poyer. London: Cass, 1971. new ed. 668p.

An attempt by a native of Barbados to present his countrymen 'with a more complete and impartial history of Barbadoes than has hitherto appeared'. Particular attention is paid to 'the civil, military, and ecclesiastical establishments of the colony, its laws and constitution', together with associated errors, imperfections and abuses. Relying on a number of secondary sources, the author traces the history of the island from early colonial days to the turn of the 19th century. The account focuses on various governors, the legislation enacted, and social conditions. Throughout the narrative, Poyer does not hesitate to indicate the extent of his approval of policies and events. This work was originally published in 1808.

355 Panama money in Barbados 1900-1920.

Bonham Richardson. Knoxville, Tennessee: University of Tennessee Press, 1985. 283p. map. bibliog.

Based on a careful analysis of archival and oral historical material. The author considers the exodus of almost a quarter of the Barbadian population to work on the construction of the Panama Canal to be a turning point in Barbados' social history. The work is essentially a 'before and after' comparison of life on the island. More specifically, it looks at the effects of emigration and remittances on such different elements as the sugar economy, friendly societies, religion and race relations. Ultimately, the Panama experience is said to have initiated the transformation of Barbados from a quasi-feudal society to a modern democracy by paving the way for the 1937 workers' riots. Although there is very little on Panama itself, as a case study of the dramatic effects of migration on contemporary Barbados the book is required reading.

356 **The history of Barbados.**
Robert Schomburgk. London: Longmans, Brown & Green, 1848. New ed., London: Cass, 1971. 722p. 2 maps.

Generally hailed as the most thorough classical treatment of the pre-emancipation period. Dissatisfied with the value judgements of earlier histories, the author seeks to base his own account more on matters of fact and official documents, thereby leaving questions of interpretation to the reader. The work is divided into three major sections. Part one provides a geographical and statistical description of the island, and includes separate chapters on climate, institutional life, political and local geography. Part two presents a chronicle of events from settlement to the administration of Sir Charles Grey. The final section supplies a wealth of detail on the island's geological formation, fossils, minerals, plants, insects, molluscs, fishes, reptiles, birds and mammals. Indeed the author indicates his desire to publish a more extensive account of the flora and fauna of Barbados. Although written by a foreigner in a language other than his maternal tongue, the value of a stranger's outlook and the careful pursuit of detail combine to make this the most comprehensive account of the period.

357 **A history of Barbados.**
Ronald Tree. London: Rupert Hart-Davis, 1972. 115p. map.

Written by a late British resident and benefactor of the island. This brief, popular narrative traces the history of Barbados from the time of the first settlers and period of slavery to independence. In many ways the account is uneven and reflects a colonial mentality. Nevertheless, it is full of interest and offers several insights into the life of the plantocracy, the sugar industry and many governors. A suggested three-day tour for visitors is also included.

Barbados our island home.
See item no. 14.

Barbados yesterday and today.
See item no. 15.

The economic geography of Barbados: a study of the relationships between environmental variations and economic development.
See item no. 70.

A descriptive list of maps of Barbados.
See item no. 107.

The natural history of Barbados.
See item no. 250.

'In search of Bim': the Barbados Museum's new permanent exhibition.
See item no. 289.

The original lists of persons of quality 1600-1700 . . .
See item no. 418.

Codrington chronicle, an experiment in Anglican altruism on a Barbados plantation 1710-1834.
See item no. 459.

Barbados diocesan history.
See item no. 466.

Background to independence.
See item no. 562.

Plantation and peasant farm – Barbados 1627-1960.
See item no. 697.

Employment in Barbados.
See item no. 724.

The history of the Barbados Workers' Union.
See item no. 729.

The 350th anniversary of Bridgetown.
See item no. 771.

History of plantocracy, peasantry and slavery

358   **After Africa.**
Edited by Roger Abrahams, John Szwed.   New Haven, Connecticut; London: Yale University Press, 1983. 444p. bibliog.

Subtitled 'Extracts from British travel accounts and journals of the seventeenth, eighteenth, and nineteenth centuries, concerning the slaves, their manners, and customs in the British West Indies'. A lengthy introduction by the editors gives the aim of this painstaking ten-year study as a search for the everyday, taken for granted elements of Afro-American culture as portrayed in the oldest available documents, together with the forced encounter of Europeans and Africans in the New World. The two anthropologists, who are frankly dissatisfied with the models offered by their colleagues, contextualize the excerpts and group them into ways of speaking, anancy tales, religion and magic, festivals and holidays, music, dance and games and miscellaneous conditions of life. There is also an appendix providing biographical details of the authors of various sources. Accounts of mainly recreational aspects of Barbadian slave life are principally based on

Richard Ligon, with additional quotations from such sources as Arthur Holt, William Lloyd, and Hans Sloane.

359   **Rebels and reactionaries: the political responses of white labourers to planter class hegemony in seventeenth century Barbados.**
Hilary Beckles. *Journal of Caribbean History*, vol. 15 (1981), p. 1-19.
Examines the exploitation of indentured servants and the strategies employed by planters to thwart their social solidarity. Rather than providing detailed descriptions of the conspiracies of 1634, 1647, 1681 and 1692, all of which failed through internal betrayal, the author prefers to underline the hatred and fear of the rival groups as characterized by escapes, planned attacks on plantations and excessive punishments.

360   **Notes on the decolonisation of West Indian history: towards the uncovering of the Barbadian revolutionary tradition.**
Hilary Beckles. *Bulletin of Eastern Caribbean Affairs*, vol. 8, no. 2 (May-June 1982), p. 13-23.
Makes the case for continuing the work begun by Elsa Goveia, Eric Williams and Walter Rodney in debunking colonial racist myths which have hitherto passed as history. More specifically, Beckles wishes to look at Barbados, since he believes that here more than anywhere else in the region 'white-sponsored racist myths are still advocated in the literature and established as facts'. The villain of the piece singled out for special attention is F. A. Hoyos, who is said to present ruling-class history as people's history. However, John Poyer, Robert Schomburgk, Vincent Harlow, J. Oldmixon and Ronald Tree are similarly dismissed along with today's crop of black politicians. With his adversaries out of the way, the author attempts to demonstrate the revolutionary consciousness of the black slave population by reference to the rebellions of 1649, 1655, 1675, 1692 and 1816, and the contribution of escaped Barbadian slaves to the Black Carib movement in the Windwards and runaway terrorist bands in Jamaica.

361   **Black rebellion in Barbados: the struggle against slavery 1627-1838.**
Hilary Beckles.   Bridgetown: Antilles Publications, 1984. 161p. bibliog.
Stemming from, and encouraged by, a lecture and discussion session held by the Barbados Creative Writers' Guild in 1983 to celebrate black civilization week, the present work is deliberately polemical in nature. It seeks to rebut Eurocentric and environmentalist interpretations of Barbadian passivity and to replace them with a radical analysis of black political consciousness. The account is chronological rather than thematic, and traces patterns of resistance from the origins of slave society to emancipation. In particular, there are examinations of marronage, the aborted uprisings of 1649, 1675 and 1692, Bussa's rebellion of 1816 and the white plantocratic reaction the risings engendered. An understanding of these early power struggles is arguably essential for an appreciation of contemporary race and class relationships in Barbados.

362 **The abortive revolution of 1876 in Barbados.**
George Belle. *Journal of Caribbean History*, vol. 18, no. 1
(1983), p. 1-34.
Written by a political scientist, this account of the opposition to Crown Colony
rule and confederation by the Barbadian plantocracy, against the wishes of
Governor Pope-Hennessy and the British government, seeks to understand the
revolutionary response of the poor black masses to the situation. At first, the
blacks were simply aligned with the colonial powers against the detested white
oligarchy. Later, however, through their own leaders, they manifested a
revolutionary class consciousness, an appreciation of which is arguably necessary
for an evaluation of race and class power relationships in contemporary Barbados.

363 **Bondsmen and bishops: slavery and apprenticeship on the
Codrington plantations of Barbados, 1710-1838.**
J. Harry Bennett. Berkeley, California; Los Angeles: University
of California Press, 1958. 176p. bibliog.
An analysis of the records and correspondence between Barbados and the Society
for the Propagation of the Gospel in Foreign Parts from the acquisition of the
Codrington estates to emancipation. The American author maintains that, largely
through ignorance, the society treated its slaves no differently from the
plantocracy, with the lone exception of religious instruction. This, he believes,
was a source of some embarrassment and controversy to the Anglican Church.

364 **Emancipation and apprenticeship in the British West Indies.**
W. L. Burn. London: Jonathan Cape, 1937. 398p. bibliog.
Based principally on an analysis of dispatches between governors and the Colonial
Office, or, in the author's terms, the 'in' and 'out' correspondence. Unlike
William Mathieson, Burn believes that the apprenticeship system introduced by
the colonial authorities was a less than useful policy instrument in effecting the
transition from slavery to freedom. In this connection, the inadequacy of the
special magistrates is highlighted. Barbados is presented as the most English and
traditionally organized West Indian territory with relatively little cruelty towards
slaves. Yet the colour bar was more rigid than elsewhere, freedom of speech more
problematic, and the slave code was one of the harshest. The Abolition Act itself
was described by Governor Lionel Smith as being 'the most cruel and sanguinary
that ever disgraced a British legislature', and the apprenticeship system was
characterized by onerous labour conditions and white intolerance.

365 **Mortality and labour on the Codrington estates, Barbados.**
Mary Butler. *Journal of Caribbean History*, vol. 19, no. 1 (1984),
p. 48-67.
Employs Codrington as a case study to illustrate the dynamics of plantation sugar
production as it adapted to the major problems relating to the survival of its
workforce. To this end mortality and production statistics are provided. The
change in policy from slave importation to local breeding is also reflected in
changing sex ratios during the 18th century.

366 **Slaves, free men, citizens: West Indian perspectives.**
Edited and introduced by Lambros Comitas, David
Lowenthal. New York: Anchor Books, 1973. 340p. bibliog.

A collection of essays which provides both an historical and a contemporary
analysis of racial, ethnic and class stratification in the West Indies from the time
of slavery. There are several references to Barbados. We are told, for instance,
that Barbados succeeded more than any other island in breeding her own slaves,
some of whom she exported to other territories, notably Jamaica. Mention is also
made of absentee proprietors, plantation attorneys, education of white children,
and the economic advantages of emancipation. Despite fairly rigid class barriers,
Barbados is said to possess an island identity based on geographical community,
and aided by an excellent road network and historic-cultural homogeneity. At the
same time, it is admitted that there is insufficient information on the island's
élites.

367 **The Barbadian diary of General Robert Haynes 1787-1836.**
Edited by Everil Cracknell. Mestead, Hampshire, England:
Azania Press, 1934. 70p.

Contains published remnants of the handwritten diary of General Haynes, one of
Barbados' largest landowners, born on the Newcastle family estate in St. John in
1769, and a descendant of a long line of Royalists. The account includes
references to the hurricanes of 1780 and 1821, the threatened invasion of the
French in 1782, sugar cultivation, the treatment of slaves, Quakers, the conditions
of the Newcastle, Clifton Hall and Bath estates, and the uprising of 1816. A
glossary and a genealogical chart of the Haynes family are appended.

368 **Sinews of empire: a short history of British slavery.**
Michael Craton. London: Temple Smith, 1974. 413p. 3 maps.
bibliog.

More philosophical than most comparable accounts and limited to a thorough
treatment of the most important variant of the slave trade and slave society – the
British version. The significance of Barbados for the market is underlined as a
major destination and subsequent transhipment point, and comparisons are made
with trade in Jamaica and the Leeward Islands. There are also details of the
preparation of slaves for auction 'by inch of candle' or by 'scramble' on board
ship, and the sale of leftovers to other ports. A description of the gang system is
provided, and references are made to poor whites, harsh slave laws, fertility and
mortality rates, and slave clothing. The 'success' of sugar production in Barbados
is attributed to greater orderliness, that is, little absenteeism, lack of labour
mobility, paternalism, low wages, and paucity of viable alternatives.

369 **Testing the chains: resistance to slavery in the British West Indies.**
Michael Craton. Ithaca, New York: Cornell University Press,
1982. 389p. 17 maps. bibliog.

A thought-provoking and critical analysis of interpretative models of slave
resistance which places the emphasis on the slaves themselves. This approach
arguably offers a more viable understanding of the varieties of reaction, ranging
from seeming accommodation and allegiance to outright rebellion. The work is

divided into five parts and respectively examines: resistance short of rebellion, marronage, African slaves, slave resistance in the age of revolution, and slave rebellions and emancipation. Two subsections are devoted to Barbados – one dealing with the early period 1645-1701 (and examining five slave plots, together with their discoveries and repercussions), and the other treating the well-known Bussa rebellion of 1816.

370   **Letters on slavery.**
William Dickson.   London: J. Phillips, 1789. Reprinted,
Westport, Connecticut: Negro Universities Press, 1970. 190p.
bibliog.

Originally intended as a treatise on the state of slavery in Barbados and the effects of abolition, this work also demonstrates the case for equality between natives of Africa and the rest of mankind. The former secretary to Governor Hay reproduces correspondence in which he pleads the abolitionist cause to Sir James Johnstone, a senator and 'a humane disinterested planter'. There is also a section on Jamaica and open letters to white inhabitants and members of the Barbadian legislature, and to the free negroes, mulattos and slaves of Barbados. This referenced account deals extensively with the life of slaves and the cruel treatment they received.

371   **Mitigation of slavery.**
William Dickson.   London: Longman, Hurst, Rees, Orme &
Brown, 1814. Reprinted, Westport, Connecticut: Negro
Universities Press, 1970. 528p. bibliog.

The work is in two parts. The first contains letters and papers of Joshua Steele, an elderly planter who arrived in Barbados in 1780, some eight years after Dickson. The second contains Dickson's correspondence to Thomas Clarkson. This lengthy collection is supplemented by 100 pages of appended notes and references. Coverage of the period after the abolition of the African slave trade concentrates on West Indian slavery with particular reference to Barbados. A middle course between immediate emancipation and unlimited slavery is recommended. The importance of Steele to Dickson lies in the former's enlightened treatment and payment of slaves, which resulted in greater productivity. In his own contribution, Dickson argues against the purchase of slaves, and for improvements in slave living conditions and methods of sugar production. He also agrees with Steele that, until laws are enacted admitting the evidence of negroes against whites, and until the quality of life is ameliorated, it makes little sense to instruct slaves in the ways of Christianity.

372   **Sugar and slaves: the rise of the planter class in the English West Indies 1624-1713.**
Richard Dunn.   Chapel Hill, North Carolina: University of North
Carolina Press, 1972. Reprinted, New York: Norton, 1973. 359p.
6 maps. bibliog.

An inquiry into how early English planters responded to the novelties of life in the tropics, sugar production and slave labour. The Barbados section relies on such accounts as those of Colt, Whistler and Richard Ligon, on poll tax returns, early maps and the correspondence of island governors, and deals with the 'success' of 'the most perfectly articulated colonial aristocracy in English America', as they switched from growing low-grade tobacco to widespread and more profitable sugar cultivation. The sugar boom, in turn, created the demand for labour, and, for economic reasons, the consequent transition from servants to slaves. As the title suggests, Dunn pays more attention to the masters than the slaves, and to this end analyses in some detail the 1680 census data. The account lacks the deadly earnestness associated with some contemporary academics, and is bolstered by the odd injection of humour.

373 **Slave society in the British Leeward Islands at the end of the eighteenth century.**
Elsa Goveia. New Haven, Connecticut: Yale University Press, 1965. 370p. map. bibliog.

Based on a doctoral thesis presented to the University of London in 1952, in which city most of the archival research was carried out by the late professor. Although most of the attention is focused on the Leewards, there are a number of references to Barbados. These include infringements of the ban on trade with America in 1800, opposition to the 4½ per cent export duty, the treatment of slaves as mere property, the 1688 Act outlining the procedure for the trial of slaves, the existence of poor white peasants, and various missions to the slaves, comprising catechesis conducted by the Society for the Propagation of the Gospel in Foreign Parts, and the work of the Moravians and Methodists.

374 **The West Indian slave laws of the eighteenth century.**
Elsa Goveia. In: *Chapters in Caribbean history, 2.* Edited by D. Hall, E. Goveia and F. Augier. St. Laurence, Christ Church, Barbados: Caribbean Universities Press; Aylesbury, England: Ginn, 1970, p. 9-53.

Contrasts the relatively humane Catholic Spanish legislation, under which slaves were considered as persons, with the more brutal English slave laws enacted by planters and reinforced by the police. The latter legislation treated slaves as property or chattels, and imposed severe penalties, mainly through fear of uprisings. The notorious Barbados Act of 1688, for instance, even permitted the death of a slave under punishment from his master, provided the killing was not wilful. However, even if it were, the penalty was only £15. The same law required the provision of clothing for slaves, but failure to comply was only punishable with a fine of 5 shillings. Furthermore, since slaves were considered 'brutish', when brought to trial, they were not entitled to a jury of twelve men. Attempts by a commissioner of legal inquiry to grant slaves rights under common law proved futile in Barbados and several other islands. Comparisons are also made with the Code Noir of the French territories and legislation under Dutch and Danish jurisdictions.

375   The Amerindian slave population of Barbados in the seventeenth
      and early eighteenth centuries.
      Jerome S. Handler.   *Caribbean Studies*, vol. 8, no. 4 (1969),
          p. 38-64.

Shortly after the initial colonization of Barbados, a small group of Arawaks from
Guyana was imported to teach the English settlers how to cultivate tropical crops
and to assist in the development of their settlements. These Amerindians came
voluntarily and as freemen. However, shortly after their arrival, they were
enslaved. This paper chronicles the story of Amerindians in Barbados, and
examines their social and legal position on the island during the 17th and 18th
centuries.

376   Aspects of Amerindian ethnography in 17th century Barbados.
      Jerome S. Handler.   *Caribbean Studies*, vol. 9, no. 4 (1970),
          p. 50-72.

A sequel to Handler's 'The Amerindian slave population of Barbados in the
seventeenth and early eighteenth centuries' (q.v.). In this paper the author
elucidates what can be deduced about the way of life of the Amerindians enslaved
in Barbados and the contribution they may have made to the island's early
culture.

377   Barbados.
      Jerome S. Handler, Arnold Sio.   In: *Neither slave nor free*. Edited
      by David Cohen, Jack Greene.   Baltimore, Maryland; London:
      Johns Hopkins University Press, 1972, p. 214-57.

Written to supplement a symposium on 'the role of the free black and free
mulatto in slave societies of the new world', held at Johns Hopkins University,
April 8-9, 1970. The study focuses on non-white freedmen in Barbados from the
end of the 18th century to emancipation. Most either lived in or gravitated
towards St. Michael and many of them were children. There is a useful discussion
on manumission and its most frequent type (for sexual services rendered). The
legal and occupational status of freedmen is also examined, together with their
relationships to the white and slave sections of the population.

378   The unappropriated people: freedmen in the slave society of
      Barbados.
      Jerome S. Handler.   Baltimore, Maryland: Johns Hopkins
      University Press, 1974. 225p. map. bibliog.

Focuses on one segment of slave society and 'describes and analyses their legal
and social status, demographic and social attributes, and especially the nature and
degree of their participation in the island's national institutions'. The period
extends from the end of the 18th century to 1834. Since these non-whites wrote no
books or pamphlets, most of the source material derives from group petitions and
addresses submitted to legislative bodies during their struggle for civil rights in the
19th century. After tracing the characteristics of the freedmen population and the
means of acquiring such status (manumission), the book examines their
contextualization at various institutional levels – the politico-judicial system, the

military, occupation, wealth, property, religion and education. A final chapter examines the social position of freedmen and their relationships to the larger white and slave populations.

379 **Freedmen and slaves in the Barbados militia.**
Jerome S. Handler. *Journal of Caribbean History*, vol. 19, no. 1 (1984), p. 1-25.
Describes the history of the island's militia from its organization in the 1640s until the arrival of the garrison in the 19th century. The strength, racial composition, regimental divisions and functions of the defence force are also analysed. Although no foreign enemy was ever engaged on Barbadian soil, fear of attack, especially by the Dutch and French, is said to have been even more worrisome to the authorities than slave uprisings. Consequently, and in the light of white emigration, several acts were passed permitting limited slave participation in the militia. The irony of the situation, as Handler points out, is that even though bravery could be rewarded by manumission, slaves were still expected to die for a society which exploited them.

380 **Notes by General Robert Haynes of Newcastle and Clifton Hall plantations, Barbados, and other documents of family interest.**
Edited by Edmund C. Haynes, Percy Haynes, Edmund S. Haynes. London: Argus Printing, 1910. 32p.
Taken from the original diary jottings of General Robert Haynes. The family tree is covered in some detail and there are also references to Haynes' various military positions, the importation of Bourbon cane, breadfruit and cinammon, the supervision of his plantations and the worries connected with the fall in the price of sugar. An appendix contains the registry of the Haynes' marriages and burials in St. John's parish church.

381 **Slave populations of the British Caribbean 1807-1834.**
B. Higman. Baltimore, Maryland; London: Johns Hopkins University Press, 1984. 781p. 18 maps. bibliog.
A monumental demographic analysis of slavery in the West Indies based on slave registration returns. The work contains chapters on physical and economic environments, the growth, distribution and structure of slave populations, rural and urban living conditions, health and reproduction. There is a statistical supplement of some 303 pages, containing 182 tables, which furnishes information on geographical distribution, ownership, birthplace, age, colour, stature, occupation, births, deaths, vital rates, manumissions, and land and labour use. About thirty of the tables refer to Barbados. One is even so detailed as to provide an analysis of slave population and ownership by street in the city of Bridgetown.

382   **Emancipation, sugar and federalism: Barbados and the West Indies 1833-1876.**
       Claude Levy. Gainesville, Florida: University of Florida, Center
       for Latin American Studies, 1980. 206p. 2 maps. bibliog. (Latin
       American Monographs).

Provides the background to emancipation from the time of settlement before
concentrating on the forty-year period that succeeded it. There are sections on the
apprenticeship system, the advent of free labour, and trade and general
conditions at the middle of the 19th century. The federation crisis is also
examined.

383   **The groans of the plantations, or a true account of their grievous
       and extreme sufferings by the heavy impositions upon sugar and
       other hardships.**
       E. Littleton. London: M. Clark, 1689. 35p.

The subtitle shows that this is not a book about slavery. Rather it is a planter tract
pleading for immediate relief from the recently imposed stamp duty with its
perceived detriment to the sugar colonies. An addendum to the subtitle indicates
that the work relates 'more particularly to the island of Barbados'. Whereas its
public services should have benefited from the tax, quite the opposite effect
obtained. Furthermore, planters had to bear the full brunt of the iniquitous
situation, since, in addition to the tax and the consequent erosion of the market,
they had to face the costs of slave purchase and upkeep, production, maintenance
and custodial services, the various details of which are provided.

384   **The West India colonies.**
       James McQueen. London: Longman, Hurst, 1825. Reprinted,
       New York: Negro Universities Press, 1969. 427p.

An anti-emancipationist tract which musters various arguments, ranging from
scriptural to economic, in favour of the retention of plantation slavery in the
colonies. References to Barbados examine in detail the 'copyhold' system of
Joshua Steele of Kendal Plantation. This elderly gentleman's revenues were
alleged to have increased due to his 'humanitarian' method of paying slaves,
allocating land and deducting living expenses. However, McQueen produces
documentary evidence, including correspondence from Barbadians, which
refutes any supposed advantages of the system. He demonstrates that Steele's
fortunes, if any, were due rather to the artificially high price of sugar on account
of the ravages of borer and hurricane. They would also have been derived from
the fact that slaves' expenses far exceeded any payments given them by Steele in
his own imported currency, which was redeemable only on his plantation.

385   **The termination of the apprenticeship in Barbados and the
       Windward Islands: an essay in colonial administration and politics.**
       Woodville Marshall. *Journal of Caribbean History*, vol. 2 (May
       1971), p. 1-45.

By focusing on apprenticeship and the reasons for its premature termination, the
author investigates the interplay between the British government and the colonial

111

legislature. In particular he examines the initiative taken by the recently appointed governor-in-chief of the Windward Islands, Sir Evan McGregor, and his relationship with the rather stubborn Barbadian assemblymen. The contribution of his spokesman, Solicitor General R. B. Clarke, is also highlighted, together with the various arguments underpinning debate on the issue both inside and outside parliament.

386 **The Colthurst journal.**
Edited by Woodville Marshall. Millwood, New York: KTO Press, 1977. 255p. 3 maps. bibliog.

The edited private journal of a retired Irish major appointed as special magistrate to Barbados and St. Vincent to oversee the period of apprenticeship. The account provides some interesting descriptions of life during the transition from slavery. Disposed to the abolitionist cause, Colthurst reveals his antipathy to the ignorance and cruelty of the planters, who unsuccessfully attempt to win him to their side by bribery and dinner invitations. His judgements read like sermons, and are occasionally full of paternalistic taunting, as he seeks to admonish this incorrigible group. The account, editorial introduction, notes and appendixes supply details of the early development of the island's police force, the administration of justice, and the duties, convictions and punishments of apprentices from 1835 to 1838.

387 **British slavery and its abolition 1823-1838.**
William Mathieson. London: Longmans, Green, 1926. Reprinted, New York: Octagon Books, 1967. 318p. bibliog.

Motivated to produce an account of slavery in the West Indian colonies, as none had been published since abolition, Mathieson draws on dispatches, official reports, and early 19th-century histories to produce a description of the conditions of slavery and the gradual movement towards emancipation. References to Barbados as 'Little England' indicate its position of privilege in terms of settlement, sugar production and trade. The account also includes descriptions of the system of food production for the slaves, the cruelty and injustice meted out to them, riots, attacks against Methodism, the arrival of Bishop Coleridge, legislation enacted in favour of the slaves, the hostility displayed by assemblymen towards emancipation, the hurricane of 1831 and the period of apprenticeship and special magistrates under Governor Sir Lionel Smith.

388 **Sins of the fathers: a study of the Atlantic slave traders 1441-1807.**
James Pope-Hennessy. London: Weidenfeld & Nicolson, 1967. 296p. 3 maps. bibliog.

An account of the slave trade and the conditions experienced during the transatlantic crossing. The journey to Barbados is characterized by the sickness of the overcrowded human cargo and the high mortality rate. There were also frequent attempted suicides, since many believed that they would be eaten on arrival. Sharks shadowed the ship throughout the voyage hoping to devour those who jumped overboard. The drunkenness and cruelty of the crew was matched only by that of the planters at the port of call, many of whom treated their slaves like domestic animals. Examples are supplied of merciless beatings and other acts of torture. There are accompanying illustrations.

389 **Little England: plantation society and Anglo-Barbadian politics 1627-1700.**
Gary Puckrein. New York, London: New York University Press, 1984. 235p. 2 maps. bibliog.

Seeks to refute the view that Barbadian society is merely a reflection of the mother country or that an understanding of the former is simply obtained by a study of the plantocracy. In contrast, Puckrein argues that Barbados in the time of slavery produced a unique blend of household familial relationships, which was neither distinctly African nor British, yet maintained aspects of both. Thus, in order to understand the political development of the island, it is necessary to appreciate its evolution from the point of view of local community or household, together with its material interests. In a sense both English and Africans were prepared for the plantation system – the former through the feudal experience of apprenticeship, the latter via bondsmen and servants. Yet the plantation had no equivalent or precedent in either English or African society. Rather it was the product of market forces and imperialism.

390 **The fall of the planter class in the British Caribbean 1763-1833.**
Lowell Ragatz. New York: American Historical Association, 1928. Reprinted, New York: Octagon Books, 520p. bibliog.

Based on a prize-winning doctoral dissertation for the University of Wisconsin. The author was one of Frank Pitman's students, and his inquiry takes over from Pitman's *The development of the British West Indies 1700-1763* (q.v.). It examines the causes for the dramatic decline in wealth experienced by the planters from the mid-18th century to the time of emancipation. While carefully denying that the end of slavery was responsible for this economic ruin, Ragatz points to such factors as extravagance of lifestyle, wastefulness of resources, individualistic conservatism, intercolonial rivalry, poor health conditions, protectionist policies, taxation and wars of the period. This rather outspoken account is at times quite racist. Nevertheless there is a useful evaluation of historical sources and a brief annotated bibliography.

391 **The development of the plantations to 1750; An era of West Indian prosperity 1750-1775.**
Richard Sheridan. Kingston: Caribbean Universities Press, 1970. Reprinted, 1976. 120p. bibliog.

The first in a series on the history of the Caribbean. The work comprises two papers. The former traces the introduction of sugar into Barbados from Brazil and the subsequent development of the industry by human and mechanical labour. Comparisons are made between Barbados, St. Dominique, Martinique and Jamaica which show differences in the racial composition of the population, size of plantations, the use of livestock and sugar mills, and the proportion of sugar products to all exports. The 'golden age' of sugar was the 1650s and 1660s; the second paper examines its 'silver age', when prices had risen from the depressions of the 1680s and 1730s, due partly to the cheapness and popularity of tea as well as rum punch in London. Production also increased as a result of the extensive manuring of previously exhausted soil. Consequently, the three-way trade between Britain, Africa and the islands also benefited during this period.

392 **Crop Over: an old Barbadian plantation festival.**
Flora Spencer.   Barbados: Commonwealth Caribbean Resource
Centre, 1974. 7p. bibliog.

Written for the Crop Over activities of the Barbados Tourist Board, this pamphlet examines the origins of the festivities. These celebrations took the form of a mill yard plantation party for the estate workers after the final procession of decorated carts bringing in the last load of sugar cane. Detailed references are made to the food and drink, accompanying games, music and dance, and the ceremonial burning of Mr Harding, symbolizing hard times ahead. In this interpretation of events, the happiness of the slaves is possibly a trifle overdone, as is the devotion of the mill gang to the windmill and the planter.

393 **The negro in the Caribbean.**
Eric Williams.   New York: Associates in Negro Folk Education,
1942. Reprinted, New York: Negro Universities Press, 1969. 119p.
bibliog.

In a rather polemical style, the author suggests that the root cause of negro slavery, and ultimately racial discrimination, is related to capitalism, and in particular the triangular trade based on sugar. Stated simply – no sugar, no negroes; no negroes, no sugar. In this respect Barbados is possibly the prime exemplar, since from 1640 to 1667 it increased its wealth forty fold and was regarded as a precious jewel in the imperial crown worth more than the American colonies put together. Sugar accounted for 95 per cent of all the island's exports. Half the land was devoted to its cultivation and two-thirds of the population directly depended on it. Yet none of this wealth would have been possible without black labour. Such a situation can only be put right when the fruits of this labour can be equitably enjoyed.

394 **Capitalism and slavery.**
Eric Williams.   London: André Deutsch, 1964. Reprinted, 1983.
285p. bibliog.

A revision of Williams' 1938 Oxford University doctoral thesis. It was first privately published in the United States some twenty-one years before it appeared in England. The period covered is from 1783 to 1833. Most of the research is based on British-housed manuscripts and parliamentary sources. The same hypothesis as that proposed in *The negro in the Caribbean* (q.v.) is offered, namely that the abolition of slavery was not due to humanitarian or Christian principles. Rather it was based on economic interest, the factor responsible for its introduction. In substantiating his case, Williams gleefully provides evidence for revising the high reputations of such names as Gladstone, Disraeli, Coleridge and even Wilberforce himself. References to Barbados include mention of sugar production, the conditions of the slaves and the opposition of the plantocracy to their amelioration, and slave revolts.

Slavery to freedom in the British Caribbean: ecological considerations.
See item no. 69.

The ordeal of free labour in the British West Indies.
See item no. 158.

An archaeological investigation of the domestic life of plantation slaves in Barbados.
See item no. 291

Plantation slavery in Barbados: an archaeological and historical investigation.
See item no. 292.

Barbadian cross currents: church-state confrontation with Quaker and negro 1660-1689.
See item no. 471.

Population

General

395 **1980/1 population census of the Commonwealth Caribbean: Barbados.**
Coordinated by Hubert Barker. Kingston: Statistical Institute of Jamaica, 1985. 3 vols. 2 maps.
Provides the most recent data base for demographers and other researchers. In volume one there are thirty-six sets of tables covering such areas as the distribution of the population by sex and age, educational achievement, economic activity, migration, vocational training, race, religion, marital status, fertility, housing and utilities. Explanatory notes are also supplied. Volume two contains fifty-seven cross-tabulations featuring the foregoing variables, and includes a copy of the questionnaire. In volume three Alyson Forte and Basia Zaba make intercensal comparisons which reflect major changes over the past two decades in Barbados.

396 **A note on the 1970 population census of Barbados.**
Joycelin Byrne. *Social and Economic Studies*, vol. 20, no. 4 (Dec. 1971), p. 431-40.
An evaluation of the reliability of the 1970 census data, given that the enumerated population falls well below projected estimates based on the previous 1960 census, and in fact has increased at a rate of only 0.26 per cent per annum. Since data for births, deaths, sex ratio and household size are found to be sufficiently reasonable, the investigation hinges on the emigration factor and the role it plays in balancing the population equation. Here problems arise because of the interpolation of visitor arrival and departure statistics, and failure of the authorities to maintain adequate external migration records.

397 **The population of Barbados.**
David Lowenthal. *Social and Economic Studies*, vol. 6, no. 4
(Dec. 1957), p. 445-501.

Investigates the phenomenon of excessive population density in Barbados, despite low birth rates and high death rates. The article looks at the island's population history during five periods, the chief of which – the 19th century – added some 100,000 to the statistics. Patterns of malnutrition and disease are analysed, along with sex ratios and literacy rates, and are compared with other territories in the region. Data are also presented for home ownership, overcrowding, internal migration, racial stratification and welfare. Barbados' resources are listed and attempts at population control briefly described. The paper is of general, as well as demographic interest, in that sections on settlement patterns, housing, agriculture and resources are also included.

398 **The population of Barbados: demographic development and population policy in a small island state.**
Joycelin Massiah. PhD dissertation, University of the West Indies, Mona, Jamaica, 1981. 2 vols. 4 maps. bibliog.

The most comprehensive analysis to date of the demographic development of Barbados from the days of slavery to 1970. From historical evidence and contemporary census data it is argued that there has been no fully integrated population policy in Barbados. Even when programmes were initiated (such as emigration and family planning), either their objectives failed to materialize, or else they were superimposed on a population which had itself taken appropriate action in the desired direction. Subjects treated in this work include assessments of record reliability, population composition and growth, patterns of internal migration, public health, life expectancy, mortality, mating, fertility and emigration. Current policies are evaluated and projections for the future are also examined.

The Barbados census of 1680: profile of the richest colony in English America.
See item no. 336.

Abridged working life tables for Barbadian males 1946, 1969 and 1970.
See item no. 732.

Demographic Yearbook.
See item no. 737.

The Caribbean basin to the year 2000: demographic, economic, and resource-use trends in seventeen countries.
See item no. 739.

Urbanization and urban growth in the Caribbean: an essay on social change in dependent societies.
See item no. 763

World urbanization 1950-1970, volume 1: basic data for cities, countries and regions.
See item no. 764.

Urbanization in the Commonwealth Caribbean.
See item no. 766.

Fertility and family planning

399 **A fertility survey in Barbados.**
Joycelin Byrne. *Social and Economic Studies*, vol. 15, no. 4 (Dec. 1966), p. 368-78.
Describes a survey of 1,512 women aged 15 to 44. Information was obtained on four sets of topics: personal data and background characteristics; pregnancy; history of sexual unions and details of partners; attitudes towards and use of birth control. Some data from the first two areas are presented and compared with those from the 1960 census in order to establish demographic profiles and to highlight the representativeness of those interviewed.

400 **The Barbadian male: sexual attitudes and practices.**
Graham Dann. London, New York: Macmillan, 1987. 225p. bibliog.
Based on 185 in-depth interviews conducted in 1985. The study explores the problems of inadequate socialization with respect to family, church and school, and the ramifications these have for sex education, gender attitudes, human relationships and responsible parenthood. Knowledge and use of family planning are also examined and related to the wider issue of overpopulation awareness. The analysis is both quantitative and qualitative.

401 **Social and demographic characteristics of family planning clients in Barbados.**
G. Ebanks. *Social and Economic Studies*, vol. 18, no. 4 (Dec. 1969), p. 391-401.
A 1 in 5 sample of the records of the Barbados Family Planning Association (giving a total sample of 2,306 respondents) is compared with the records of the Population Council Research Project, a sample survey of 461 of its patients, and the female population as a whole, as detailed in the 1960 census. The four sets of data are compared with respect to the profile variables of age, education, occupation, religion, marital status and area of residence. Information dealing with diffusion agents, pregnancies, duration of contraceptive usage and number of methods employed is also examined.

402 **Barbados.**
    G. Ebanks. In: *Population policies in the Caribbean.* Edited by
    A. Segal. Lexington, Massachusetts: D. C. Heath, 1975, p. 25-47.
    bibliog.

An excellent summary of population growth and fertility decline in Barbados with
particular reference to the part played by emigration and the work of the
Barbados Family Planning Association. There are some interesting, though
debatable, observations regarding political unanimity and the role of élites on
population policy, minimal religious opposition to birth control, and lack of
urban/rural differences in Barbados. Prospects for the future are said to look
promising provided that present trends continue, that costs per averted birth can
be reduced, and that there are improvements in record keeping.

403 **The modern demographic transition: an analysis of subsistence**
    choices and reproductive consequences.
    W. Penn Handwerker. *American Anthropologist*, vol. 85 (1983),
    p. 5-27; vol. 88 (1986), p. 400-17.

Severely criticizes modernization and transition theories in their attempts to
explain fertility reduction. Instead of using nature or types of relationships,
unbalanced sex ratios or expected intergenerational income demand from
children, Handwerker employs a modified wealth flows model, which places
greater emphasis on changes in the opportunity structure, rewarding educationally
acquired skills. The study is all the more significant since it raises fundamental
questions about a great deal of Caribbean research, and includes in the critique a
number of works on Barbados. The author hopes to demonstrate his conclusions
empirically with the completion of analysis of recent surveys conducted in
Barbados and St. Lucia.

404 **Metropolitan dominance and family planning in Barbados.**
    H. Jones. *Social and Economic Studies*, vol. 26, no. 3 (Sept.
    1977), p. 327-38.

Demonstrates that there are very real differences in Barbadian fertility which are
predicated on area of residence. This socio-geographical differential is due to the
fact that economic development and modernization in urban areas usually go
hand in hand with a reduction in fertility. In order to test this hypothesis still
further, the effects of space and allied variables on fertility are examined
statistically with reference to the census data of 1960 and 1970. With the
relationship once more validated, it is consequently ironic that most family
planning clinics and fieldwork activity are concentrated in the urban parishes and
that more disadvantaged rural dwellers find themselves without adequate
facilities.

405 **Abortion and public opinion in Barbados.**
    Joycelin Massiah. *Bulletin of Eastern Caribbean Affairs*, vol. 3,
    nos. 11-12 (Jan.-Feb. 1978), p. 11-17.

A content analysis of newspaper clippings during the period 1973-77. Of the forty
featured Barbadian articles, most tended to reflect the generally liberal opinion of

the press rather than the more conservative views of the public. In this connection, two columnists argue that abortion is one area where public opinion would not be forthcoming. By way of significant omission, Massiah notes that silence also characterized the attitude of youth and of legal and women's organizations. The author contrasts the Barbadian reticence to speak out on controversial matters with the number of submissions on abortion made to the National Commission on the Status of Women in Barbados. The views of spokesmen from the Anglican, Catholic and Methodist churches are also examined, along with those from the Barbados Association of Medical Practitioners. The merits and disadvantages of a recommended committee approach to the problem are analysed in some detail.

406 **The pattern of mating behaviour, emigration and contraceptives as factors affecting human fertility in Barbados.**
Moni Nag. *Social and Economic Studies*, vol. 20, no. 2 (June 1971), p. 111-33.
Compares the 1946 and 1960 census data to corroborate an hypothesis validated elsewhere in the Caribbean that stability of union and fertility are positively associated. Further confirmation is gained from a sample of 124 women health clinic patients in which non-union time is calculated. The emigration factor is also examined from 1861, together with its effects on the sex ratio and fertility. Since the post-1962 decline in emigration, contraceptives have played a more important role in the reduction of fertility.

407 **Fertility and family planning in Barbados.**
Neal Kar Nair. Bridgetown; Columbia, Maryland: Barbados Family Planning Association and Westinghouse Health Systems, 1982. 144p. map. bibliog.
Contains the results of a contraceptive usage survey conducted in 1980-1981 among a sample of 1,463 Barbadian women aged between 15 and 49. The report includes a useful introduction which provides recent demographic information on the female population. It also deals with objective fertility rates before examining more subjective data, such as fertility desire, and the associated knowledge and use of various contraceptive methods. Sources of supplies are discussed and an evaluation of the thirty-year-old Barbados Family Planning Association is presented. This comprehensive work contains fifty-eight tables and a questionnaire.

408 **The problems of teenage pregnancies in Barbados.**
Beverly Norville. *Bulletin of Eastern Caribbean Affairs*, vol. 10, no. 5 (Nov.-Dec. 1984), p. 21-28.
Presents data to show that the percentage of teenage births is increasing in Barbados, and stands at 28.6 per cent (1980). This may be due to the Barbados Family Planning Association's failure to provide adequate counselling in its outreach services or to counteract misinformation. Nor are educational programmes in schools or through family life education sufficiently comprehensive or fertility-focused. They also tend to neglect male attitudes and the negative influence of Rastafarianism. Contact with adolescents reveals that the majority of teenage pregnancies are either unplanned or unwanted, and that many do not see

themselves as being at risk in casual encounters. Noting the associated health problems for both mother and child, the article concludes with a number of recommendations for local authorities.

409   Some aspects of mating and fertility in the West Indies.

George Roberts. *Population Studies*, vol. 8, no. 3 (1955), p. 20-47.

A technical demographic paper which examines the effects on fertility of diversity of family forms and the imbalance between the sexes. Declining sex ratios are said to be not only characteristic of West Indian territories, such as Barbados, but they are reinforced by the emigration factor. Probabilities for different types of union are also calculated, along with such indicators as the average age for motherhood, proportions of unmarried mothers and average numbers of children. Statistical tables derived from early 20th century census data accompany the presentation.

410   Knowledge and use of birth control in Barbados.

George Roberts, G. Cummins, J. Byrne, C. Alleyne. *Demography*, vol. 4, no. 2 (1967), p. 576-600.

Based on a 1964 sample survey of 1,512 female respondents aged between 15 and 50. Knowledge and use of birth control are analysed with respect to the independent variables of union status, age, educational attainment and religion. High differentials are recorded between knowledge and practice. However, the latter increases with encouragement from partners and family planning agencies.

411   Fertility and mating in four West Indian populations.

George Roberts. Mona, Jamaica: Institute of Social and Economic Research, University of the West Indies, 1975. 341p. bibliog.

A comparative demographic analysis of Jamaica, Trinidad and Tobago, St. Vincent and Barbados, based largely on the 1960 census, for which the author provided considerable input. The account begins with an historical introduction outlining five stages of demographic development. It then examines fertility trends, mating patterns and types of union, and studies the way these are affected by variables such as education and religion. In many senses Barbados is regarded as unique with respect to high density, fertility control, racial composition, religious persuasion and uninterrupted British colonial rule. The Barbados data are supplemented with those from a 1964 survey of fertility and family planning, and a special set of tables relating to motherhood cohorts is calculated for the island.

412   Family unions in the West Indies and some of their implications.

George Roberts. In: *Nuptiality and fertility*. Edited by L. Ruzicka. Liège, Belgium: Ordina Editions, 1979, p. 243-69.

Outlines the methodological difficulties of categorizing union status and patterns of fertility in the West Indies. Comparative census data reveal that, for over a century, Barbados has had one of the lowest female marriage rates in the region and one of the highest singulate mean ages at marriage. An explanation is suggested in its negro population of over 90 per cent. The racial factor is also said to account for variations in household headship and childbearing.

413 **A cohort analysis of fertility decline in Barbados.**
Sara Seims.   PhD dissertation, University of Pennsylvania, Philadelphia, 1978. 206p. map. bibliog. (Available from University Microfilms, Ann Arbor, Michigan, order no. GAX78-24754).

Based on a 1976 household survey of 328 men and 459 women. The author compares age cohorts with respect to differences in generational fertility patterns. Fertility decline is explained in terms of a diffusion process dependent on the interaction between cohorts. Demographic transition theory is modified to incorporate two middle stages. While women approve of contraceptives in both stages, only in the second do they become socialized acceptors. The conclusion is that Barbados will only reach the final level of demographic development with the decline of a pre-natalist culture which emphasizes young motherhood.

414 **An evaluation of the economic cost and effectiveness of the Barbados Family Planning Association.**
Stephen Slavin.   PhD dissertation, New York University, 1973. 364p. bibliog. (Available from University Microfilms, Ann Arbor, Michigan, order no. GAX74-01967).

Fertility decline in Barbados is examined with respect to twelve variables: infant mortality, female emigration, the age distribution of women between 15 and 49, population density, industrialization, the participation rate of women in the labour force, changes in per capita real income, unemployment trends, urbanization, educational attainment and literacy, community network, and the effect of the Barbados Family Planning Association (BFPA). Of these factors, the last is found to be the most significant. The thesis seeks to discover how many births the BFPA has averted and the dollar cost of each. The aversion factor is calculated by converting woman years of contraceptive use into woman years of protection and by multiplying the latter by age-specific fertility rates of BFPA users. Expenditure is estimated on an opportunity cost, rather than an accounting cost, basis. By 1971 the cost per averted birth in Barbados was calculated to be 447 US dollars.

415 **A family planning service in the West Indies.**
Christopher Tietze, Charles Alleyne.   *Fertility and Sterility*, vol. 10, no. 3 (May-June 1959), p. 259-71.

A follow-up study of 555 women who had attended clinics of the Barbados Family Planning Association during its first year of operation. Even though the sample is somewhat atypical, in that 72 per cent are married, and urban-rural differences are minimized, the account is interesting for its discussion of the effectiveness of early programmes, with limited methods of contraception at their disposal. Attendance at clinics is estimated to reduce the pregnancy rate by three-fifths.

Migration

416 **Working class emigration from Barbados to the United Kingdom, October 1955.**

G. Cumper. *Social and Economic Studies*, vol. 6, no. 1 (March 1957), p. 76-83.

An analysis of interviews conducted among emigrants bound for the United Kingdom showed that the outward movement of Barbadians predominantly comprised young males who were single and from rural areas. However, for both men and women who were parents, there was a tendency to leave children behind, thus creating a potential welfare problem. By contrast, a greater proportion of temporary overseas farm workers were married and from urban areas. When compared with the census data of 1946, both groups of emigrants were found to possess above-average skills.

417 **Emigration from Barbados, 1951-1970.**

G. Ebanks, P. George, C. Nobbe. *Social and Economic Studies*, vol. 28, no. 2 (June 1979), p. 431-49.

Due to the inadequacy of emigration statistics, the authors sought details of relatives who had emigrated from respondents participating in three fertility studies conducted in 1971, together with official figures taken from the major countries of destination – the United Kingdom, Canada and the United States. In each case it was possible to establish emigrant profiles, and the effect on the sex ratio and, ultimately, fertility in Barbados.

418 **The original lists of persons of quality 1600-1700 . . .**

John Camden Hotten. London: the author, 1874. Reprinted, New York: Empire State Book Company, [n.d.]. 580p.

The subtitle of this book indicates that the lists of various categories of emigrants who left Britain for the American colonies are derived from manuscripts in the Public Record Office. For instance, there are details of those sent to Barbados after the Monmouth Rebellion of 1685, complete with their jails and ships of origin, as well as information on tickets granted to those from Barbados wishing to emigrate to North America and Jamaica. There is also a wealth of minutiae derived from the island's parish registers, recording not only baptisms and burials, but additionally lists of landowners, slaves and Jews.

419 **Migration as an agent of change in Caribbean island ecosystems.**

Dawn Marshall. *International Social Science Journal*, vol. 34, no. 3 (1982), p. 451-67.

The small islands of the East Caribbean have experienced 150 years of almost continuous out-migration, to the extent that emigration has to be regarded as a fundamental aspect of the social environment. The author here pursues this theme and presents passages on migration to Panama in the 19th century, referring to Barbadian workers in particular, and on London Transport's recruitment programmes in Barbados in the 20th century. The paper stems from a study of migration from four Eastern Caribbean countries, including Barbados. In the second half of the paper, the geographical-ecological impact of such out-migration is considered.

420 **Emigration from the island of Barbados.**
George Roberts. *Social and Economic Studies*, vol. 4, no. 3 (1955), p. 245-88.

Traces the history of emigration from the post-emancipation period to 1921. As Barbados had no indentured labour to speak of, the island faced the dilemma of high population density on the one hand, and a flight of agricultural workers on the other. While early legislation sought to avoid the latter eventuality, and thereby to protect planter interests, with the collapse of sugar prices the pendulum inevitably swung in the opposite direction. Barbados thus witnessed heavy external migration to other West Indian colonies and to Panama, which had the twin desirable effects of increasing remittances to the island and of controlling population growth.

Migration and rural development in the Caribbean.
See item no. 65.

Panama money in Barbados 1900-1920.
See item no. 355.

Diggers and silver men (part I).
See item no. 427.

Diggers and silver men (part II).
See item no. 428.

Race and labour in London Transport.
See item no. 429.

West Indian migrants: social and economic facts of migration from the West Indies.
See item no. 430.

Emigrants who come home, part I.
See item no. 431.

Emigrants who return, part II: adaptation and readjustment.
See item no. 432.

The impact of return migration, part III.
See item no. 433.

Barbadians and Barbadian house forms in the Brazilian Amazon.
See item no. 434.

Some aspects of Barbadian emigration to Cuba 1919-1935.
See item no. 435.

The silver men: West Indian labour migration to Panama 1850-1914.
See item no. 436.

Factors affecting the distribution of West Indians in Great Britain.
See item no. 437.

West Indian migration to Britain: a social geography.
See item no. 439.

British unemployment cycles and West Indian immigration.
See item no. 440.

Go west young man: black Barbadians and the Panama Canal.
See item no. 442.

Minorities

421 **Barbados press comment on the local Rastafari movement.**
Bulletin of Eastern Caribbean Affairs, vol. 3, nos. 7-10 (Sept.-Dec. 1977), p. 26-36.

An analysis of press debate after a group of brethren in October 1977 had approached a government minister requesting the acquisition of land for agricultural purposes. The discussion focused on three aspects of the Rastafarian movement: its origins, views, and implications for Barbadian society. The emergence of Rastafari was generally attributed to prevailing poverty and unemployment, the spread of reggae music and the Barbadian tendency to mimic outsiders. While commitment to peace and unity, together with certain dietary habits, were often commended, the smoking of marijuana and lack of hygiene were universally condemned. Most commentators were of the opinion that the followers of Haile Selassie were simply 'drop-outs' and were likely to have a negative social impact, although some agreed that they could contribute to the development of arts, crafts and small farming. One observer considered that if the movement began to attract middle-class members, protests against the evils of society would assume serious proportions.

422 **Recent developments on the Rastafari movement in Barbados.**
Eudine Barriteau. *Bulletin of Eastern Caribbean Affairs*, vol. 6, no. 4 (Sept.-Oct. 1980), p. 21-24.

Examines the controversy linking Rastafari with crime (particularly housebreaking and street robbery) following an appeal in October 1980 by a government senator (also the chairman of the Board of Tourism) to eradicate the approximately 2,000-strong membership of the local movement. The article looks at press commentary at that period and the ambivalent position taken by the government and the opposition as evidenced by debates in the House of Assembly on The Petty Trespass Act.

423 **The position of poor whites in a color-class hierarchy: a diachronic study of ethnic boundaries in Barbados.**
Karen Davis. PhD dissertation, Wayne State University, Detroit, Michigan, 1978. 365p. 4 maps. bibliog. (Available from University Microfilms, Ann Arbor, Michigan, order no. GAX79-08903).
Based on participant observation and interviewing in a small east coast Barbadian village comprising 720 residents, 27 per cent of whom were white. The study provides ethnographic information concerning poor whites. At the same time it contextualizes the group within the general West Indian colour-class hierarchy and supplies a useful comparison of class and cultural pluralism models in analysing colour and class relationships. The account provides a worthwhile history of this group as well as highlighting problems of contemporary social mobility.

424 **The redlegs of Barbados.**
Thomas J. Keagy. *Américas*, vol. 24 (1975), p. 14-21.
Following a series of general descriptive remarks about the island, the paper focuses on the history and contemporary character of the poor whites or 'redlegs' who are descended from thousands of indentured Europeans sent to Barbados during the 17th and 18th centuries. The present-day primary location of the redleg community is the Churchview-Newcastle area of the parish of St. John on the windward side of the island. It is estimated that the redleg population in this locality numbers a little less than 120 people, most of whom are employed in agriculture. This article is adapted from Keagy's Master's thesis, produced for the American University, Washington, DC, which was based on two months' field work. The paper includes some interesting and informative photographs taken in the Newcastle area.

425 **The redlegs of Barbados.**
Edward T. Price. *Journal of the Barbados Museum and Historical Society*, vol. 29, no. 2 (1962), p. 47-52.
The history of the redlegs in Barbados since the 17th century is considered. The name used to describe the group first attracted the author's attention because it is also occasionally used in South Carolina to refer to a racial group of mixed blood. Since South Carolina was settled by Barbadians, the author considered the possibility that the two redleg groups might conceivably be related. No concrete evidence of this was found, however. Interestingly, the establishment of resettlement communities of Barbadian redlegs in St. Vincent, Grenada and Bequia in the 19th century is described.

426 **The 'redlegs' of Barbados: their origins and history.**
Jill Sheppard. Millwood, New York: KTO Press, 1977. 147p.
map. bibliog.
Explores the origins and subsequent history of the redlegs of Barbados, the poor whites who are descended from early indentured servants. This definitive account includes the following chapters: 'Settlement (1627-1642)'; 'Consolidated immigration (1643-1659)'; 'Decline in the white population (1660-1703)'; 'From indentured servants to poor whites (1704-1839)'; 'Disbandment of the military

tenants (1839)'; 'The problem of degeneration'; 'The era of reform'; 'Redistribution of the poor whites'. These are followed by a brief conclusion.

Rastafarian language in St. Lucia and Barbados.
See item no. 448.

Jewish presence, enterprise and migration trends in the Caribbean.
See item no. 460.

New life for old synagogue.
See item no. 464.

A review of the Jewish colonists in Barbados in the year 1680.
See item no. 467.

Jewish monumental inscriptions in Barbados.
See item no. 468.

The Jewish synagogue, Bridgetown, Barbados.
See item no. 469.

Overseas Populations

427 Diggers and silver men (part I).
Mark D. Alleyne. *Bajan* (Jan. 1985), p. 6-9.
West Indians first emigrated to Panama in 1850 as labourers constructing the Panama railway. Early in the 20th century they worked on the Panama Canal. It is estimated that between 1900 and 1904, some 19,000 Barbadians went to work in Panama.

428 Diggers and silver men (part II).
Mark D. Alleyne. *Bajan* (Feb. 1985), p. 10-11.
This second part of the article looks at aspects of labour organization up to 1940.

429 Race and labour in London Transport.
Dennis Brooks. London: Oxford University Press, 1975. 389p. bibliog.
This study of immigrants working for London Transport is substantially based on a sample of 195 immigrants, of whom 34 per cent were from Barbados, and 91 per cent from the Caribbean as a whole. London Transport operated a planned system of recruitment in Barbados from 1956 onwards, and the efficacy of this scheme and the associated training provided is discussed in detail in chapter thirteen.

430 West Indian migrants: social and economic facts of migration from the West Indies.
R. B. Davison. London: Oxford University Press (under the auspices of the Institute for Race Relations), 1962. 89p. bibliog.
Includes sections on the characteristics of migration and migrants, the economic background to their moves and the social problems left behind on the islands.

129

Includes a quite detailed section on emigration from Barbados, with statistics on the government-sponsored emigration scheme (1955-60) and the loans scheme (1955-60) given on p. 27-30. Unfortunately, the book lacks an index.

431 Emigrants who come home, part I.

George Gmelch. *Bajan* (April 1985), p. 8-9.

Briefly reports the findings of a survey of 135 return migrants, carried out in 1983-84 under the supervision of Gmelch, an American anthropologist. The article focuses on the reasons for return migration; chief among these were the desire to live in one's own society and to be near family and friends, and the climate.

432 Emigrants who return, part II: adaptation and readjustment.

George Gmelch. *Bajan* (May-June 1985), p. 4-5.

Considers the principal problems faced by the sample of Barbadian return migrants. These were mainly the slow pace of life, the high cost of living, personal relationships, the climate, limited entertainment and limited range of goods available.

433 The impact of return migration, part III.

George Gmelch. *Bajan* (July-Aug. 1985), p. 4-6.

This third article in the series considers the contribution that return migrants make to the society, in terms of work skills, new ideas and attitudes. The author finds evidence of the acquisition of new skills, but the migrants make less impact as brokers of new ideas. Those returning mainly spend their repatriated earnings on housing and other forms of consumerism.

434 Barbadians and Barbadian house forms in the Brazilian Amazon.

Sidney M. Greenfield. *Journal of the Barbados Museum and Historical Society*, vol. 36, no. 3 (1981), p. 253-65.

The Madeira-Mamore railway was built during the first decade of the 20th century and some 22,000 workers were brought in, including 5,000 West Indians recruited in Bridgetown. This paper records how these Barbadians introduced Barbadian vernacular architecture to the settlement of Porto Velho. Some well-preserved examples of rectangular-shaped, gable-roofed houses made of clap-board survive today. The only local adaptation was the building of some of these houses on stilts.

435 Some aspects of Barbadian emigration to Cuba 1919-1935.

Basil Maughan. *Journal of the Barbados Museum and Historical Society*, vol. 37, no. 3 (1985), p. 239-75.

Initially prepared as an undergraduate dissertation at the University of the West Indies, this article studies both the push and pull factors promoting the emigration of Barbadians to Cuba just after the First World War.

436 **The silver men: West Indian labour migration to Panama 1850-1914.**

Velma Newton. Mona, Jamaica: Institute of Social and Economic Research, 1984. 218p. bibliog.

The aim is to provide a comprehensive study of the background against which the movements of labour from the West Indies to construct the Panama railway during the 1850s and the Panama Canal from 1881 to 1914 occurred. The central theme is the far-reaching economic and demographic consequences that this had for the British West Indies. In particular, it is argued that the movements led to the establishment of the idea that extra-regional migration is one of the better avenues of social and economic betterment. At the time of publication, the author was the Acquisitions Librarian of the Faculty of Law Library at the University of the West Indies, Cave Hill Campus, Barbados.

437 **Factors affecting the distribution of West Indians in Great Britain.**

G. C. K. Peach. *Transactions of the Institute of British Geographers*, vol. 38 (1966), p. 151-63.

Much of the material in this article is a summary account of the author's *West Indian migration to Britain: a social geography* (q.v.).

438 **West Indians as a replacement population in England and Wales.**

Ceri Peach. *Social and Economic Studies*, vol. 16 (1967), p. 289-94.

The author, a geographer, elucidates the argument that West Indian migrants took jobs that the indigenous population regarded as unacceptable. This is, of course, a very important observation given the causal link between the presence of immigrant groups and unemployment that is all too frequently made in popular arguments in Britain.

439 **West Indian migration to Britain: a social geography.**

Ceri Peach. London: Oxford University Press for the Institute of Race Relations, 1968. 122p. 2 maps. bibliog.

This account covers the background to the emigration of West Indians to Great Britain, along with the influence of British political and economic conditions on immigration, and features of the geographical distribution of West Indian immigrants. It is concluded that migration from the West Indies largely depended on the external demand for labour, rather than on internal conditions such as population density and growth. West Indians tended to move to the largest urban areas, especially London and Birmingham, filling jobs and areas that others found undesirable, so that West Indians acted as a true replacement population. Barbados is frequently referred to both in the text and in many of the supporting statistical tables.

440 **British unemployment cycles and West Indian immigration.**

Ceri Peach. *New Community*, vol. 7 (1978-79), p. 40-43.

The key role played by British employment levels in determining the volume of migration from the West Indies at different times is stressed in this article.

441 **The force of West Indian island identity in Britain.**
Ceri Peach. In: *Geography and ethnic pluralism.* Edited by Colin Clarke, David Ley, Ceri Peach. London: George Allen & Unwin, 1984, p. 214-30.

Barbadians are frequently referred to in this account which looks at the plurality and segregation of West Indian groups, which are perceived as highly homogeneous by Britons. Many of the data relate to the distribution of West Indians in the Greater London boroughs in the 1970s. Barbadians are demonstrated to be the most scattered and mixed of all West Indian groups.

442 **Go west young man: black Barbadians and the Panama Canal.**
Bonham C. Richardson. *Caribbean Review*, vol. 14, no. 2 (1985), p. 10-13; 41.

Altogether 20,000 Barbadian men travelled to Panama as contract workers between 1905 and 1911. In fact, the overwhelming majority of British West Indian contract workers were from Barbados. This paper looks at why they went to work on the Panama Canal and the demographic and social changes that resulted in Barbados. Includes some interesting black-and-white historical photographs.

443 **The West Indians in Britain.**
Dave Saunders. London: Batsford Academic & Educational, 1984. 72p. map.

Uses the example of three families, the parents of which came to England between 1957 and 1964, to illustrate the overall picture of West Indians in Britain today. These are the Davis and Curtis families from Jamaica and the Burke family from Barbados. Although intended for schools, this short book offers some interesting insights and good illustrations. The chapters entitled 'Welcome to the mother country', 'A new life in Britain', and 'Education and discipline' are especially interesting.

Migration and rural development in the Caribbean.
See item no. 65.

Migration as an agent of change in Caribbean island ecosystems.
See item no. 419.

Remittance impacts on development in the Eastern Caribbean.
See item no. 601.

The impact of Panama money in Barbados in the early twentieth century.
See item no. 626.

Languages and Dialects

444 A dictionary of Caribbean English usage: selected entries.
S. R. R. Allsopp.   Detroit, Michigan: Gale Research, 1982. 97p.
bibliog.

Prepared by the coordinator of the Caribbean Lexicography Project as a preprint of the major work to come. There are about 200 entries, together with thorough explanations and details of pronunciation, usage and sources. Some of the Barbadian expressions are provided by Timothy Callender, Austin Clarke, Frank Collymore, George Lamming and John Wickham, and from a private collection of barbadianisms compiled by the late Herman Boxill.

445 Bajan proverbs.
Margot Blackman.   Montreal: Margot Blackman, 1982.
Reprinted, Bridgetown: Cedar Press, 1985. 18p.

This collection of proverbs dates back some twenty years. Many of the sayings are derived from the rural area of St. John and contain references to animals, such as 'Two smart rats can live in one hole', 'Evah boar hog got he Saturday' and 'Wherevah a monkey come from, he still a monkey'. Some come from the urban areas of local folk oral history, such as 'A beggah beggin' from a beggah mek God laugh', 'When t'ief t'ief from t'ief, Satan laugh' and 'Today is a funny night'. There are introductions by the late Frank Collymore and the current editor of *Bim* magazine, John Wickham. The text is illustrated by Virgil Broodhagen.

446 Notes for a glossary of words and phrases of Barbadian dialect.
Frank Collymore.   Bridgetown: Advocate, 1965. Reprinted,
Bridgetown: Barbados National Trust, 1976. 3rd ed. 122p.

This work had its origins in an amateur exercise. Thus, despite not knowing whether the expressions were standard English, whether they existed elsewhere, or what were their exact historical and etymological derivations, the author nevertheless decided to publish his notes in the hope that others more qualified might continue his work. There are approximately 900 entries. Some are quite amusing (e.g. 'piss to windward' signifies ineptitude). Items include examples of verbal mongrels, clipping, double negatives, echo words, and the infamous compound redundant. There are surprisingly few Africanisms. However, certain mysteries still remain to be revealed to the non-Barbadian, the chief of which seem to be 'up' and 'down', 'above' and 'below', to indicate spatial directions.

447 **Black talk, being notes on negro dialect in British Guiana with (inevitably) a chapter on the vernacular of Barbados.**
J. Graham Cruickshank. Demerara, Guyana: Argosy, 1916. 76p.

The 'inevitability' of including Barbados is said to be due to the fact that Demerara blacks obtained their English at second hand from Barbadian negroes emigrating to Guyana. They in turn learned their English from white bondservants originating in Devon, Ireland and Scotland, where remnants of local expressions can still be heard. Cruickshank, after giving a brief description of the Scotland District, claims that no African words have survived in Barbados (with the possible exceptions of ku-ku and unna). By contrast, one encounters several living examples of otherwise obsolete English and Irish phrases (eg. pension meaning present, a good set of rain, etc.). An appendix contains a number of further examples and a note on vowel pronunciation.

448 **Rastafarian language in St. Lucia and Barbados.**
Velma Pollard. *Bulletin of Eastern Caribbean Affairs*, vol. 10, no. 1 (March-April 1984), p. 9-20.

Explains the spread of Rastafari in the Eastern Caribbean in terms of a common cultural heritage and contemporary experience of deprivation. Not surprisingly the language of the Rastaman has accompanied the movement. Looking first at Jamaican dread talk, the author makes the connection between positive 'ai' words and the 'eye' of the far-seeing adherent. By contrast, negative words often contain the prefix 'blain' or 'blind'. Thus in Barbados 'blindza', meaning money, displays a negative attitude. However, the opposite to 'aital', a high word meaning vital, pure or natural (food) is 'lotal' or 'low tal', of low vitality. 'Haits' or 'heights' has come to mean 'understand' among Barbadian brethren, whereas in Jamaica it signifies the heights of spirituality, and can be used either to describe the supreme colour red or as a greeting. Other changes include 'to sip' (eat and drink in Barbados, smoke in Jamaica) and 'to dally' (leave in Barbados, weave in and out of traffic in Jamaica).

Barbados.
See item no. 17.

Folk songs of Barbados.
See item no. 867.

Religion

449 Handbook of churches in the Caribbean.
Edited by Joan Brathwaite.   Bridgetown: Christian Action for
Development in the Caribbean (Caribbean Conference of
Churches), 1973. 234p.

A document prepared for the inaugural assembly of the Caribbean Conference of
Churches. An historical section provides details of the Salvation Army and the
African Methodist Episcopal, Anglican, Methodist, Moravian, Roman Catholic,
Congregational and Presbyterian churches. In Barbados, instead of the last two,
one finds the Church of God, Fundamental Baptists, the New Testament Church
of God and the United Church of America. Statistics for these and the foregoing
are supplied in a second section of the handbook. There is also a brief country-by-
country profile, a listing of national councils of churches and a clerical directory.
In addition, the structure of the Caribbean Conference of Churches is described
together with its affiliated ecumenical organizations.

450 The church in the West Indies.
A. Caldecott.   London: Cass, 1898. Reprinted, 1970. 275p. map.
bibliog.

As much a social as an ecclesiastical history, since several descriptions of colonial
life are provided. The position of the governor as Anglican 'ordinary' is
highlighted, and examples are given of Governor Bell's religious legislation in
Barbados. The origin of the limited power of the Bishop of London is questioned,
as is the delay in appointing bishops to the West Indies or in extending church
offices beyond the ranks of a predominantly English, poorly educated, though
upper-class clergy. Among other topics covered are the refusal of the sacraments
to slaves, the work of nonconformists, the arrival of Barbados' first bishop –
Coleridge – and the role of the church in education. As regards the latter, there is
a short section on the foundation and early history of Codrington College.

451 **The church in Barbados in the seventeenth century.**
P. F. Campbell. The Garrison, St. Michael, Barbados: Barbados
Museum and Historical Society, 1982. 188p. maps. bibliog.

After an introductory background to the complex religious situation in England,
Campbell attempts to fill a current void in the religious history of Barbados. He
investigates the various problems of settlement, the establishment of the parish
system, and the differences between Anglicans and Puritans, as mirrored in
respective Royalist and Roundhead allegiances. The impact of nonconformists,
principally Quakers, is also examined, along with the differing policies of
Catholics and Protestants *vis-à-vis* the baptism of slaves. Additionally, there is a
section on the church and clergy which discusses questions of ecclesiastical
administration and individual clerics, fuller biographical details of whom are
provided in an appendix.

452 **A history of the West Indies.**
Thomas Coke. London: A. Paris, 1808-11. Reprinted, London:
Cass, 1971. 3 vols.

As much a sacred as a profane history of the islands by a noted Wesleyan
missionary. The Barbados material is found in chapters eighteen and nineteen of
volume two. The first of these deals with the discovery, settlement, constitution,
legislature, military, population and resources of the island. The second, and
more original, account concentrates on the ups and downs of the early period of
evangelization. It is based on correspondence dating from 1790, and on the
author's own missionary activities, which commenced in 1788 in the company of a
Mr Pearce. Despite some initial small-scale success, the main opposition to their
mission seems to have come from several planters who refused to allow their
slaves access to the preaching on pain of corporal punishment. Additionally many
meetings were disrupted by stone-throwing mobs, and their tiny, mainly white
congregations became the butt of local ridicule. As a result of its religious
indifference, Barbados is thus described as a populous but unfruitful island, an
ungrateful territory, for which divine pestilence is seen as a fitting punishment on
account of its neglect of the gospel.

453 **Cross and crown in Barbados.**
Kortright Davis. Frankfurt, GFR: Peter Lang, 1983. 187p.
bibliog.

Examines the interrelationship of church and state in Barbados with particular
reference to established Anglicanism. The brief history views the church to which
the planters adhered, and which supported them, as a major bastion of the status
quo, despite the efforts of Bishop Mitchinson to disentangle the alliance. Even
though there have been many social changes between that period and the present
era of independence and disestablishment, the author warns that appearances can
be deceptive.

454 **Caribbean Quakers.**
Harriet Durham. Hollywood, Florida: Dukane Press, 1972. 133p.
4 maps. bibliog.
In seeking to avoid persecution in England, and at the same time wishing to
proselytize abroad, the Quakers naturally looked to Barbados as a first port of
call. It also became a transit point to and from the American colonies. The first
arrivals were Mary Fisher and Anne Austin in 1655. Some sixteen years later, the
founder of the Friends, George Fox, paid a visit to the island. The rather uneven
Barbados section of this book (p. 11-32) ranges back and forth through history,
highlighting the nonconformity and dissent of the Quakers, the various petitions
they wrote, the legislation passed against them and the penalties they suffered for
conscientious objection. A useful table is provided giving the names, occupations,
and other details of the Quakers around the year 1680. From this listing one can
see that, despite the hardship, many Friends were clearly very affluent.

455 **The Jews in Barbados.**
P. Farrar. *Journal of the Barbados Museum and Historical
Society*, vol. 9, no. 3 (May 1942), p. 130-33.
Summarizes the work of Darnell Davis and Wilfred Samuel. Most of the
Portuguese-speaking Jews came to Barbados from Brazil and Surinam after their
respective capture by the Dutch in the 17th century. The majority kept to
themselves and lived and worked in Swan St. or Jew St. in Bridgetown as
merchants, usurers and coin clippers, and became the target of discrimination in
the legislation of the period. Even the practice of offering every new governor
'Jew pie', a crust covering a pile of gold coins, failed to ingratiate them with the
authorities. The writer laments the current secular usage of the synagogue and the
poor state of the Jewish cemetery.

456 **The toiler of the sees: a life of John Mitchinson, Bishop of
Barbados.**
John Terence Gilmore. Belleville, St. Michael, Barbados:
Barbados National Trust, (forthcoming). ca. 150p. bibliog.
Provides a complete biography of this distinguished educationalist and church-
man. Particular attention is paid to the years which Mitchinson spent in the West
Indies as Bishop of Barbados (1873-1881), and his role as chairman of influential
commissions on education and poor relief. Mitchinson's attitudes towards racial
matters and social questions are also treated at some length.

457 **Facing the challenge of emancipation: a study of the ministry of
William Hart Coleridge, first Bishop of Barbados 1824-1842.**
Sehon Goodridge. Bridgetown: Cedar Press, 1981. 112p. map.
bibliog.
Deals with the establishment of the first Anglican diocese in Barbados and the
Leeward Islands as part of colonial strategy to ameliorate the conditions of slaves.
The account explores the state of the church from the time of settlement. It also
examines the various reforms introduced by Coleridge, covering such areas as
ecclesiastical buildings, recruitment of clergy, education and pastoral care. The

last-mentioned is considered to have been particularly challenging in the light of prevailing slave customs and their exclusion hitherto from the sacraments. The archival material researched by this former Principal of Codrington College includes Coleridge's original correspondence.

458   **Church and society in Barbados in the eighteenth century.**
Keith Hunte.   In: *Social groups and institutions in the history of the Caribbean, paper presented to the VIth annual conference of Caribbean historians, Puerto Rico, April 7, 1974.* n.p.: Association of Caribbean Historians, 1975, p. 13-25.

Examines the relationship between the Anglican (mainly English) clergy and society prior to the installation of a resident bishop in Barbados. During the period under review clerical appointments were made by the Bishop of London, and assignation of benefices and other church matters dealt with by the governor acting as ordinary, while the rather ineffectual office of commissary was established principally as a link between the island and the mother country. Hunte traces the ecclesiastical politics of the day with particular reference to the power of the plantocracy in relation to the vestries and the legislature. He also looks at the implications of declining morality and limited missionary activities aimed at the majority slave population.

459   **Codrington chronicle, an experiment in Anglican altruism on a Barbados plantation 1710-1834.**
Edited by Frank Klingberg.   Berkeley, California; Los Angeles: University of California Press, 1949. Reprinted, Millwood, New York: Kraus Reprint, 1974. 157p. bibliog.

Based on the analysis and research of a seminar group at the University of California (Los Angeles) investigating the microfilmed documents of the Codrington plantations. In an editorial introduction, Klingberg sees Codrington as a philanthropist bridging the old world of 18th-century liberalism and the new world of the sugar planter intent on making a profit via slave labour. The bequest of the Codrington estates posed a serious problem for the Society for the Propagation of the Gospel, which as administrator attempted to reconcile servitude and Christianity, a policy which eventually paved the way for emancipation. There are six contributions to the volume: Samuel McCulloch and John Schutz consider Codrington and the interpretation of his will; Maud O'Neil describes the difficulties encountered in the construction of Codrington College; John Schutz and Maud O'Neil examine the management of plantations; Hazel Hartley focuses on the processes of sugar production; Harry Bennett emphasizes the slaves themselves; and Jean Bullen and Helen Livingston highlight the educational role of the colonizers.

460   **Jewish presence, enterprise and migration trends in the Caribbean.**
Zvi Loker.   In: *Cultural traditions and Caribbean identity: the question of patrimony.* Edited by S. J. K. Wilkersen. Gainesville, Florida: Center for Latin American Studies, 1980, p. 177-204.

Offers some fascinating insights concerning the establishment of Jewish communities in the Caribbean after 1654. For example, it is explained that the Hebrew family name 'Baruch', meaning blessed, became 'Barrow' in both Barbados and Jamaica. Barbados is frequently mentioned in this readable account.

461   **A history of the Moravian Church, Eastern West Indies province.**
G. Oliver Maynard.   Port of Spain: Yuille's Printerie, 1968. 175p.
7 maps. bibliog.

Based on research in the archives of the Moravian Church at Bethlehem, Pennsylvania, as well as the diaries and correspondence of four Caribbean mission stations, this account by a Moravian minister seeks to enlighten his colleagues and other interested persons regarding the history of the church. Although these missionaries arrived first in the Danish West Indies in 1732, they did not reach Barbados until 1765. The author explains the Moravian mission to the slaves hitherto ignored by the established church. He also describes the problems faced by the missionaries (sickness, death, poverty, hurricanes and planter hostility) in establishing their first of many churches at Sharon in St. Thomas, together with a number of schools.

462   **New mission for a new people: voices from the Caribbean.**
Edited by David Mitchell.   New York: Friendship Press, 1977.
144p.

This collection of essays discusses the work of the Barbados-based Caribbean Conference of Churches, together with its development arm (Christian Action for Development in the Caribbean), its monthly newspaper (*Caribbean Contact*), and publishing house (Cedar Press). The book examines the historical and economic conditions of the region and the ecumenical role of the churches in establishing a Caribbean identity free from metropolitan dominance.

463   **The Moravian mission in Barbados: historical sketch of the past hundred years.**
Journal of the Barbados Museum and Historical Society, vol. 31, no. 2 (May 1965), p. 73-78.

These extracts from *The Times* of 2 and 5 May 1865 describe the coming of the first two Moravian missionaries to Barbados in 1765, Andrew Rittmansberger and John Wood, the death of the former just one month after his arrival, and the lapsing of the latter. There are quotations from the diary of Benjamin Brookshaw in 1767 and his account of preaching to the slaves on the estate of a Quaker, a certain Mr Jackman.

464   **New life for old synagogue.**
Bajan (April 1985), p. 7.

Relates the history of the old Jewish synagogue, located in central Bridgetown. This was built in 1654, but sold in 1928 when only a single Jew was left on the island. The building was to be demolished, but the government now plans to restore it.

465   The monumental inscriptions in the churches and churchyards of
the island of Barbados, British West Indies.
Edited by Vere Langford Oliver.   London: Mitchell Hughes &
Clarke, 1915. 223p. map.

A total of 1,472 inscriptions were transcribed by the author on a visit to Barbados
from 1913 to 1914. They include all those found in churches, chapels and
churchyards, but not those in sectarian establishments or modern cemeteries.
Additionally there were some belonging to plantations and some 100 Jewish
inscriptions. Beginning with St. Michael's Cathedral (the largest set of entries),
the physical condition and location of each tombstone is supplied, and, where
possible, the pedigree of the deceased is also provided.

466   **Barbados diocesan history.**
Edited by J. E. Reece, C. G. Clark-Hunt.   London: West India
Committee, 1925. 136p.

A publication commemorating the first centenary of the Anglican diocese in
Barbados. After a brief history of the established church in the island, there are
chapters on a number of bishops and notes from parish church records supplied
by the incumbents. There are also details of various district and country churches,
providing such information as fittings, plate, lists of clergy and registers.
Additionally, there are separate entries on education and the occult in Barbados.

467   **A review of the Jewish colonists in Barbados in the year 1680.**
Wilfred S. Samuel.   *Transactions of the Jewish Historical Society
of England*, vol. 13 (1932-35), p. 1-111.

This lengthy and highly detailed account is the text of a paper read before the
Jewish Historical Society of England on 19 May 1924. The paper is accompanied
by plates showing early maps and census lists. Detailed appendixes listing wills
and other documents relating to Jews in Barbados in 1620 may also be of interest.

468   **Jewish monumental inscriptions in Barbados.**
Introduced by E. M. Shilstone.   London: Jewish Historical
Society, University College, 1956. 205p. bibliog.

Contains the Hebrew, English, Spanish and Portuguese transcripts of tombstone
inscriptions found in the burial ground (*beth haim*) of the Bridgetown synagogue
as evidence of the fluctuating Jewish presence in the island from 1654 or earlier.
A documented preface by Wilfred Samuel provides a brief history of the
Sephardim, their near extinction in the 19th century, and regrowth after the Nazi
persecutions. Included is the interesting fact that Quakers attempted to convert
Barbadian Jewry. Shilstone's introduction is even more informative, as it
examines various records of Jewish presence, before commencing analysis of the
cemetery itself and the first burial there, which was probably in 1660.

469 **The Jewish synagogue, Bridgetown, Barbados.**
E. M. Shilstone. *Journal of the Barbados Museum and Historical Society*, vol. 32, no. 1 (1966), p. 3-15.
Describes, in some considerable detail, the history of the Jewish synagogue located in Bridgetown which was consecrated in March 1833.

470 **History of the Catholic Church in Barbados during the nineteenth century.**
Francis Shorrocks, S. J. *Journal of the Barbados Museum and Historical Society*, vol. 25, no. 3 (May 1958), p. 102-22.
Examines the minutes of the meetings of Catholic committees held at the house of the first military chaplain and resident priest, Rev. William Rogers, after his transference from Guyana in 1839. The analysis extends to those meetings held by his successors, and in particular the attempts to raise funds for the construction of the church of St. Patrick, which opened in 1848. There are also references to various episcopal visitations and to correspondence between bishops and laity.

471 **Barbadian cross currents: church-state confrontation with Quaker and negro 1660-1689.**
Winnifred Winkelman. PhD thesis, Loyola University, Chicago, 1976. 299p. bibliog.
An examination of divergent attitudes towards slavery, abolition and the question of baptism by Quakers and Anglicans. There are liberal quotations from Fox and Godwyn (the latter seems to be the only clerical exception to the rigid Anglican position). The history of settlement, the introduction of sugar cane, and the emergence of a planter class provide the necessary back-drop to the study. A well-documented work and a useful account of early nonconformity.

The quality of life in Barbados.
See item no. 12.

Barbados press comment on the local Rastafari movement.
See item no. 421.

Recent developments on the Rastafari movement in Barbados.
See item no. 422.

Social Conditions

472 **Social problems we face: a symposium.**
Academy of Politics of the Democratic Labour
Party. Bridgetown: Democratic Labour Party, 1980. 40p. bibliog.

A collection of published lectures which includes: 'The social implications of tourism' by Farley Brathwaite, 'The challenge of the young' by David Mitchell, 'Perspectives on education in Barbados' by Leonard Shorey, and 'Our cultural heritage and its future' by Kathleen Drayton. Each of the contributions takes a critical look at specific Barbadian institutions and is followed by a list of references.

473 **The question of Barbadian culture.**
Richard Allsopp. Bridgetown: Bajan Magazine, 1972. 20p.
(Bajan Booklet, no. 1).

Originally three newspaper articles appearing in the *Advocate* of the previous year and entitled 'Culture, patriotism and personality', 'Culture and the university' and 'How vital is the matter of our culture?' The reflections are occasioned by an incident at the university when a visiting opera group had been heckled by a number of students, which illustrated for the author the clash of two cultures. As specific instances of Barbadian culture, Allsopp cites the Landship, tea meetings, cou-cou, jug-jug, some folk songs and proverbs, and a few place names. Nevertheless, he considers that most of the true manifestations lie submerged after 350 years of imitation of English life. Consequently the question of culture is even more important in the context of a new university and its attempts to bestow a Caribbean identity.

474 **Reputation and ranking in a Barbadian locality.**
Christine Barrow. *Social and Economic Studies*, vol. 25, no. 2
(June 1976), p. 106-21.

An observational study of a lower-class 'village' located in the suburbs of Bridgetown. When 129 respondents were questioned as to the criteria for social class, most mentioned wealth and occupation (very few spoke of colour), and, in some cases, the persons with whom one associated. These answers led to a detailed investigation of the more subjective characteristics of 'respect' and 'shame', qualities which turn out to be gender-predicated. Gossip, rumour, and the tendency to 'lower rate' persons, are all explored in this typical microcosm of Barbadian society.

475   **Ownership and control of resources in Barbados, 1834 to the present.**
Christine Barrow.   *Social and Economic Studies*, vol. 32, no. 3 (Sept. 1983), p. 83-120.

Traces the survival of a white economic élite in Barbados in spite of the crises of emancipation, the collapse of sugar prices and the upheavals of the 1930s. Through manipulation of legislation, corporatization and intermarriage, this minority continues today to wield economic power. An analysis of the four major parent companies currently operating, Barbados Shipping and Trading, Plantations, Goddards and Commercial and Industrial Enterprise Limited, reveals a pattern of interlocking directorships and a virtual colour bar. The network becomes complete with the inclusion of education at élite schools and membership of exclusive clubs.

476   **Wayside sketches: pen pictures of Barbadian life.**
George Bernard (*pseud.*).   Bridgetown: Advocate, 1934. Reprinted, Bridgetown: Nation Publishing Company, 1985. 2nd ed. 89p.

A collection of *Advocate* newspaper articles written by the late Gordon Bell under a *nom de plume*. The material is divided into ten chapters which deal respectively with Barbados and the Barbadian, the communities of Barbados, the masses, the girls, the boys, the teaching profession, law and order, the legal profession, the plantations and Bridgetown. The booklet includes some rare, and often humorous, observations on the redlegs, the Landship movement, friendly societies and the aspiring middle classes. The abstractive-inductive case study approach permits the author to typologize his subjects and to use the definite article when speaking for instance of the beachcomber, the cow specialist, the sweet man, the sheikh or the Tudor Street girl. The work reveals an entertaining view of life in Barbados over fifty years ago.

477   **Growing up stupid under the Union Jack.**
Austin Clarke.   Havana: Casa de las Américas, 1980. 188p.

Probably the best known of Clarke's works, this autobiographical novel received the 'Premio Casa de las Américas' in 1980. At the same time it can equally be considered as a social history of colonial Barbados, as seen through the eyes of the author as a child growing up during the Second World War. Nowhere else is the 'Little England' theme played out to such an extent as in this schoolboy world of King George, Churchill, the BBC, Lord Nelson, and Major Noot, the headmaster of Combermere, or with such 'made in England' items as Pears soap and Quink ink. Sociologically, the account describes the struggle for social mobility via the unique avenue of education. Consequently, there is a constant shuttling between the primary sphere of the village, with its chattel houses, rum shop and mission hall, and the secondary world of Bridgetown, academe and St. Michael's Cathedral.

478 **Sovereignty, dependency and social change in the Caribbean.**
Colin Clarke. In: *South America, Central America and the Caribbean*. London: Europa Publications, 1986, p. 20-25.

A thoughtful and interesting review of current social and economic conditions in the Caribbean. The account contains numerous references to Barbados, for example describing its role in the inauguration of the West Indies Federation in 1958. The author ranges over problems of dependent development, the quest for social equality and geopolitics, especially CARIFTA and CARICOM. In conclusion it is argued that 'social statuses and standards of living for the majority of Caribbean peoples remain both disappointing and unacceptable'.

479 **Topics from yesteryear.**
E. L. Cozier, selected and arranged by J. Wickham, F. A. Hoyos. Bridgetown: Public Relation Associates (Caribbean), 1975. 108p.

A collection of about fifty articles and some poems, published between 1967 and 1975 in the *Advocate News*. This often outspoken and widely-read daily columnist presents a regular intellectual challenge to the Barbadian public as he reflects on local and international issues. A confessed liberal and defender of the capitalist cause, Cozier allows his journalistic pen to range far and wide over a whole gamut of social conditions and events, and his topics underline these catholic interests.

480 **Contemporary Caribbean: a sociological reader.**
Edited by Susan Craig. Maracas, Trinidad: College Press, 1982. 2 vols. map. bibliog.

A collection of essays by various scholars, which examines from several perspectives the structural changes which have taken place since the riots of the 1930s and the achievement of independence of many territories. Subject areas in volume one include: population and migration, class and race, agrarian structures and peasant movements. Volume two studies developments within the working class, theory and ideology and societies in crisis. Of the thirty-one contributions, one by Cecilia Karch deals specifically with Barbados. Entitled 'The growth of the corporate economy in Barbados: class and race factors 1890-1977', the essay summarizes many of the arguments presented in the author's earlier PhD thesis.

481 **Racism in Barbados.**
Kathleen Drayton. *Bulletin of Eastern Caribbean Affairs*, vol. 9, no. 2 (May-June 1983), p. 1-5.

After examining various definitions, the author pinpoints slavery as giving birth to racism and the discrimination of one race against another for economic reasons. However, she believes that racism is manifested today in Barbados in articles and letters appearing in newspapers, and in admission procedures to certain hotels and clubs. Acceptance of the cultural values of the perceived (white) dominant group is also evidenced in the role of standard English, mainstream religion and the Westminster model of government. Historically, the 1628 Act for the Governance of Negroes, which remained in force until the 1820s, deliberately set out to destroy black culture. Moreover, the 1841 Masters and Servants Act (passed after emancipation), requiring labourers to work some free days for the plantation under threat of eviction, continued the oppressive situation, as did the subsequent consolidation of power between the plantocracy and the new commercial élite. In contemporary Barbados economic power is still principally in the hands of whites, as can be seen from examining the management structure of hotels, banks and such companies as Barbados Shipping and Trading. Furthermore, both income and employment (and hence class) are predicated on racial lines. The author concludes that Barbados cannot call itself a democratic society while racism still exists.

482 **Family organization in Barbados.**
Sidney Greenfield. PhD dissertation, Columbia University, New York, 1959. 225p. bibliog. (Available from University Microfilms, Ann Arbor, Michigan, order no. GAX60-01140).
The result of fifteen months' fieldwork in a Barbadian village community. The author applies structural-functional and cultural-historical analysis to examine the matrifocal and nuclear forms of family encountered. He concludes that the former is a lower-class variant of the latter, since males in such relationships, unable to fulfill their obligations, become marginal to the daily operations of the family. However, with the attainment of middle-class status, the nuclear form is adopted. Greenfield argues that a similar pattern can be found in industrialized countries, a position not widely endorsed by researchers today. A revision of this dissertation has been published under the title *English rustics in black skins* (New Haven, Connecticut: College and University Press, 1966).

483 **Land exploitative activities and economic patterns in a Barbados village.**
Jerome S. Handler. PhD dissertation, Brandeis University, Waltham, Massachusetts, 1965. 355p. 2 maps. bibliog. (Available from University Microfilms, Ann Arbor, Michigan, order no. GAX65-14422).
This study of the village of Chalky Mount focuses on the use of land resources and the relationships formed through such agricultural activity. It also examines the extent to which land-based and other economic activities meet their cash and subsistence needs. The account provides interesting insights into Barbadian rural life and the struggle for survival of the small sugar cane farmer. There are also descriptions of subsidiary pursuits, such as the production of arrowroot, pottery, subsistence crops and livestock. Additionally, the structure of a contemporary sugar plantation is provided.

484 **More than a word.**
Gladstone Holder. Wildey, St. Michael, Barbados: Coles Printery, 1978. 90p.
A collection of articles which originally appeared in the *Nation* and *Advocate News*, and a couple of short stories from the *Weymouth Magazine*. It is freedom

which is 'more than a word' and one of the prevailing themes. Self-respect, excellence and humaneness are other issues which Barbados' most penetrating journalist constantly puts before readers in a weekly column. Indeed, the incisive commentaries from this watchdog of national liberty have always kept successive governments and politicians on their toes. At the same time, Holder is a true craftsman of language and widely read.

485 **Class formation and class and race relations in the West Indies.**
Cecilia Karch. In: *Middle classes in dependent countries*. Edited by Dale Johnson. Beverly Hills, California: Sage, 1985, p. 107-36.

Traces the development from societies characterized by master-slave relationships to those replacing the power of the plantocracy with a new, but nevertheless white, agro-commercial bourgeoisie, an emergent black middle class and a residual peasantry. Explanations are sought in the changes from mercantile to industrial modes of international capitalism and their effects on local monopolies and relations of production. The analysis focuses on Barbados, Trinidad and Jamaica. In the case of the former, such idiosyncratic factors as lack of absentee proprietorship, and alternative lands for emancipated small-holders or indentured labour, yielded different class-colour relationships than in other territories. Even the riots of the 1930s seemed only to excite the quest for political power, with the result that, apart from the manufacturing sector, economic structures have remained virtually the same in contemporary Barbados.

486 **Race, class and development in Barbados.**
Anthony Layne. *Caribbean Quarterly*, vol. 25, nos. 1-2 (March-June 1979), p. 40-51.

After an historical analysis of the racial/occupational structure of Barbados, the author demonstrates from the census data of 1960 and 1970 that similar élitist divisions still exist between whites and blacks. However, with increases in educational opportunity for the black majority, it is hoped that aspirations can be channelled towards fulfilment. Layne argues that the alternative is political instability.

487 **The growth of the modern West Indies.**
Gordon Lewis. London: MacGibbon & Kee, 1968. 506p. bibliog.

A classic socio-historical analysis of the West Indies from the end of the First World War to independence by this well-known Puerto Rico-based Caribbeanist. In his own inimitable style, Lewis variously describes Barbados as the 'Clapham Junction of the West Indies' and 'a tropical society modelled on the sort of English life that passed away in 1914 . . . Cheltenham with tropical overtones' whose women are 'rigid with starch and Anglicanism, but not so rigid that they do not possess a healthy resistance against the Judeo-Christian fear of sex life'. Convinced that Barbados deserves to be the butt of regional humour, the author takes mischievous delight in making fun of the arrogance, ignorance, traditionalism and philistinism of the inhabitants with respect to class, race, education, politics and religion, and in fact every conceivable cultural institution. The text is thus full of witticisms, some original, some derived from the works of travellers and others. The only organization to escape the verbal pillorying is the Barbados Workers' Union, and the only individuals who are spared are Clennel Wickham,

Frank Walcott and Errol Barrow. Altogether a monumental ridiculing of 'Little England', including its sacred cows of the church, the professions, élite schools and sugar estate capitalism.

488 Some issues facing the working class in contemporary Barbadian society.

Linden Lewis. *Bulletin of Eastern Caribbean Affairs*, vol. 4, no. 5 (Nov.-Dec. 1978), p. 1-19.

Investigates the plight of the working class in a predominantly capitalist society administered by successive anti-socialist governments. According to the author, the working class, as gauged by occupation, accounts for roughly 34 per cent of the labour force, and is constantly exploited in Barbados. In particular he looks at the small farmers (who number 25,788 and own 7,944 acres) and the landless farmers and the discrimination they suffer at the hands of the plantations which own 86 per cent of all arable land. Religion and the working class is also analysed with reference to the psychological support provided by 'roots churches', which, unlike Rastafari, have now regrettably begun to imitate the institutionalized religion of their more orthodox counterparts. Additionally, mention is made of Barbadian individualism nurtured by capitalism. Cooperative movements are seen as a way of combating this unfortunate characteristic.

489 West Indian societies.

David Lowenthal. London: Oxford University Press, 1972. 385p. map. bibliog.

Seeks to account for the origin and nature of West Indian identity and the relationship with external forces. Since race affects so many areas of institutional life, that theme is extensively treated as a significant variable in understanding social structure. Barbados is no exception to this rule, and almost half the references to the island deal with colour and class. The remainder are taken up with local pride and the 'Little England' theme, and such matters as government, sugar, slaves, family life and tourism. The inclusion of a forty-four page bibliography makes this excellent book required reading for all those wishing to study West Indian social conditions. Until his recent retirement the author was Professor of Geography at University College London.

490 Warning from the West Indies.

W. M. Macmillan. London: Faber & Faber, 1936. 213p. map. bibliog.

This work is founded on the premise that centuries of colonial rule have merely served the interests of planter settlers and done little, if anything, for the inhabitants. The warning is issued from the West Indies to Africa that there is no hope for development unless health, wealth, education, agriculture and social conditions are drastically improved. In this connection, and in spite of good agricultural management, the author points to the situation of Barbados in the mid-1930s – poor representation, inadequate vestry and tenantry systems, colour consciousness, overpopulation and overcrowded housing, substandard health administration, insanitary conditions, and a high incidence of venereal disease and illegitimacy. The book was written just two years before riots broke out in the island protesting against these very conditions as experienced by the black masses.

491   **Race, class and power in Barbados.**
Raymond Mack.   In: *The democratic revolution in the West Indies*.
Edited by Wendell Bell. Cambridge, Massachusetts: Schenkman,
1967, p. 140-64.

Based on six months of general observation and interviews with individuals from all strata of Barbadian society in 1961-62. Here, the author expands on the resulting paper presented to the American Sociological Association in 1963. Mack as an outsider believes that since the transference of political power to the black majority in Barbados, racial distinctions do not so clearly demarcate boundary behaviour as does social class based on occupation. 'Pass-as-whites' can thus choose those with whom they associate and thereby select their own racial alternatives. In the meantime whites protect their own economic interests by accommodating to black political power. The conclusion that racial discrimination has diminished in Barbados is unlikely to be accepted by those who can point to more subtle and less overt forms of the phenomenon.

492   **Class, culture and politics in a Barbadian community.**
Susan Makiesky-Barrow.   PhD dissertation, Brandeis University,
Waltham, Massachusetts, 1976. 294p. bibliog. (Available from
University Microfilms, Ann Arbor, Michigan, order no. GAX76-
25314).

A study of the social and political behaviour of black residents in a changing plantation community. The work also examines the tension between a national ideology of individual achievement and that of community-based worker solidarity, where the latter stresses the unity and equality associated with poverty and low status. The research is based on a twenty-seven-month period of participant observation in the representative village of Endeavour. During this time the author visited homes and meeting places, attended dances and religious gatherings, and came into contact with about one-third of the adult population. However, most of the data are derived from frequent association with seventy-five individuals and close friendship with half a dozen. In particular the author was able to concentrate on relationships between locals and outsiders during the run-up to a general election, and observe the formation of a political pressure group.

493   **Social stratification in Barbados: a study in social change.**
Joseph Manyoni.   PhD dissertation, University of Oxford,
Oxford, 1973. 269p. map. bibliog.

This study focuses on the period 1630 to 1970 by examining select theories of stratification (plural, class and élite), both historically and from the perspective of contemporary observation. The underpinning hypothesis is that present-day stratification is derived from early patterns of social relationships in Barbados. The author is particularly critical of the application of plural society and Marxist terminology to the Barbadian situation, since, in his view, they are both too unwieldly and ahistorical.

494   **The establishment of a peasantry in Barbados 1840-1920.**
Woodville Marshall, with Trevor Marshall, Bentley Gibbs.   In:
*Social groups and institutions in the history of the Caribbean, paper
presented to the VIth annual conference of Caribbean historians,
Puerto Rico, April 6, 1974.* n.p.: Association of Caribbean
Historians, 1975, p. 85-104.

A working paper which seeks to explain why Barbados, unlike most other
Caribbean territories after emancipation, witnessed only a modest growth in self-
sufficient small-holding farming and the establishment of peasant villages. Among
the various factors investigated, the most salient was probably the abundance of
labour combined with a paucity of good arable non-plantation land, which served
to perpetuate a tenantry system well into the 20th century. Only when sugar
prices fell dramatically were planters (reluctantly) prepared to subdivide, and
then for considerable profit. Of course there were exceptions, and these too are
examined in some detail.

495   **Barbados and St. Lucia: a comparative analysis of social and
economic development.**
Coleman Romalis.   PhD dissertation, Washington University,
Washington, DC, 1969. 250p. bibliog. (Available from University
Microfilms, Ann Arbor, Michigan, order no. GAX69-22554).

This study compares Barbados and nearby St. Lucia on a number of topics,
ranging from colonization and local political organizations to ideology. Included
in the analysis is a treatment of the early administrative and developmental
histories of both territories, together with an examination of education and
religion. Colour, class, parties, ideologies and trades unions are dealt with, and
the economic and commercial élites compared and contrasted. The relationship
between economic and political élites is also explored.

496   **Geh muh back muh mind.**
Eddie da Silva.   Bridgetown: Carib Printers, 1985. 47p.

A tract seeking to educate politically the 'poor man class'. Written by the founder
of the Barbados Peace Movement 'Ploughshares for Life', the booklet attempts to
alert the masses to the dangers of United States militarism in the Caribbean and
the threat of nuclear war in the region. Reference is made to a telephone survey
conducted in Barbados on the foregoing themes. Using local examples, the author
argues that an even greater obstacle to freedom is posed by aping the lifestyle of
the rich, with its emphasis on luxury, gambling and pornography.

497   **The plural society in the British West Indies.**
M. G. Smith.   Berkeley, California; Los Angeles; London:
University of California Press, 1965. 359p. bibliog.

A collection of essays written between 1952 and 1961, during which time the
author was attached to what was then the University College of the West Indies.
The volume examines the nature and character of West Indian society, using the
ideas of J. S. Furnivall on the 'plural society as a unit of disparate parts which
owes its existence to external factors, and lacks a common social will'.

149

498   **Industrial employment and inter-spouse conflict: Barbados West Indies.**
Richard Stoffle.   PhD dissertation, University of Kentucky, Lexington, Kentucky, 1972. 229p. bibliog. (Available from University Microfilms, Ann Arbor, Michigan, order no. GAX73-07372).

Employing role theory, and based on interviews with 120 industrial workers, this study seeks to test the hypothesis that rapid industrialization leads to marital stress. It is also anticipated that interspouse conflict will increase as a result of economic male marginality and female-biased hiring policy. Contrary to expectation, Stoffle finds that role strains are being managed successfully. However, it is argued that female adjustment to industry can be improved where there is a greater male willingness to undertake traditional household duties.

499   **An account of a West Indian sanatorium and a guide to Barbados.**
Rev. J. H. Sutton Moxly.   London: Sampson Low, Marston, Searle & Rivington, 1886. 209p.

Based on nine years' residence as a chaplain to the British forces, this book, which is expanded from a magazine article, covers such topics as Barbados' (undeserved) reputation as an unhealthy place, how it became a sanatorium, the low incidence of contagious diseases, the climate, the necessity for medical qualifications, entertainment, sights of interest, the white and black populations, and the dishonesty, ignorance, fatalism, fundamentalism and immorality of the latter. The role and effectiveness of religion in the island are also discussed by the clergyman. A concluding section and an appendix provide general information on such topics as education, rents, wages, hotels, the telephone system, current prices of food (with fresh lobsters ranging from ten to twenty-four cents each!), and the fares for the railway and tram.

Everyday life in Barbados: a sociological perspective.
See item no. 11.

The quality of life in Barbados.
See item no. 12.

The social structure of the British Caribbean (excluding Jamaica).
See item no. 30.

Black power in the Caribbean context.
See item no. 38.

The United States and the Caribbean.
See item no. 42.

Spatial inequalities in Barbados, West Indies.
See item no. 68.

West Indian Eden: the book of Barbados.
See item no. 191.

The Barbados book.
See item no. 192.

The Barbadian male: sexual attitudes and practices.
See item no. 400.

The position of poor whites in a color-class hierarchy: a diachronic study of ethnic boundaries in Barbados.
See item no. 423.

Indicators of women in development: a preliminary framework for the Caribbean.
See item no. 526.

The West Indies and their future.
See item no. 617.

Consumer choice in the Third World: a study of the welfare effects of advertising and new products in a developing country.
See item no. 619.

Multinational corporations and black power.
See item no. 664.

Urbanization and urban growth in the Caribbean: an essay on social change in dependent societies.
See item no. 763.

Folk songs of Barbados.
See item no. 867.

Social Services, Health and Welfare

500 The bush teas of Barbados.
Iris Bayley. *Journal of the Barbados Museum and Historical Society*, vol. 16, no. 3 (May 1949), p. 103-12.

A study of over 150 different plant species known for their medicinal properties. One called 'duppy basil' is used for chest colds, but was originally employed to ward off yellow fever. Hence its alternative name 'mosquito bush'. Then there is 'miraculous bush' for influenza, and a host of others (many of them quite toxic) to cure all kinds of 'bad feels'. Some roots and leaves are applied externally, but they often leave the patient in a worse condition than before and sometimes necessitate limb amputation. The roles of obeah, hawkers, pharmacists and bush doctors are also briefly discussed.

501 Patterns of drinking in Barbados.
Graham Dann. Bridgetown: Cedar Press, 1980. 157p. bibliog.

The report of an island-wide random sample survey of 437 residents aged eighteen and over. The research examines the three principal groups of teetotallers, ex-drinkers and drinkers of alcohol, together with the reasons for their current status. Drinkers are self-ranked as occasional, regular and heavy. A more objective assessment employs a composite index comprising annual consumption, duration and expenditure rates, and the incidence and extent of drunkenness. Predictor variables are arranged in a path-analytical framework, and include sex, age, marital status, area of residence, religion, and the age drinking commenced. The respective influences of family, friends and workmates are also contained in the model. Additionally there is an examination of types of drink imbibed, their frequencies, and locational preferences. There are 119 tables, a questionnaire and a codebook accompanying the report.

502   **Child care and family services in Barbados.**
Juliet Edmonds.   *Social and Economic Studies*, vol. 22, no. 2
(June 1973), p. 229-48.

Traces the development of social services in Barbados since the recommendations of the Moyne Commission in 1945. Since then, there have been improvements in family planning, antenatal care, maternity benefits and care, child care and day care, nutrition, children's homes, the social welfare department, probation service and care of the handicapped. However, there are still dietary problems due to the unwillingness of Barbadians to grow their own food, and the difficulty posed by welfarism, as opposed to a self-help mentality and self-help projects. The latter, it is argued, are of limited success in Barbados on account of pronounced social divisions and lack of sufficient community spirit. Edmonds feels that, even though many social problems are attributable to the high prevalence of one-parent families, it is unrealistic in the short term to tackle this island-wide phenomenon at source.

503   **The imagery of madness in village Barbados.**
Lawrence Fisher.   PhD dissertation, Northwestern University,
Evanston, Illinois, 1973. 411p. bibliog. (Available from University
Microfilms, Ann Arbor, Michigan, order no. GAX74-07740).

Based on research conducted at the Barbados Mental Hospital and a west coast fishing village. The study investigates views of madness among children, medical practitioners and mental inmates and their staff. The ways by which various community beliefs and myths are generated and sustained are also examined.

504   **Health education needs in the Caribbean.**
Henry Fraser.   *Bulletin of Eastern Caribbean Affairs*, vol. 4, no. 3
(July-Aug. 1978), p. 1-5.

Argues that the development of health education beyond the traditional areas of antenatal care and communicable diseases to those of sex education, malnutrition and drug abuse, can both improve health standards and reduce the escalating costs of curative medicine. In Barbados, for instance, data from the 1970s show that fifty-three per cent of 'healthy' women and sixty-three per cent of female patients of the Queen Elizabeth Hospital are obese. This is probably a result of the mistaken belief that 'fat is beautiful' or that it indicates prosperity. Not surprisingly, nearly half of the adult admissions to the hospital are cases of hypertension, diabetes, or an associated complication. Fraser suggests that a multifaceted approach be undertaken with respect to health education, one which involves doctors, nurses, schools, the media and churches. The example set by the Seventh Day Adventists is a good one to follow.

505 **Public attitudes to the proposed National Health Service scheme in Barbados: implications for policy implementation.**
Doyle Jordan, Michael Maycock, Philip Pilgrim, Sharon Wilson, assisted by Farley Brathwaite. *Bulletin of Eastern Caribbean Affairs*, vol. 9, no. 2 (May-June 1983), p. 24-42.
Describes a quota sample survey of 126 persons which sought to gauge public awareness, knowledge and attitudes towards the proposed National Health Service in Barbados. While most respondents had heard about the scheme (rather than read of it), they were less certain as to how free it would be. The majority were in favour of the proposal and felt confident about the quality of care it would provide. However, apprehension was expressed with respect to abuse of the service by patients, its mismanagement and the reluctance of doctors to participate.

506 **Study findings and recommendations for the establishment of the National Health Service for Barbados.**
Kaiser Foundation International. Oakland, California: Kaiser Foundation International, 1979. 50p.
The summary of a report made to the Ministry of Health and National Insurance during the 1976-1981 administration of the Barbados Labour Party. Since the party's manifesto had proposed a National Health Service (under which all persons ultimately would receive free medical attention from the doctor of their choice), it was only natural that Kaiser, after reviewing existing conditions, would also recommend adoption of the scheme. Given that this plan never came to fruition, beyond the first stage of free drug prescriptions for the disadvantaged sector of the population, it is interesting to examine the educational strategies, together with financial and fiscal arrangements, set out in the report.

507 **Cancer mortality in the Commonwealth Caribbean.**
N. D. McGlashan. *West Indian Medical Journal*, vol. 30 (1981), p. 142-48.
The preliminary findings of a cancer mortality investigation in ten islands of the English-speaking Caribbean, including Barbados, are described. Data from death certification are believed to provide consistent results which show major differences of site-specific cancer mortality between the islands.

508 **Causes of death in ten English-speaking Caribbean countries and territories.**
N. D. McGlashan. *Bulletin of the Pan American Health Organization*, vol. 16, no. 3 (1982), p. 212-23.
Provides a preliminary comparison of mortality data from ten island countries in the Caribbean. Major differences are observed between the mortality due to cancer, ischemic heart disease, diabetes mellitus and car accidents.

509 **Mental health in Barbados and the Eastern Caribbean.**
George Mahy. *Bulletin of Eastern Caribbean Affairs*, vol. 9,
no. 6 (Jan.-Feb. 1984), p. 1-4.

After defining mental health, Mahy criticizes the twenty-seven-year-old Caribbean
Federation for Mental Health as being too preoccupied with the mentally ill, and
the Caribbean Psychiatric Association for concentrating too much on programmes
for the mentally ill. Such negativism may derive from those who stress that the
insecure and dependent personality is traceable to slavery, or those whose
religiosity is centred on the banishment of evil spirits via church attendance or
obeah. While most of the islands in the Eastern Caribbean have no trained
permanent psychiatrists, Barbados is fortunate in having four, plus eight
community psychiatric nurses. However, Mahy still claims that the majority of
those with mental health problems (who fail to see the connection between
psychological stress and physical disorder) present themselves to general
practitioners. Reluctance to consult trained psychiatrists is largely due to the
stigma associated with madness. Consequently, short of conducting house-to-
house surveys, it is difficult to ascertain the prevalence of impaired mental health
in Barbados.

510 **Protein-energy malnutrition in Barbados.**
Frank Ramsey. New York: Josiah Macy Jr. Foundation, 1979.
173p. map. bibliog.

Based on an analysis of the first 340 child admissions to the Queen Elizabeth
Hospital in 1965, and 1,394 total admissions for 1966. In the latter case, 143 had
protein energy malnutrition (PEM), and the majority were under the age of 2
years. The readmission rate was 25 per cent. Since 89 per cent were lost to follow-
up, it was necessary to introduce a system for continuity of care in management,
or more specifically a nutrition intervention programme. The data base for the
programme was a longitudinal epidemiological study of 448 children recuperating
from PEM from 1967-70, who were compared with a 1 per cent sample of a 1969
national nutrition survey. The establishment of a target profile called for
improvements in nutrition education and child feeding practices. As a result of
these measures, there were dramatic reductions in PEM hospital days,
readmission rates, case fatality and mortality rates. Similar progress was reported
at the community level in the worst affected parish – St. Thomas. In addition to
an account of the foregoing research, the work also contains an interesting
historical introduction in which Barbados progresses from being the unhealthiest
colony in the Empire to providing one of the highest standards of public health
care in the Caribbean.

511 **Welfare and planning in the West Indies.**
Thomas Spensley Simey. London: Oxford University Press, 1946.
267p. map.

The focus is on social welfare provision and associated planning, and the need for
well-conceived and carefully executed planning during the transition from
colonialism to independent status is stressed as the overarching theme.

512   **Budgets and nutrition in Barbados.**
K. Straw.   *Social and Economic Studies* vol. 3, no. 1 (June 1954),
p. 5-38.

The results are presented of a random sample survey of 1,417 households
conducted in 1951 and 1952 during the crop season and hard times in order to
determine patterns of domestic budgeting and the nutritional content of diets.
From the 94.3 per cent whose incomes ranged from 0 to 49 dollars per week, the
first set of information was used to construct a retail price index. In these cases it
transpired that 51 per cent of all expenditure was allocated to food items.
Separate analysis revealed that there were significant deficiencies in the per capita
consumption of calcium, riboflavin, vitamin A and protein of animal origin.

513   **The opinions and proposals of the Barbados Association of Medical**
Practitioners for improvement of health care in Barbados.
E. Walrond.   *Bulletin of Eastern Caribbean Affairs*, vol. 4, no. 3
(July-Aug. 1978), p. 5-9.

Briefly traces the development of health care in Barbados from the time of the
planters, when their own serious cases were sent to England while slaves were
treated by local 'doctors'. Whereas public health and preventative services have
reduced infant mortality through the growth of clinics, polyclinics and hospitals,
the same high standards have not been maintained for free public primary care for
the indigent, who are either treated at the casualty department, or by parish
medical officers in the case of those on welfare. Consequently, in order to cater
for the needs of those unable to pay a private practitioner, there has been a call
by government for a National Health Service. The rest of the essay shows the
clash of opinion between the then ruling Barbados Labour Party and the
Barbados Association of Medical Practitioners as to the value of such a proposal.
The latter considers the adoption of a National Insurance Scheme (NIS), such as
exists in Britain, to be unrealistic for a developing country. Instead it recommends
a system of primary care catering mainly for the elderly, chronically ill, infants
and young children.

514   **West Indies Royal Commission 1938-39: statement of action taken**
on the recommendations.
London: HM Stationery Office, 1945. 108p. (Cmd 6656).

A state-of-the-art report presented to the British Parliament by the Colonial
Secretary in June 1945. The document provides details of progress made during
the Second World War since the original sitting of the Moyne Commission, which
investigated conditions in the West Indies in the aftermath of the 1937-38 regional
riots. Areas examined include social services (education, health, housing and
labour), the economic situation, and problems connected with agriculture and
land settlement. Action to be taken is spelt out on a country-by-country basis.
Consequently, improvements in Barbados' position can be noted.

515 **Malnutrition in children attending a Barbadian polyclinic.**
Louis Whittington. MSc thesis, University of the West Indies,
Mona, Jamaica, 1985. 149p. bibliog.

Seeks to explain the relatively high rate (8.8 per cent) of malnutrition in Barbados
as recorded by the 1951 National Health and Nutrition Survey. The study
compares 52 malnourished children with an equal number of normal children.
Anthropometric data are collected from clinic files and maternity records and
supplemented with interviews of the parents. Significant differences between the
index and comparison groups are registered with respect to mother's employment,
water supply, condition of housing, amenities, birth weight and feeding habits.
However, contrary to trends observed elsewhere, there are no significant
differences in relation to mother's age, union status or educational attainment.
Nor for that matter does family size or presence or employment of the male head
of household account for variation in nutritional status.

516 **The Caribbean: its health problems.**
Edited by A. Curtis Wilgus. Gainesville, Florida: University of
Florida Press, 1965. 273p. map. bibliog.

The fifteenth in an annual published series of Caribbean conferences hosted by
the University of Florida. The contributions comprise sections on climate,
housing, food and nutrition, sanitation, diseases, health administration and
agencies. Brief references are made to Barbados with respect to fisheries, the
government marketing corporation, poverty and courses for sanitary inspectors.

The quality of life in Barbados.
See item no. 12.

Geographic notes on the Barbados malaria epidemic.
See item no. 59.

**A West Indies geographic pathology survey: causes of death in some
English-speaking Caribbean countries.**
See item no. 63.

An epidemiological spectrum in the Caribbean.
See item no. 64.

An account of a West Indian sanatorium and a guide to Barbados.
See item no. 499.

Legal services for the poor in Barbados.
See item no. 547.

**The ecology of development administration in Jamaica, Trinidad and
Tobago, and Barbados.**
See item no. 575.

**Consumer choice in the Third World: a study of the welfare effects of
advertising and new products in a developing country.**
See item no. 619.

Social Services, Health and Welfare

Government expenditure in Barbados, 1946-79.
See item no. 627.

Income redistribution through public transport in Barbados, 1955-1979.
See item no. 715.

Women's Studies

517 **Perceptions of Caribbean women.**
Erna Brodber, edited by Joycelin Massiash. Cave Hill,
St. Michael, Barbados: Institute of Social and Economic Research,
University of the West Indies, 1982. 62p. bibliog. (Women in the
Caribbean Project, no. 4).

A documentation of stereotypes of Caribbean women as gleaned from two
sources: the church and the press. There are separate sections on Barbados,
Jamaica and Trinidad, which follow the same format: images, role performance
1838-1900, images 1901-independence, stereotypes, images post-independence,
cultural prescriptions, internalized stereotypes, and images, stereotypes and
cultural prescription. The Barbadian material is drawn from articles and
advertisements in *The Barbadian*, *Times* and *Barbados Advocate* newspapers,
records of Moravian missionaries, and Warren Alleyne's *Historic Bridgetown*
(q.v.). While references are made to women of different racial background, there
is a strong Eurocentric bias in professed models of role behaviour as housewife
and mother, in spite of changes in employment patterns and the advent of the
feminist movement.

518 **Caribbean resource book.**
Coordinator for Women's Programmes. Cave Hill, St. Michael,
Barbados: Extra-Mural Department, University of the West
Indies, 1977. 213p. bibliog.

The result of a regional seminar on 'The integration of women in development in
the Caribbean' (Jamaica, 1977). This loose-leaf resource book encourages ideas
for change with follow-up sheets. It lists women's organizations in each territory
(Barbados is covered on p. 8-17), and shows how to attract funds from several
identified sources. There is a select bibliography covering various areas of
institutional life as they affect women. The book concludes with a seventeen-page
supplement entitled 'Regional plan of action for the Caribbean.'

519 **Report of the National Commission on the Status of Women in Barbados.**
Edited by Norma Forde. Bridgetown: Government Printery, 1978. 2 vols. bibliog.

The work of a multidisciplinary commission appointed by the government in 1976 to examine various pieces of legislation (on immigration, marriage, taxation, labour and political rights) as they affect women in employment, sexual discrimination, mental and physical health, education and the one-parent family. The report is based on papers prepared by one or more commissioners, memoranda, public hearings, interviews, surveys and statistical data. It includes an historical background, an examination of traditional attitudes towards women, and chapters on women and the law, education, employment, health and the family. A miscellaneous section deals with abortion and women in the church, in politics and in the media. In most cases chapters conclude with a series of recommendations for official consideration.

520 **The status of women in Barbados: what has been done since 1978.**
Norma Forde. Cave Hill, St. Michael, Barbados: Institute of Social and Economic Research, University of the West Indies, 1980. 53p. bibliog. (Occasional Paper, no. 15).

This monograph examines official and unofficial reaction to the 212 recommendations of the much hailed *Report of the National Commission on the Status of Women*, which appeared in September 1978. Interviews with senior personnel in five out of seven government ministries reveal that little action, far less implementation, has been taken in the major institutional areas of the report: the law, education, employment, health, family, church, abortion, the media, women's organizations and the Department of Women's Affairs. An appendix provides a brief recommendation-by-recommendation assessment of what, if anything, has been done. The paper makes rather depressing reading, and could well have adopted as its subtitle 'a study of bureaucratic inertia'.

521 **Women and the law in the Commonwealth Caribbean.**
Norma Forde. Cave Hill, St. Michael, Barbados: Institute of Social and Economic Research, University of the West Indies, 1982. 125p. bibliog. (Women in the Caribbean Project, no. 1).

Collates and presents legislation as it affects women in the Caribbean. Areas treated include constitutional guarantees, marriage – contract, dissolution, maintenance and property rights – succession, domicile, employment, sexual offences and citizenship. Recent Barbados legislation (the Succession Act, Married Women (Amendment) Act, Status of Children Act, and Family Law Act) has been realistic to the extent that it recognizes the rights and liabilities of those in non-marital unions, together with their offspring. The divorce laws have also been brought in line with modern thinking in that counselling is provided in an attempt to reconcile the partners.

522 **Women of Barbados: Amerindian era to mid twentieth century.**
Jill Hamilton. Wildey, St. Michael, Barbados: Letchworth Press,
1981. 91p. map. bibliog.
Using 'classical' sources, the author traces the development of women in
Barbados from pre-settlement times to the 1970s and the championing of women's
rights by former attorney general Henry Forde. The work necessarily focuses on
famous women whose various contributions to the island are described, together
with the honours they received. The text is accompanied by illustrations and
photographs and there are notes to each chapter.

523 **Women and the family.**
Introduced by Hermione McKenzie. Cave Hill, St. Michael,
Barbados: Institute of Social and Economic Research, University
of the West Indies, 1982. 162p. bibliog. (Women in the Caribbean
Project, no. 2).
This volume contains five papers: 'Women and the family in Caribbean society' by
Hermione McKenzie, 'The realm of female familial responsibility' by Victoria
Durant-Gonzalez, 'Stresses affecting women and their families' by Jean Jackson,
'Women who head households' by Joycelin Massiah, and 'Network analysis: a
suggested model for the study of women and the family in the Caribbean' by
Dorian Powell. While only the second and fourth articles refer directly to
Barbados, from a variety of perspectives, all the contributions are quite
applicable.

524 **The status of women in Barbados – some considerations.**
Joycelin Massiah. *Bulletin of Eastern Caribbean Affairs*, vol. 2,
no. 9 (Nov. 1976), p. 1-5.
Contextualizes the relatively late establishment of the National Commission on
the Status of Women in Barbados and a Department of Women's Affairs to assist
in its deliberations. Problems of researching status qualitatively as well as
quantitatively are highlighted in the hope that the commission will make a
significant contribution to Caribbean social scientific knowledge.

525 **Women as heads of households in the Caribbean: family structure
and feminine status.**
Joycelin Massiah. Paris: UNESCO, 1983. 69p. bibliog. (Women
in a World Perspective Series).
Discusses female-headed households from the perspective of the woman.
Quantitative data are taken from the 1970 census, where it is seen that 42.9 per
cent of households in Barbados are headed by women, some 10.9 per cent in
excess of the regional mean. These women also demonstrate the highest median
age (54.9 years) and 58.9 per cent have received secondary education while
45.5 per cent are participating in the labour force. In the case of Barbados
additional qualitative data are derived from a pilot study seeking to identify
women's strategies for survival. There is also a section which examines
governmental response to the situation by analysing various forms of financial
assistance and thirty-eight case histories of national assistance recipients. Clearly,

161

problems still remain in the areas of sources of income, diversification of employment and employment opportunity, child care facilities, education, emotional support and self-esteem.

526 **Indicators of women in development: a preliminary framework for the Caribbean.**
Joycelin Massiah. In: *Women and Work*. Cave Hill, St. Michael, Barbados: Institute of Social and Economic Research, University of the West Indies, 1984, p. 41-129. bibliog. (Women in the Caribbean Project, no. 6).

An objective social indicator approach is suggested for the study of women's development in the Caribbean. Indicators are grouped into three major categories or panels: resources, status or autonomy of women, and national institutions. Together these are modelled to yield a composite index of female well-being. Within each panel there are various subcategories, each with their own battery of physical indicators. For example, resources comprise human, physical, economic and social mobility. Human resources in turn contain indicators referring to population, education, health and social conditions. In each case it is possible to calculate an index of femaleness and to make intra-Caribbean comparisons between territories. In this connection, a number of appended tables show the position of Barbados relative to other countries in the region.

Women and politics in Barbados 1948-1981.
See item no. 530.

Gender versus ethnic pluralism in Caribbean agriculture.
See item no. 693.

Women, work and development: Barbados 1946-1970.
See item no. 728.

Employed women in Barbados: a demographic profile 1946-1970.
See item no. 733.

Official ideology and the education of women in the English-speaking Caribbean 1835-1945.
See item no. 815.

Women in the Caribbean: an annotated bibliography.
See item no. 946.

Women in the Caribbean: a bibliography.
See item no. 954.

Women in the Caribbean: a bibliography. Part two.
See item no. 955.

Politics

527 Political socialisation among adolescents in schools: a comparative study of Barbados, Guyana and Trinidad.
W. Anderson, R. Grant. *Social and Economic Studies*, vol. 26, no. 2 (June 1977), p. 217-33.

The results of a survey of 539 schoolchildren aged between 11 and 19, 144 of whom were in Barbados, 189 in Guyana and 206 in Trinidad. The administered questionnaire sought to ascertain student awareness of, and attitudes towards, the political and economic system in their own country, trade unions and the Caribbean Common Market. At the same time opinions were requested on alternative career choices. Significant territorial differences emerged with respect to estimated self-sufficiency in food and government control of agriculture, trade unions and cooperatives (where greater Barbadian antipathy was recorded), and attitudes towards CARICOM and entering the University of the West Indies, which received more support from Barbadians.

528 Caribbean integration: the politics of regionalism.
W. Andrew Axline. London: Frances Pinter; New York: Nichols Publishing Company, 1979. 233p. bibliog.

Deals with the theory and the practice of regional integration in the Caribbean. Chapter one considers the economic basis for integration, whilst chapter two translates this into political requirements. Basic information on Caribbean countries and the region as a whole are provided in chapter three. Chapters four to seven consider the actual application of integration in the Caribbean. Chapter four deals with the original decision to establish CARIFTA and chapter five studies the creation of CARICOM.

163

529 **Political decolonization and the future of state sovereignty in the anglophone Caribbean.**
Neville Duncan. *Transafrica Forum*, vol. 1, no. 2 (1982), p. 73-87.

Argues that so-called 'independence' in the Caribbean has merely seen a transfer of leadership, while the more fundamental structures of society remain in a condition of neo-colonial capitalist dependency. Here the state continues to be subservient to metropolitan domination as it eventually develops through three stages in firstly, preparing the economic infrastructure for the operation of foreign monopolies; secondly, partnering outside interests; and thirdly, owning such joint ventures. Barbados is said to be halfway between the first and second stages in that it is undertaking an intensive capital works programme, and, at the same time, paving the way for national health and welfare schemes. As a model for development, such a situation is however described as illusory, since concomitant increased balance of payments difficulties will soon lead to stages two and three of the state monopolist relationship. There are also references to the excessive power wielded by island prime ministers, and to Barbados' armed cooperation in the repressive policies of nearby St. Vincent in dealing with the Union Island uprising.

530 **Women and politics in Barbados 1948-1981.**
Neville Duncan, Kenneth O'Brien. Cave Hill, St. Michael, Barbados: Institute of Social and Economic Research, University of the West Indies, 1983. 68p. (Women in the Caribbean Project, no. 3).

Provides initial and partial research findings in five areas of women's political involvement: participation in local government and in the Legislative Council, House of Assembly and Senate, membership of statutory boards, commissions and public corporations, party affiliation, and engagement in electoral politics from 1951 to 1981. As in most developing countries, women are disproportionately underrepresented, their voices are not adequately heard in political decision making, and they have little or no ideology or power base of their own which can be channelled to serve women's interests or causes.

531 **Dr. Ralph Gonsalves and the socialist debate in Barbados: a comment.**
Bentley Gibbs. *Bulletin of Eastern Caribbean Affairs*, vol. 3, nos. 11-12 (Jan-Feb. 1978), p. 26-29.

Describes the significant impact of a Vincentian Marxist university lecturer in political science and newspaper columnist on the people and government of Barbados. Having pointed out certain unpleasant home truths (e.g. that one per cent of the population owns about eighty per cent of the land, and that government simply perpetuates poverty and inequality by succumbing to external imperialist and capitalist pressure), Gonsalves came under severe attack in the press and from the Prime Minister in Parliament. According to Gibbs, Gonsalves faced two possible alternatives: either recant or risk deportation. The latter possibility duly became reality at the end of 1979.

532 **Some eminent contemporaries.**
F. A. Hoyos.   Bridgetown: Advocate Company, 1944. 134p.
In contrast to *Builders of Barbados* (q.v.), this slim volume focuses on recent personalities who have contributed to the enhancement of the island, whether or not they were nationals. The entries are either reprints or modifications of articles written by Hoyos for the *Advocate* newspaper. Since they all commence with the death of the subject, they tend to read like obituaries.

533 **The rise of West Indian democracy.**
F. A. Hoyos.   Bridgetown: Advocate Press, 1963. 228p. bibliog.
Deals with the life and times of Grantley Adams up to the dissolution of the West Indian Federation in 1962. The author's personal closeness to the Adams family proves invaluable when he traces Grantley's early childhood days, and he is able to provide the inside story of this former statesman. Of particular interest are the various controversies which arose during his political ascendancy. The reader is also told about Adams' conversion from the liberalism of Oxford and Asquith to defence of the cause of the poor against the might of the plantocracy.

534 **Grantley Adams and the social revolution: the story of the movement that changed the pattern of West Indian society.**
F. A. Hoyos.   London: Macmillan Caribbean, 1974. 280p.
bibliog.
The most complete biography of this former premier of Barbados and the West Indies Federation. The author also traces the events surrounding the 1937 riots and the transference of power on the island. He provides useful insights into the formation of the Progressive League, trades unions and political parties in Barbados. The book includes several references to available source material.

535 **The origins and development of political parties in the British West Indies.**
Charles Henry Kunsman, Jr.   PhD thesis, University of
California, Berkeley, 1963. 785p. 6 maps. bibliog. (Available from
University Microfilms, Ann Arbor, Michigan, order no. 63-5523).
Claims to be the first work to describe and analyse party systems of the West Indies. As such, it relies extensively on regional newspapers and magazines, together with interviews with seventy-five political and trade union leaders. After a general introduction to the West Indies, there is an account of the historical development of the various governments and constitutions, in which the period 1945-1955 in Barbados is featured. A separate analysis of the island's political parties is contained in part four of the thesis (p. 475-540). Here the origins of the political parties are traced and their characteristics described.

536 **The aftermath of sovereignty: West Indian perspectives.**
Edited by David Lowenthal, Lambros Comitas.   Garden City,
New York: Anchor Press, Doubleday, 1973. 422p. bibliog.
The fourth volume in a series, this collection contains nineteen essays appearing since the 1950s and written predominantly by nationals and residents of the West

Indies. The focus is mainly on the shared experiences of Commonwealth Caribbean territories, together with the common problems they face. There is one contribution by a Barbadian, Sir Hugh Springer, the present Governor General, dealing with the experiment of the West Indies Federation. Additionally, there are several references to Barbados in the various essays, including those of Williams on slavery, Proctor on government in transition, Ayearst on political parties, Ramphal on West Indian nationhood, and Lewis on independence, after rejection of alternative federation with the LDCs of the Eastern Caribbean.

537 Political development in the mini-state Caribbean: a focus on Barbados.

Will Wilbur Marvin. PhD dissertation, University of Missouri System, Columbia, Missouri, 1972. 373p. 2 maps. bibliog. (Available from University Microfilms, Ann Arbor, Michigan, order no. GAX73-21844).

The independence celebrations of Barbados in 1966 cause the author to reflect on the problems associated with the transition from statehood to nationhood. More specifically, he wishes to examine four interrelated aspects of political development – feelings of national identity, the establishment of national authority patterns, institutionalization of authority, and the ability of the political system to adjust to demands for participatory equality. His investigation looks at the Barbadian economic environment, racial stratification, the colonial heritage, the crises of the 1930s, and the emergence of party and personality politics to the point of institutionalization.

538 Confederation of the British West Indies versus annexation to the United States of America.

Louis Meikle. New York: Sampson Low, Marston & Company, 1912. Reprinted, New York: Negro Universities Press, 1969. 279p.

A political discourse arguing in favour of a responsible federal government and against annexation to the United States or dominion status with Canada. After an examination of the various pros and cons, the author provides an island-by-island account of colonial maladministration. In this respect, Barbados attracts more praise than criticism for its representative system of government and intelligent labour force. However, the historical details of its discovery and settlement provided here are inaccurate.

539 Caribbean patterns: a political and economic study of the contemporary Caribbean.

Harold Mitchell. Edinburgh; London: W. & R. Chambers, 1967. 520p. 9 maps. bibliog.

An overview of the Commonwealth Caribbean with sections on Cuba, Haiti, the Dominican Republic, Puerto Rico, the French departments, Dutch dependencies, the former British Honduras and a number of other islands such as the Virgins, the Bahamas and Cayman. The brief Barbados section (p. 156-60) contains details of the constitution, political parties, the failure of Federation, and the economy immediately after independence. Some information is inaccurate (e.g. the island's rapid population growth), and a few expectations are unwarranted (e.g. the short life of the natural gas supply).

540 **The West Indies: the federal negotiations.**
John Mordecai. London: George Allen & Unwin, 1968. 484p. map. bibliog.

Focuses on the creation and ultimate demise of the West Indies Federation during the period 1958 to 1962. The role of Errol W. Barrow as the Prime Minister of Barbados at that juncture is highlighted.

541 **People, parties and politics.**
Edited by Elton Mottley, Roderick Broome. Bridgetown: Yoruba Press, 1976. 120p.

A collection of essays intended as political education, and produced prior to the 1976 general elections in Barbados. Contributions include an analysis of manifestoes by Neville Duncan, election statistics by Patrick Emmanuel, the role of lawyers in Barbadian politics by Robert Morris and Ronald Hughes, the church and political development by Andrew Hatch, sport and political development by Nigel Harper, youth and politics by Claudette Franklin, and politics and the civil service by Leonard St. Hill. Manifestoes of the People's Political Alliance and the People's Progressive Movement are also supplied, together with the calypso lyrics of the two major parties and a 'who's who' of electoral candidates.

542 **The Caribbean Commission.**
Bernard Poole. Columbia, South Carolina: University of South Carolina Press. 1951. 303p. map. bibliog.

Examines the post-emancipation social and economic conditions of the Caribbean, the measures taken to alleviate the hardship and regional efforts to ameliorate the situation. Interesting details are provided of the Anglo-American Commission, the Caribbean Research Council and West Indian conferences (the first of which was held in Barbados in 1944), and the expanded Caribbean Commission including French and Dutch territories. The account also examines the various measures undertaken to improve communication and transport, fishing, agriculture and tourism. Comparisons are made between the system of 'responsible' government of Barbados and the administration of Crown Colonies.

543 **Caribbean power.**
Colin Rickards. London: Dennis Dobson, 1963. 247p. map. bibliog.

A leader-by-leader political profile of those land masses and islands bordering the Caribbean Sea. In Barbados' case, the analysis is of Errol Walton Barrow. A brief, accurate biography is presented and Barrow's distrust of Grantley Adams is highlighted. The story of the emergence of Barrow's Democratic Labour Party is also told, and this is all the more relevant today in the light of its resounding victory and return to power in the 1986 general elections.

544 **Understanding Third World politics and economics.**
Carl Stone. Brown's Town, Jamaica: Earle Publishers, 1980.
105p. bibliog.

An interdisciplinary study which examines the relationships between political systems and economic performances in the developing world. Barbados, with a pro-Western stance, and characterized by both competitive party politics and a free market economy, is ranked among the most mature Third World régimes with one of the highest levels of individual freedom. Specific comparisons are made with Jamaica, Chile and Costa Rica on a number of economic indicators, including income growth, food production, calorie intake, infant mortality and car ownership. Here again Barbados outscores its rivals, and, along with Taiwan, Argentina, Singapore and Cuba, is described as an outstanding Third World country.

545 **Government of the West Indies.**
Hume Wrong. Oxford: Clarendon Press, 1923. Reprinted, New York: Negro Universities Press, 1969. 190p. map. bibliog.

Written to provide an account of a neglected phase of constitutional history, and at the same time to supply the necessary background for understanding the contemporary political realities of the British West Indian colonies. Descriptions of Barbados are given in the early days of settlement under proprietary rule. These include references to the dissipated life of the planters and the cruel treatment meted out by them to their servants and slaves. After 1663, in common with the Bahamas and Bermuda, the Old Representative system was adopted (that is, there was an elected House of Assembly and nominated Legislative Council). The clashes between the assemblymen and governors are noted, especially those occurring during the governorship of Pope-Hennessy. Problems of representative government and political federation are also examined.

Geopolitics of the Caribbean: ministates in a wider world.
See item no. 43.

West Indian opposition to British policy: Barbadian politics 1774-82.
See item no. 332.

Class, culture and politics in a Barbadian community.
See item no. 492.

Barbados and St. Lucia: a comparative analysis of social and economic development.
See item no. 495.

Constitutional and political development in Barbados 1946-66.
See item no. 552.

Britain and the United States in the Caribbean.
See item no. 574.

U.S. policy in the Caribbean.
See item no. 584.

The politics of the dispossessed.
See item no. 734.

Constitution and the Legal System

546 Commonwealth Caribbean legal essays.
Edited by Francis Alexis, P. K. Menon, Dorcas
White. Cave Hill, St. Michael, Barbados: Faculty of Law of the
University of the West Indies, 1982. 303p. bibliog.

A collection of addresses by current and former members of staff marking the celebration of a decade of teaching at the Faculty of Law of the University of the West Indies in Barbados. Papers relating to Barbados include: 'The labour movement and the law in Barbados' by Francis Alexis, 'University of the West Indies' Faculty of Law Library: ten years (1970-80) assessment and projection' by John Dyrud and 'Juveniles in the Barbados society' by Sandra Mason.

547 Legal services for the poor in Barbados.
Francis Alexis. *Bulletin of Eastern Caribbean Affairs*, vol. 8,
no. 3 (July-Aug. 1982), p. 1-11.

Examines state legal aid (there are no alternative private schemes) in Barbados before and after November 1981, when the Community Legal Services Act came into being. Before that time legal aid could only be awarded by a magistrate or judge in cases where the applicant was deemed indigent by the appropriate authorities, and then only for certain major criminal offences requiring defence counsel. Since the passing of the 1981 Act, however, a community legal services commission deals with applications from the needy on the recommendation of the courts, and provides such services from its own established panel of attorneys and a number of partially trained lawyers. The main advantage of the new situation is that services are provided for certain civil matters, including maintenance under family law, security of tenure for tenants and human rights litigation.

548 **Changing Caribbean constitutions.**
Francis Alexis.   Bridgetown: Antilles Publications, 1983. 281p.
bibliog.
Studies changes to the constitutions of Caribbean countries in the post-independence period. Neither a chronological nor a nation-by-nation account is provided: rather, stress is placed on contemporary constitutional change in a thematic manner. However, tables of page references to constitutional Acts and Statutes are provided in the preliminaries (for those relating to Barbados see p. xii, xx, xxi). With particular regard to Barbados, the 1974 amendments to the constitution are discussed (p. 7); the Electroal and Boundaries Commission (p. 71-74); republicanism (p. 108–09); and property rights in Barbadian tenantries (p. 170-77).

549 **The constitution of Barbados.**
Bridgetown: Attorney General's Chambers, 1966. 92p.
Sets out the draft constitution for an independent Barbados. The chapters are as follows: 'Preliminary'; 'Citizenship'; 'The recognition and protection of human rights and fundamental freedoms'; 'The Governor General'; 'Parliament'; 'Executive powers'; 'The judicature'; 'The public service'; 'The services commissions'; and 'Finance'.

550 **Aspects of Barbados land tenure 1627-1663.**
P. F. Campbell.   *Journal of the Barbados Museum and Historical Society*, vol. 37, no. 2 (1984), p. 112-48.
This detailed paper considers the land tenure system established during the first thirty-six years after the original settlement of the island in 1627.

551 **General outline comparison of some main features of the constitution of Barbados with those of the constitutions of Guyana, Jamaica and Trinidad and Tobago.**
A. R. Carnegie.   St. Michael, Barbados: Barbados Government Printing Office, 1978. 21p.
This brief pamphlet contains the following sections: 'The head of state'; 'The Governor-General's Privy Council'; 'Parliament'; 'The Prime Minister and Cabinet'; 'The courts'; 'The civil service'; 'The police'; 'The armed forces'; 'Judicial review and the human rights provisions'; 'Citizenship'; and 'The party system and elections'.

552 **Constitutional and political development in Barbados 1946-66.**
Richard L. Cheltenham.   PhD thesis, University of Manchester, Manchester, 1970. 2 vols. bibliog.
Traces two decades of political development leading up to independence. After providing a background to the constitution, the author examines the Bushe experiment and the forces of reaction which opposed it, the advent of adult suffrage, the emergence of Grantley Adams as a political hero, the subsequent decline and fall of the Barbados Labour Party, the birth of the Democratic

Labour Party, the collapse of the West Indies Federation and the path to independence. A final chapter provides an overview of the major political and constitutional trends of the period, and considers likely future developments. The account draws liberally from the press and House of Assembly debates as it paints a detailed picture of disputes and intrigue, and presents information on the colourful personalities involved.

553 **Reforming the criminal law in Barbados.**
Delroy Chuck. *Bulletin of Eastern Caribbean Affairs*, vol. 5, no. 1 (March-April 1979), p. 18-26.

Discusses the recent initiatives of the Attorney General in the direction of updating criminal law in Barbados from its antiquated colonial condition; it was still almost identical to the common law and statutes received from England prior to independence in 1966. Yet while that country had considerably updated, modified or repealed most of its criminal law during the past fifteen years, Barbados had implemented no such changes. Drawing on several cases, some of which are quite amusing, Chuck examines several anomalous areas requiring immediate attention: homicide, provocation, sexual offences, abortion, other offences against morality and larceny. Even in 1986 many of the author's proposals have still not been adopted. Women, for instance, must continue to demonstrate lack of consent in the matter of rape, and capital punishment is retained for murder. Chuck maintains that, instead of being externally imposed, the law should reflect the conscience and behaviour of the people.

554 **The constitutional crisis of 1876 in Barbados.**
Charles P. Clarke. Bridgetown: Herald Press, 1896. 154p.

A collection of articles which previously appeared in the *Herald* newspaper. These were originally printed, complete with errors, for a few friends of publisher C. P. Bowen, a firm believer in the independence of the Barbados House of Assembly. The contributions deal with the colonial attempt to bring about federation of the Windward Islands and the subsequent conflict between governors and assemblymen on the issue. There are detailed references to many speeches, gubernatorial addresses, rumours and newspaper reports, and to the great amount of heat and energy that the controversy generated.

555 **Report of the commission appointed to review the constitution and to consider a system of national honours and a national table of precedence.**
M. E. Cox, E. E. Alleyne, C. A. Burton, J. S. B. Dear, F. A. Hoyos, E. I. Payne. Bridgetown: Constitution Review Commission, 1979. 194p.

The major part of this document considers those sections of the 1966 constitution, amended in 1975, which, after consultation with individuals, organizations and members of the public, the commissioners believe require revision. Examples of recommended change include such areas as repatriation of the constitution, citizenship, an increase in membership of the House of Assembly, the formation of an independent boundaries commission, and the powers of the Governor General. Other matters outside the scope of the constitution, though still requiring amendment, concern local government, the office of ombudsman, protection for staffs of statutory boards, the Officials Secrets Act, and standing tribunals relating to the right of personal liberty and freedom of movement. Minority reports are also attached, as are extensive memoranda prepared by the consultant to the commission, Professor Ralph Carnegie.

556 **The Third World and modern international negotiations: the case of the Third United Nations Conference on the Law of the Sea (with a focus on Commonwealth Caribbean positions).**

Winston Extavour. In: *Issues in Caribbean international relations.* Edited by Basil A. Ince, Anthony T. Bryan, Herb Addo, Ramesh Ramsaran. Lanham, Maryland: University Press of America, 1983, p. 209-33.

Aims to identify the principal issues which are facing the Third United Nations Conference on the Law of the Sea, and to establish the positions adopted by Third World countries, either as a single pressure group or individually as sovereign states. Barbados' support for the concept of the exclusive economic zone is emphasized and the country is mentioned in several other connections in this chapter.

557 **The evolution of marriage law in Barbados.**

Norma Forde. *Journal of the Barbados Museum and Historical Society*, vol. 35, no. 1 (1975), p. 33-46.

A detailed article looking at 18th- 19th- and 20th-century developments in the marriage laws of Barbados. The author stresses the need for reform in the light of changing social conditions, but also notes that this would be dependent on a review of all family law, including maintenance and custody.

558 **Report of the Barbadian constitutional conference 1966.**

Great Britain. Colonial Office. London: HM Stationery Office, 1966. 15p. (Cmnd. 3058).

This command paper presents a report on the activities of the conference convened in London between 20 June and 4 July 1966 in order to discuss the granting of independence to Barbados within the Commonwealth in 1966. A draft of the proposed constitution of Barbados is presented as Annex B, p. 11-15.

559 **Barbados Independence Act, 1966.**

Great Britain. Commonwealth Office. London: HM Stationery Office, 1966, Chapter 37, p. 677-83.

The text of the Act to make provision for the attainment by Barbados of fully responsible status within the Commonwealth.

560 **The Barbados Independence Order 1966.**
Great Britain – laws, statutes, etc. London: H.M. Stationery
Office, 1966. 69p.

The instrument of Barbados' independence, which was put before the British
Parliament on 22 November 1966, and came into effect on 30 November. The
document establishes the constitution of the island and revokes conflicting
legislation. Areas covered include citizenship, fundamental rights and freedoms,
the Governor General, parliament, executive powers, the judicature, the public
service and finance.

561 **Ten years of constitutional development in Barbados 1944-1954.**
J. M. Hewitt. Wildey, St. Michael, Barbados: Coles Printery,
1954. 41p.

Commences with the Representation of the People (Amendment) Act of 1943
and the reduction of the franchise qualification to a £20 per annum income. The
author also deals with the advent of adult suffrage some eight years later and
ministerial government in 1954. The booklet is dedicated to the martyrs of 1937,
those who lost their lives in the Barbados riots protesting against unemployment
and poverty, and who ultimately prompted not only economic, but also political
reform. That their discontent was taken very seriously is evident from the
recommendations of the Deane Commission of 1938-39, and the experiment
conducted by Governor Bushe in the method of nominating members to the
executive committee of government. Also emphasized in these reforms are the
roles of the Barbados Labour Party, the Progressive League and the Barbados
Workers' Union.

562 **Background to independence.**
F. A. Hoyos. Bridgetown: Advocate Press, 1967. 80p.

An amended collection of articles which first appeared in the *Sunday Advocate*
under the caption 'Towards independence'. The booklet traces the Barbadian
system of government from the signing of the Articles of Agreement in 1652 to
the collapse of the Federation and the electoral success of the new Democratic
Labour Party in 1961.

563 **Behind the mace: an introduction to the Barbados House of
Assembly.**
Lionel C. Hutchinson. Bridgetown: Advocate Press, 1951. 47p.

Provides a brief history of the House of Assembly before examining its various
officials, rules, parliamentary privileges and the question of prorogation. As the
booklet was written before the introduction of ministerial government, descriptions of the administration are confined to the development of the executive
committee and the Bushe experiment. Hutchinson's lively style brightens up an
otherwise dull topic and illuminates the mysteries of Westminster ritual in the
tropics.

564 **Civics for Barbados.**
W. LeRoy Inniss. Kingston: Kingston Publishers, 1982. 119p.
maps. bibliog.
A textbook written to familiarize Barbadian schoolchildren with the workings of their society. After a general introduction to the history of the island, there are chapters featuring the path towards contemporary democracy, citizenship, the constitution, elections, government, representation of the people, laws, public officers, the judiciary, revenue, non-governmental institutions and organizations, symbols of independence and relations with the Caribbean and the rest of the world. Exercises appear after several of the chapters, and essay topics and a quiz are included at the end of the book.

565 **The laws of Barbados in force on the 31st day of December 1971.**
O. R. Marshall, K. W. Patchett. Bridgetown: Government Printery; London: Eyre & Spottiswoode, Sweet & Maxwell, 1974.
7 vols. Supplement, 1978. 2 vols.
The first edition of this work seems to have been in one volume collected by W. Rawlin, clerk of the Assembly, and published in 1699. The current edition is in loose-leaf format, and was commissioned in 1967; it replaces the previous edition of the revised and consolidated laws of 1944. Statutes are classified alphabetically by subject rather than chronologically as was done previously. The two supplementary volumes comprise enactments during the period 1 July 1972 to 31 December 1976, including both new and amending legislation. Until the current edition the laws ran to over forty volumes. In the 19th century they were usually published by the Official Gazette Office, but from 1928 onwards this responsibility fell to the Advocate Company, Bridgetown.

566 **Law in Caribbean society: an annotated guide to University of the West Indies law in society dissertations 1973-77.**
Velma Newton, Sylvia Moss. Cave Hill, St. Michael, Barbados: Research and Publications Fund Committee of the University of the West Indies, 1980. 151p.
Contains short descriptions of 177 dissertations deposited in the law library. Appendixes include West Indian statutes, cases and secondary sources cited. Main topics comprise constitutional and administrative law, courts and the legal profession, criminal law, family law, international law, labour law and land law. The Barbadian entries include 'Control of land use in Barbados' by Jeannette Dellimore, 'The identification of pollutants in Barbados and an assessment of the legal framework within which environmental policies operate' by Lystra Haynes, 'Trade unions, the law and Barbadian society' by Sandra Mason, 'The status of women in Barbadian society – a sociolegal view' by Marston Gibson, 'The evolution of certain aspects of law in relation to marriage in Barbados' by Norma Forde, 'A critique of the Adoption Act in Barbados' by Rhonda Bain, 'The criminal sanction in Barbados with special reference to certain offences' by Elneth Kentish, 'Probation and aftercare with particular reference to Barbados' by C. Lashley, 'H.M. Prison Glendairy: an analysis' by M. Castagne, 'Law enforcement, the police and public relations in Barbados' by Richard Byer, 'The administration of criminal justice in Barbados' by Arden Clarke, 'Aspects of

consumer protection in Barbados' by Manuel Sosa, and 'A case for judicial review of administrative action in Barbados' by M. Atwell.

567 **Constitutional development of the West Indies 1922-1968.**
Ann Spackman. St. Lawrence, Christ Church, Barbados: Caribbean Universities Press; Epping, Essex, England: Bowker, 1975. 619p. bibliog.

An ordered presentation of major documents, which traces the various stages of constitutional development from colonial status to independence. There are also extracts from the 1922 Wood Report, the Moyne Commission, conferences pertaining to closer regional association and a number of colonial despatches. Independence constitutions are examined in detail, and a comprehensive list of references is provided for each territory. Barbados entries follow the foregoing pattern, the main exception being its Old Representative system of government. The documents are accompanied by useful well-researched introductions, thus rendering this extensive work a *vade mecum* for students of West Indian political science.

568 **Early West Indian government.**
Frederick Spurdle. Palmerston North, New Zealand: Frederick Spurdle, printed by Whitcombe & Tombs, Christchurch, New Zealand, [n.d.]. 275p. bibliog.

Traces the growth of popular assemblies in the West Indies and the corresponding decline in the power of the governors up to 1783. A great deal of the book is devoted to Barbados. Topics examined include representative government from 1640 to 1660, the devolution of government, the courts, the militia, assembly organization, financial administration, public works – fortifications, defensive expeditions, harbour works and public buildings – and appointments to offices. An appendix contains a list of the island's governors during the period under review.

Barbados our island home.
See item no. 14.

A short history of Barbados from its first discovery and settlement to the end of year 1767.
See item no. 339.

Governors and generals: the relationship of civil and military commands in Barbados 1783-1815.
See item no. 340.

A general account of the first settlement and of the trade and constitution of the island of Barbados.
See item no. 342.

Barbados and the confederation question, 1871-1885.
See item no. 343.

Our common heritage.
See item no. 345.

Builders of Barbados.
See item no. 346.

The history of Barbados from the first discovery of the island, 1605, till the accession of Lord Seaforth, 1801.
See item no. 354.

Women and the law in the Commonwealth Caribbean.
See item no. 521.

The rise of West Indian democracy.
See item no. 533.

The origins and development of political parties in the British West Indies.
See item no. 535.

Caribbean patterns: a political and economic study of the contemporary Caribbean.
See item no. 539.

Government of the West Indies.
See item no. 545.

The West Indies and their future.
See item no. 617.

Acquisition of legal materials, with special reference to the Caribbean: problems and prospects.
See item no. 888.

A bibliographical guide to law in the Commonwealth Caribbean.
See item no. 949.

Administration and Local Government

569 **Report on local government in Barbados.**
Richard M. Jackson. Bridgetown: Government Printing Office,
1964. 90p.
In December 1963, Dr Jackson was appointed as a commissioner to examine all
aspects of the working of the three local government councils of Barbados,
namely the Bridgetown City Council, the Southern District Council, and the
Northern District Council. These had been in existence since the Local
Government Act of 1958. A useful summary of the highly detailed recommendations made is to be found on p. 80-83.

570 **Development administration: field research in Barbados.**
Jamal Khan. Fontabelle, Bridgetown: Yoruba Press, 1976. 203p.
This volume comprises a collection of studies on development administration in
Barbados which were carried out during the early 1970s. The main topics dealt
with in the twelve chapters are: administrative change and development, planning
and budgeting in poor countries, administrative planning, public development
corporations, development projects, community development projects, agricultural development, the development of science and technology, trade unionism
and international relations.

571 **Public management: the Eastern Caribbean experience.**
Jamal Khan. Leiden, The Netherlands: Royal Institute of
Linguistics and Anthropology, 1982. 348p. map. bibliog.
Although basically a study of the less developed countries of the Eastern
Caribbean, this work contains a number of references to Barbados which serve to
contextualize its historical, constitutional and economic development in relation
to its island neighbours. The importance of Barbados as a headquarters for
several regional organizations, training and conference centres, is also emphasized.

572 **Report on local government in Barbados.**
John Maude. Bridgetown: Advocate Press, 1949. 68p.

Based on a survey of the eleven vestries and discussions with parish treasurers, medical officers and members of the business community, undertaken during the summer and autumn of 1948. The report deals with the existing local government system and its perceived weaknesses, and goes on to provide a series of recommendations and a summary of the same. Maude strongly believes that the former system of parish administration and taxation, derived from English practice which originated in the Middle Ages, should be replaced by a more modern system of local government based on three regional councils (one northern, one southern, and one comprising Bridgetown and its environs).

573 **Administering agricultural development through a public corporation: the case of Barbados.**
John M. Mayers. *Agricultural Administration*, vol. 12, no. 3 (1983), p. 155-71.

In accordance with the government's policy of reducing dependence on sugar cane by diversifying into other types of agriculture, the Agricultural Development Corporation (ADC) was set up. This paper considers the role of the ADC in promoting agricultural development, reviewing the financial, technical and administrative problems that face a statutory corporation of this type.

574 **Britain and the United States in the Caribbean.**
Mary Proudfoot. London: Faber & Faber, 1954. Reprinted, Westport, Connecticut: Greenwood Press, 1976. 434p. map. bibliog.

A comparison of the methods of administration of colonies and dependencies employed by Great Britain and the United States, on the basis of field research conducted in Barbados, Jamaica, Trinidad, St. Lucia, Puerto Rico and the US Virgin Islands from 1949 to 1950. Areas covered include metropolitan organization, economic relationships, race and class structure, central and local government, political and economic life, health, housing, religion, education, population problems and the possibility of federation. In addition, the Barbados sections refer to colonial welfare programmes, the rum and sugar industries, industrialization, illiteracy and the colour bar. The work contains a number of detailed appendixes based mainly on 1946 census returns. An informative study for those interested in Caribbean social conditions in the post-Second World War period.

575 **The ecology of development administration in Jamaica, Trinidad and Tobago, and Barbados.**
Jean-Claude Garcia-Zamor. Washington, DC: Organization of American States, 1977. 122p.

This book is divided into two parts, one theoretical, the other descriptive. In the latter, the author looks at such areas as education, trade unionism, unemployment, housing, health and family planning. There is also a section on public enterprise in the Caribbean, based on interviews with thirty-two senior civil servants, four of whom are from Barbados.

The colonial agents of the British West Indies: a study in colonial administration mainly in the eighteenth century.
See item no. 317.

A short history of Barbados.
See item no. 334.

Women and politics in Barbados 1948-1981.
See item no. 530.

Public policy.
See item no. 648.

The West Indies chooses a capital.
See item no. 768.

Foreign Relations

576 ACP, EEC and Lomé: a layman's guide.
Mark D. Alleyne. *Bajan*, (May-June 1986), p. 7-9.
Written following the meeting of the Council of Ministers of the African,
Caribbean and Pacific Group (ACP) and the European Economic Community
(EEC) in Barbados in April 1986, which preceded the start of the Lomé III
agreement between the ACP and EEC in May 1986, this report seeks to explain
the links existing between these organizations.

**577 The theory of integration and the Caribbean community process:
ten years on.**
Havelock R. Brewster. In: *Issues in Caribbean international
relations*. Edited by Basil A. Ince, Anthony T. Bryan, Herb Addo,
Ramesh Ramsaran. Lanham, Maryland: University Press of
America, 1983, p. 77-110.
Seeks to evaluate the revived process of integration in the Caribbean now that it
has completed its first decade. Barbados features prominently in a number of
places in this interesting and carefully written chapter.

578 Where the power is wielded.
S. R. Elliot, Ian Lee. *Geographical Magazine*, vol. 53, no. 13
(1981), p. 843-46.
Ranges widely over the disposition of strategic military power in the Caribbean. It
is argued that direct military hostilities between the USA and Cuba would be
counterproductive. However, the article suggsts that the United States cannot
tolerate loss of political leadership and influence in the Caribbean region. Thus,
the United States should work with other states such as Mexico and Venezuela to
further the economic standards of all countries in the region.

579 **Issues in Caribbean international relations.**
Edited by Basil A. Ince, Anthony T. Bryan, Herb Addo, Ramesh Ramsaran. Lanham, Maryland: University Press of America, 1983. 349p. bibliog.

In May 1977, the Institute of International Relations of the University of the West Indies at St. Augustine, Trinidad and Tobago, convened a conference on Caribbean international affairs. A selection of thirteen papers from the conference are presented in this volume, which is divided into four parts reflecting the major concerns under consideration: small size and foreign policy, regional integration, negotiation and decision-making.

580 **Commonwealth Caribbean relations with hemispheric middle powers.**
Vaughan A. Lewis. In: *Dependency under challenge: the political economy of the Commonwealth Caribbean.* Edited by Anthony Payne, Paul Sutton. Manchester, England: Manchester University Press, 1984, p. 238-58.

Primarily examines the relationships existing between the members of the Commonwealth Caribbean and the middle powers of Venezuela, Mexico and Brazil. Concludes that with regard to economic aid relationships, the most important single power has been Venezuela, which has sought to grant assistance through a mixture of bilateralism and multilateralism.

581 **The West Indian Federation: perspectives on a new nation.**
Edited by David Lowenthal. New York: Columbia University Press, 1961. 142p. map. bibliog. (American Geographical Research Series, no. 23).

Presents four essays on the birth of the West Indies Federation resulting from a symposium held at Carleton University, Ottawa in April 1959. The essays are as follows: H. W. Springer, 'The West Indies emergent: problems and prospects'; Gordon Merrill, 'The survival of the past in the West Indies'; Douglas G. Anglin, 'The political development of the West Indies'; David Lowenthal, 'The social background of West Indian Federation'. Finally, on p. 101-35 there is a useful partially annotated 'Selected West Indian reading list' prepared by David Lowenthal.

582 **The Barbados-America connection: the story of a mini-country and a giant.**
May Lumsden. Bedford, Nova Scotia: Layne, 1982. 70p.

The author, a native American who has lived in Barbados since 1970, explores the connections between Barbados and America from the 17th century to the early part of the 20th century. The book serves to stress that although the close connections between 'Little England' and Great Britain are well known, its linkages with the United States from the early days have not been loudly proclaimed or discussed. The chapters are as follows: 'Establishing identity'; 'Population source for American colonies'; 'To the Carolinas'; 'The Northward trek'; 'Some more historic Barbadian names'; 'Pioneer freedom fighters and

preachers'; 'Character of Barbadian immigrants'; 'How Bajans adapted to the
new environment'; 'Contribution to medicine'; 'George Washington, tourist';
'Trade ties'; 'Reverse migration attempt'; 'Panama Canal'; 'Negative factors';
'Appreciation from a giant'.

583   **The dissolution of the West Indies Federation: a study in political
geography.**
Paul Firmino Lusaka.   MA dissertation, McGill University,
Montreal, 1963. 222p.

Argues that the dissolution of the West Indies Federation in 1962 resulted from
factors of location, communications, trade, population, contrasting levels of
economic development, politics, history and social customs. A comparative study
is provided between the West Indies Federation and the then proposed
Federation of Greater Malaysia.

584   **U.S. policy in the Caribbean.**
John Martin.   Boulder, Colorado: Westview Press, 1978. 420p.
bibliog.

Written by a former United States ambassador to the Dominican Republic. The
author seeks to understand the current 'love-hate relationship' that exists between
the Caribbean and the United States against the backdrop of the latter's vested
strategic, economic and political interests in the region. In order to do this, he
traces the history of the relationship from the enunciation of the Monroe Doctrine
through a number of administrations varying in attitude from active collaboration
to benign neglect. Barbados, once more important to Britain than New York,
Carolina, Pennsylvania and New England together, is today evaluated by the
writer as a fairly safe pro-US democratic mini-state. Martin reaches this
conclusion by examining the island's attitude to Black Power and left-wing
politics, voting patterns in the OAS and UN, relations with Cuba, and adoption
of USAID policies.

585   **Europe in the Caribbean.**
Harold Mitchell.   Stanford, California: Hispanic American
Society, Stanford University, 1963. 211p. 3 maps. bibliog.

Subtitled 'The policies of Great Britain, France and the Netherlands towards their
West Indian territories in the twentieth century', much of the book is taken up
with British policy in general, and the ill-fated federation experiment in
particular. Barbados' system of government, when compared with other West
Indian territories, probably rendered it the most prepared constitutionally to take
the first step towards regional integration. At the same time, its opposition to
federation in the Eastern Caribbean in 1876, combined with its individualism and
traditionalism, tended to militate against such an initiative. Added to these
difficulties were problems of poor communication and competition in trade.
Mitchell is quite critical of Grantley Adams as the first and last (Barbadian) prime
minister of the federal government and blames him for his glib talk of West
Indian dominion status before he had resolved the issues of equitable representation, immigration, taxation and customs union. Additionally, his over-reliance
on small island support at the expense of the larger territories is said to have been

partially responsible for the rift with Manley, the withdrawal of Jamaica and later Trinidad, and the ultimate collapse of the Federation.

586   **The politics of the Caribbean Community 1961-79: regional integration amongst new states.**
Anthony J. Payne.   Manchester, England: Manchester University Press, 1980. 299p. map. bibliog.

In the first part of this book, the history of intra-regional relations in the Caribbean, from the days of early British rule to the collapse of the West Indies Federation in 1961, is considered. This provides the framework for the ensuing account of contemporary Caribbean integration, which focuses especially on the Caribbean Free Trade Association (CARIFTA) and the Caribbean Community (CARICOM).

587   **The international crisis in the Caribbean.**
Anthony J. Payne.   London: Croom Helm, 1984. 177p. bibliog.

The foreign policy of Barbados is considered in some detail in this account of the intensified competition for influence in the Caribbean region, involving the external powers of the United States, Britain, France, the Netherlands, Venezuela, Mexico, Colombia and Brazil.

588   **Britain's pro-Federation policy in the Caribbean: an inquiry into motivation.**
Jesse H. Proctor, Jr.   *Canadian Journal of Economics and Political Science*, vol. 22 (1956), p. 319-31.

Provides a detailed analysis of Britain's reasons for supporting the West Indies Federation.

589   **Issues in Commonwealth Caribbean-United States relations.**
Ramesh F. Ramsaran.   In: *Dependency under challenge: the political economy of the Commonwealth Caribbean*. Edited by Anthony Payne, Paul Sutton. Manchester, England: Manchester University Press, 1984, p. 179-203.

The nature and meaning of Commonwealth Caribbean-United States relations are reviewed in this chapter. The author begins by setting out the extent of the region's dependence on the US, with respect to trade, private investment, aid and emigration. He then looks at the implications of this for national development in the area. The Caribbean Basin Initiative (CBI) launched by President Reagan in 1982 is examined in depth. Contains many useful and up-to-date statistics. For example, Ramsaran records that in 1978, 27.9 per cent of Barbados' total trade was with the United States.

590 **From neo-colonialism to neo-colonialism: Britain and the EEC in the Commonwealth Caribbean.**
Paul Sutton. In: *Dependency under challenge: the political economy of the Commonwealth Caribbean.* Edited by Anthony Payne, Paul Sutton. Manchester, England: Manchester University Press, 1984, p. 204-37.

This lengthy account seeks to assess the degree to which countries of the Commonwealth Caribbean have gained from the first and second Lomé Conventions held in 1975 and 1979 respectively. Argues that for the Commonwealth Caribbean, Lomé seems to preserve the past within a new set of arrangements.

591 **Trouble in Uncle Sam's backyard.**
Ralph Lee Woodward, Jr. *Geographical Magazine*, vol. 53, no. 13 (1981), p. 838-43.

Woodward examines the political development of the Caribbean, which has long been regarded as a zone within the hegemony of the USA. Particular attention is paid to the Cuban Revolution and the establishment of a Soviet territorial base in the region. Accompanied by very useful colour graphic maps depicting Caribbean military arsenals and foreign relations.

Geopolitics of the Caribbean: ministates in a wider world.
See item no. 43.

The Third World and modern international negotiations: the case of the Third United Nations Conference on the Law of the Sea (with a focus on Commonwealth Caribbean positions).
See item no. 556.

Britain and the United States in the Caribbean.
See item no. 574.

Economy

592   **The Caribbean Basin Initiative and the Commonwealth Caribbean.**
Eudine Barriteau.   *Bulletin of Eastern Caribbean Affairs*, vol. 7,
no. 6 (1982), p. 11-20.

This article was prepared before President Reagan's address concerning the
Caribbean Basin Initiative was delivered on 24 February 1982. In it, the author
traces the origin of the Caribbean Basin Initiative (CBI) and discusses its most
salient proposals. The paper concludes with the cautionary warning that the
countries of the Eastern Caribbean will gain relatively little assistance from the
plan.

593   **The other side of paradise: foreign control in the Caribbean.**
Tom Barry, Beth Wood, Deb Preusch.   New York: Grove Press,
1984. 405p. map. bibliog.

Examines how foreign corporate and government control has shaped the
contemporary Caribbean economy and politics. Part one deals with foreign
influences on the major sectors of the economy and presents an overview of
regional finances and international aid programmes and the expanding influence
of the United States in the region. In part two, profiles of all the Caribbean states
and nations are presented and Barbados is featured on p. 264-67 in an account
covering agriculture, industry and economy.

594   **Caribbean economy: dependence and backwardness.**
Edited by George L. Beckford.   Mona, Jamaica: Institute of
Social and Economic Research, University of the West Indies,
1975. 180p.

This volume of essays based in the dependency school of thought is certain to
be of interest to those considering the economic situation of Barbados.

595 **Caribbean rural economy.**
George L. Beckford. In: *Caribbean economy: dependence and backwardness*. Edited by George L. Beckford. Mona, Jamaica: Institute of Social and Economic Research, 1975, p.77-91.

Argues that underdevelopment in Caribbean economies stems directly from excessive dependence on foreign capital for resource development. This is felt most acutely in the rural sector, where it is argued that the peasantry remain at subsistence levels as a direct consequence. A stimulating account.

596 **The Commonwealth Caribbean and the New International Economic Order.**
Denis Benn. In: *Dependency under challenge: the political economy of the Commonwealth Caribbean*. Edited by Anthony Payne, Paul Sutton. Manchester, England: Manchester University Press, 1984, p. 259-80.

This useful account considers the role of Commonwealth Caribbean states in the debate on the establishment of the New International Economic Order. Although all Caribbean states have been committed to the principle of promoting a more equitable international economic system, it is argued that Guyana and Jamaica have played the most active part in these discussions, whilst Barbados, along with the Bahamas and Trinidad and Tobago, has traditionally adopted what are described as low-key stances.

597 **A national accounts study of the economy of Barbados.**
Jeanette Bethel. *Social and Economic Studies*, vol. 9 (1960), p. 123-252.

Provides a statistical study of the economic structure of Barbados, as of 1960, along with an account of recent changes and development.

598 **Some critical issues in Caribbean economic development.**
Courtney N. Blackman. *Central Bank of Barbados Economic Review*, vol. 9, no. 3 (1982), p. 9-13.

The text of a paper delivered to a symposium in Curaçao. Stresses the role of information, computer technology, democracy, corporate independence and small size in enhancing future economic development in the region.

599 **Latin America and the Caribbean: economic problems.**
Robin Chapman. In: *South America, Central America and the Caribbean*. London: Europa Publications, p. 3-9.

Economic problems since the onset of economic crisis in the early 1980s are reviewed. There are sections on external debt, inflation, trade and integration, energy, employment and urbanization. Although much space is devoted to the main economies of Argentina, Brazil and Mexico, the commentary is of direct relevance to Barbados and the Caribbean. A useful postscript on developments in 1984 is included towards the end.

600 **The Commonwealth Caribbean: the integration experience (report of a mission sent to the Commonwealth Caribbean by the World Bank).**
Sidney E. Chernick (co-ordinating author). Baltimore, Maryland; London: Johns Hopkins University Press for the World Bank, 1978. 521p.

This volume considers the twelve territories that are in the process of forging an integrated community. Its themes are the vexing problems of small size, economic fragmentation and poorly coordinated strategies for economic development. Particular emphasis is placed on the four productive sectors of agriculture, industry, tourism and transport, which are crucial to the success of the Caribbean Free Trade Association and the Caribbean Common Market. The main chapters are followed by a vast statistical appendix (p. 237-513) presenting a mass of basic data for the twelve territories. In short, this is an invaluable source book of both statistics and ideas on Caribbean economic development.

601 **Remittance impacts on development in the Eastern Caribbean.**
Dennis Conway. *Bulletin of Eastern Caribbean Affairs*, vol. 11, nos. 4-5 (1985), p. 31-40.

Discusses one salient consequence of contemporary overseas migration, namely the impact of remittances, or the homeward transfer of cash and kind. It is suggested that previous studies of remittances have tended to be negative and thus the author calls for a reorientation of approach to their analysis. In so doing, he examines annual estimates of private transfer payments from individuals overseas to Barbados.

602 **The economics of development in small countries with special reference to the Caribbean.**
William G. Demas. Montreal: McGill University Press, 1965. 150p.

This volume is based on the four Keith Collard lectures that Demas delivered at McGill University in March 1964. The argument is that work done so far on economic development has not taken into account sufficiently the influence of the size of countries. Chapter one deals with the concepts of underdevelopment and self-sustained growth, whilst chapter two considers their nature in small countries. In chapters three and four the characteristics of Caribbean economies and problems of economic planning in the Caribbean are covered.

603 **Situation and change.**
William G. Demas. In: *Caribbean economy: dependence and backwardness*. Edited by George L. Beckford. Mona, Jamaica: Institute of Social and Economic Research, 1975, p. 61-76.

Presents a strong dependency theory approach to the analysis of the Commonwealth Caribbean economy, and although Barbados is not discussed individually, the text provides much general food for thought concerning the contemporary economic structure of the region.

604 **Some distinguishing characteristics of island states.**
Edward Dommen. *World Development*, vol. 8 (1980), p. 931-43.
Barbados is included in the sample of island countries that is compared with a
sample of continental countries, with regard to economic structure and quality of
life. The author's conclusion that island countries are often particularly fortunate
places provides food for thought and debate.

605 **Barbados: *Financial Times* survey.**
Financial Times (15 Jan. 1970), p. 21-25.
An interesting document published only four years after independence. It argues
that the economic problems of small size can be overcome by the growth of the
Caribbean Free Trade Association (CARIFTA). The article covers a range of
topics, including economic balance, development planning, tourism, family
planning, land values, home food growth, the sugar industry and 'Operation
Beehive', the country's industrialization programme.

606 **Barbados: *Financial Times* survey.**
Financial Times (29 Feb. 1972), p. 24-27.
This detailed report focuses on attempts to boost the growth of the tourist
industry and also considers the economy in general, the sugar industry and
development planning.

607 **Barbados: *Financial Times* survey.**
Financial Times (27 Nov. 1974), p. 12-15.
Pays specific attention to the general economic condition of the country, banking,
tourism, the property market, sugar and the 1973-1977 Development Plan.

608 **Barbados: *Financial Times* survey.**
Financial Times (30 Nov. 1976), p. 35-38.
Provides summaries of economic growth, agricultural decline, the provision of
infrastructure (especially in subsidiary urban areas), tourism and bank liquidity.

609 **Barbados: *Financial Times* survey.**
Financial Times (30 Nov. 1978), p. 32-35.
An in-depth analysis of the economy in general and manufacturing industry,
sugar, development planning and tourism in particular.

610 **Barbados: *Financial Times* survey.**
Financial Times (3 Dec. 1980), p. 11-13.
Includes sections on the economy, basic statistics, agriculture, banking, tourism,
industry and energy. The article stresses that although Barbados is economically
vulnerable at the global level, its political stability aids economic performance
considerably at the regional level.

611 **Barbados:** *Financial Times* **survey.**
Financial Times (29 Nov. 1983), p. 31-34.
A recent overview of Barbados' economy, industrial activities, foreign policy,
tourism and agriculture. The introduction argues that the future of CARICOM
may have been jeopardized by the US invasion of Grenada.

612 **Barbados:** *Financial Times* **survey.**
Financial Times (27 Nov. 1985), p. 21-24.
Appearing eight months after Bernard St. John became Prime Minister following
the sudden death of Tom Adams, this report surveys the state of the economy,
arguing that unemployment will be the principal front on which future political
battles are likely to be fought. Includes sections on economy and trade, sugar,
foreign investment, the Caribbean Development Bank, tourism, rum and cricket,
in addition to the general introduction.

613 **Caribbean economic handbook.**
Edited by Peter D. Fraser. London: Euromonitor Publications,
1985. 241p. maps.
One of a new series of handbooks which aim to provide a comprehensive picture
of the economic situation of a particular region, specifically looking at its role in
the world economy and its future prospects. Chapter one examines the Caribbean
in a world context, whilst chapter two provides an overview of the region.
Particular islands and island groups are dealt with in chapters three to eleven. The
account of Barbados, covering agriculture, industry, energy, industrial finance,
tourism and trade constitutes chapter four.

614 **The development of dependency economics in the Caribbean and**
Latin America: review and comparison.
Norman Girvan. *Social and Economic Studies*, vol. 22 (1973),
p. 1-33.
The search for an acceptable economics of development in Latin America and the
English-speaking Caribbean is the focus of this paper. This search has evoked the
joint concepts of external dependence and the institutionalization of underdevelopment. The paper is divided into two parts. The first examines the
emergence of a post-war development model which represented a rejection of the
primary product exporting model and the case for industrialization, as propounded
by W. Arthur Lewis. The second half examines in some detail the emergence of
the dependency school, which essentially uses an historical-structural approach to
diagnose the causes of underdevelopment and poverty. This is a thoughtful and
eminently readable piece.

615 **Rural development in the Caribbean.**
Edited by P. I. Gomes. London: Hurst; New York: St. Martin's
Press, 1985. 246p. 2 maps.
Consists of twelve chapters covering rural development strategies in the
Caribbean region. Two chapters deal with Barbados in some detail: chapter one,
'Peasant development in the West Indies since 1838', by Woodville K. Marshall,

and chapter two, 'The agri-business bourgeoisie of Barbados and Martinique', by Michael Sleeman. The book's basic message is the need for an 'integrated approach' to rural development.

616 Barbados development plan 1983-1988.
Government of Barbados. Bridgetown: Ministry of Finance and Planning, Government Headquarters, [n.d.]. 206p.

This five-year sectoral economic development plan is geared, as stated by its subtitle, to 'change plus growth'. The plan outlines the government's goals, policies, and associated programmes up to 1988. Recent economic developments are dealt with in part one, whilst part two sets out planning objectives, strategies and targets. Part three covers public sector investment. Part four presents sectoral plans and programmes for major sectors such as agriculture and fisheries, tourism, industry, trade, energy, housing, etc.

617 The West Indies and their future.
Daniel Guérin, translated by Austryn Wainhouse. London: Dennis Dobson, 1961. 192p. map. bibliog.

A rather bitter and pessimistic account of life in the West Indies under colonial rule. Overpopulated Barbados is criticized for its excessive dependence on sugar. This commodity is said to represent between 98 and 99 per cent of the island's exports in 1950, while its yield is only two-thirds of that of Cuba, and over 90 per cent of the land is allocated to sugar cultivation. Consequently, the colonial power is fully aware that, should it remove its price support mechanism, the economy would collapse overnight. The author grudgingly admits that the political situation has somewhat improved since 1939, when only 3.4 per cent of the population was eligible to vote, as a result of the constitutional revisions of 1943 and 1950 and the advent of adult franchise. Nevertheless, the stranglehold on the economy by the white plantocracy, and their attitudes towards the black majority, have led to a racism which, Guérin argues, is similar to that of Martinique, and is nothing short of grotesque.

618 The economic development of Barbados, 1946-1980.
Michael Howard. PhD thesis, University of the West Indies, Barbados, 1986. 636p. bibliog.

A comprehensive and critical evaluation of the application of Arthur Lewis' 'industrialization by invitation' Puerto Rican model to the post-war economy of Barbados. After a sector-by-sector historical and contemporary analysis of agriculture, tourism and manufacturing, and an examination of such externally dependent development, the author concludes that capital gains in output and income are not matched by those in employment. While Barbados must continue to be export-oriented, at the same time it should adopt import substitution policies, particularly with respect to self-sufficiency in food. The text is accompanied by 152 tables and a detailed list of references.

619 **Consumer choice in the Third World: a study of the welfare effects of advertising and new products in a developing country.**
Jeffrey James. London: Macmillan, 1983. 178p. bibliog.

Seeks to assess the welfare aspects of advertising in developing countries; the empirical work is based on a case study of laundry cleaning products in Barbados. The volume offers an interesting combination of marketing theory and field research. Semantic differential scales are used to collect data on 330 respondents' perceptions of competing products in chapter four. Such perceptions are then related to advertising in chapter five. It is concluded that advertising may lead to absolute welfare losses amongst the poor, as a consequence of their being induced to buy products which otherwise they might not have. The appendix details the survey method and the characteristics of the respondents.

620 **Transnational corporations and Caribbean inequalities.**
David Kowalewski. New York: Praeger, 1982. 235p. bibliog.

A very interesting volume which takes a broad view of the economic and social consequences of the operation of transnational corporations (TNCs) in the Caribbean Basin, excluding Cuba and the Venezuelan Antilles. Broadly speaking, the period covered is from 1960 to 1980, when many transnational corporations were established in the region. Barbados is considered in numerous places in the text, for example, with respect to tourism. The book includes an island-by-island listing of TNCs (Barbados is dealt with on p. 167-68) and a most useful thirty-nine page bibliography.

621 **Character of Caribbean economy.**
Kari Levitt, Lloyd Best. In: *Caribbean economy: dependence and backwardness.* Edited by George L. Beckford. Mona, Jamaica: Institute of Social and Economic Research, 1975, p. 34-59.

Barbados is referred to at several junctures in this account of economic theory and policy in the post-war period. The account stresses the central policy issue of getting the economy to grow sufficiently fast. The promotion of industrial development by tax concessions and the provision of social infrastructure is discussed in relation to Barbados and other Caribbean countries. Barbados is also considered with respect to the Caribbean Plantation Economy.

622 **The search for unity in the Commonwealth Caribbean (Caricom, Carifta, Caribe).**
Abdelkader Marquez. PhD dissertation, University of Miami, 1984. 260p. maps. bibliog.

This doctoral thesis examines the various moves towards economic integration that have occurred in the Commonwealth Caribbean as a whole.

623 **Caribbean dependence on the United States economy.**
Ransford W. Palmer. New York: Praeger, 1979. 173p. bibliog.

Considers the nature of the dependence of four major English-speaking Caribbean countries, Jamaica, Trinidad and Tobago, Guyana and Barbados, on

191

the economy of the United States. The volume deals with four principal facets of Caribbean dependence on the US economy: trade dependence, financial dependence, dependence on emigration and the dependence of local economic policies. Barbados features prominently throughout. The lack of an index seems strange in a volume of this length.

624   **U.S. investment in Latin America and the Caribbean.**
Ramesh F. Ramsaran.   London: Hodder & Stoughton, 1985.
196p. bibliog.

Bearing in mind the United States' Caribbean Basin Initiative (CBI) announced by President Reagan in 1982, this monograph examines the historical growth of American investment in the region, along with the problems and issues which surround the role of private foreign capital in the development process. The volume contains numerous references to Barbados, including its balance of payments situation. The author was Senior Lecturer in International Relations at the University of the West Indies, St. Augustine, Trinidad and Tobago at the time of publication.

625   **The Caribbean Basin Initiative.**
Ronald Reagan.   *Bulletin of Eastern Caribbean Affairs*, vol. 8,
no. 1 (1982), p. 23-30.

This is the full text of an address to the Organization of American States on the Caribbean Basin Initiative delivered by President Reagan on 24 February 1982. The Caribbean Basin Initiative is an economic and military assistance programme for Caribbean and Central American countries, the main plank of which is the creation of free trade for Caribbean products entering the United States.

626   **The impact of Panama money in Barbados in the early twentieth century.**
Bonham Richardson.   *Nieuwe West-Indische Gids*, vol. 59,
nos. 1-2 (1985), p. 1-26.

This paper focuses on the social and economic impact of money remitted by Barbadians and the money brought home from the Panama Canal Zone in the early 20th century. The reasons behind Barbadian migration to the Panama Canal are considered before the effects produced by the remittances are enumerated.

627   **Government expenditure in Barbados, 1946-79.**
Muriel Saunders, De Lisle Worrell.   *Central Bank of Barbados Quarterly Review*, vol. 8, no. 2 (1981), p. 30-79.

Surveys the allocation of government expenditure and shifts in its emphasis during the post-war period. In the fiscal year 1946-47, government expenditure amounted to 14.5 per cent of GDP. By 1978-79, it had risen to 48.3 per cent. This detailed paper explains why this change has occurred. There are useful sections on education, health, social welfare, water, housing, the infrastructure and other sectors of the economy.

628 **Development policy in small countries.**
Edited by P. Selwyn. London: Croom Helm in association with
the Institute of Development Studies, Sussex, 1975. 284p.

Presents the papers prepared for a conference organized by the Institute of
Development Studies in August 1972, and held at the Centre for Multi-Racial
Studies at the University of the West Indies, Cave Hill, Barbados. The central
issues covered concerned the nature of the constraints faced by small countries on
account of their size, and their scope for independent action.

629 **Marketing activities and household activities of country hawkers in
Barbados.**
Eleanor Spence. MA dissertation, McGill University, Montreal,
1964. 123p. bibliog.

The field work for this social anthropological dissertation was carried out in six
selected villages of the Scotland District from May to September 1963; the author
looks in detail at the marketing and household activities of women hawkers in
these areas.

630 **Some preliminary results of a survey of income and consumption
patterns in a sample of households in Barbados.**
K. H. Straw. *Social and Economic Studies*, vol. 1 (1953), p. 5-40.

Examines seasonal variations in the income and expenditure on food and other
commodities induced by the sugar crop.

631 **The economy of Barbados 1946-1980.**
Edited by De Lisle Worrell. Bridgetown: Central Bank of
Barbados, 1982. 199p. bibliog.

This basic source work for all those interested in the economy and economic
history of Barbados was published to mark the tenth anniversary of the Central
Bank of Barbados. The essays, all written by staff of the Bank, focus on the post-
war period, and begin with De Lisle Worrell's analysis of the economy as a whole
from 1946 to 1980 (p. 1-46). Winston Cox then considers the performance of the
manufacturing sector of the economy (p. 47-80), whilst Cleviston Hayes analyses
the role of sugar (p. 81-105). Edsil Phillips examines the development of the
tourist industry (p. 107-39), Carlos Brathwaite and Harold Codrington look at the
external sector of the economy (p. 141-66). A particularly useful feature is the
inclusion of references at the end of each of the chapters, plus a select
bibliography on the economy of Barbados (p. 167-95).

**The Caribbean community in the 1980s: report by a group of Caribbean
experts.**
See item no. 31.

**The economic geography of Barbados: a study of the relationships
between environmental variations and economic development.**
See item no. 70.

Effects of the tourist industry in Barbados, West Indies.
See item no. 197.

A structural analysis of the Barbados economy, 1968, with an application to the tourist industry.
See item no. 198.

Perceived effects of international inflation and recession on tourism in Barbados.
See item no. 212.

Tourism and development: the case of Barbados, West Indies.
See item no. 214.

Caribbean tourism markets: structures and strategies.
See item no. 218.

The future of tourism in the Eastern Caribbean.
See item no. 219.

The transformation and consolidation of the corporate plantation economy in Barbados 1860-1977.
See item no. 349.

Panama money in Barbados 1900-1920.
See item no. 355.

Ownership and control of resources in Barbados, 1834 to the present.
See item no. 475.

Land exploitative activities and economic patterns in a Barbados village.
See item no. 483.

Barbados and St. Lucia: a comparative analysis of social and economic development.
See item no. 495.

Caribbean patterns: a political and economic study of the contemporary Caribbean.
See item no. 539.

The Caribbean Commission.
See item no. 542.

Understanding Third World politics and economics.
See item no. 544.

The ecology of development administration in Jamaica, Trinidad and Tobago, and Barbados.
See item no. 575.

The external debt of Barbados.
See item no. 654.

The construction industry in the economy of Barbados 1960-1980.
See item no. 657.

Women, work and development: Barbados 1946-1970.
See item no. 728.

Wages, productivity and employment in Barbados 1949-82.
See item no. 731.

The Caribbean basin to the year 2000: demographic, economic and resource-use trends in seventeen countries.
See item no. 739.

Statistical Yearbook.
See item no. 740.

An analysis of the housing market in Barbados.
See item no. 788.

Select bibliography on the economy of Barbados.
See item no. 958.

Finance, Banking and Trade

632 The proposed national commercial bank for Barbados: an assessment.
Frank Alleyne. *Bulletin of Eastern Caribbean Affairs*, vol. 3, nos. 3-4 (1977), p. 12-16.

The author, who at the time of publication was a lecturer in economics at the Cave Hill Campus of the University of the West Indies, considers the government's intention at that time to amalgamate all public sector credit institutions except the Central Bank of Barbados, to form a national commercial bank. Given the traditional domination of the commercial banking sector by large foreign banking concerns, it is argued that special powers should be given to the proposed national bank.

633 A critical evaluation of the impact of credit union activity upon the social and economic development of Barbados 1961-83.
Frank Alleyne. *Bulletin of Eastern Caribbean Affairs*, vol. 11, nos. 4-5 (Sept.-Dec. 1985), p. 41-47.

Traces the growth of credit unions in Barbados, particularly during the last five years. Today the movement has gained more respectability and is viewed as more than simply a sophisticated 'meeting turn'. Additionally, with increased professionalism, better surroundings and the encouragement of trade unions and government, credit unions should continue to play a vibrant role in the economy, especially catering to the needs of young people. Their greatest strength, however, seems to lie in their ability to offer loans at attractive rates to those otherwise disqualified on grounds of income from borrowing from commercial banks.

634   **The stock of fixed capital in Barbados, 1958-1981: some exploratory estimates.**
Daniel O. Boamah.   *Central Bank of Barbados Economic Review*, vol. 11, no. 3 (1984), p. 8-20.

Presents the results of an effort to estimate the stock of fixed capital in Barbados, that is the sum total, at constant prices, of all past investments in plant, machinery, buildings and other capital assets. An estimate of $1.21 billion in 1981 at real 1972 values is obtained. The limitations of the perpetual inventory method employed are also noted.

635   **Commercial banking.**
Edmond Bradshaw.   *Bajan* (June-July 1985), p. 12-15.

This article looks at the histories of and services currently provided by three of Barbados' leading banking institutions: the Canadian Imperial Bank of Commerce, the Bank of Nova Scotia and the Barbados National Bank.

636   **Tax incentives for offshore banks in Barbados: a survey of the provisions of the Off-Shore Banking Act, 1979-1981.**
Andrew Burgess.   *Canadian Tax Journal*, vol. 33, no. 3 (1985), p. 559-66.

The Act passed in 1979 seeks to encourage the development of Barbados as an offshore financial centre, principally through the provision of tax reductions, exemptions and other benefits to offshore banks and investors in offshore banks in Barbados. Details of the precise tax benefits available under the Off-Shore Banking Act are given in this paper.

637   **The regulatory framework of accounting in Barbados.**
Robertine Chaderton.   Bridgetown: Carib Printers, 1986. 128p.

Based on financial accounting and auditing courses taught at the University of the West Indies, Cave Hill, this book is targeted not only at students but also fellow professionals. The need for such a publication is apparent given the recent effects of the Companies Act 1982-84 and difficulties in interpretation of various British, North American and international standards. All these are discussed in an easy pedagogical style with several illustrations drawn from the balance sheets of well-known Barbadian enterprises, including: Goddards, Barbados Shipping and Trading, Plantations, Banks Breweries, Industrial Development Corporation, Rediffusion and the utility companies. A brief historical section traces the development of accountancy in the island from the formation of Thomas & Bovell in the 1860s, and a financial statement from Drax Hall Plantation in 1853 is also reproduced.

638   **The terms of trade experience of Barbados and Trinidad and Tobago 1955-1980.**
Harold Codrington, Carlos Holder.   *Central Bank of Barbados Economic Review*, vol. 11, no. 1 (1984), p. 15-23.

Most poor countries exhibit a high degree of openness, since they depend on the export of surplus commodities to finance the import of raw materials, machinery and foreign consumer goods. This paper considers the terms of trade ratio (export price index to import price index) of Barbados and Trinidad and Tobago over a twenty-five-year period. It is concluded that export expansion is the most feasible way to combat the deteriorating net terms of trade.

639 Doing business with Barbados.
South, no. 72 (Oct. 1986), p. 57-64.

Despite the inaccuracy of an introductory map which depicts both Speightstown and Holetown as located well inland, this survey provides an up-to-date overview of the economic and political complexion of the country. The account includes an interview with Prime Minister Errol Barrow, who swept to power in the May 1986 elections. There are also sections on tourism, trade, offshore finance and agricultural diversification.

640 15 helpful years.
Bajan (April 1985), p. 20-24.

Examines the record of the Barbados Development Bank since its establishment in April 1969, following the transferral of the financial function of the former Barbados Development Board to the Development Bank.

641 The governor from Wall Street.
Bajan (March-April 1986), p. 10-11.

Examines the policies and views of Dr. Courtney Blackman, the Central Bank's first and, at the time of writing, only governor.

642 The Barbadian monetary base.
Michael Howard. *Bulletin of Eastern Caribbean Affairs*, vol. 4, no. 6 (1979), p. 5-7.

The author aims to explain the Barbadian monetary base and to examine whether it is an appropriate target variable for monetary policy. The relationship between the monetary base and the balance of payments is also considered.

643 The fiscal system of Barbados 1946-1965.
Michael Howard. Cave Hill, St. Michael, Barbados: Institute of Social and Economic Research, University of the West Indies, 1979. 84p. bibliog. (Occasional Paper, no. 12).

A technical paper which empirically examines patterns of revenue and expenditure during the final phase of colonial rule. The author highlights the clumsiness and excessive cost of maintaining a largely centralized bureaucratic administration at the expense of health, education, social and welfare services. In the period under review, the skewed nature and under-reporting of income tended to militate against the maximization of revenue from personal taxation, leading in turn to a corresponding overutilization of customs and excise duties as an alternative fiscal measure. The perceived need and mechanisms to balance accounts naturally precluded any modern system of deficit financing.

644   **Post-war public policy in Barbados 1946-1979.**

Michael Howard. *Social and Economic Studies*, vol. 31, no. 3 (1982), p. 95-128.

An historical inerpretation of public policy in Barbados during the post-war period is provided. The account is divided into two periods, the colonial era (1946-1966) and the post-independence era (1966-1979). The paper contains a wealth of information concerning taxation and fiscal and budgetary policy.

645   **Investing in Barbados.**

Tony Hoyos, Vivien Morgan. *Canadian Tax Journal*, vol. 33, no. 3 (1985), p. 550-59.

Provides a summary of the legislation which surrounds the provision of tax incentives to firms and banks, and also reviews the general business environment of Barbados.

646   **Inside the Central Bank.**

Bajan (March-April 1986), p. 17-21.

Considers the functions of the Central Bank of Barbados, established on 2 May 1972. Today the Central Bank staff has grown to 1,980, and at the time of writing, the bank was just about to move to its new ten-storey building in the Church Village area of Bridgetown.

647   **The foreign sales corporation and its relevance to Barbados.**

David King. *Central Bank of Barbados Economic Review*, vol. 12, no. 1 (1985), p. 20-22.

In November 1984, the United States Department of the Treasury announced that Barbados was eligible for the establishment of Foreign Sales Corporations (FSC). FSCs, subsidiaries of United States manufacturers, gain tax exemption on 32 per cent of their foreign trade income. By May 1985, some 180 FSCs had been attracted to Barbados.

648   **Public policy.**

Maurice A. Odle. In: *Caribbean economy: dependence and backwardness*. Edited by George L. Beckford. Mona, Jamaica: Institute of Social and Economic Research, 1975, p. 130-46.

This chapter examines public policy measures, especially those concerned with fiscal policy, as they have affected dependence over time. The national insurance scheme and the local government system of Barbados are specifically discussed in this account.

649   **Credit and the agricultural sector in Barbados.**

David Sheppard. *Bulletin of Eastern Caribbean Affairs*, vol. 2, no. 12 (Feb. 1977), p. 13-19.

Highlights the generally poor performance of agriculture in Barbados during the first half of the 1970s. Sugar production had declined with respect to land under cultivation, tons per acre and overall yield. In the non-sugar sector, with the exception of meat and dairy products, there had been a similar decline. Suggested reasons for the failure include a plethora of governmental, banking and other institutions involved in agriculture, inadequate financial support of the sector in terms of budgeting and loans, low wages, changes in consumer tastes due to tourism, and the westernization of the local diet. Proposals for the amelioration of this state of affairs include a more scientific approach for gauging the agricultural situation, the formulation of programmes by experts from a variety of disciplines, and ongoing research in this neglected area.

650 **Aspects of finance and the balance of payments in the Barbadian economy.**
A. Wendell A. McClean. *Bulletin of Eastern Caribbean Affairs*, vol. 4, no. 5 (1978), p. 20-25.

The relationships between the balance of payments, public budgeting, savings and investment are examined. It is concluded that the balance of payments problem must be dealt with via a combination of direct methods of foreign exchange rationing, export promotion, socially acceptable methods of expenditure reduction and the redistribution of income in favour of those who have a higher propensity to spend locally.

651 **Some evidence on the demand for money in a small open economy: Barbados.**
A. Wendell A. McClean. *Social and Economic Studies*, vol. 31, no. 3 (1982), p. 155-70.

An investigation into the existence and form of the money-demand function in Barbados is presented, using data for the years 1966 and 1979. Although somewhat technical, the paper should be of interest to those concerned with finance and banking.

652 **Protection in the manufacturing sector of Barbados 1960-80.**
Peter Whitehall. *Central Bank of Barbados Economic Review*, vol. 11, no. 2 (1984), p. 9-23.

This study quantifies the level of protection available to manufacturing firms as a result of tariffs and forms of tax relief. It contains some useful background information on the growth of manufacturing in Barbados since the 1960s.

653 **Development of the financial sector in Barbados 1946-1980.**
De Lisle Worrell, Ronald Prescod. *Central Bank of Barbados Economic Review*, vol. 10, no. 2 (1983), p. 9-26.

Covers the evolution and nature of financial institutions and the financial system in Barbados in the post-war period.

654 **The external debt of Barbados.**
Mary G. Zephirin. *Central Bank of Barbados Quarterly Review*,
vol. 7, no. 4 (1980), p. 24-67.
Discusses the external debt situation of Barbados, in terms of the history of public
debt growth since 1960 and the country's current foreign debt situation.

War and trade in the West Indies 1739-1763.
See item no. 315.

A history of Barbados 1625-1685.
See item no. 344.

The Caribbean Basin Initiative and the Commonwealth Caribbean.
See item no. 592.

Barbados development plan 1983-1988.
See item no. 616.

The Caribbean Basin Initiative.
See item no. 625.

Financing industrial development in Barbados.
See item no. 659

**Report of the committee appointed to report on the action to be taken to
establish a deep water harbour in Barbados.**
See item no. 716.

**Report to his excellency the Governor on the deep water harbour at
Bridgetown.**
See item no. 720.

The Port of Bridgetown handbook.
See item no. 721.

**Handbook for international trade and development statistics: 1984
supplement.**
See item no. 741.

Industry

655 Our bubbling budding oil industry.

Mark D. Alleyne. *Bajan and South Caribbean*, no. 358 (Sept. 1983), p. 4-5.

In Barbados, petroleum exploration dates back to the 1870s. The complexity of the geological structure makes the assessment of oil reserves difficult. This article notes that the drilling operations were nationalized in 1982 with the setting up of the National Petroleum Corporation. It also discusses the Woodbourne oil field and the likelihood of similar discoveries elsewhere on the island.

656 Barbados Industrial Development Corporation development plan.

Bridgetown: Industrial Development Corporation, [n.d.]. 39p.

This, the first development plan of the Industrial Development Corporation, deals with the late 1970s and the early 1980s. There are sections covering the structure of the manufacturing sector of the economy, goals and objectives, development strategy, factors of industrial development, the handicraft industry, sources and resources.

657 The construction industry in the economy of Barbados 1960-1980.

Carlos Brathwaite. *Central Bank of Barbados Economic Review*, vol. 9, no. 2 (1982), p. 10-29.

A consideration of the role of the construction sector in the economy of Barbados since 1960. The contribution of the sector to Gross Domestic Product (GDP) is discussed, followed by the factors affecting its growth. Subsequently, the role of labour and capital in the sector, the costs of the building industry, and the influence of construction costs on the general levels of prices and the balance of payments are all explored.

658 **Secondary agrobased industries: ECCM and Barbados.**
Jeffrey Dellimore, Judy Whitehead. Mona, Jamaica: Institute of
Social and Economic Research, University of the West Indies,
1984. 296p. bibliog. (Caribbean Technology Policy Studies Project
Series).

The authors investigate the problem of the (largely unnecessary) regional
dependence on imported foodstuffs by focusing on production and consumption
patterns in the islands of Barbados, Antigua, St. Kitts, St. Lucia and Montserrat.
There are surveys of a small number of mainly secondary agrobased industries
and engineering services. Complementary data are also assembled from various
territorial censuses and household budgetary surveys. A content analysis of
advertisements appearing in local newspapers is conducted as well in order to
examine the manipulation of consumer taste. Readers may be surprised to learn
that Barbados imports some bananas and sugar, peas and rice, and even
quantities of flying fish!

659 **Financing industrial development in Barbados.**
Andrew S. Downes. *Bulletin of Eastern Caribbean Affairs*, vol. 5,
no. 4 (1979), p. 1-10.

The author observes that in 1976-77 approximately ninety-four per cent of
investment capital in new industrial endeavours was provided by foreign
investors. Although it is accepted that small, open economies like Barbados need
foreign investments to some extent, it is suggested that the phasing out of the
dependence on foreign finance should be a central aim of governmental financial
policy.

660 **A vital industry battles the recession.**
Norma Faria. *Bajan* (May-June 1985), p. 22-27.

Stresses that tourism is the island's most significant economic sector, despite its
current recessionary problems.

661 **Manufacturing: a beleaguered industry.**
Norma Faria. *Bajan* (Nov.-Dec. 1985), p. 16-18.

Includes a brief résumé of the history of industrial development in Barbados in
the post-war period, before examining the effects of the current spate of closures
and reduced employment. Considers the prospect that, in the future, new
manufacturing concerns are likely to be less labour-intensive, a fact which
the government will have to consider carefully in evaluating its policy of
'industrialization by invitation'. This is a short but useful summary.

662 **Will light industry pull us through?**
Debra Hughes. *Bajan and South Caribbean*, no. 335 (Oct. 1981),
p. 12-22.

Although this is a rather generalized view of current industrialization trends in
Barbados, it includes some informative photographs.

663 **The industrialisation of the British West Indies.**
W. Arthur Lewis. *Caribbean Economic Review*, vol. 2, no. 1
(1950), p. 1-61.

A seminal paper which extols the virtues of development by industrialization in the Caribbean. Accordingly, the greater part of the paper is given over to the identification of the types of industries that might be introduced in the region. These are classified into three sub-sets according to their assessed favourability. The latter part of this early paper is given over to a discussion of what are referred to as the 'techniques of industrialisation', that is the economic needs and requirements of such a path.

664 **Multinational corporations and black power.**
Harry G. Matthews. Cambridge, Massachusetts: Schenkman,
1976. 124p. bibliog.

A research monograph which seeks to examine the racial implications of multinational businesses in the Eastern Caribbean, drawing on the cases of Barbados and Trinidad and Tobago. Unfortunately, the volume lacks an index.

665 **Regional industrial programming in CARICOM.**
Anthony Payne. In: *Dependency under challenge: the political economy of the Commonwealth Caribbean*. Edited by Anthony Payne, Paul Sutton. Manchester, England: Manchester University Press, 1984, p. 131-51.

Describes the initial progress in industrialization in the Commonwealth Caribbean during the post-war period, and the attempts which have been made to put into practice the concept of regional industrial development. The latter is an avowed intention of the Caribbean Community, in order to encourage the economies achieved by large-scale production for the wider regional market.

666 **Industrial development and urban planning in Barbados.**
Robert B. Potter. *Geography*, vol. 66, no. 3 (1981), p. 225-28.

This short article outlines the progress of industrial development since 1959, with particular reference to the major industrial parks established by the Industrial Development Corporation. Trends in industrial development are finally related to recent urban planning policies, particularly that of decentralization from metropolitan Bridgetown.

667 **Seventy-five years of light and power.**
Bajan (April-May 1986), p. 24-31.

Considers the history of electric power generation in Barbados, specifically from 17 June 1911 when the Barbados Electricity Supply Corporation was established.

The tourist industry in Barbados: a socio-economic assessment.
See item no. 206.

The other side of paradise: foreign control in the Caribbean.
See item no. 593.

The Commonwealth Caribbean: the integration experience . . .
See item no. 600.

Barbados development plan 1983-1988.
See item no. 616.

The economic development of Barbados, 1946-1980.
See item no. 618.

Transnational corporations and Caribbean inequalities.
See item no. 620.

Character of Caribbean economy.
See item no. 621.

The economy of Barbados 1946-1980.
See item no. 631.

The foreign sales corporation and its relevance to Barbados.
See item no. 647.

Protection in the manufacturing sector of Barbados 1960-80.
See item no. 652.

Industrial growth and employment in a small developing country: the case
of Barbados 1955 to 1980.
See item no. 726.

Barbados Industrial Development Corporation Annual Report.
See item no. 923.

Agriculture and Fishing

668 **Agricultural co-operation in CARICOM.**
W. Andrew Axline. In: *Dependency under challenge: the political economy of the Commonwealth Caribbean.* Edited by Anthony Payne, Paul Sutton. Manchester, England: Manchester University Press, 1984, p. 152-73.
Starts by arguing that 'the fundamental problem of Caribbean dependence and underdevelopment remains the agricultural sector'. The author looks at the efforts which have been made to overcome this, and at some of the main issues currently facing the agricultural sector in the region.

669 **The Barbados fishing industry: the development and economic importance of a fishing industry in the tropics.**
Roslyn Annette Bain. MA dissertation, McGill University, Montreal, 1962. 86p.
Attempts a general assessment of the fishing industry in Barbados, looking at its nature, scope and development. Issues of balanced diet and adequate employment are subsidiary themes. The dissertation includes some interesting photographs, although the text is by now very dated.

670 **Peasant agriculture in Barbados: a case study of a rural system.**
David M. Brack. MA dissertation, McGill University, Montreal, 1964. 148p.
Endeavours to explain the landscape of the peasant agricultural system, identifying the factors that influence it and appraising its overall efficacy. The dissertation is based on two months' field work in the summer of 1960, among small-holders in the village of Hillaby.

671   **Agricultural research and agricultural development in small plantation economies: the case of the West Indies.**
Carlton G. Davis.   *Social and Economic Studies*, vol. 24 (1975), p. 117-49.

Set in the context of the 'Green Revolution' based on research systems which have developed high-yielding cereal varieties, this paper examines the organizational and institutional frameworks within which agricultural research is carried out in the West Indies. Indigenous research systems are required which will help to 'break the dynamic self-perpetuating stranglehold of the plantation economy' within the region.

672   **Markets and marketing in Barbados.**
J. Donoghue.   MA dissertation, McGill University, Montreal, 1965. 150p.

This economic geographical study examines the distribution of local agricultural commodities. The author urges strongly that every effort should be made to produce agricultural items locally and to improve marketing systems to facilitate this.

673   **Long range fishing vessels.**
Norma Faria.   *Bajan* (March 1985), p. 12-15.

The introduction in the 1970s of larger launches fitted with ice holds and sleeping accommodation in the cabin is examined. Such craft can stay out on the fishing banks for a week or longer. It is estimated that there are presently 35-40 such 'ice boats' out of a total fishing fleet of 350 vessels.

674   **Sugar: sweet or sour.**
Norma Faria.   *Bajan* (Aug.-Sept. 1985), p. 12-13.

A brief survey of the problems and prospects of the sugar industry, focusing on the views of sugar economist Gerry Hagelberg who has acted as an advisor to the Barbadian government. Hagelberg's views are outlined in 'Some current questions of sugar policy and implementation in Barbados' (q.v.)

675   **Fishing fleet safety record at stake.**
Norma Faria.   *Bajan* (March-April 1986), p. 36-38.

Written after a period when eight long-range fishing vessels or 'ice boats' ran into difficulties within one week, this short paper looks at some of the problems of safety facing the modern fishing fleet.

676   **Are alternative crops viable?**
Norma Faria.   *Bajan* (Sept.-Oct. 1986), p. 5-9.

Observing at the outset that 'a drive through what was once a blanket of sugar cane fields, covering the country's interior, will today reveal several crops such as cotton, hot peppers, watermelons, eggplants – even red ginger lily flowers', the author ranges widely over matters concerning agricultural diversification. In concluding, she stresses the need for governmental leadership in promoting non-sugar crops in the immediate future.

207

677   **The sugar industry in Barbados during the seventeenth century.**
J. H. Galloway. *Journal of Tropical Geography*, vol. 19 (1964),
p. 35-41.

An interesting paper which, with the aid of three maps and two black-and-white plates, describes the introduction of sugar cane, the plantation system, cultivation of the crop particularly by the cane-hole method, the manufacture of sugar and the extent of plantation agriculture and sugar cane cultivation in the 17th century.

678   **The modern plantation in the Third World.**
G. E. Graham with I. Floering.   London: Croom Helm, 1985.
256p. bibliog.

Barbadian plantations are considered in several places in this recent volume which primarily argues that the plantation estate is an efficient unit of agricultural production in less developed countries.

679   **Crop diversification in Barbados.**
E. G. B. Gooding.   *World Crops*, vol. 20, no. 1 (1968), p. 34-39.

The difficulties of breaking the one-crop economic dependence of Barbados are stressed, as is the need to reduce food import bills. The author reports on research conducted into increasing the yield per acre of yams, sweet potatoes and corn. Several tables and black-and-white photographs are included.

680   **Progress of agricultural diversification in Barbados.**
E. G. B. Gooding.   *World Crops*, vol. 23 (1971), p. 186-89.

A further report on the progress of agricultural diversification in Barbados in which it is argued that in the five years previous to writing, a distinct change in the domestic climate of opinion had occurred in favour of crop diversification. The author presents sections on cotton, root crops, maize, potatoes, peanuts, vegetables, meat production and dairying, along with associated marketing problems.

681   **Land tenure and transmission in rural Barbados.**
Sidney M. Greenfield.   *Anthropological Quarterly*, vol. 33 (1960),
p. 165-76.

This article is based on data collected from a survey conducted in the rural village of Enterprise Hall in the parish of St. George in the years 1956-57. The traditional systems of land tenure, use and transmission among the rural folk of the island are discussed; these are based on a principle of seed to seed inheritance.

682 The organization of large scale agricultural labor in Barbados and
Minas Gerais, Brazil: a comparison of two responses to
emancipation.
Sidney M. Greenfield. *Anthropological Quarterly*, vol. 40 no. 4
(1969), p. 201-16.

In this expanded version of a paper presented at the annual meeting of the
American Anthropological Association in 1963, Greenfield compares the systems
of organizing large-scale agricultural labour that are employed in Barbados and in
the *Zona da Mata* of the state of Minas Gerais in Brazil. Both areas specialized in
the production of agricultural staples from their first settlement, producing sugar
and coffee respectively. Similarly, in both areas, the planters depended primarily
upon slave labour. With emancipation, new systems of recruiting and organizing
agricultural labour were needed; in Barbados it took the form of institutionalized
wage labour, whilst in Minas Gerais a form of sharecropping developed.

683 Some current questions of sugar policy and implementation in
Barbados.
Gerry B. Hagelberg. *Central Bank of Barbados Economic
Review*, vol. 12, no. 1 (1985), p. 23-30.

Considers sugar policy in the period since 1980. The following topics are studied:
environmental factors, scale and market constraints, structural and social aspects,
land productivity, the industry's viability, marginal costs and returns, and income
redistribution of crop returns.

684 The history of arrowroot production in Barbados and the Chalky
Mount Arrowroot Growers' Association, a peasant marketing
experiment that failed.
Jerome S. Handler. *Journal of the Barbados Museum and
Historical Society*, vol. 31, no. 3 (1965), p. 131-52.

Over the years, efforts to diversify agriculture away from sugar have resulted in
different crops being introduced, generally on a highly localized basis. Arrowroot
was thus introduced into the village of Chalky Mount in the Scotland District. The
Chalky Mount Arrowroot Growers' Association, in existence from 1936 to 1942,
was the first attempt in Barbados to produce an organization for the processing
and marketing of a crop grown by small farmers or 'peasants'.

685 Some aspects of work organization on sugar plantations in
Barbados.
Jerome S. Handler. *Ethnology*, vol. 4, no. 1 (1965), p. 16-38.

Opens with the observation that there have been few studies dealing with the
types of tasks plantation workers perform and the ways in which they are
organized to perform them. The materials for the paper were drawn from the
plantations for which the inhabitants of Chalky Mount, a village in the Scotland
District, work. There are sections on plantation staff and the workers, work tasks
and the agricultural cycle, earnings and employment, and the Barbados Workers'
Union and labour shortages.

686 **Small-scale sugar cane farming in Barbados.**
Jerome S. Handler. *Ethnology*, vol. 5 (1966), p. 264-83.

The author seeks to elucidate some of the prominent social and cultural aspects of sugar cane farming on small agricultural holdings. It is demonstrated that the Barbadian small farmer 'is strongly oriented toward the acquisition of cash and is deeply immersed in a market economy. Small-scale sugar cane farming in Barbados cannot be understood without taking these factors into consideration and without a full appreciation of the small farmer's system of cash needs'.

687 **A reassessment of the 'traditional' in Caribbean small-scale agriculture.**
Theo L. Hills, Stanley Iton. *Caribbean Geography*, vol. 1, no. 1 (1983), p. 24-35.

Noting that the small-scale sector has only become significant in the Caribbean landscape since emancipation and more particularly over the past century, the authors' central argument is that Caribbean small-scale farmers are practical ecologists with an overall record of success. Thus, what are seen as the limitations of modernization programmes for such agricultural systems along industrialized lines are examined in this paper.

688 **Computer simulation of combine harvesting and handling of sugar cane in Barbados.**
Winston O'Neale Harvey. PhD dissertation, Michigan State University, East Lansing, Michigan, 1983. 226p. maps. bibliog.

Two computer simulation models are developed to examine the field sub-system and the factory yard sub-system of sugar cane handling. The broad aim of the study is to improve the efficiency of the combine harvesting of sugar cane in Barbados.

689 **The spatial structure of Barbadian peasant agriculture.**
Janet D. Henshall. MSc dissertation, McGill University, Montreal, 1964. 143p.

This interesting and well-researched thesis is based on field work carried out between May and September 1963. It examines the development of peasant agriculture, geographical conditions, the ecology of individual crops, land use patterns and the recognition of regions. A stratified sample of areas under peasant agriculture is used in connection with a questionnaire survey.

690 **The demographic factor in the structure of agriculture in Barbados.**
Janet D. Henshall. *Transactions of the Institute of British Geographers*, vol. 38 (1966), p. 183-95.

Based on data collected as a part of Henshall's MSc dissertation. *The spatial structure of Barbadian peasant agriculture* (q.v.), a factor analysis is undertaken in relation to thirty-two farm characteristics. In conclusion, it is argued that both the peasant farming and plantation systems are strongly influenced by the demographic variable. Thus, the influence of metropolitan Bridgetown on the pattern of agriculture is stronger than either physical or institutional factors.

691   **Some structural characteristics of peasant agriculture in Barbados.**
Janet D. Henshall, Leslie J. King.   *Economic Geography*, vol. 42,
no. 1 (1966), p. 74-84.

Also based on Henshall's *The spatial structure of Barbadian peasant agriculture*
(q.v.) and again using multivariable statistical procedures, this paper discusses the
main features of peasant agriculture. Perhaps of rather more methodological than
substantive interest.

692   **Farmers of 'Little England'.**
Janet D. Henshall.   *Geographical Magazine*, vol. 11, no. 5 (1967),
p. 398-406.

Stresses the possible contribution of the peasant farmer at a time of agricultural
diversification. By local legal definition, such small-holdings comprise less than
twenty-five acres, but most are in fact less than five acres and have at least
seventy-five per cent of their land given over to sugar cane. The author also
discusses current economic trends and chattel housing. The article is accompanied
by some fine colour photographs.

693   **Gender versus ethnic pluralism in Caribbean agriculture.**
Janet D. Henshall.   In: *Geography and ethnic pluralism*. Edited
by Colin Clarke, David Ley, Ceri Peach.   London: George Allen
& Unwin, 1984, p. 173-92.

Starts from the argument that the demands of colonial agriculture created the
basis of the ethnic pluralism found in the contemporary Caribbean. Women have
been part of this process of capitalist expansion throughout, a point reflected in
much previous research. Although based mainly on the cases of Trinidad and
Nevis, Barbados is referred to quite frequently. In conclusion it is maintained that
sexual pluralism has been consistently overlooked in studies of small-scale farming
in the Caribbean.

694   **Resource development in the Caribbean.**
Introduced by Theo Hills.   Montreal: Centre for Developing Area
Studies, McGill University, 1972. 337p. bibliog.

The edited proceedings of a multidisciplinary seminar held in the 1970-71
academic session at McGill University to familiarize and bring together
researchers working on Caribbean development and to stimulate collaborative
ventures in the future. Topics range from marine resources to theatre. Specific to
Barbados are papers on 'The potential of horticultural development' by G.
Mason, and 'A pilot study of moisture conditions' by K. Swami. The first argues
for greater agricultural diversification and import substitution, with more input in
policy making by the small farmer. The second calls for increased sophistication in
rainfall measurement techniques.

695   **The Barbados sugar industry fights back.**

Colin Hudson.   *Sugar y Azucar* (Dec. 1984), p. 14-22.

This short article covers the recent history of sugar production in Barbados before describing some of the adaptations of sugar-related equipment that have occurred. Includes modifications to combine harvesters, reaping aids, planters and loaders.

696   **The availability of soil water: with reference to studies with sugarcane growing in clay soils in Barbados.**

J. C. Hudson.   PhD dissertation, University of the West Indies, St. Augustine, Trinidad, 1967. 142p. bibliog.

A detailed thesis describing experimental work and field studies designed to examine the relations between sugar cane growth rate and soil-water deficit. For a given soil-water deficit, growth rate was shown to increase as a result of small showers of rain at night or cloudy periods during the day, and to decrease as the root system ages.

697   **Plantation and peasant farm – Barbados 1627-1960.**

Frank Cecil Innes.   PhD dissertation, McGill University, Montreal, 1967. 291p. maps. bibliog.

Examines historically the division of land in Barbados between plantation and peasant farmers. Employs published topographical maps and other descriptive data to build up the picture of estates from 1627. The thesis commences with a useful introduction to the relief, rainfall, soils and general physical geography of Barbados.

698   **Peasant agriculture in Barbados: a sample study.**

John Peter Mbogua.   MA dissertation, McGill University, Montreal, 1961. 152p. maps. bibliog.

Stresses that only a few acres of marginal land are available for the peasantry, as most of the arable land is used for the production of sugar cane on a large commercial scale. The peasant agricultural system also revolves around sugar cane, which is the main cash crop, although other crops are grown, chiefly for subsistence. It is concluded that the only solution to the problems of peasant agriculture lies in comprehensive land reform.

699   **Fish hunters of the Caribbean.**

Henri Menjaud.   *Geographical Magazine*, vol. 11, no. 5 (1967), p. 386-97.

At the time of writing in 1967, eighty per cent of all the fish eaten in the Caribbean was salted cod brought from the North Atlantic. At that stage, major offshore (pelagic) fish reserves had never been tapped and the marketing system was poorly developed. This article discusses the Caribbean Fishery Development Project, carried out by the Food and Agriculture Organisation on behalf of the United Nations Development Programme, which was based in Bridgetown, Barbados.

700　**Crisis in the Caribbean sugar industry.**
　　Janet D. Momsen.　*Geography*, vol. 56 (1971), p. 338-40.
The crisis prevailing in the sugar industry since the late 1960s is chronicled in this short paper. It is maintained that specific problems have been brought about by labour difficulties, rising costs of production, uncertainty as to future preferential sugar quotas and unfavourable weather conditions in 1970. Poor harvests, the use of migrant workers, the process of mechanization, labour dissatisfaction, cane fires and controlled burning are all discussed with respect to Barbados.

701　**Peasant farming in Barbados.**
　　Cecil J. Morrison.　*The Farmer*, (Jan.-March 1951), p. 31-35.
Noting that in Barbados the term 'peasant farm' refers to any cultivated holding of ten acres and under, this paper outlines the characteristics of such units, focusing for instance on their patterns of land use, systems of land tenure, the outlook of peasant farmers, the main crops grown, improvement measures, agricultural credit and cooperation.

702　**Rainfall evaporation and sugar cane yields in Barbados.**
　　J. S. Oguntoyinbo.　MSc dissertation, McGill University,
　　Montreal, 1964. 72p. maps. bibliog.
The empirical research, based on thirteen plantations, demonstrates the significant statistical association that exists between sugar yields and moisture deficiency.

703　**Evapotranspiration and sugar cane yields in Barbados.**
　　J. S. Oguntoyinbo.　*Journal of Tropical Geography*, vol. 22
　　(1966), p. 38-48.
Based on the author's MSc dissertation *Rainfall evaporation and sugar cane yields in Barbados* (q.v.), this paper presents the findings in a shorter and somewhat more accessible format.

704　**The cultivation of food crops in Barbados.**
　　J. O. Oyelese.　MA dissertation, McGill University, Montreal,
　　1964. 179p. maps. bibliog.
Considers the cultivation of commonly grown root crops (ground provisions), fruit trees, vegetables and seasonings in Barbados. Based on a random sample survey of ten per cent of the area of peasant agricultural practice, fifty-eight sample units were selected to cover the island. It is concluded that the production of food crops falls short of potential, due principally to the emphasis placed on sugar cane.

705　**Some aspects of food crop cultivation in the plantations of
　　Barbados, West Indies.**
　　J. O. Oyelese.　*Nigerian Geographical Journal*, vol. 9 (1966),
　　p. 55-70.
Argues that hopes for increased local food production and agricultural diversification depend on the plantations rather than on the peasant farmers. In fact, in

213

Barbados, a law passed in 1938 and amended in 1942, 'The Local Food Production (Defence) Order' exists specifically to encourage plantations to devote some of their land to the cultivation of food crops. The author considers the success of this order in promoting crop diversification.

706   **The impact of agricultural diversification policies in Barbados in the post-war period.**
Bishnodak Persaud, Lakshmi Persaud.   *Social and Economic Studies*, vol. 17 (1968), p. 353-64.

Endeavours to assess the degree to which progress has been made in agricultural diversification up to 1965. It is concluded that little or no progress has been made to date and the second part of the paper advances reasons for this lack of success. These are given as: lack of knowledge, marketing needs, existing farming structure, smallness of farms and the shortage of underground water.

707   **The need for and the possibilities of agricultural diversification in Barbados.**
Lakshmi Persaud.   PhD thesis, Queen's University Belfast, 1969. 469p. bibliog.

A scholarly examination of the issues involved in the process of encouraging greater agricultural diversification in Barbados.

708   **Climatic control of distribution and cultivation of sugar cane.**
S. Ivan Smith.   PhD dissertation, McGill University, Montreal, 1962. 137p. bibliog.

Seeks to explain the distribution and cultivation of sugar cane by climatic factors. The existing literature is first reviewed and then climatic variables such as solar energy, sunshine, light and moisture are assessed.

709   **Important issues of agricultural diversification and its implementation in Barbados.**
Basil G. F. Springer.   *Central Bank of Barbados Economic Review*, vol. 12, no. 3 (1985), p. 24-30.

Sets out to identify the major issues involved in the promotion of agricultural diversification in Barbados. The author also makes recommendations for the implementation of a stable agricultural diversification system, stressing the need for public sector support in the early stages of such a programme.

710   **Sugar cane varieties in Barbados: an historical review.**
G. C. Stevenson.   *Journal of the Barbados Museum and Historical Society*, vol. 26, no. 2 (1959), p. 67-92.

A detailed account of the varieties of sugar cane that have been grown in Barbados since sugar became the staple crop of the island in the 1640s, up to the time of varietal trends in commercial planting, inbreeding and cytogenetics research in the 1950s.

711 **Origins of Barbadian cane hole agriculture.**
David Watts. *Journal of the Barbados Museum and Historical
Society*, vol. 32 (1968), p. 143-51.

Describes the practice of planting sugar cane in square depressions, or 'holes'
approximately five feet in size, marked out by hand hoes. It is argued that the
system was introduced as an erosional control during the first decade of the 18th
century. The system, it is observed, controls downward soil wash, as any material
which moves accumulates in the holes.

Caribbean views of Caribbean land.
See item no. 62.

**A comparative study of some soil nutrients in the coralline sugarcane
soils of Barbados.**
See item no. 80.

Caribbean soils: a soil study for agricultural science.
See item no. 84.

The presugar era of European settlement in Barbados.
See item no. 348.

Land exploitative activities and economic patterns in a Barbados village.
See item no. 483.

Aspects of Barbados land tenure 1627-1663.
See item no. 550.

**Administering agricultural development through a public corporation:
the case of Barbados.**
See item no. 573.

Rural development in the Caribbean.
See item no. 615.

Barbados development plan 1983-1988.
See item no. 616.

The economic development of Barbados, 1946-1980.
See item no. 618.

Character of Caribbean economy.
See item no. 621.

**Marketing activities and household activities of country hawkers in
Barbados.**
See item no. 629.

The economy of Barbados, 1946-1980.
See item no. 631.

Credit and the agricultural sector in Barbados.
See item no. 649.

Agriculture and Fishing

Soil conservation and future land use in the Scotland District, Barbados.
See item no. 806.

Land use in the Scotland District, Barbados.
See item no. 812.

Transport

712 **The history of our roads.**
Warren Alleyne. *Bajan and South Caribbean*, no. 310 (Sept. 1979), p. 21-24.
This short article provides an historical overview of the development of roads in 17th-century Barbados, along with associated legislation. Ligon's and other maps are reproduced as illustrations.

713 **Barbados: utilities and communications.**
Bridgetown: Barbados Industrial Development Corporation, 1979. 30p.
Provides summary information on the basic utilities of electricity, water and gas along with telephone and telegram services, before presenting information on air, sea and road transport, and media and postal communications. The pamphlet is aimed principally at potential industrialists.

714 **Caribbean Airways is taking off.**
Bajan and South Caribbean, no. 368 (July 1984), p. 4-10.
A special cover feature examining the history of Caribbean Airways, the Barbadian national flag carrier, from its launch on 29 September 1970, through the problems of the Laker collapse in early 1982, to the introduction of the new scheduled service to Frankfurt in June 1984. Caribbean Airways carried a total of 34,519 passengers in 1983.

715   **Income redistribution through public transport in Barbados, 1955-1979.**
Harold Codrington.   *Bulletin of Eastern Caribbean Affairs*,
vol. 10, no. 5 (1984), p. 8-20.
It is argued that the Transport Board in Barbados has performed an income distributive role by keeping bus fares below cost. Government has been more concerned with the social value of public transport than with its financial viability. However, a shortage of buses and their poor condition have served to counter these potential welfare gains.

716   **Report of the committee appointed to report on the action to be taken to establish a deep water harbour in Barbados.**
Deep Water Harbour Committee, chaired by Frank
Walcott.   Bridgetown: Advocate Company, 1954. 26p.
The report of a prestigious committee established to examine the financial viability of a self-supporting deep water harbour for Barbados. In particular the committee endorsed most of the recommendations of Sir Douglas Ritchie, vice-chairman of the Port of London Authority, and his choice of a land reclamation scheme from two options set forth by the consultant engineers in 1947. Members also looked at the questions of levies, administration, labour, and repercussions of the harbour for the sugar industry. Six technical appendixes are added to the report, including the observations of an official delegation visiting the facilities offered by nearby Trinidad.

717   **The Barbados railway.**
W. E. L. Fletcher.   *Journal of the Barbados Museum and Historical Society*, vol. 28, no. 3 (1961), p. 86-98.
A jaunty and interesting historical account of the origins, development, operation and eventual demise of the Barbados railway system. The author gives details of the original Act of 1846, which provided for a railway from Bridgetown to Speightstown with several branches. However, this never came to fruition, and an Act of 1873 provided for a Bridgetown to St. Andrew line. This line opened from Bridgetown to Carrington in 1881 and was finally completed around 1882. The system eventually closed in 1937 owing to structural and financial problems. This is the text of a paper read to the members of the Barbados Museum and Historical Society on 28 February 1961. It includes eight black-and-white photographs of the railway in the 1880s and of rolling stock.

718   **Caribbean airline connectivity and development.**
Gary L. Gaile, Dean M. Hanink.   *Caribbean Geography*,
vol. 1, no. 4 (1984), p. 272-83.
This paper presents an analysis of the changing inter-island connectivity of the Caribbean airline network since 1934. By 1983, Bridgetown was jointly the third most connected airport, with nine non-stop links to other Caribbean airports.

719 **LIAT moves to improve service.**
Bajan (July-Aug. 1985), p. 11.

LIAT (Leeward Island Air Transport) serves twenty-two islands and is owned by the Caribbean Community (CARICOM) governments. This short article looks at its acquisition of new planes, its revenue from passenger traffic, cargo and small packages ('Quick pac service'), and its future plans.

720 **Report to his excellency the Governor on the deep water harbour at Bridgetown.**
P. Eric Millbourn. Bridgetown: Advocate Company, 1955. 6p.

A brief follow-up report to *Report of the committee appointed to report on the action to be taken to establish a deep water harbour in Barbados* (q.v.). A number of cost-cutting suggestions are made with respect to the deep water harbour construction proposals, including a reduction in water depth. However, the authorities are alerted to the fact that provision will be necessary for access roads and a berthing tug, points neglected in the earlier submission.

721 **The Port of Bridgetown handbook.**
Compiled by Monica Quintyne, Donald Marshall, edited by Monica Quintyne. Bridgetown: Barbados Port Authority, 1979. 37p. 2 maps.

An information booklet with twenty-two accompanying black-and-white photographs, containing technical and general details on port development, management, navigation and entry, pilotage and other services, bunkering, berthing, customs, security, coast guard, crews, salvage, storage and medical facilities, water, electricity, etc. There are also listings of ship chandlers, customs brokers, commercial warehouses, shipping agents and stevedore companies.

722 **The roads of Barbados.**
Bajan and South Caribbean, no. 310 (1979), p. 6-20.

After a highly vitriolic account of national misconceptions about roads, a brief history and critique of recent road building projects is provided. The article bemoans the emphasis placed on the East Coast Road, despite the lack of a Bridgetown ring road and a dual carriageway to the Grantley Adams Airport. Finally, problems of general road construction and maintenance are considered.

The pocket guide to the West Indies.
See item no. 181.

Caribbean cruise industry study.
See item no. 217.

Long range fishing vessels.
See item no. 673.

The 350th anniversary of Bridgetown.
See item no. 771.

Employment, Labour and Trade Unions

723 Barbados: the worker.
Bridgetown: Barbados Industrial Development Corporation, 1979. 20p.

Intended as a guide for potential industrial investors in the island, this small pamphlet includes sections on labour supply, employment levels, employers' organizations, workers' organizations, legislation and industrial relations.

724 Employment in Barbados.
G. Cumper. *Social and Economic Studies*, vol. 8, no. 2 (June 1959), p. 105-46.

In the regrettable absence of an economic history of the island, the author briefly traces employment patterns since the time of emancipation. In addition he provides data from a government-commissioned employment survey in 1955, which show increases in unemployment as a result of progress in technology, particularly among women, whose traditional job as domestics and seamstresses have similarly declined. The report from which the article is drawn dwells on a number of methodological issues in researching unemployment, underemployment and seasonal employment. Certain recommendations are made with respect to these social problems, especially as they affect young persons.

725 Household and occupation in Barbados.
G. Cumper. *Social and Economic Studies*, vol. 10, no. 4 (Dec. 1961), p. 386-419.

Based on the only island-wide household survey (n = 1,294) ever to have been conducted during a hurricane. Occupation is treated under eight categories (white collar, skilled wage earner, own account worker, non-farm labourer, domestic, peasant, renter and landless labourer) and cross-tabulated with economic characteristics. Household is classified according to type of occupation, and a profile of each type is supplied. There is also a section on intragenerational mobility. Problematic to the research is the unbalanced sex ratio of the population and the omission of questions on marital status.

726 **Industrial growth and employment in a small developing country: the case of Barbados 1955 to 1980.**
Andrew Downes. PhD thesis, University of Manchester, Manchester, England, 1985. 703p. bibliog.

Uses Barbados as a case study to examine a very small developing country's efforts at industrialization as a means to economic expansion and generation of employment. The thesis investigates the effect of small size on growth by examining three strategies of industrial development. Components analysis, input-output analysis and regression analysis are then utilized to determine the relative strengths of various sources of growth and allied interactive factors, and subsequently to test a number of hypotheses focusing on growth and development based on surveys of industrial establishments and overseas trade statistics. Governmental development programmes for the future are also critically examined.

727 **Trade union development and trade union education in the British Caribbean.**
Rawle Farley. Georgetown: Daily Chronicle Press, 1957. Reprinted, 1958. 64p. bibliog.

Outlines the growth of Caribbean trade unionism. By examining its past and present positions, the author attempts to evaluate the role of education in promoting further progress. The Barbados Workers' Union features as a case study of educational efforts and organized evolution. In particular, the roles played by Grantley Adams, Hugh Springer and Frank Walcott are emphasized. Statistics and the contents of annual reports are provided as evidence of the Union's success.

728 **Women, work and development: Barbados 1946-1970.**
Margaret Gill. In: *Women and Work*. General editor Joycelin Massiah. Cave Hill, St. Michael, Barbados: Institute of Social and Economic Research, University of the West Indies, 1984, p. 1-40. bibliog.(Women in the Caribbean Project, no. 6).

Raises a number of questions about traditional approaches, concepts and methods related to women and development. The author examines sources of livelihood, power and authority, and emotional support, within the equally controversial context of the role and status of women in Barbados. The account is based on census data, various national development plans and case studies conducted under the auspices of the Women in Development Project. From these sources changes are discovered in patterns and attitudes of labour force participation. In particular there has been a shift in emphasis from agriculture to service occupations.

729   **The history of the Barbados Workers' Union.**
Francis Mark.   Bridgetown: Barbados Workers' Union, [n.d.].
168p.

Traces the history of the Barbados Workers' Union from its emergence in the aftermath of the 1937 riots, when workers were inspired by the fiery speeches of Clement Payne, and their awakened consciousness of the exploitative nature of their conditions was subsequently endorsed by the Moyne Commission. The role of Grantley Adams and the Progressive League in their struggle for trade union legislation is also examined, as is the formation of the Barbados Workers' Union in 1941 and its early years of development. Problems of political allegiance are discussed, together with the transition of the power bases from the Barbados Labour Party to the Democratic Labour Party, in which veteran Frank Walcott played a significant part. The overall picture is one of the development of a prosperous and vibrant organization which today exerts a strong and mature influence in the areas of workers' rights and collective bargaining.

730   **Tourism and employment in Barbados.**
Dawn Marshall.   Cave Hill, St. Michael, Barbados: Institute of
Social and Economic Research, University of the West Indies,
1978. 66p. bibliog. (Occasional Papers Series, no. 6).

Based on a 1975 survey of Barbadian accommodation establishments, this paper questions the conventional wisdom concerning tourism as a generator of significant employment. It is also critical of government development policy in this area, claiming that it is passive or reactive rather than active. Problems of definition, together with those relating to access to and reliability of data, are discussed, as is the finding that, while visitor arrivals increase, generated employment in the industry appears to decline. Additionally, there are sections on the cost of job creation, labour expenses, employee/room ratios, classification of hotels and guest houses, and the problems of seasonality, package tour dependency, and lack of dialogue between managers and policy makers.

731   **Wages, productivity and employment in Barbados 1949-82.**
Clyde Mascall.   *Central Bank of Barbados Economic Review*,
vol. 12, no. 3 (1985), p. 10-17.

This paper explores wage trends in the economy since 1949, breaking the period into a number of distinct phases.

732   **Abridged working life tables for Barbadian males 1946, 1969 and
1970.**
Joycelin Massiah.   In: *Human Resources 2*. Edited by Jack
Harewood. St. Augustine, Trinidad: Institute of Social and
Economic Research, University of the West Indies, p. 69-108.
bibliog. (Occasional Papers Series).

A technical demographic analysis of past trends and future projections of male labour force participation in Barbados. The introduction discusses questions of definition of employment and the methodology of census data comparisions. The major variables contributing to change in employment patterns are also examined. Particular reference is made to differences in life expectancy, education, and the all-important emigration factor.

733 **Employed women in Barbados: a demographic profile 1946-1970.**
Joycelin Massiah. Cave Hill, St. Michael, Barbados: Institute of Social and Economic Research, University of the West Indies, 1984. 131p. bibliog. (Occasional Papers Series, no. 8).

A revised and updated version of a background paper prepared for the National Commission on the Status of Women in Barbados. The work analyses census data, but more specifically those factors which permit an understanding of variation in participation by women in the labour force over time, namely: age, area of residence, education, union status and fertility. Comparisons are also made between male and female patterns of employment with respect to age differentials, hours of work and worker status. There is a useful discussion of suggested areas for further research.

734 **The politics of the dispossessed.**
Winston Murray. Port of Spain: Beacon, 1971. 139p. bibliog.

Deals with the political behaviour of the labour movement in the Caribbean by tracing its evolution from post-emancipation days. Social and labour legislation is examined in various critical periods, since arguably it is this, or sometimes the lack of it, which has determined the psychology of the worker, and ultimately the character of trade unionism in the West Indies. The riots of the late 1930s and the subsequent working-class struggle are said to receive little sympathy from emerging native politicians whose middle-class Europeanized values seem more geared towards preserving a Westminster model of democracy than instigating radical change in the Caribbean. Grantley Adams and Errol Barrow of Barbados are cast among these 'chief protagonists of the right', the former for being an 'apologist of British colonialism' in promoting the pro-Western International Confederation of Free Trade Unions at the expense of the Communist-inspired World Federation of Trade Unions. The introduction of the word 'labour' in the name of his own political party is alleged to have been done in the hope that the British Labour Party would be more generous to the colonies. There is a strange neglect of the great contribution made by Frank Walcott to trade unionism in Barbados, and many will consider Murray's passionate account as a trifle too dismissive of indigenous statesmen.

735 **Occupational handbook for Barbados.**
C. Stoffle, D. George, A. Pignataro, P. Fields,
A. Young. Barbados: no publisher cited, 1967. 170p.

A somewhat dated careers guide for students and counsellors compiled by a number of Peace Corps workers and Barbadian secondary school teachers. Job descriptions are partly based on those provided by the business community. The object of the handbook is to make known the range of employment available, the qualifications required and the salaries offered. There are also short sections on application procedures and training opportunities. The greatest prospects seem to lie in tourism and manufacturing, but little hope is offered in the realm of agriculture.

The quality of life in Barbados.
See item no. 12.

The tourist industry in Barbados: a socio-economic assessment.
See item no. 206.

Industrial employment and inter-spouse conflict: Barbados West Indies.
See item no. 498.

The ecology of development administration in Jamaica, Trinidad and Tobago, and Barbados.
See item no. 575.

Manufacturing: a beleaguered industry.
See item no. 661.

The organization of large scale agricultural labor in Barbados . . .
See item no. 682.

Some aspects of work organization on sugar plantations in Barbados.
See item no. 685.

Urbanization in the Commonwealth Caribbean.
See item no. 766.

Secondary school students' employment aspirations and expectations and the Barbados labour market.
See item no. 826.

Statistics

736 **Barbados Blue Book.**
Bridgetown: Advocate Company, 1930- .
A collection of usually annual volumes dealing with various details of government administration, including taxes, duties, fees, sources of revenue, imports, exports, public officers, the church, the population, education, shipping, crime statistics, health and transport. This provides a wealth of official statistics for researchers from the latter half of the 19th century to the middle of the 20th century. Approximately 50 volumes have been published to date.

737 **Demographic Yearbook.**
New York: United Nations, Statistical Office, 1948- . annual.
The main source for worldwide demographic statistics, including data for Barbados.

738 **Statistical Yearbook for Latin America Annuario/Estadistíco de América Latina 1983.**
Economic Commission for Latin America. New York: United Nations, 1984. 749p.
Data on Barbados are provided in several of the sections. The principal tables cover social development and welfare, economic growth, capital formation and financing, external trade, external financing, population, national accounts, domestic prices, balance of payments, natural resources, employment and social conditions. This publication began in 1973 and was the successor to the *Statistical Bulletin of Latin America* (1964-72).

739   **The Caribbean basin to the year 2000: demographic, economic, and resource-use trends in seventeen countries.**
Norman A. Graham, Keith L. Edwards.   Boulder, Colorado; London: Westview Press, 1984. 166p. bibliog.

Described as a compendium of statistics and projections, this book presents, in over one hundred tables and figures, information on topics such as population, fertility, income distribution, energy consumption, arable land per capita, tourism receipts, foreign trade, oil and mineral resources and United States military assistance. Most statistics of importance are projected through to the year 2000. The country profile for Barbados is on p. 28-33 and includes subdivisions on demography, economy, oil, population growth and structure, Gross National Product (GNP) and income distribution. A useful repository of current statistics.

740   **Statistical Yearbook.**
New York: United Nations, Statistical Office, 1948- . annual.

A vast repository of statistical data of all sorts, particularly on economic production and social structure. Statistics for Barbados are given in many of the tables.

741   **Handbook for international trade and development statistics: 1984 supplement.**
United Nations Conference on Trade and Development.   New York: United Nations, 1984. 497p.

Intended to provide a complete basic collection of statistical data relevant to the analysis of world trade and development. Details of the international trade situation of Barbados are to be found in a number of the statistical tables which constitute the volume.

Environment

Town and country planning

742 Planning for 1980: an environmental study of Barbados.
Barbados National Trust.   Bridgetown: Barbados National Trust,
1970. 35p.

The report of a seminar held at the Cave Hill campus of the University of the
West Indies on 27 April 1970. This comprises the text of papers given by Lord
Llewellyn-Davies (on planning for 1980), Dr. John Lewis (on marine pollution),
E. G. B. Gooding (on preserving natural features), Stephen E. Emtage (on the
role of the planner), Richard C. Gill (on traffic and housing), Eric Armstrong (on
the economy in 1980), Leonard St. Hill (on the triangle of development),
Dr. Keith Hunte (on planning for growth and leisure), and Dr. Elsie Payne (on
the example of Switzerland). The booklet finishes with twelve resolutions that
were to be put forward to the government after the meeting.

743 Physical Development Plan for Barbados.
Barbados Town and Country Development Planning
Office.   Bridgetown: Government Printing Office, 1970. 134p.
maps.

In this first ever physical development or land use plan for Barbados, a blueprint
for the future settlement pattern of the island was outlined. The plan covered the
period up to 1985 and its principal objective was to decentralize population and
economic activities from the primate capital of Bridgetown. In order to achieve
this, a planned hierarchy of national settlements was envisaged. Although the
regional centres of Speightstown and Oistins have indeed experienced much
growth and expansion during the plan period, much less progress has been made
with regard to the expansion of the numerous designated district and village
centres. However, this rather idealistic and dated plan still merits attention as it
presents a great deal of basic social and economic data.

744 **Barbados Physical Development Plan Amended 1983.**
Bridgetown: Barbados Town and Country Development and
Planning Office, Ministry of Finance and Planning, 1983. 132p.
24 maps.

This second physical development plan updates the 1970 one. It is split into two
parts: the basic report of survey (p. 2-68), and the plan itself (p. 69-126). The
former presents a useful summary of recent population, economic, housing and
transport trends. The plan acknowledges the rather utopian nature of the 1970
plan. It thus seeks to focus future settlement growth into what is described as the
emerging 'linear urban corridor' running from Speightstown in the north, via
Holetown, Bridgetown and Oistins, through to St. Philip in the south-east. The
maps alone provide a mine of information on the basic spatial features and
characteristics of the country. This is an essential starting point for all those
concerned with town and country and wider environmental planning matters.

745 **A fishing harbour and marina: will it materialise?**
Bajan and South Caribbean, no. 320 (July 1980), p. 14-16.

Discusses the development of the Bridgetown wharf proposed in the 1970
Physical Development Plan for Barbados (q.v.) and includes a sketch map of the
marina.

746 **A new southern town.**
Debra Hughes. *Bajan and South Caribbean*, no. 353 (April
1983), p. 8-21.

A short text looks at the planned redevelopment of Oistins as the regional centre
for the southern area of Barbados. The article is accompanied by an excellent set
of photographs of, for example, the new fish market and jetty.

747 **State policies and labour migration.**
Peter Peek, Guy Standing. In: *State policies and migration:
studies in Latin America and the Caribbean.* Edited by Peter Peek,
Guy Standing. London: Croom Helm, 1982, p. 1-26.

Although not discussed in the text, Barbados is included in table one, which
summarizes a United Nations study of governmental perceptions of the
acceptability of their overall population distributions. Of twenty-seven countries
in the Latin American and Caribbean region, Barbados is listed as the only one
regarding its own population distribution as being entirely acceptable. This, of
course, runs counter to the accepted idea of the need to decentralize population
from the Bridgetown area.

748 **Recent developments in planning the settlement hierarchy of
Barbados: implications concerning the debate on urban primacy.**
Robert B. Potter, Muriel L. Hunte. *Geoforum*, vol. 10 (1979),
p. 355-62.

Provides a résumé and critique of the main recommendations of the 1970 *Physical
Development Plan for Barbados* (q.v.). In order to combat the primacy of

Bridgetown, the plan advocated the creation of a tiered hierarchy of settlements below the capital. Progress towards this goal is reviewed and it is concluded that the plan, based on classical central place theory, was somewhat unrealistic in the first place. An alternative suggestion for a more limited and feasible pattern of spatial decentralization is finally presented.

749 **Mental maps of Barbados, part II: how Barbadians perceive planning issues.**
Robert B. Potter. *Bajan and South Caribbean*, no. 360 (Nov. 1983), p. 30-31.

Presents a non-technical summary of the results of a sample survey of Barbadians' views of environmental planning issues and their reactions to current planning proposals.

750 **The hand analysis of repertory grids: an appropriate method for Third World environmental studies.**
Robert B. Potter, John T. Coshall. *Area*, vol. 16, no. 4 (1984), p. 315-22.

The purpose of this paper is to present a worked example of a method that can be employed to analyse people's evaluative perceptions of their environment or surroundings. The method, which is based on the theory of personal constructs, is demonstrated by means of one person's perceptions of the eleven parishes which constitute Barbados. The principal argument set forth in the paper is that the method offers a suitable analytical approach for planners interested in finding out how their clients view the environment. In short, it is argued that the method represents an 'appropriate technology' for Third World planners and environmentalists.

751 **Spatial perceptions and public involvement in Third World urban planning: the example of Barbados.**
Robert B. Potter. *Singapore Journal of Tropical Geography*, vol. 5, no. 1 (1984), p. 30-44.

After stressing the general need to establish genuine and effective public involvement in the planning process in Third World countries, this paper examines some aspects of the physical development planning policies of Barbados. In the empirical section of the paper, the results of a social survey based on some 207 respondents are considered. These analyse the respondents' environmental perceptions of Bridgetown and the planning issues which the capital faces, their awareness of planning policies and reactions to them.

752 **Environmental planning and popular participation in Barbados and the Eastern Caribbean: some observations.**
Robert B. Potter. *Bulletin of Eastern Caribbean Affairs*, vol. 11, nos. 4-5 (1985), p. 24-30.

Stresses the important potential role that environmental and particularly physical planning can play in the Third World, as well as in developed countries. This is especially true in the case of small nations which have a narrow resource base, highly uneven population distributions and marked spatial inequalities in both income and welfare levels – features very characteristic of the Eastern Caribbean. The issues surrounding relations between planners and public, and public participation in planning are then raised. Throughout, these arguments are linked with the author's research undertaken in Barbados, St. Lucia and Trinidad and Tobago.

753 **Evaluating environmental structure and change in the Caribbean context: the potential of personal construct theory.**
Robert B. Potter. *Bulletin of Eastern Caribbean Affairs*, vol. 12, no. 4 (1986), (in press).

After a brief consideration of the environmental concerns and pressures that face Barbados, this paper outlines an approach which may be employed to look equally effectively at both human and physical aspects of environmental structure and change. Reference to research carried out in Barbados seeks to demonstrate how well such an approach fits with a people-based conception of economic development and environmental change.

754 **Physical development or spatial land use planning in Barbados: retrospect and prospect.**
Robert B. Potter. *Bulletin of Eastern Caribbean Affairs*, vol. 12, no. 1 (1986), p.24-32.

The intention is to review the proposals contained in the *Barbados Physical Development Plan Amended 1983* (q.v.). It is argued that this document represents an important step in the evolution of spatial land use planning in Barbados. On a retrospective level, the paper commences with a summary of the development of physical planning in Barbados. The first island-wide plan produced in 1970 is reviewed and the rather idealistic nature of the proposals it embodied is stressed.

755 **The Speightstown Plan.**
Bajan and South Caribbean, no. 354 (May 1983), p. 30-32.

Considers measures for the development of the town following the publication of the Speightstown Plan in September 1980.

756 **Planning in the West Indies.**
Peter H. M. Stevens. *Town and Country Planning*, vol. 25 (1957), p. 503-08.

This short paper examines town and country planning in the British Caribbean, emphasizing that most countries at the time of writing lacked comprehensive physical development or land use planning systems. The author finishes by stressing the problems that are faced by small islands which cannot economically justify the employment of a permanent planning staff. It is argued that many of the smaller islands of the Windward and Leeward groups must, therefore, look elsewhere for technical planning assistance.

Landscape as resource for national development: a Caribbean view.
See item no. 60.

Congruence between space preferences and socio-demographic structure in Barbados, West Indies: the use of cognitive studies in Third World urban planning and development.
See item no. 67.

Rural development in the Caribbean.
See item no. 615.

Industrial development and urban planning in Barbados.
See item no. 666.

Urbanization in the Caribbean.
See item no. 760.

Urban development, planning and demographic change 1970-80, in Barbados.
See item no. 769.

Urbanisation and planning in the Third World: spatial perceptions and public participation.
See item no. 770.

Planning and preservation.
See item no. 796.

Urbanization

757 **Speightstown down the centuries.**
Warren Alleyne. *Bajan and South Caribbean*, no. 354 (May 1983), p. 18-20.
Published as part of a special issue on the past, present and future of Speightstown, this article examines the development of the settlement since its establishment as a port and commercial centre in the 17th century.

758 **Speightstown renewal.**
Céline Barnard. *Bajan and South Caribbean*, no. 354 (May 1983), p. 22; 26-27.
Considers the commercial development of Speightstown, principally since 1959, up to the building of the new shopping mall in October 1980.

759 **Urban research in the British Caribbean: a prospectus.**
L. Broom. *Social and Economic Studies*, vol. 1 (1953), p. 113-19.
An early and thus somewhat dated attempt to assess the need to understand urbanization processes in the Caribbean. However, a number of pertinent issues are touched upon. It is stressed that the then relatively low level of urbanization and high overall population densities in the Caribbean sharply distinguish the region from the rest of the Western Hemisphere. The irrationality of lumping the Caribbean with Latin America is thus emphasized. The density of settlement of Barbados is particularly stressed on p. 114-15 and in Table 3 on p. 118.

760 **Urbanization in the Caribbean.**
Colin G. Clarke. *Geography*, vol. 59, no. 3 (1974), p. 223-32.
A good summary of the causes and consequences of urban development in the Caribbean since the Second World War. The paper includes sections on historical perspectives, urban definitions, capital city populations, urban primacy, internal migrations, employment, unemployment, housing, squatting, public housing, urban ecology and regional development planning. Barbados is referred to in several of the sections.

761 **The Commonwealth Caribbean.**
Colin G. Clarke. In: *Essays on world urbanization*. Edited by Ronald Jones. London: George Philip, 1975, p. 341-51.
Written to meet the need for a survey of urbanization trends in the Commonwealth Caribbean as a whole, this account is disappointing in its almost total concentration on Jamaica and Trinidad. However, Barbados receives some scant attention with respect to its overall level of urbanizaton (Table 49, p. 344).

762 **Urbanization.**
Colin G. Clarke. In: *A geography of the Third World*. Edited by J. P. Dickenson (et al.). London: Methuen, 1983, p. 169-207.
There is direct reference to Barbados only in a table showing the growth of manufacturing in selected developing countries. However, the reader interested in Caribbean urbanization in general will find plenty here concerning the history of urban development in the region, migration, urban-rural wage differentials, informal sector jobs, unemployment, urban primacy, slums, shanty towns and rent yards.

763 **Urbanization and urban growth in the Caribbean: an essay on social change in dependent societies.**
Malcolm Cross. Cambridge, England: Cambridge University Press, 1979. 174p. map. bibliog.
Presents a primarily sociological examination of urban development in the wider Caribbean region. A large number of data tabulations are presented, many of which refer to Barbados. After a general introduction the chapters cover theories of urbanization and dependence, the economic order, population structure and change, social structure and organization, race, class and education, politics and policies. Barbados is mentioned under most of these headings. The volume as a

whole offers a stimulating overview of the Caribbean urban process, albeit an almost entirely aspatial one.

764 **World urbanization 1950-1970, volume I: basic data for cities, countries, and regions.**
Kingsley Davis. Berkeley, California: Institute of International Studies, University of California, 1969. 318p.
Provides comparative data on urbanization trends in 1950, 1960 and 1970 for all the world's countries, Barbados included.

765 **Urban population growth in the Caribbean.**
Kempe Ronald Hope. *Cities*, vol. 1, no. 2 (1983), p. 167-74.
Although at the outset purporting to analyse rapid urbanization in the four Caribbean territories of Barbados, Guyana, Jamaica and Trinidad and Tobago, hardly any specific facts or details concerning urban development in Barbados are given. Virtually the entire paper is taken up with a useful but highly generalized account of Caribbean urbanization processes and trends. The author concludes with a call for a more explicitly rural-based approach to economic and social development.

766 **Urbanization in the Commonwealth Caribbean.**
Kempe Ronald Hope. Boulder, Colorado; London: Westview Press, 1986. 129p. bibliog.
Notwithstanding the title, this volume provides a discussion of the general issues and processes involved in Caribbean urbanization, but the territorial focus of attention is limited to Barbados, Trinidad and Tobago and Guyana. The five substantive chapters focus on Third World urbanization in general, urban population growth in the Caribbean, unemployment and labour force participation, policies and a summary.

767 **Urbanisation and planning in the West Indies.**
Brian J. Hudson. *Caribbean Quarterly*, vol. 26, no. 3 (1980), p. 1-17.
Although the author focuses on the history of urbanization and planning in Cuba, Puerto Rico and Jamaica, his general discussion of trends in urban development in the Caribbean will be of direct relevance to those interested in Barbados. Notes, in particular, that Barbados exhibits a very high degree of urban primacy.

768 **The West Indies chooses a capital.**
David Lowenthal. *Geographical Review*, vol. 48, no. 3 (1958), p. 336-64.
Considers the problems involved, and the images evoked, in the choice of a capital for the Federation of the West Indies. The author concentrates on the three main contenders – Barbados, Trinidad and Tobago and Jamaica, particularly the first two, which are noted for their rivalry. The West Indies Federation, the Capital Commission Report and West Indian reactions are examined in some detail.

769 **Urban development, planning and demographic change 1970-80, in Barbados.**
Robert B. Potter. *Caribbean Geography*, vol. 1, no. 1 (1983), p. 3-12.

This short paper describes the town and country planning machinery of Barbados and examines its aims and achievements since 1959. In the second half, urban trends in the period 1970-1980 are considered with respect to the policy aim of decentralization. It is demonstrated that whilst St. Michael is decreasing its relative share of national population, the wider south-eastern urban corridor is still gaining in relative terms.

770 **Urbanisation and planning in the Third World: spatial perceptions and public participation.**
Robert B. Potter. London: Croom Helm; New York: St. Martin's Press, 1985. 284p. maps. bibliog.

Although primarily providing an overview of urbanization trends in Third World countries in general, this book draws heavily on the author's empirical work carried out in Barbados, Trinidad and Tobago and St. Lucia. Thus, the development and structure of Caribbean settlement patterns are covered in chapter three (p. 66-79), and this relates especially to Barbados (p. 70-79). The housing structure of Bridgetown receives attention in the same chapter (p. 107-109), whilst Barbadian settlement planning is covered in chapter four (p. 130-33). Research into Barbadian nationals' perceptions of their country and its environmental problems is reported in chapters six and seven.

771 **The 350th anniversary of Bridgetown.**
Bajan and South Caribbean, no. 296 (July 1978), p. 4-59.

An extended introduction to the history and present-day structure of the Bridgetown area in the form of seventeen short essays penned by various authors: 'Who built the Indian Bridge?'; 'The town of the merchants'; 'The Bay Plantation'; 'The history of the Careenage'; 'The oldest building in Bridgetown'; 'Bridgetown's unique dry dock'; 'The church that made Bridgetown a city'; 'Representation in the house'; 'The conscience of the city'; 'Some patterns and personalities'; 'Sport in Bridgetown'; 'The vibrant days in Bridgetown'; 'The trade unions come to town'; 'The church leaders'; 'Plans for the future promise revival'; 'Bridgetown roundabout'; and 'Buildings under siege'.

Historic Bridgetown.
See item no. 330.

The population of Barbados.
See item no. 397.

Metropolitan dominance and family planning in Barbados.
See item no. 404.

Government expenditure in Barbados, 1946-79.
See item no. 627.

Housing and architecture

772 Report to the Barbados Government and the Barbados Housing Authority on land tenure, housing policy and home finance.
Charles Abrams. New York, 1963. 51p.

Although this is an unpublished mimeographed report it is of some importance as it details an acknowledged expert's views concerning the land and housing markets of Barbados. Abrams makes some interesting suggestions, including, for instance, the likely utility of core-housing schemes rather than self-help programmes in Barbados. It would not be uncharitable to suggest that Abrams' recommendations appear to have received relatively little attention until quite recently.

773 Housing in the modern world: man's struggle for shelter in an urbanizing world.
Charles Abrams. Cambridge, Massachusetts: Massachusetts Institute of Technology, 1964; London: Faber & Faber, 1966. 307p. bibliog.

A classic work on the housing problems and policies of fast-growing Third World cities. Abrams worked in Barbados in the early 1960s as a consultant to the Barbadian Government. Hence, the Barbadian housing system is referred to in several sections, and photographs are included of chattel houses (Fig. 11) and government-built low-income apartments (Fig. 20).

774 Treasure in the Caribbean: a first study of Georgian buildings in the British West Indies.
Angus Whiteford Acworth. London: Pleiades Books, 1949. 36p.

Describes a number of Georgian buildings in Jamaica, the Leeward and Windward Islands, Trinidad and Tobago and Barbados. Sixty black-and-white photographs are included, thirteen of which are of Barbadian houses. The text concerning Barbados (p. 29-35) notes that as a conseqeunce of fires and hurricanes, few pre-1831 buildings survive in anything like their original form. Among the buildings discussed and depicted are St. Lucy parish church, Holborn (Fontabelle), the Savannah and Codrington College.

775 Buildings of architectural or historic interest in the British West Indies.
Angus Whiteford Acworth. London: HM Stationery Office, 1951. 21p.

Barbados is considered on p. 6-7 of this short summary of historic buildings and their preservation in the British West Indies. Some interesting photographs of Barbadian buildings are to be found between p. 4 and p. 5.

776 **Kaz antiye jan moun ka rete.** (Caribbean popular dwellings.)
Jack Berthelot, Martine Gaume. Pointe-à-Pitre, Guadeloupe:
Editions Perspectives Creoles, 1982. 167p. map. bibliog.

Highly recommended for all those interested in popular or vernacular achitecture
in the Caribbean. The book is unusual in that it is published in three languages:
Creole, French and English. Although there is a very strong accent on
Guadeloupe, examples and illustrations are drawn from throughout the
Caribbean, and Barbadian house forms feature prominently throughout the text.
The volume covers the distinctive aspects of Caribbean architecture, including
such topics as how huts are built, materials and evolution, façades and decoration.
The text is illustrated by a large collection of fine photographs, many of them in
full colour, and useful architectural drawings. The English prose text is somewhat
disappointing, with a tendency towards looseness of expression.

777 **Historic architecture of the Caribbean.**
David Buisseret. London, Kingston, Port of Spain: Heinemann
Educational, 1980. 93p. map. bibliog.

Illustrated with some 175 black-and-white photographs, this recent volume
surveys the architecture of the Caribbean under five separate headings: domestic
buildings, commercial structures, industrial buildings, military and naval works,
churches and public buildings. Although there is a heavy emphasis on Jamaica,
Barbados receives attention in several of the chapters.

778 **St. Ann's Fort and the Garrison.**
P. F. Campbell. *Journal of the Barbados Museum and Historical
Society*, vol. 35, no. 1 (1975), p. 3-16.

Describes the building from ca. 1705 of St. Ann's Garrison which comprises the
former military buildings bordering the Savannah.

779 **Colonial calypso.**
Observer Magazine, (26 Jan. 1986), p. 39-43.

Adapted from the book *Caribbean style* (q.v.) written by Suzanne Slesin et al.
This short article, which includes excellent colour photographs, considers whether
there is a distinctive Caribbean architecture, and pursues the argument of the
book in stressing that 'Caribbean style represents a vernacular architecture
without official agreement or approval' and that 'Today's West Indian houses are
amalgams of classical architecture on the one hand and, on the other, the rural
architecture of both Europe and Africa'.

780 **The windmills and copper walls of Barbados.**
J. Sydney Dash. *Journal of the Barbados Museum and Historical
Society*, vol. 31, no. 2 (1965), p. 43-60.

This résumé of a talk given by Professor Dash to members of the Barbados
Museum and Historical Society on 16 March 1964 notes that the windmill has
endured in Barbados for more than 200 years, and is as Barbadian as its national
dishes of flying fish and cou-cou, rice and peas and jug-jug. Although windmills

are found on other West Indian islands, they are not as numerous. The author looks at the history of windmills, their evolution, structure and performance.

781 **The West Indian hip-roofed cottage.**
Edwin Doran, Jr. *California Geographer*, vol. 3 (1962),
p. 97-104.

A hip roof is one that slants in four directions, whereas a gable roof slopes in only two. This paper establishes that the distinctive hip-roofed cottage is almost ubiquitous in the West Indian islands, except for Cuba and Puerto Rico. It is shown that the cottage type occurs most frequently in the British and Netherlands West Indies. Evidence suggests that the house type probably originated within a hundred miles of the English Channel and was introduced to the West Indies between 1625 and 1700, since when it has been disseminated among the islands. R. Ligon's 17th-century work *A true and exact history of the island of Barbadoes* (q.v.) is quoted in this connection.

782 **How to make your building withstand strong winds.**
Keith J. Eaton. *Bajan and South Caribbean*, no. 332 (July 1981),
p. 26-28.

The author, who is a member of the Overseas Division of the Building Research Establishment (UK), presents twenty-five points relevant to the sound construction of buildings to help them withstand hurricanes.

783 **The evolution of vernacular architecture in the Western Caribbean.**
Jay D. Edwards.   In: *Cultural traditions and Caribbean identity: the question of patrimony*. Edited by S. J. K. Wilkersen.
Gainesville, Florida: Centre for Latin American Studies, 1980,
p. 291-339.

Despite the regional emphasis indicated in the title, much of this essay is appropriate to the Eastern Caribbean. The development of Caribbean vernacular architecture is divided into five broad historical stages, the first four being characteristic of the entire British West Indies, only the final one unique to the Western Caribbean region. Thus, the form and development of houses in Barbados receive some attention, partly via Richard Ligon's *A true and exact history of the island of Barbadoes* (q.v.).

784 **Historic houses of Barbados: a collection of drawings, with historical and architectural notes.**
Henry S. Fraser, Ronnie Hughes.   St. Michael, Barbados:
Barbados National Trust, 1982. 68p. bibliog.

This set of pen-and-wash drawings by Henry Fraser aims to present the vernacular architecture of Barbados. Each drawing is accompanied by a descriptive account. Sections included are: The oldest survivors, Plantation houses, Town houses, Suburban houses, The chattel house, Houses of governors, Military residences, Romantic ruins and Sam Lord's Castle. The book stresses the uniformity of architectural style, which stems from the continuous British presence and the essentially Georgian type of buildings. Affords an excellent starting point for those interested in urban design and architecture.

785 **Our architectural heritage – an S.O.S.**
Henry S. Fraser. *Bajan and Souith Caribbean*, no. 338 (Jan. 1982), p. 21-22.
Argues the case for urban rehabilitation to save the country's architectural heritage, involving a more wide-ranging grading and listing of buildings and the identification of specific areas of historic character.

786 **Our architectural heritage.**
Henry S. Fraser. *Bajan and South Caribbean*, no. 348 (Nov. 1982), p. 6-8.
Suggests that Barbados probably has the finest surviving heritage of 19th-century domestic architecture in the Caribbean. The author describes such houses as 'old suburban Bajan vernacular'. The basic style is characterized by several distinctive features, including: perfect symmetry of the front façade, a low hurricane-resistant rectangular shape, a front gallery or verandah and a central porch. Fraser argues that there are pressing social and economic reasons for the careful conservation of this architectural heritage. An interesting and well-written short article.

787 **Historic churches of Barbados.**
Barbara Hill, edited by Henry Fraser.   St. Michael, Barbados: Art Heritage Publications, 1984. 128p. map. bibliog.
The author, an architect, lived and worked in Barbados between 1958 and 1982 and was responsible, among other things, for the remodelling of the Barbados Museum. The present text grew from a draft written by Barbara Hill in 1977, which was illustrated with her own black-and-white photographs and pen sketches. She died in London in February 1983, and the present book has been produced as a tribute to her. Thus, the text has been edited and amplified by Henry Fraser and additional photographs provided by Willie Alleyne. With the aid of some sixty illustrations and fourteen colour plates, the historic churches of Barbados are reviewed in considerable detail; a map on p. 117 shows the location of those described.

788 **An analysis of the housing market in Barbados.**
Carlos Holder.   *Central Bank of Barbados Economic Review*, vol. 12, no. 1 (1985), p. 13-19.
Basic information on housing conditions, the structure of the housing market and mortgage availability is presented, followed by a statistical model of housing demand. A regression model is calibrated using empirical data relating to the period 1960-81. Yearly housing demand is related to income levels, the price of housing, the general price level of other goods, the mortgage interest rate and population level. The model explains eighty-seven per cent of yearly variation in housing demand. The level of income and the price level of goods are found to be the most powerful influences on housing demand.

238

789 **White Paper on Housing.**
Housing Planning Unit, Ministry of Housing and
Lands. St. Michael, Barbados: Barbados Government Printing
Office, 1984. 26p.

Describes the nature and history of the present-day housing problem in Barbados
before outlining the government's policies and strategies for housing since 1976,
and for the near future. Chapter five provides a résumé of the Tenantries Freehold
Purchase and Tenantries Development Acts of 1980. The aim of involving private
sector developers and financing agencies in housing programmes rather than the
public sector is stressed in this policy document for the 1980s.

790 **Sugar windmills in Barbados, part 1.**
Maurice Bateman Hutt. *Bajan and South Caribbean*, no. 326
(1981), p. 48-49.

There are approximately 120 surviving windmill towers, referred to locally as
'millwalls', in Barbados. In 1960-61, the author and his wife carried out a survey
of these. Used for milling sugar cane, they vary in size, and some are as tall as
fifty-five to sixty feet, as at Drax Hall in St. George. An interesting although brief
account.

791 **Sugar windmills in Barbados, part 2.**
Maurice Bateman Hutt. *Bajan and South Caribbean*, no. 327
(1981), p. 22-23.

In this second article, the author describes the location and character of millwalls
in the northern parish of St. Peter.

792 **New technology in Barbados.**
Bajan (Jan.-Feb. 1986), p. 22-25.

This short piece describes the introduction of a pre-cast concrete modular housing
system in Barbados. The system has been developed by Caribbean Concrete
Construction Limited, whose factory is located at Newton industrial park. The
first such houses were built at West Terrace Gardens.

793 **Residential subdivisions of Barbados 1965-1977.**
Lionel L. Nurse. Cave Hill, St. Michael, Barbados: Institute of
Social and Economic Research, University of the West Indies,
1983. 119p. maps. bibliog. (Occasional Papers Series, no. 14).

This study attempts to examine the question of residential land subdivision in
Barbados. The author considers why it occurred so rapidly between 1965 and 1977
on green field sites, frequently replacing sugar, although subsequently many of
these subdivisions were not built on.

794 **Mental maps and spatial variations in residential desirability: a**
Barbados case study.
Robert B. Potter. *Caribbean Geography*, vol. 1, no. 3 (1984),
p. 186-97.

Along with some of the author's other work this paper considers aspects of the
environmental perceptions of Barbadian nationals, but the emphasis here is
placed on the contrasts which exist in the perceived residential desirability of the
parishes. The work was carried out using a sample of 207 Barbadians. The major
contrast is revealed between the low imageability of the northern parishes and the
enhanced residential desirability of the south-western coastal strip, especially the
parish of Christ Church.

795 **Housing upgrading in Barbados: the tenantries programme.**
Robert B. Potter. *Geography*, vol. 71, no. 3 (1986) p. 255-57.

Explains the historical evolution of the housing tenure system in Barbados with
particular reference to the structure and development of plantation tenantries and
chattel houses. Subsequently, the tenantries programme, launched in 1980 in
order to afford all tenants the opportunity of purchasing their house spots, and to
improve the wider environment of the tenantry, is explained and discussed.

796 **Planning and preservation.**
Peter Stevens. *Journal of the Barbados Museum and Historical
Society*, vol. 26, no. 3 (1959), p. 111-19.

The text of a lecture delivered to a meeting of the Barbados Museum and
Historical Society in which the need for architectural preservation is emphasized.
The paper includes four pages of black-and-white photographs.

797 **Caribbean style.**
Suzanne Slesin, Stafford Cliff, Jack Berthelot, Martin Gaume,
Daniel Rozensztroch, photographs by Gilles de
Chabaneix. London: Thames & Hudson, 1986. 290p. map.

A photographic record of the diversity of architectural styles to be found in the
Caribbean region. This superbly produced book contains over 600 colour
photographs. The chapters cover the overall appearance of the Caribbean,
outside views of houses, island influences, foreign influences, the plantation
house, the town house, the popular house, the contemporary house, and gardens.
The volume ends with an architectural notebook (p. 279-88) which shows
representations of popular house types on the various islands (see p. 282 in
relation to Barbados). Villa Nova and St. Nicholas Abbey are considered on
p. 66-75 and p. 76-81 respectively.

798 **Some early buildings of Barbados.**
Thomas T. Waterman. *Art Bulletin of the College Art Association
of America*, vol. 27 (1945), p. 146-49.

Provides a brief examination of the early rural and urban architecture of
Barbados. Drax Hall and St. Nicholas Abbey are described as the finest British
Colonial dwellings of the period in America; both were built around 1650.

The quality of life in Barbados.
See item no. 12.

Caribbean views of Caribbean land.
See item no. 62.

Barbadians and Barbadian house forms in the Brazilian Amazon.
See item no. 434.

Barbados development plan 1983-1988.
See item no. 616.

Government expenditure in Barbados, 1946-79.
See item no. 627.

Urbanization in the Caribbean.
See item no. 760.

Environmental conservation

799 **Save the Graeme Hall Swamp.**
Mark D. Alleyne. *Bajan and South Caribbean*, no. 327 (Feb. 1981), p. 4-6.
The Graeme Hall Swamp, situated close to the island's south coast and covering seventy-eight acres, forms a natural bird sanctuary and has extensive mangrove vegetation. Its ecology, however, is increasingly affected by human activities and this article stresses the case for its environmental protection against possible private development.

800 **Emerging environmental problems in a tourist zone: the case of Barbados.**
Ewart Archer. *Caribbean Geographer*, vol. 2, no. 1 (1985), p. 45-55.
Argues that in Caribbean islands such as Barbados, ecological damage to shallow water corals, nutrient enrichment and bacteriological contamination of coastal waters, and beach erosion are environmental problems that could pose long-term problems for the tourist industry. It is argued that environmental regulations already on the statute books must be implemented more rigorously if such damage is to be reduced and controlled.

801 **The problems relative to soil conservation in the Scotland District.**
W. J. Badcock. *Journal of the Barbados Museum and Historical Society*, vol. 27, no. 4 (1960), p. 126-29.
Summarizes the geology of Barbados and goes on to consider the question of its soil characteristics, particularly those of the Scotland District. It is argued that

early agriculture led to slipping and slumping which was ignored so that there are now 'thousands of acres of degraded lands in the Scotland area'. The remedy is seen as nothing short of a complete change in the management of agricultural enterprises in the area.

802 **The land conservation conundrum of Eastern Barbados.**
M. A. Carson, Sai-Wing Tam. *Annals of the Association of American Geographers*, vol. 62, no. 2 (1977), p. 185-203.

An examination of severe land erosion in the Scotland District, detailed field work having been carried out in the Joe's River basin. It is stressed that the problem has been aggravated by clearance of the natural vegetation, thereby allowing increased overland flow, and more recently, by inappropriate conservation strategies. The paper contains some useful maps, sketches and aerial photographs.

803 **Guarding our health, enhancing our beauty: a look at the Ministry of Tourism and Environment.**
Wilton Conliffe. *Bajan* (June-July 1985), p. 4-5.

Records the establishment of the new Ministry of Tourism and Environment on 1 February 1985 and stresses the need for environmental protection and public education.

804 **An assessment of the soil conservation scheme, Scotland District, Barbados, 1957-1969.**
E. H. St. J. Cumbarbatch. *Journal of the Barbados Museum and Historical Society*, vol. 33, no. 1 (1969), p. 14-24.

Explains the long-standing problem of soil erosion in the Scotland District before considering the Scotland District Soil Conservation Scheme which commenced in 1957. At the time of writing, the author was Deputy Chief Agricultural Officer, Ministry of Agriculture, Barbados.

805 **CCA doing a good job.**
Norma Faria. *Bajan* (Jan-Feb. 1986), p. 5-6.

Examines the work of the Caribbean Conservation Association (CCA), an organization which is based in Barbados, although its membership includes some seventeen regional governments. Some poor expression and typographical errors serve, however, to obscure the meaning of several passages.

806 **Soil conservation and future land use in the Scotland District, Barbados.**
Henry Teck Pong. MSc dissertation, McGill University, Montreal, 1964. 132p. maps. bibliog.

Examines the long-standing problem of soil erosion in the Scotland District, affording an inventory of the area's land use and an assessment of its potential for agriculture. The area is described in chapter one, whilst the problem of soil erosion is discussed in chapters two and three. Chapter four presents the inventory of land resources and future potential. The dissertation contains some useful maps and photographs.

807 **Towards a new environment.**
Geoffrey M. Ramsay. *Bajan* (June-July 1985), p. 6-7.

Written by a landscape architect, this short article argues the need for gradual environmental improvement via streetscaping, vegetation preservation, tree planting, the creation of mini-parks and the removal of derelict buildings.

808 **Managing our ecology.**
Yvonne L. St. Hill, Ronald Baynes. *Bajan* (May-June 1986), p. 14-16.

The authors, an environmental education officer at the Ministry of Tourism and Environment, and a University of the West Indies graduate respectively, argue that there is increasing realization on the part of decision makers in the small developing islands of the Caribbean that sustained socioeconomic growth and development is dependent on maintaining adequate standards of environmental quality via effective programmes of environmental management. The text focuses on the issues surrounding Long Pond, the Scotland District, Graeme Hall Swamp and Turner's Hall Woods. Government initiatives since 1981 are briefly considered, specifically in relation to the St. James marine reserve and the Barbados National Park.

809 **Canadian tropical research in the West Indies.**
Finn Sander. *Nature*, vol. 244 (1973), p. 201-02.

This short paper summarizes the research work carried out at the Bellairs Institute of McGill University, much of which was of a marine biological-ecological nature.

810 **Mechanisms and spatial patterns of erosion and instability in the Joe's River basin, Barbados.**
Sai-Wing S. Tam. PhD dissertation, McGill University, Montreal, 1975. 211p. maps. bibliog.

Intensive morphological mapping of the Joe's River basin, St. Joseph, in the Scotland District revealed that instability and badland terrain are associated with areas underlain by overconsolidated muds of Eocene age. It is shown that inappropriate land use and forest clearing led to increased run-off after colonization in the 17th century. The final part of this thesis considers corrective and conservation measures. A well-documented thesis which contains some excellent photographs.

811 **Causes of environmental deterioration in Eastern Barbados since colonization.**
Sai-Wing S. Tam. *Agriculture and Environment*, vol. 5 (1980-81), p. 285-308.

A detailed article which examines the severe erosion of the Joe's River basin of the Scotland District. Experimental run-off plots were established in the basin to represent three different environments: revegetated hill slopes, cane fields and abandoned down-hill furrows. Data show a statistical relationship between land use type and run-off. The article supports the hypothesis that large-scale deforestation and cane growing since colonization have changed the hydraulic regime, leading to accelerated erosion. The so-called conservation practice of down-hill furrows is aggravating the erosion problem further.

812 **Land use in the Scotland District, Barbados.**
Carolyn C. Weiss. MA dissertation, McGill University, Montreal, 1966. 262p. maps. bibliog.

Examines the problems posed by the Scotland District of Barbados by virtue of its land use complex and land tenure system. The dissertation looks at the historical development and present nature of land use in the area, particularly focusing on peasant and plantation agriculture. The author calls for a considerable degree of replanning of land use in the district, particularly the reduction of the dependence of the economy on a single export crop and the development of a more diversified system of agriculture.

Land use change in Western Barbados.
See item no. 71.

Beach changes and recreational planning on the west coast of Barbados.
See item no. 72.

Physical changes in Barbados since 1627.
See item no. 78.

The geology and mineral resource assessment of the island of Barbados.
See item no. 111.

Geological background to soil conservation and land rehabilitation measures in Barbados, W.I.
See item no. 131.

Effects of the tourist industry in Barbados, West Indies.
See item no. 197.

Assessing the environmental effects of tourism development on the carrying capacity of small island systems: the case for Barbados.
See item no. 211.

Turner's Hall Wood, Barbados.
See item no. 240.

Marine life of the Caribbean.
See item no. 252.

The cattle egrets and mangroves of Graeme Hall Swamp.
See item no. 277.

Our architectural heritage – an S.O.S.
See item no. 785.

Our architectural heritage.
See item no. 786.

Planning and preservation.
See item no. 796.

Education, Science and Technology

813 Computing in Barbados 1969-1979: a review.
Stewart Bishop   *Bulletin of Eastern Caribbean Affairs*, vol. 6, no. 6 (Jan.-Feb. 1981), p. 8-23.

Traces the history of computing in Barbados from the establishment of International Systems Associates and the installation of the first IBM (1401) machine in 1969. Apart from the Government Data Processing Unit (also using IBM equipment), the pioneers of computerization in the island were the Barbados Light and Power Company and Barbados Shipping and Trading, both employing ICL hardware. Expansion of computing in manufacturing, banking etc. soon followed, though mostly for purposes of payroll and accounts. Except for the introduction of the Statistical Package for the Social Sciences (SPSS) in 1976, computers in Barbados have rarely been used for research. A useful appendix is included providing names of organizations, types of computer models, dates of acquisition and major applications.

814 Tackling the literacy problem in the Eastern Caribbean: some considerations.
Desmond Clarke.   *Bulletin of Eastern Caribbean Affairs*, vol. 5, no. 5 (Nov.-Dec. 1979), p. 14-26.

After discussing problems of definition, Clarke opts for a functional literacy approach which comprises the minimum standards for coping adequately with the practical tasks of living. An examination of educational data for Barbados reveals that in 1979, of 8,152 males aged 15 to 19 only 1,150 or 14.1 per cent had matriculated and that for females the comparable figure was 18.7 per cent. Furthermore, of the handful taking a school leaving examination, the pass rate was just 56 per cent. While these depressing statistics are better than those presented for St. Lucia, Grenada and St. Vincent, they nevertheless highlight problems associated with poor reading ability. These difficulties are a continuation of those discovered by Leonard Shorey when evaluating the failures of the 'eleven plus' common entrance examination. Clarke concludes by looking at a number of strategies for remedying the situation.

815 **Official ideology and the education of women in the English-speaking Caribbean 1835-1945.**
Joyce Cole. In: *Women and education.* Cave Hill, St. Michael, Barbados: Institute of Social and Economic Research, University of the West Indies, 1982, p. 1-34. (Women in the Caribbean Project, vol. 5).

Argues that education promotes the status quo of class and gender stratification. In the case of former colonies, such as Barbados, female education is predicated on the traditional women's roles of wife and mother. Consequently, while there is generally equality of opportunity between the sexes as regards access to schooling, the same cannot be said with respect to curricular differences and eventual employment options. The argument is based on historical evidence with particular reference to the Mitchinson (1875), Bree (1894), Marriott-Mayhew (1932) and Moyne (1939) Commissions, and the Hammond (1940) and Hayden (1945) Reports.

816 **Toward the formulation of policies for the utilization of science and technology in CARICOM States. Part II – A conceptual framework for planning industrial development in the food producing sector.**
Jeffrey Dellimore, June Gibbons. *Bulletin of Eastern Caribbean Affairs,* vol. 3, nos. 1-2 (1977), p. 9-14.

Outlines an approach to the development of a desirable food-producing sector for Caribbean countries. It is stressed that food processing should be kept to a minimum as unprocessed food crops are of much greater nutritional value. The need for research and development for the design of an appropriate level of technology for food production is also emphasized.

817 **Coming of age in the computer age.**
Helen Fisher. *Bajan and South Caribbean,* no. 371 (Oct. 1984), p. 20-22.

Stresses that computerization in Barbados will change the way businesses are run, and emphasizes the need for businesses to choose the right systems and supporting software.

818 **The development of higher education in the West Indies with special emphasis on Barbados.**
Christopher Hunte. PhD dissertation, Washington State University, Pullman, Washington, 1976. 210p. bibliog. (Available from University Microfilms, Ann Arbor, Michigan, order no. GAX76-27736).

Provides an overview of higher education in three periods: pre-emancipation (1710-1834), post-emancipation (1835-1945), and expansion (1946-1974) with the advent of the University College of the West Indies. Specific reference is made to Barbadian tertiary institutions: Codrington College, Erdiston Teachers' Training College, the Homecraft Centre, Labour College, Hotel School, the Polytechnic and the Community College. By employing a social and manpower methodology, the policy-oriented research examines three questions in reference to higher education: accessibility, types of curriculum and effectiveness in responding to national goals. The author concludes that such education is too limited and academic in nature and fails to cater for regional manpower needs. A series of recommendations is made to remedy the encountered difficulties, including a lowering of the birth rate and the establishment of more community colleges based upon the American model.

819 **The Bellairs Research Institute.**
John Lewis. *Journal of the Barbados Museum and Historical Society*, vol. 29, no. 2 (Feb. 1962), p. 41-44.

Describes the establishment of the institute in 1954 as a centre for research in the tropics, due to the generosity of Commander Carlyon Bellairs, a resident of Barbados. When McGill University in Montreal expressed an interest in the venture, it was decided to expand operations from Bellairs' former seaside home to enlarged new premises. Since then the residential centre has hosted local and overseas researchers specializing in marine biology. Notable success has been achieved, for instance, in studies of the sea urchin, flying fish, crayfish and various reef fauna. A climatological section at Waterford was also set up and the Brace Experimental Station for research into solar and wind energy and desalinification was established.

820 **Ritual as ideology: an analysis of Barbados public school songs.**
Cameron McCarthy. *Cimarrón*, vol. 1, no. 1 (Spring 1985), p. 69-90.

Examines the hypothesis that school songs not only promote social solidarity, but are also vehicles of latent imperialism. The content of eight songs is analysed under the themes of imperial predominance, class, gender and colour. Afro-Barbadian culture is seen to be played down and that of the mother country emphasized as the prime exemplar to be imitated. Racism, élitism and sexism are also evident in the texts. The author believes that his hypothesis is validated since the micro-neocolonial aspects of school life, as symbolized in song, reflect asymmetrical relationships in society at large.

821 **Educational research: the English-speaking Caribbean.**
Errol Miller. Ottawa: International Development Research Centre, 1984. 199p. bibliog.

A critical evaluation of educational research in the Caribbean. The assessment contextualizes education in a wider social framework before examining the existing research capacity in various territories, the training of researchers, funding possibilities and types of projects undertaken. Barbados has five educational research institutions – the School of Education and Institute of Social and Economic Research (both at the University of the West Indies), the Ministry of Education, the Caribbean Examinations Council, and the National Nutrition

Centre. However, these are said to face a number of constraints, including inadequate funding, over-emphasis on teaching and curricula, lack of journals, poor professional communication among academics, and unwillingness to accept criticism based on empirical evidence. The general Caribbean problem of political interference is also found in Barbados.

822   **Educational development in the Eastern Caribbean primary, secondary, and tertiary levels 1966-1977.**
      R. M. Nicholson.   *Bulletin of Eastern Caribbean Affairs*, vol. 4, no. 3 (July-Aug. 1978), p. 24-28.

Examines an era of expansion of educational facilities in the Eastern Caribbean. In addition to its Erdiston Teachers' Training College, Barbados reinforced its tertiary education with the establishment of the Samuel Jackman Prescod Polytechnic, Community College and the Cave Hill campus of the University of the West Indies. The School of Education of the university has since 1972 not only produced research, but also witnessed the development of projects, programmes, workshops, in-service training, and curricula reform, particularly in the subject areas of science and mathematics. Degree programmes in education were also envisaged at the time of this study and are now available.

823   **Leisure hours at the pier, or a treatise on the education of the poor in Barbados.**
      J. W. Orderson.   Liverpool, England: Thomas Kaye, 1827. 56p.

Based on the philosophical premise that education is primarily concerned with happiness, morality, social usefulness and industry, this rather tedious discourse considers the educational needs of poor whites. There is also an evaluation of the work of the Central School, as evidenced in the reports of the Barbados Society for Promoting Christian Knowledge.

824   **Age differences in the content and style of cognitive maps of Barbadian schoolchildren.**
      Robert B. Potter, Mark G. Wilson.   *Perceptual and Motor Skills*, vol. 57 (1983), p. 332.

Presents the results of an exercise where groups of Barbadian schoolchildren of different ages were asked to provide details of all the features and places they deemed important on the island. The results suggest a clear contrast in both the complexity and overall style of the cognitive maps typical of children of different ages.

825   **The University of the West Indies and the Caribbean Community.**
      Aston Preston, Sidney Martin, Randolph Cato.   *Bulletin of Eastern Caribbean Affairs*, vol. 1, no. 12 (Feb. 1976), p. 1-19.

A joint presentation of three individual contributions. The first is based on a lecture delivered by the late vice-chancellor on the financial structure and problems of the university. The second is the summary of an address given by the first principal of the Cave Hill campus, Barbados, on the historical development of the institution in the region, including its establishment in Barbados in 1963.

The third is a critique presented by a graduate student which focuses on the colonial nature of the institution, its middle-class image and excessive bureaucracy. Fortunately, he argues, questions of greater relevance to the region have been asked since the belated appearance of a social science faculty.

826 Secondary school students' employment aspirations and expectations and the Barbados labour market.
J. Sackey, T. Sackey. *Social and Economic Studies*, vol. 34, no. 3 (Sept. 1985), p. 211-58.

Reports the findings of a 1981 sample survey of 499 secondary school students. The data reveal that over two-thirds wished to continue their education, males stressing universities and technical colleges, and females commercial colleges and nursing schools. Gender typing by subject area was also evident, with girls choosing the arts and clerically oriented courses, and boys opting for professional, scientific and technical disciplines. Occupational prestige ranking and perceived income followed the trend of most Western societies, with aspirations pointing in the same direction. Significantly no one was interested in agriculture. Finally, the foregoing data were compared with more realistic expectations and the actual situation in the job market.

827 A functional role of teachers' organisations in Barbados.
Leonard Shorey. *Caribbean Quarterly*, vol. 18, no. 3 (Sept. 1972), p. 34-42.

An article which points out the potential benefits of a vibrant and united national teachers' association in Barbados to replace the current plethora of small particularist organizations. Of approximately 3,000 teachers in Barbados, only 12.4 per cent are both graduates and professionally trained. A teachers' association could encourage professional training and have some say regarding the content of the programme. Additional benefits could accrue from fostering personal growth and academic development, research, preparing appropriate indigenous aptitude tests to replace the largely ineffective common entrance examination, reviewing current teaching methods, assessing colleagues, acting as an arbiter in disputes, and performing the role of a consultant body to the Ministry of Education.

828 The primary education project.
Leonard Shorey. *Bulletin of Eastern Caribbean Affairs*, vol. 7, no. 3 (July-Aug. 1981), p. 22-25.

A preliminary description of a four-year (1980-84) project funded by the United States Agency for International Development for the Eastern Caribbean and Jamaica. The objective was to enhance primary school education and the quality of administration and educational planning by concentrating on five schools in each territory and three of the following subject areas: language, arts, mathematics, science and social studies. To this end, implementation and evaluation officers were appointed for each territory aided by four specialists in the foregoing subject areas. Additionally, resource materials were to be produced and a series of workshops conducted at the territorial and regional level. After less than one year's operation, Dr. Shorey, the University of the West Indies coordinator, was satisfied with the initial success of the venture. In particular, he was pleased with the way in which benefits had also spread to non-project schools.

The quality of life in Barbados.
See item no. 12.

Barbados our island home.
See item no. 14.

Mapping educational disparities in the Caribbean.
See item no. 66.

Government expenditure in Barbados, 1946-79.
See item no. 627.

New technology in Barbados.
See item no. 792.

Dialog Information Retrieval Service in a Third World library: a case study.
See item no. 884.

The role of libraries in developing countries: focus on libraries in Barbados and Jamaica.
See item no. 887.

Education in the Eastern Caribbean: a select bibliography.
See item no. 957.

Literature

829 **Caribbean stories. Cuentos del Caribe.**
Selected, edited and introduced by Blanca Acosta, Samuel
Goldberg, Ileana Sanz. Havana: Casa de las Américas, 1977.
274p./ 284p.

Produced by a group of lecturers and graduates of the School of Modern
Languages at the University of Havana, in back-to-back English and Spanish
versions. The lengthy introduction notes that, in spite of historical similarities
arising from a common experience of colonialism, it was not until 1972 that Cuba
and the MDCs of the West Indies established diplomatic relations. The
coincidence of nationalism and a literary spirit in Trinidad, Jamaica, Guyana and
Barbados is then detailed. In the latter case, such a quest for identity was all the
more problematic owing to the continuation of servitude to the land and the white
oligarchy after emancipation. Class and race differences are therefore still more
pronounced in Barbados than elsewhere in the Caribbean. As examples of
liberation from the colonial mentality, the volume includes an excerpt from
George Lamming's *In the castle of my skin* and a story by Edward Brathwaite
entitled 'The Black Angel'.

830 **Barbados Independence Issue.**
New World Quarterly, vol. 3, nos. 1-2 (Dead Season 1966 and
Croptime 1977).

This special issue of a now defunct West Indian journal is entirely dedicated to
Barbados' Independence (30 November 1966). The edition comprises a number
of essays (some of which have appeared elsewhere), including: 'What the
Barbadian means to me' by John Hearne, 'Clennel Wickham: a man for all time'
by John Wickham (his son), 'The struggle for freedom' by Gordon Lewis,
'Harrison College and me' by Austin Clarke, 'An education in retrospect' by
Geoffrey Drayton, 'The legitimacy of Codrington College' by George Simmons,
'The home of the heroes' by Clyde Walcott, 'Samuel Prescod: the birth of a hero'

by H. A. Vaughan, 'Conrad Reeves: a kind of perfection' by Lionel Hutchinson, 'On Barbadians and minding other people's business' by Richard Moore, 'Duncan O'Neale: apostle of freedom' by Keith Hunte, 'Health and freedom' by Mickey Walrond, 'The poor man and his land' by Theo Hills, 'Lamming and the search for freedom' by Wilfred Cartey, and 'Frank Collymore and the miracle of *Bim*' by Edward Baugh. There are also a number of short stories and poems by well-known Barbadian authors and tributes from Puerto Rico.

831 Critics on Caribbean literature.
Edited by Edward Baugh.   London: Allen & Unwin, 1978. 164p. bibliog.

As much an introduction to a youthful West Indian literature (the earliest entry was published in 1960) as an exposure of the literature to a body of criticism. The main themes are colonialism, the nature of community and the vexing problem of dialect versus standard English. The essays are united by a common perception of the fragmentation of relationships under the broader sociological perspective of the tension between the individual and society. The two Barbadian writers featured are novelist George Lamming and poet Edward Brathwaite.

832 West Indian poetry.
Lloyd Brown.   Boston, Massachusetts: Twayne, 1978; London: Heinemann, 1984. 202p. bibliog.

Covers all the major and most of the minor West Indian poets from 1759 to the present day. Included is a rarely cited Barbadian planter, M. J. Chapman, whose 'Barbadoes' (1833) epitomizes the Caribbean pastoral tradition with clichés on the local landscape and the happiness of the slaves. Needless to say, there is a special chapter devoted to the 'cyclical vision' of Edward Brathwaite with references to his most important works. Brown takes the view that Brathwaite and Derek Walcott should be compared rather than contrasted, since both share the quest for an expression of West Indian identity.

833 Race and colour in Caribbean literature.
G. Coulthard.   London: Oxford University Press under the auspices of the Institute of Race Relations, 1962. 152p. bibliog.

Highlights the social and political awareness of writers who take racial identity as a central theme. The *engagé* nature of Latin American, and later West Indian, literature, is thus exemplified in the anti-slavery novel, the theme of Africa, the rejection of European culture, and negritude. Consequently, the Barbadian George Lamming is included among the featured 'propagandist' authors. His preoccupation with colour in *In the castle of my skin* (1953) is likened to Joseph Zobel's autobiographical novel *Rue Cases Nègres*, while the notion of self-discovery in an alien culture in Lamming's *The emigrants* (1954) is considered to have a greater insight than other comparable Caribbean works examining the emigration experience, such as Cotto-Thorner's *Tropico en Manhattan*, Zobel's *La Fête à Paris* and Samuel Selvon's *Lonely Londoners*. This work was originally published in Spanish under the title *Raza y color en la literatura Antillana* (Seville, Spain: Escuela de Estudios Hispano-Americanos de Sevilla, 1958).

834 **Caribbean narrative.**
Edited and introduced by O. Dathorne. London: Heinemann,
1966. 247p.

A collection of excerpts from thirteen Caribbean novelists, designed to give the
pre-university and university student a taste for West Indian literature. Only one
Barbadian, George Lamming, is featured, with extracts from *In the castle of my
skin* and *Season of adventure*. However, the introduction makes several
references to other Barbadian authors including Frank Collymore, John Wickham
and Geoffrey Drayton. The editor's opening essay is additionally useful for
tracing the historical development of West Indian literature, and for thereby
contextualizing Barbadian contributions. Specific references are also made to
Lamming's self-imposed exile, his ear for dialect, difficulty with humour and
penchant for history through myth.

835 **Place and nature in George Lamming's poetry.**
Arturo Maldonado Díaz. *Revista Interamericana*, vol. 4, no. 3
(1974), p. 402-10.

Focuses on Lamming the poet, rather than on his more celebrated role as novelist.
In 'Birthday poem', 'The sculptor', 'The boy and the sea', 'Swans' and
'Dedication from afar', warm nature is felt in terms of loss, once life has been
experienced in northern white cities or even the semi-urban sophistication of a
yacht club. There is a sense of hopelessness and alienation about the aspirations
of the black man when artificial physical and intellectual relationships replace the
true communion with nature enjoyed in innocent adolescence.

836 **West Indies number.**
Guest edited by Arthur Drayton. *Literary Half-Yearly*
(University of Mysore), vol. 11, no. 2 (1970), 199p.

A collection of West Indian literary contributions. The Barbadian entries are
'Point of reversal', a short story by Timothy Callender, and 'Seven poems' by
Edward Brathwaite. The issue also includes a review of Brathwaite's 'Islands' by
Gordon Rohlehr entitled 'The historian as poet'. In addition, there are two
critiques by Barbadian graduates of the University of the West Indies: 'The
novelist as historian' (on V. S. Naipaul's *The loss of El Dorado*) by C. Alan
Wade, and 'George Lamming: the historical imagination' by Gloria Yarde. Jane
Walkley provides 'A decade of Caribbean literary criticism: a select annotated
bibliography', featuring Edward Brathwaite, George Lamming, Frank Collymore
and the literary journal *Bim*.

837 **Spectrum and prism: the language of contemporary Caribbean
anglophone poetry.**
Elaine Fido. *Bim*, vol. 18, no. 69 (Dec. 1985), p. 73-78.

A sympathetic review which examines the work of two Caribbean poets, Edward
Kamau Brathwaite and A. L. Hendriks. The former is indirectly acknowledged to
be the leading contemporary practitioner of Caribbean anglophone poetry and
Fido feels it is worthwhile to look at some of Brathwaite's theoretical ideas as
expounded in his *History of the voice* (1984), the transcript of a 1979 Harvard
lecture. The major point highlighted in this essay is that there is a 'nation

language' in the Caribbean which is predominantly oral and African. Furthermore, such a language, which transcends mere dialect, possesses a rhythm of its own, one which is a folk maroon interpretation of a subjectively apprehended socio-cultural experience ultimately grounded in the twin curses of poverty and oppression. This is a far cry from the typical ideal colonial pentameter, which is problematic to say the least in describing the aftermath of a hurricane, whether physical or psychological.

838   **Caribbean voices: an anthology of West Indian poetry. Vol. 1. Dreams and visions.**
Selected and introduced by John Figueroa.   London: Evans Brothers, 1966. Reprinted, 1974. 119p. bibliog.
A collection of approximately one hundred poems appropriate for schoolchildren. Many selections are derived from the BBC's programme 'Caribbean Voices' and the Barbadian literary journal *Bim*. The poems are grouped under six headings: People, Nature, Art, In our land, Interlude and Beyond. Barbadian contributions are from William Arthur, Frank Collymore, Geoffrey Drayton, A. N. Forde, George Lamming, Alfred Pragnell and H. A. Vaughan.

839   **Forgotten limericks.**
Journal of the Barbados Museum and Historical Society, vol. 16, nos. 1-2 (Nov. 1948-Feb. 1949), p. 12-13.
Some examples of limericks are provided dating from 1865. Most are targeted at assemblymen, and illustrate the popularity of lampooning prominent figures. The anonymous person who introduces the verse believes that this literary form should be preserved from oblivion.

840   **The West Indian novel.**
Michael Gilkes.   Boston, Massachusetts: Twayne, 1981. 168p. bibliog.
Traces the historical evolution of the West Indian novel through four stages: pioneers (de Lisser, C. L. R. James, Roger Mais and Edgar Mittelholzer); the background to exile (George Lamming, V. S. Naipaul and St. Omer); a kind of homecoming (V. S. Reid and George Lamming); and new directions (Hudson, Williams and Wilson Harris). The Barbadian writer Lamming receives extensive treatment. His themes of childhood, alienation, the quest for identity, exile and return are thoroughly analysed with reference to other comparable West Indian (Reid, Harris, Naipaul) and extraregional (James Joyce and Mark Twain) authors.

841   **Dr. M. J. Chapman.**
F. A. Hoyos.   *Journal of the Barbados Museum and Historical Society*, vol. 16, nos. 1-2 (Nov. 1948-Feb 1949), p. 14-20.
A sympathetic account of the life and work of a distinguished Barbadian scholar, medical practitioner and poet. Examples of his verse are presented including some which appear to extol the happiness of the slaves. Hoyos points out that this attitude should be understood in the context of the improvement of their

conditions in the period between abolition and emancipation and the perceived danger in granting immediate freedom.

842   **A companion to West Indian literature.**
Michael Hughes.   London: Collins, 1979. 135p. bibliog.

Provides a brief account, with critiques, of the lives and major works of 106 West Indian authors. Twenty-two literary journals are also featured in the compilation. Writers from Barbados for whom there are entries include Edward Brathwaite (described as probably the finest poet the West Indies have so far produced), Timothy Callender, Austin Clarke, Frank Collymore, Geoffrey Drayton, J. B. Emtage, A. N. Forde, Lionel Hutchinson, George Lamming and John Wickham. The journal which Wickham edits, *Bim*, is also mentioned. A true companion and bibliography in its own right.

843   **The islands in between: essays on West Indian literature.**
Edited and introduced by Louis James.   London: Oxford University Press, Three Crown Books, 1968. 166p. bibliog.

This volume of literary criticism comprises evaluations of West Indian writers by their contemporaries. A lengthy, but informative, introduction takes up one-third of the text and includes comments on the following works by Barbadian authors: Austin Clarke's *The survivors of the crossing* (1964), Geoffrey Drayton's *Christopher* (1959), Edward Brathwaite's *Rights of passage* (1967) and *Masks* (1968), and George Lamming's *The pleasures of exile* (1960). There is also a separate chapter on the latter entitled 'The poet as novelist: the novels of George Lamming' by Mervyn Morris, who critically reviews the author's major works.

844   **The re-presentation of history in the literature of the West Indies.**
Jackie Kaye.   In: *Caribbean societies, vol. 1.* Edited by Christopher Abel, Michael Twaddle. London: Institute of Commonwealth Studies, University of London, 1952, p. 1-7. (Collected Seminar Papers, no. 29).

Examines the complex manner in which four West Indian writers (V. S. Reid, Jean Rhys, Edward Brathwaite and George Lamming) deal with history from a Caribbean perspective. The last two, both Barbadians, tackle the problem through poetry and prose respectively. Brathwaite in *Masks* travels into his ancestral past by focusing on the guilt of the Akan people of the 'Gold Coast', as they migrate from the fallen empire of the interior 'through weakened thoughts' and lack of god, only to be caught up in the horrors of slavery. Lamming also employs the allegory of voyage in *Natives of my person*, this time a mythical 17th-century trip from repressive Limestone in Europe to the imaginary island of San Cristobal, in which the guilt of slavery and genocide is expiated. The themes of guilt, complicity, fear of commitment and feminine love, are also explored in some other works by Lamming, namely *In the castle of my skin* and *Season of adventure*.

845 West Indian literature.
Edited and introduced by Bruce King. London: Macmillan, 1979. 247p. bibliog.

Seeks to fill a void by presenting the historical development of West Indian literature and literary criticism of major English-speaking Caribbean writers. While the first six essays attend to the former, the remaining eight deal with the latter. In the second section there are two critical reviews of Barbadian authors: 'George Lamming' by Ian Munro, and 'Edward Brathwaite' by J. Michael Dash. Both emphasize these authors' common themes of alienation, exile and search for identity.

846 Critical approaches to West Indian literature.
Introduced by Roberta Knowles, Erika Smilowitz. St. Thomas, US Virgin Islands: Humanities Division, College of the US Virgin Islands, 1981. 282p. bibliog.

A compilation of fourteen edited position papers presented at a joint conference involving the College of the Virgin Islands and the University of the West Indies. Two of the contributions focus on the Barbadian poet Edward Brathwaite. The first, 'Aspects of technique in Brathwaite's "Rights of Passage" ' is presented by Gordon Rohlehr. Here the functions of various art forms are examined – the metaphor of architecture in 'Judas of Barcelona', music in 'Rights of passage', and carving and sculpture in 'The making of the drum' and 'Ogun'. The second, 'Edward Brathwaite as critic' by Edward Baugh, examines Brathwaite's critical essays (before he became an established poet) in literary journals such as *Bim*. Other essays in this volume include 'Sir Galahad and the islands', 'The new West Indian novelists', 'Roots: a commentary on West Indian writers', 'Jazz and the West Indian novel' and 'West Indian prose fiction in the sixties: a survey'.

847 Notes to *Masks*.
Maureen Lewis. Benin: Ethiope Publishing Corporation, 1977. 88p. 2 maps.

A guide to Edward Brathwaite's celebrated 'roots' poem which, in its inimitable way, seeks to explore West Indian African ancestry. The author first contextualizes the Barbadian's contribution in relation to his own work and to other literary works relating to Africa, before examining the central themes, symbols and techniques of *Masks* (1968). Thereafter the text assumes an exegetical character, providing commentary for each section of the poem.

848 Special issue of *Caribbean Quarterly* on Edward Brathwaite and Derek Walcott.
Introduced by Rex Nettleford. *Caribbean Quarterly*, vol. 26 nos. 1-2 (June 1980).

After an opening essay by Laurence Breiner comparing the Barbadian and St. Lucian writers, there are a number of contributions focusing on specific works. Items about Barbadian writers include 'Bridges of sound, an approach to Edward Brathwaite's "Jah" ' and 'Background music to "Rights of Passage" ' by Gordon

Rohlehr, and 'The dust – a tribute to the folk' by Velma Pollard. The issue concludes with a poetic tribute to 'Eddy' by Pam Mordecai.

849   **The novels of George Lamming.**
Sandra Pouchet Paquet.   London: Heinemann, 1982. 130p.
bibliog.

In a novel-by-novel critique, Paquet examines Lamming's six major works. From her analysis of the novels and from interviews with the author she concludes that Lamming is very much a political writer who treats the colonial experience as a unitary theme, and as a situation from which West Indians must be liberated in consciousness. In all his novels, even the autobiographical *In the castle of my skin* where G, the central character, becomes in a sense the whole village, Lamming is said to examine private experience in relation to public events. His technique is based on the use of the collective character. There are thus three levels of analysis – the individual, social relations and the community of men. It is the latter world which the author primarily addresses as a prophetic reformer, one who can symbolically relate the present to both past and future, just as the priest of voodoo consults the ancestral gods in order to determine a course of action.

850   **Poetry in the Caribbean.**
Julie Pearn with an introduction by Louise Bennett.   London:
Hodder & Stoughton, 1985. 60p. bibliog.

A textbook encouraging students to familiarize themselves with regional poets. Among the Barbadians featured are Frank Collymore and his playful sketches of birds, beasts and plants, and Bruce St. John with his use of proverbs and the litany style of the gospel hall. Edward Brathwaite shares a chapter with Derek Walcott, and in it the influence of jazz, T. S. Eliot, the sea and Rastafari on his work is discussed.

851   **Anansesem.**
Edited by Velma Pollard.   Kingston: Longman, 1985. 89p.

In the words of the subtitle, this is 'a collection of Caribbean folk tales, legends and poems for juniors'. Anansesem, a Twi word from the Akan language of the people of Ghana, literally means 'anancy stories', and several of the contributions relate to this cunning African spider and his animal-cum-human friends. The Barbadian selections comprise two poems by Edward Brathwaite, one by Phyllis Inniss, and seven by Frank Collymore. Among the latter is the classic two-liner: 'The winged part of the flying fish/Is not required in the dish'.

852   **West Indian narrative: an introductory anthology.**
Compiled and introduced by Kenneth Ramchand.   London:
Nelson, 1966. Reprinted, 1971. 226p.

The compiler appeals to Caribbean schoolchildren to relate their experiences to those of West Indian authors. By asking a series of questions about the featured excerpts, he hopes to tackle this problem of relevance. In this sense, the two contrasting Barbadian selections, *In the castle of my skin* by George Lamming and *Christopher* by Geoffrey Drayton, both of which are about growing up in the island (albeit from differing racial perspectives), would find an automatic identification response from children.

853   **An introduction to the study of West Indian literature.**
Kenneth Ramchand.   Sunbury-on-Thames, Surrey, England: Nelson Caribbean, 1976. Reprinted, 1980. 183p. bibliog.

Based on a course of university lectures, tutorials and seminars. Eleven Caribbean authors are 'introduced', along with critiques and supplementary readings, in order to facilitate comparisons with other writers who have treated similar themes. The volume includes studies of Lamming's *In the castle of my skin* and Brathwaite's trilogy *The Arrivants*. While the former is highlighted for its treatment of childhood alienation in a colonial society, the focus of the latter is more explicitly on a search for an understanding of black West Indian culture. Both novelist and poet achieve their aims through a mastery of dialect and rhythm.

854   **Best West Indian stories.**
Introduced by Kenneth Ramchand.   Walton-on-Thames, Surrey, England: Nelson, 1982. 186p.

The introduction to this anthology of twenty items contextualizes the short story in West Indian literature as the bridge between oral tradition and the novel, the former drawing on the folk-tale, fairy story, humorous tale, tall tale and anecdote. Strangely, only one Barbadian author is featured: Geoffrey Drayton, noted for his novels *Christopher* (1959) and *Zohara* (1961) and his book of poems *Three meridians*, is represented by a piece entitled 'Mr Dombey, the zombie'. This is a bizarre tale of a man who murders his hounsi wife and survives the hangman's noose three times. Evidently this story reflects the author's unpublished research on obeah and voodoo.

855   **Pathfinder.**
Gordon Rohlehr.   Maracas, Trinidad: College Press, 1981. 343p. bibliog.

Subtitled 'Black awakening in *The Arrivants* of Edward Kamau Brathwaite', this book is a critical analysis of the Barbadian poet's well-known trilogy. An introductory chapter, some of which is based on personal communication between author and poet, traces Brathwaite's life and the various forces and personalities which shaped his contribution to Caribbean literature. Thereafter Rohlehr examines the background, context, technique and language of 'Rights of Passage', *Masks* and 'Islands'. Appendixes provide details of the influence of music on Brathwaite's poetry, the writer's own essays and critical reviews of his work.

856   **Lionel Hutchinson: Barbados' forgotten novelist.**
Roydon Salick.   *Bim*, vol. 18, no. 69 (Dec. 1985), p. 66-72.

A review of Hutchinson's two novels: *Man from the people* (1969) and *One touch of nature* (1971). The first is about Barbadian politics of the early 1960s, and the unsuccessful attempt of an honest upright community man, Sam Martin, to overcome the vulgarity, vindictiveness and sexual exploitation so characteristic of his rivals. The second is the only local novel to deal with redlegs. It does so through the eyes of Harriet Jivenot and her sister Judy. The former yearns to escape from her oppressive existence through a series of affairs; the latter settles for love with a black man. Salick considers that, while neither of the two novels is a masterpiece, both capture neglected portions of Barbadian social history. In particular, the female characters are strong, the commentary is witty, and there is a strong grasp of dialect.

857 Caribbean prose.
Edited and introduced by Andrew Salkey. London: Evans Brothers, 1967. 126p.

An anthology of short stories compiled for readers in the fourteen to seventeen age range. Of the thirteen recognizable 'slices of West Indian life', which can later serve as introductions to the themes of novels, two Barbadian works have been selected. One is an excerpt from *In the castle of my skin* entitled 'The Preacher'. The other is a prose-poetry anecdote, 'Cricket', by Edward Brathwaite, which alternates between a beach game and a match against the MCC at Kensington. In the latter, the local heroes become victims of Jim Laker's spin bowling, in spite of all the advice offered to the batsmen by the vociferous home crowd.

858 Caribbean essays: an anthology.
Edited and introduced by Andrew Salkey. London: Evans Brothers, 1973. 131p.

A collection of sixteen previously published essays by Caribbean writers, introduced by a well-established Jamaican novelist. The book includes a contribution from George Lamming, 'The West Indian people', and a piece by John Hearne entitled 'What the Barbadian means to me'. The latter dwells on the characteristics of Englishness, thrift, hard work, orderliness and compromise, which other West Indians, though secretly admiring, find quite infuriating. There is also an interesting essay by the sociologist and novelist Orlando Patterson on 'The ritual of cricket', which examines the symbolism of the game. At the same time it attempts to answer the quetion of why riots take place at Test matches against the former colonial power.

859 New writing in the Caribbean.
Edited and introduced by A. J. Seymour. Georgetown: Guyana Lithographic Company, 1972. 319p.

The origins of this book lay in two conferences of Caribbean Authors and Artists (1966 and 1970) and the 1972 Caribbean Festival of Creative Arts, all held in Guyana. The selections emphasize a growing awareness of intercultural common ground shared by Dutch-, French-, Spanish-, Portuguese- and English-speaking peoples of the Caribbean and South America. The material included provides evidence of a rejection of European values and the need to experience and communicate with folk realities. Among the English-language authors represented are four Barbadian poets: Edward Brathwaite, Elizabeth Clarke, Frank Collymore and Bruce St. John. There are also two examples of Barbadian prose: A. N. Forde's 'The women of Breadfruit Alley' and John Wickham's 'The fellow travellers'. While the former tells us something of the Bajan male view of women, the latter looks at Barbadians through the eyes of Trinidadians stranded at Seawell Airport.

860 **Aftermath: an anthology of poems in English from Africa, Asia and the Caribbean.**
Edited by Roger Weaver, Joseph Bruchac. New York: Greenfield Review Press, 1977. 257p.

Seeks to expose Commonwealth writers from smaller countries to a wider international readership. The Caribbean section is introduced by Barbadian author Bruce St. John; he pinpoints the overall theme of search for identity and the problem posed by skin colour in a creole society. The volume includes nine selections from six Barbadian poets: Edward Brathwaite, Frank Collymore, A. N. Forde, Margaret Gill, H. A. Vaughan and St. John himself.

West Indian literature: an index to criticism 1930-1975.
See item no. 934.

Caribbean writers: a bio-bibliographical-critical encyclopedia.
See item no. 941.

The Arts

861 **A photographic display.**
Barbados Professional Photographers' Association. *Bajan and South Caribbean*, no. 279 (Feb. 1977), p. 26-27.
Describes the contents of the exhibition held on the 10th anniversary of Independence mounted by the island's leading photographers. Brief biographies of eleven professional photographers are supplied, along with some examples of their work.

862 **From Kensington to Carnegie Hall.**
Céline Barnard. *Bajan and South Caribbean*, no. 281 (April 1977), p. 4-9.
Describes the rise to international fame of the popular white Barbadian group known as the Merrymen. Formed in 1962 by Emile Straker, along with Robin Hunte and Stephen Fields, the initial trio began singing folk songs on the Barbados radio station Rediffusion. After the addition of Chris Gibbs to the group, they entered the hotel circuit. Local acceptance came in 1963 with their performance at the Carnival Queen Show at Kensington Oval. From that point progress was rapid and several North American and European engagements soon followed. The band expanded, there were a few changes and new recruits, but the appeal of the right sound combined with original and traditional material ensured the group's success. Today the Merrymen often act as overseas ambassadors for the Barbados Board of Tourism, they have their own recording studio, and still play to capacity crowds in Barbados.

863 **Guy O'Neal, cartoonist.**
Céline Barnard. *Bajan and South Caribbean*, no. 292 (March 1978), p. 41-42.

Outlines the life and work of one of Barbados' youngest cartoonists. In particular, the influence of the much-acclaimed Winston Jordan is readily acknowledged, and the commercial possibilities of such art are also discussed.

864 **Report of the second conference of Caribbean dramatists.**
Coordinated by Ken Corsbie. Barbados: Theatre Information Exchange, 1978. 109p.

An important 'state of the art' conference involving several Caribbean writers and producers. Ken Corsbie's introduction includes accounts of the establishment of Theatre Information Exchange in Barbados, the work of Cave Hill staff in drama-related activities, and various theatre groups in the island, such as Rontana, Yoruba, Stage One, Adventure Theatre and Green Room Players. In his keynote address, John Wickham queries the usefulness of establishing a national auditorium, and discusses the manipulation of the arts by politicians and the response to cultural events by members of the Barbadian public.

865 **Directory of artists in Barbados.**
Compiled by Joyce Daniel, Bill Grace. Collymore Rock, St. Michael, Barbados: Cedar Press, 1984. 37p.

A production of the Visual Arts Committee of the Barbados Arts Council. The directory contains information on about forty resident artists, including details of biography, exhibitions, awards and work media. Home addresses and telephone numbers are also provided for those wishing to contact the artists.

866 **Lamentable loss of Yoruba.**
Trevor Marshall. *Bajan and South Caribbean*, no. 308 (July 1979), p. 23-24.

The author traces the nine-year history of the only overt Afro-Barbadian cultural movement from 1970 to its collapse as a commercial venture through indebtedness. Founded by Elton 'Elombe' Mottley, the activities of Yoruba focused on printing and publishing on the one hand, and Afro-Caribbean presentations on the other. The latter operated from Yoruba Yard in Fontabelle, an intimate theatre and cultural training centre blessed with the services of a Nigerian master dancer and master drummer. Yoruba Presents was the production arm of the Yard, while Yoruba People was an associated cultural performing group. Marshall regrets the passing of this source and inspiration of black identity, and hopes for its resurrection through various local, regional and international funding agencies. Although his hope has not yet materialized, there is now a government-run National Cultural Foundation of which Mottley was until recently director.

867 **Folk songs of Barbados.**
Compiled by Trevor Marshall, Peggy McGeary, Grace
Thompson. Barbados: Macmarson Associates, 1981. 108p.
bibliog.

A pioneering work which collectively represents about twenty-five years of
research. In some ways it may be considered an oral history project, since the
compilers spent many hours tramping through working-class villages of the more
genuinely Barbadian eastern and northern districts of the island. There is a useful
introduction for those interested in comparative culture or simply for those who
wish to know more about a rapidly disappearing unsophisticated folk tradition.
The songs themselves have been classified under the headings of narrative social
songs, children's songs, tuk band songs, work songs, social songs, songs about
men, songs about women and recent songs about the folk. Each is presented with
music and an historical commentary. Although not a complete collection, since
extraneous foreign matter had to be discarded and obscene material deleted, this
is nevertheless an extremely worthwhile effort.

Sports and Recreation

868 The 'Big Bird': life off the wicket.

Mark D. Alleyne.   *Bajan* (Dec. 1984), p. 18-21.

An interview with Joel Garner, the 6′8″ fast bowler from Barbados. The account begins with details of his upbringing by his grandmother, Editha, and his early performances for South Point Cricket Club and Boys Foundation School, where he earned the nickname 'Big Bird'. He later joined Wes Hall, his mentor, who was playing his last season with Cable and Wireless, where Garner landed his first job. His professional career began in 1976 in the Lancashire League where he represented Littleborough, and in the same year he represented his country. In 1977 he joined the West Indies side, and, apart from missing games through shoulder and knee injuries, has been in the Test side ever since. In spite of world fame, and the many demands of overseas tours, Joel still enjoys relaxing in the Christ Church neighbourhood where he has lived all his life.

869 Sir Gary, a biography.

Trevor Bailey.   London: Collins, 1976. 190p.

On the basis of a close relationship both on and off the field, the author is convinced that Sobers 'has quite simply been the greatest of all time, the most complete all-rounder ever, with the figures to substantiate the claim'. Consequently, the biographer makes no apology for being oversympathetic in his treatment of a man he admires so much. The rags-to-riches story of Barbados' most illustrious cricketer is spiced with anecdotal material and occasional glimpses of growing up in the island during the 1940s. For the enthusiast, a set of Sir Garfield's career statistics is also included.

265

870   **Frank Worrell.**
       Ernest Eytle.   London: Hodder & Stoughton, 1963. Reprinted,
       1964. 194p.

Commences with the famous final Test of the 1960-61 series at Melbourne with
the post-match cries of 'Well played boys!' and 'Come back soon!', which Worrell
confesses 'brought a lump to my throat and tears to my eyes'. The author then
goes back over the career of this West Indian captain, the only one of the
legendary 3 Ws (Weekes, Walcott and Worrell) still playing at the time of writing.
Starting with childhood days, when Worrell played in shorts at the age of thirteen
for Combermere School's First XI, the reader is taken on a journey which
culminates in the triumphant tour of England in 1963. Frank, later knighted, adds
a personal postscript to each chapter.

871   **West Indians at the wicket.**
       Clayton Goodwin, with a foreword by Clive Lloyd.   London:
       Macmillan Caribbean, 1986. 200p. map.

A sympathetic and knowledgeable overview of the historical and contemporary
progress of the world's top cricket team. Separate chapters are devoted to the
writer's hero, batsman Gordon Greenidge, to the seemingly never-ending stream
of Barbadian fast bowlers, and to Kensington Oval. Amid a wealth of statistics,
the author, like so many others before him, makes the point that the island has
contributed more to regional cricket than any other territory, so much so that it
now combines cricket with tourism. Even the taxi drivers, who regularly escort
international reporters to hotels, are reckoned to know more about the finer
points of the game than some members of the press covering the events.
Goodwin's comments are aptly echoed by former England captain, David Gower:
'Barbados, of course, has long had a reputation for being capable of producing a
side of Test match standard all by itelf, and it does not take long, when you visit
the island, to find out why. Everywhere people are playing cricket, from the dusty
lanes through the sugar cane fields, through the many rough and ready grounds
dotted round the island, plus of course the more elegant and historical clubs such
as Wanderers, to the beaches that we all know so well from the travel brochures.
This is the heart of Caribbean cricket, the origin of all the talent that springs from
the region'.

872   **Chucked around.**
       Charlie Griffith with an introduction by David
       Simmons.   London: Pelham Books, 1970. 160p.

A self-defence by the well-known and controversial Barbadian bowler, believed
by some to be a thrower of the ball, and remembered for his injuring of Indian
Nari Contractor in 1962. Apart from accounts of various tours and Test matches,
there are sections about Barbados itself and growing up in St. Lucy during the
Second World War. The organization of the game in Barbados is also briefly
described, together with the prevailing racial prejudice in the cricket clubs.

266

873 **Playing to win.**
Conrad Hunte.   London: Hodder & Stoughton, 1971. 160p.

Like Ernest Eytle in his biography *Frank Worrell* (q.v.), Conrad Hunte opens his
account with the famous 1960-61 Test series in Australia. There is then a similar
flashback to childhood days, this time to cricket in a St. Andrew village with a
coconut palm frond for a bat, and a cork wrapped with cloth and twine for a ball.
Thereafter the story of Hunte's life becomes more personal, as readers are told
about the feelings of a black man working in England, with reflections on black
power and Powellism. They are also provided with details of his conversion to
Moral Rearmament and his joining of Rajmshan Gandhi's march on wheels
across India.

874 **Gary Sobers: cricket crusader.**
Garfield Sobers with R. A. Martin.   London: Pelham Books,
1966. 171p.

This autobiography is intended not so much to elaborate on cricketing technique,
as to tell enthusiasts about the man Gary Sobers. Personal reflections on the game
and feelings experienced at various turning points of his life are expressed in a
curious blend of the past tense and present historic. The style ranges from
conversational to confessional, seeming to reveal all while typically keeping back
his innermost thoughts.

875 **Gary Sobers' way of cricket.**
Garfield Sobers, Patrick Smith.   Hawthorn, Victoria, Australia:
Five Mile Press, 1985. 78p.

This booklet includes forewords by Bob Hawke and Ian Chappell, together with a
brief biography of the 'greatest all-round cricketer in Test history', who was born
in Barbados on 18 July 1936. The remainder of the volume is dedicated to
batting, bowling and fielding techniques, and is accompanied by several
illustrations and photographs.

876 **West Indies revisited.**
E. W. Swanton.   London: Heinemann, 1960. 288p.

Basically a book about the 1959-1960 MCC tour of the West Indies, including the
game against Barbados and the first Test at Kensington Oval. The former was a
famous ten-wicket victory for the home side. The win was all the more
convincing, given that Everton Weekes, placing himself at number seven, was not
even required to bat, yet still managed to collect four wickets while resting his
main bowlers. The celebrated commentator notes that 'there are no more
hospitable folk than the Barbadians, nor any with a deeper pride in their island
and in its cricket achievements . . . The essence of cricket as produced in
Barbados is an incomparable distillation. There is nothing quite like it anywhere
in the world'. This volume also provides a number of personal and nostalgic
impressions as well as recollections about cricket.

Everyday life in Barbados: a sociological perspective.
See item no. 11.

Sports and Recreation

The quality of life in Barbados.
See item no. 12.

The Barbados book.
See item no. 192.

Crop Over: an old Barbadian plantation festival.
See item no. 392.

Caribbean newspaperman – an autobiography.
See item no. 890.

Food and Drink

877 Cooking the West Indian way.
Dalton Babb.   Wildey, St. Michael, Barbados: Letchworth Press, [n.d.]. 48p.

Written by a former chef of the Bagshot House, and one-time housekeeper to Lord and Lady Rothschild at Sandy Lane, this recent publication contains over 100 recipes comprising appetizers, salads and vegetables, seafood, meat and poultry, desserts, special menus and brunches. Several of the dishes are original preparations of the author and incorporate his surname in their titles.

878 What's cooking? Favourite recipes of cooks in Barbados.
Members of the Barbados Red Cross Society St. George Branch.   Ellerton, St. George, Barbados: Caribbean Graphics, 1983. Reprinted, 1985. 145p.

Recipes have been contributed to this book by various members of the Red Cross as a fund-raising effort for that institution's meals-on-wheels programme. Dishes are arranged under seven main headings: starters (including birds on toast!); meat and poultry; fish; luncheon and supper dishes; vegetables and salads; desserts; cookies and cakes. However, only a few of the 193 entries are strictly Barbadian in origin.

879 Barbados rum book.
Researched by Peter Campbell.   London: Macmillan Caribbean, 1985. 46p. map.

After a brief introduction to the island, the booklet traces the history of rum production in Barbados. Recipes are supplied for various daiquiris, cocktails, juleps, highballs and punches, along with some cake and dessert dishes. The accompanying photographs are well produced.

880   **Jill Walker's cooking in Barbados.**
Charlotte Hingston, illustrated by Jill Walker.   St. Thomas,
Barbados: Best of Barbados Limited, 1983. Reprinted, 1984. 98p.

This was very much a family effort, since the daughter and mother respectively
compiled and illustrated the booklet, while the father published it. The recipes
have all been 'tested' and are not too expensive. They are divided into the
following categories: appetizers and soups, fish, chicken, meats, vegetables,
desserts, baking, drinks, and preserves and beauty hints. There is even one entry
on bush tea. This publication is also interesting for its presentation of various
rural and street scenes of Barbados.

881   **100 favourite old-tyme molasses recipes made with pure Barbados
fancy molasses.**
V. A. Layne.   Halifax, Nova Scotia, Canada: the author, [n.d.].
29p.

Accompanied by a brief history of molasses, the recipes include meats,
vegetables, pies, cakes, cookies, gingerbreads, desserts, frosting, toppings,
sauces, breads, candies and special treats.

882   **Caribbean cookbook.**
Rita Springer.   London: Evans Brothers, 1968. Reprinted,
London: Pan Books, 1979; 1983. 235p.

Written by a leading Barbadian culinary expert, who writes a weekly column on
food preparation for the *Nation* newspaper. In addition to providing recipes for
various regional fish, meat and vegetarian dishes, Springer includes drinks, home-
baked bread, jams and preserves, and Caribbean adaptations of Oriental,
European, African and American cuisine. Typically Barbadian entries feature
conkies, cou-cou, doved peas, falernum, fowl down-in-rice, jug-jug, and the
ubiquitous pudding and souse.

883   **The Barbados cook book.**
Compiled by Peggy Sworder, Jill Hamilton.   Wildey, St. Michael,
Barbados: Letchworth Press, 1983. Reprinted, 1986. 104p.

A booklet published in aid of the Barbados Military Cemetery (a brief history of
which is also included). In addition to the customary fish, meat and vegetable
preparations, there are entries on drinks, cakes, biscuits, breads, sweets, jams and
preserves. A useful glossary and cook's tips are also provided.

Barbados.
See item no. 17.

Some observations on the snappers of Barbados.
See item no. 228.

Some notes on the crustacea of Barbados.
See item no. 268.

Some notes on the echinoderms (starfish, sea eggs) of Barbados.
See item no. 269.

A true and exact history of the island of Barbados.
See item no. 351.

Libraries

884 **Dialog Information Retrieval Service in a Third World library: a case study.**
Nel Bretney. *Bulletin of Eastern Caribbean Affairs*, vol. 8, no. 6 (Jan.-Feb. 1983), p. 1-8.

Discusses the benefits of the United States National Aeronautics and Space Administration's retrieval system, DIALOG, used in the Cave Hill library of the University of the West Indies since December 1981 as a possible alternative to periodical subscriptions in gathering research information. The computer commands for the search strategies are briefly analysed and a number of examples provided dealing with topics related to library information, law, social science, management and agriculture. The merits and disadvantages of DIALOG are compared with those of hard-copy indexing services, and the six months' experience of the system's operation in Barbados is evaluated.

885 **Libraries and librarianship in the Commonwealth Caribbean.**
Alma Jordan. *Caribbean Quarterly*, vol. 18, no. 3 (Sept. 1972), p. 43-50.

Compares the growth of library services in the member countries of the former West Indies Federation and the problems they face in terms of staff, training, manpower and finance. Barbados, with a ninety-two per cent literacy rate in 1946, instituted a free public library by law three years before England and one year before the United States. Today it has a reasonably good library system in operation, with a bookmobile service, a university library (established in 1967), and an association of librarians (formed in 1969).

886   **The problems of specialist libraries.**
Dawn Marshall.   *Bulletin of Eastern Caribbean Affairs*, vol. 3,
nos. 1-2 (March-April 1977), p. 17-20.

An account of a seminar hosted by the Institute of Social and Economic Research
(Eastern Caribbean) to examine the problems facing specialist libraries in
Barbados. Participants included representatives from the Library Association of
Barbados and libraries of the University of the West Indies, Central Bank of
Barbados, Caribbean Development Bank and Christian Action for Development
in the Caribbean. In a background paper prepared by Audine Wilkinson,
librarian of the Institute of Social and Economic Research, the problems of small
size, and limited space, staff and budget, were outlined. Additional difficulties
concerned the acquisition of unpublished papers and government reports, and
collaboration with other special libraries in the region. The question of purging
dated and irrelevant material was also discussed.

887   **The role of libraries in developing countries: focus on libraries in
Barbados and Jamaica.**
Velma Newton.   *Bulletin of Eastern Caribbean Affairs*, vol. 2,
no. 12 (Feb. 1977), p. 1-7.

After stressing the educational need for an efficient library service, the author
describes the pitiful state of those found in the Leeward and Windward Islands.
By contrast, Jamaica and Barbados are more fortunate. The latter has a central
library in Bridgetown, seven branch libraries, and a bookmobile service to eighty-
three primary and three secondary schools. There are also special collections at
the Queen Elizabeth Hospital and Glendairy Prison. Even though the Barbados
Public Library has since 1958 been financed by government, salaries still account
for sixty per cent of expenditure, and in 1976/77 only fifty cents per head of the
population was allocated for books. At that time records showed that one in four
Barbadians borrowed at least one book per year. Other libraries in the island are
briefly described, including those found in schools, some government departments
and statutory boards, the Archives and the University of the West Indies.

888   **Acquisition of legal materials, with special reference to the
Caribbean: problems and prospects.**
Velma Newton.   *Bulletin of Eastern Caribbean Affairs*, vol. 9,
no. 5 (Nov.-Dec. 1983), p. 17-22.

Describes how the law library of the University of the West Indies in Barbados,
commencing with just a few hundred books in 1970, by 1982 housed roughly
50,000 volumes. Among these are collections of Commonwealth Caribbean
legislation, regional law reports and judgements, law reports and other primary
materials from non-Caribbean Commonwealth countries, Commonwealth law
reform commission reports and working papers, and a reasonable number of
periodicals. Deficiencies comprise primary legal materials for English-speaking
Africa and the United States, monographs and textbooks published in many areas
of law for the Commonwealth outside the United Kingdom and the Caribbean,
law reports, monographs and periodicals dealing with natural resources, public
utilities and commercial law, collections of annual departmental and other reports
from the Commonwealth Caribbean. Such omissions are due in the main to

budgetary constraints, limitations of space, and difficulties in acquisition from source.

A guide to records in Barbados.
See item no. 926.

Mass Media

General

889 **To local media power.**
Nigel Barrow. *Nation Independence Special* (27 Nov. 1981),
p. 34.

Records highlights of a speech by the then minister of information at the opening
of the Voice of Barbados radio broadcasting station the previous May. From this
address and the booklet published to celebrate the golden anniversary of
Rediffusion, the following sequence of events is constructed for the electronic
media in Barbados: 1935, Radio Distribution wired service established; 1951,
Name changed to Barbados Rediffusion Ltd; 1959, First experimental television
production by Rediffusion; 1963, Commencement of radio and television by the
government-owned Caribbean Broadcasting Corporation; 1979, Rediffusion
acquired by Nation Company; 1981, Voice of Barbados – 790 begins transmissions; 1982, Barbados Broadcasting Service to commence FM transmissions.
FM Radio Liberty, which is targeted mainly at youth, and is the sister station to
CBC Radio 900, has since come on the air.

890 **Caribbean newspaperman – an autobiography.**
E. L. Cozier with an introduction by Sir Hugh
Springer. Bridgetown: Literary Features (Caribbean), 1985.
182p.

Subtitled 'the life and times of Jimmy Cozier', this is the tale of one of Barbados'
most well known and popular journalists. The autobiography ranges through most
of the Caribbean from St. Croix to Trinidad, and includes several glimpses of
Barbados as seen through the eyes of a white man brought up on a plantation.
There are also references to bridge as played on the island, and Cozier's
invaluable contribution to the game as founder president of the Barbados Bridge
League.

275

891 **Early printing in Barbados.**
Douglas McMurtrie. London: the author, 1933. 15p.
Traces the development of printing from the early days of Samuel Keimer and David Harry of Philadelphia. Although McMurtrie finds no evidence that the erratic Harry printed anything locally, he reproduces the earliest surviving issue of the semi-weekly *Barbados Gazette* (no. 120, 1733) to demonstrate the work of this one-time master. However, Keimer apparently experienced difficulty in collecting the debts of subscribers, and there was an outburst by him to this effect in the 4 May 1734 edition of that newspaper. He was succeeded by William Beeby, who had the paper printed for him at the rate of 5 shillings per quarter. Beeby also managed to publish *Memoirs of the first settlement* (q.v.) in 1741, of which only two first editions still survive. George Esmand was the next to appear on the scene. He printed the *Barbados Mercury* in 1762, though the earliest recorded issue of this paper is February 1766. He was joined by W. Walker, and together they published some pamphlets. John Orderson followed as printer of the *Mercury*, accompanied by Isaac, who was probably his son. Thomas Perch is also mentioned as publisher of the *Gazette* during the years 1787 and 1788.

892 **What makes Cana tick?**
Harry Mayers. *Bajan* (Dec. 1984), p. 12-13.
Relates the coming into being of the Caribbean's own regional news communication agency in January 1976, following recommendations of the 1967 Heads of Government Conference and three UNESCO feasibility studies. Today CANA is housed in new high-tech offices in Barbados, and employs the latest in computer and video equipment. Helped by a grant from the West German government, the agency also prepares daily radio news and sports programmes. Additionally, there is a public relations wire service circulating press releases to major national and international companies. The board of directors comprises media managers throughout the region.

893 **Rediffusion Star Radio: 50 golden years, 1935-1985.**
Staff of Rediffusion, with features by Gary Duesbury, Michael Laing, Peter Campbell, John Wickham, John Marshall, Harold Tudor. Bridgetown: Nation Publishing Company, 1985. 16p.
Traces the history of Barbados' first wired service, Radio Distribution, from its early operations at Wildey and Trafalgar Street. In 1951 it became a subsidiary of a London-based company, and has been known since as Barbados Rediffusion Ltd. However, it was not until 1979 that it became a local concern, when its assets were acquired by the Nation Ltd. Some two years later the new company opened a popular wireless broadcasting station called the Voice of Barbados. There are still many subscribers to Rediffusion, which broadcasts for about 125 hours per week. Older residents fondly remember its broadcast of King George V's jubilee, the events of the Second World War and the announcements about Hurricane Janet in 1955. Interestingly, Rediffusion was the first to demonstrate television to the island, in 1959.

894   **Some notes on early printing presses and newspapers in Barbados.**
E. Shilstone. *Journal of the Barbados Museum and Historical Society*, vol. 26, no. 1 (Nov. 1958), p. 19-33.

Outlines the early history of printing and publishing in Barbados from the establishment of the first printing press in the island in 1730 by the spendthrift David Harry of Philadelphia, apprentice of a notorious glutton, one Samuel Keimer, and former associate of no less a person than Benjamin Franklin. For over one hundred years the only means of publishing official documents had been to send them to the United States. Now, with a printing press installed, the government could itself disseminate reports. The first newspaper, commencing in the following year, was a two-page weekly known as the *Barbados Gazette*, which, in 1783, became the *Barbados Gazette and General Intelligencer*. Keimer's successor, William Beeby, published the first book in the island, *Memoirs of the first settlement*. In 1762 there appeared a rival newspaper, the *Barbados Mercury*, later to be called the *Barbados Mercury and Bridgetown Gazette*.

895   **Through the years: The *Nation* 10th anniversary special.**
Bridgetown: Nation Publishing Company, 23 November 1983. 64p.

A supplement which traces the exciting 'rags to riches' story of Barbados' leading daily newspaper. Readers are also taken around the various departments, shown the inner workings of production and introduced to members of staff and columnists. Additionally, there are two informative articles by E. L. Cozier and John Wickham about the development of the press in the island.

Newspapers

896   **Barbados Advocate.**
Bridgetown: Advocate Company, 1895- . Monday to Saturday.

Formerly the *Advocate News*. A facsimile of the very first number is reproduced in the 1 October 1983 edition. This sober and solid newspaper, with possibly an above-average coverage of international events, has recently been losing out to competition from its more popular rival, the *Nation*. The *Advocate* carries a weekend supplement targeted at teenagers. The paper had circulation figures of 21,516 in Dec. 1985 and its managing editor is Robert Best.

897   **Caribbean Contact.**
Bridgetown: Caribbean Conference of Churches, 1971/72- . monthly.

An ecumenical newspaper edited by Colin Hope and featuring news and views of people and events around the region. This publication, which tends to reflect the various opinions of the Caribbean Conference of Churches, is probably more independent and radical than other sections of the press in Barbados. Circulation is approximately 20,000 to 22,000.

898 **The Nation.**
Bridgetown: Nation Publishing Company, 1973- . Monday to
Friday.
This paper started as a weekend issue on 25 November 1973 from a tiny one-door
building in St. Mary's Row and with an initial working capital of only 30,000
Barbadian dollars. Originally it was printed in Trinidad by Syncreators Ltd., later
by Express Newspapers Ltd. Since 1977 it has operated from ultra-modern
computerized offices in Fontabelle. The *Nation* has been a daily tabloid since
1981, with a colour supplement on Friday. The newspaper has a circulation of
about 24,884 (Monday to Thursday) and 36,384 on Friday. The managing editor
and founder is Harold Hoyte.

899 **The Sun Seeker.**
Bridgetown: Advocate Company, 1985- . fortnightly.
A tabloid for tourists with print runs averaging 12,000 to 15,000 depending on the
season. It provides customary information on hotels, restaurants, entertainment
and other topics of interest to the holidaymaker.

900 **Sunday Advocate.**
Bridgetown: Advocate Company, 1946- . weekly.
The sister publication of the *Barbados Advocate* (q.v.). It contains a supplement
carrying a review of the previous week's news and an extensive classified
advertisement section. There are also a number of feature articles, many of which
focus on such topics as local architecture and the environment. It is edited by
Ulric Rice and has a circulation given in Dec. 1985 as 23,345.

901 **Sunday Sun.**
Bridgetown: Nation Publishing Company, 1979- . weekly.
Aims to be less political and controversial than its daily counterpart the *Nation*
(q.v.). This newspaper, with a greater accent on sport, was first offered to
Barbadians as a paper which would 'go down well with peas and rice'. Today it is
the best-selling tabloid in the island. The *Sunday Sun* is edited by Tony
Vanterpool and has a circulation given in Dec. 1985 as 39,242.

902 **The Visitor.**
Bridgetown: Nation Publishing Company, 1979- . fortnightly.
A fortnightly tabloid sponsored by a number of advertisers and issued gratis to
tourists. Contains information on major events, hotels, restaurants and entertainment. Circulation tends to be seasonal, but the average print run in 1986 was
roughly 13,000.

Professional
Periodicals

903   **The Bajan.**
Bridgetown: Carib Publicity Company, 1953- . monthly.
Originally called *The Bajan and South Caribbean*, this periodical was started by
George Hunte (who is still its London correspondent). It was originally intended
primarily for tourists. In 1971 Charles McKenzie became the editor and extended
coverage to local and regional affairs. Three years later, the present editor,
Trevor Gale (grandson of Valence Gale, founder of the Barbados *Advocate*
newspaper), took over. Both he and his daughter, Céline Barnard, have seen
their publication win a number of awards for journalism.

904   **Barbados Sugar Review.**
Bridgetown: Barbados Sugar Industry Limited, 1969- . biannual.
Originally the quarterly publication of the Barbados Sugar Producers' Association, this review is now the biannual journal of Barbados Sugar Industry Limited,
after the merger of the Association with Barbados Sugar Factories Limited. It
features short articles, including personnel news, abstracts from overseas
publications, and technical reports on such matters as soil compaction, rainfall
records and agricultural diversification.

905   **Bim.**
St. Michael, Barbados: the journal, 1942- . biannual.
The Barbados-based leading Caribbean literary journal. In receipt of a Barbados
government publication subsidy for the past decade, and a grant from the
Organization of American States, *Bim* appears spordically subject to additional
funding. Former editors include Frank Collymore and E. L. Cozier. The present
incumbent is John Wickham, author, literary editor of the *Nation* newspaper, and
weekly columnist in the *Sunday Sun*. *Bim* is one of the few sources of literary
criticism in the region, and over the years has featured several well-known West
Indian writers.

906 **Bulletin of Eastern Caribbean Affairs.**
Cave Hill, St. Michael, Barbados: Institute of Social and Economic
Research, University of the West Indies, 1975- . bimonthly.
Contains short articles, commentaries, reviews, bibliographies and documents,
which focus primarily on the Eastern Caribbean. There are also special issues
dedicated to common themes. An up-to-date listing of past titles can be found in a
recently published index to volumes 1-10 (1975-85).

907 **Caribbean Geography.**
Mona, Jamaica: Longman, 1984- . annual.
This recently established journal aims to publish articles in all areas that will be of
scholarly interest to geographers, educators and individuals interested in other
closely related fields. To this end it publishes major articles, short articles, reports
and news items. It also includes book reviews. The journal is edited in the
Education and Geography Departments at the Mona Campus of the University of
the West Indies.

908 **Caribbean Issues.**
St. Augustine, Trinidad: Department of Extra-Mural Studies,
University of the West Indies, 1975- . 3 or 4 times per year.
This journal of Caribbean affairs is generally edited by the departmental tutor.
Each number has a guest editor, is dedicated to a specific Caribbean theme, and
given a multidisciplinary treatment by regional scholars. The topics covered have
included poverty, unemployment and tourism, and a number of original articles
on Barbados have been presented.

909 **Caribbean Journal of Education.**
Mona, Jamaica: School of Education, University of the West
Indies, 1974- . biannual.
Covers matters related to education in the Caribbean. Recently the publication
has become rather sporadic.

910 **Caribbean Quarterly.**
Mona, Jamaica: Department of Extra-Mural Studies, University of
the West Indies, 1951- . quarterly.
Under the influence of the indefatigable Rex Nettleford, this publication invites
manuscripts on subjects which people would like to see discussed, particularly
those of Caribbean relevance. It contains a number of articles on Barbados, and
sometimes has special issues devoted to the island. Back copies may be obtained
from Kraus-Thomson Reprints, Route 100, Millwood, New York 10546 or from
University Microfilms.

911   **Caribbean Review.**
Tamiami Trail, Miami, Florida: Florida International University,
1972- . quarterly.
The aim of this review is to promote greater understanding among the Americas
by articulating the culture and ideals of the Caribbean and Latin America and the
emigrating groups originating therefrom.

912   **Caribbean Studies.**
Rio Piedras, Puerto Rico: Institute of Caribbean Studies,
University of Puerto Rico, 1961-62- . quarterly.
This journal specializes in articles of Caribbean interest with an interdisciplinary
or intercultural focus. Research notes and book reviews are also included. Back
issues may be obtained from Johnson Reprint Corporation, 111 5th Avenue, New
York, New York 10003.

913   **Cimarrón.**
New York: CUNY Association of Caribbean Studies, 1985- . three
times per year.
A recently initiated journal with an emphasis on new contributions to history, the
environment, and the issues of race, class, social change and ideological
pluralism.

914   **Family.**
Bridgetown: Nation Publishing Company, 1978- . three times per
year.
More than simply a newsletter of the Barbados Family Planning Association, this
tabloid also publishes short articles of contemporary relevance to Barbados and
the Caribbean, which, in addition to family planning issues, cover subjects
relating to physical and social well-being, such as health and nutrition and the
environment. Soon to be issued biannually.

915   **Journal of the Barbados Museum and Historical Society**.
St. Michael, Barbados: Barbados Museum and Historical Society,
1933- . irregular.
This well-established publication contains articles mainly, though not exclusively,
of historical interest, by a number of authoritative contributors. A very useful,
and sometimes unique, source of information on many aspects of island life
varying from bush teas and Quakers to butterflies and printing presses. An index
to early issues is also available.

916   **Journal of Caribbean History.**
Mona, Jamaica; Port of Spain; Cave Hill, Barbados: Department
of History of the University of the West Indies, 1970- . biannual.
Editorial responsibilities are rotated among the three campuses of the University
of the West Indies. In addition to articles, the journal also publishes book

reviews. The focus is predominantly Caribbean, and there have been a number of contributions from Barbados.

917 **Journal of Caribbean Studies.**
Coral Gables, Florida: Association of Caribbean Studies, 1980- .
two or three times per year.

The official publication of the Association of Caribbean Studies, this journal covers all aspects of Caribbean studies from a broad multidisciplinary social scientific perspective.

918 **Revista/Review Interamericana.**
San Juan: Inter American University, 1971- . quarterly.

Features articles of general Caribbean interest, plus short stories, poetry and book reviews. There have also been a number of special issues on such topics as education, population, sociolinguistics and literature. The journal is also available from University Microfilms, Ann Arbor, Michigan.

919 **Social and Economic Studies.**
Mona, Jamaica: Institute of Social and Economic Research,
University of the West Indies, 1953- . quarterly.

Presents papers of a broad social scientific interest which focus on the Caribbean. Back issues contain a number of articles on Barbados, particularly relating to population studies.

920 **Transafrica Forum.**
New Brunswick, New Jersey: Periodicals Consortium, Rutgers University, 1982- . quarterly.

Deals with matters pertaining to Africa and the Caribbean. More specifically, the journal treats political, economic and cultural issues affecting black communities, topics traditionally excluded from American public opinion and debate.

921 **West Indian Medical Journal.**
Mona, Jamaica: Faculty of Medicine, University of the West Indies, 1952- . quarterly.

Contains short articles on the sciences, and on clinical and community medicine. Also featured are review articles and brief case reports. Back numbers include several technical papers on Barbados.

Directories, Yearbooks and Handbooks

922   Barbados Year Book 1964.
Advocate Company.   Bridgetown: Advocate Company, 1964.

This is of interest not so much for the historical and touristic information provided, but rather for such items as the local and political 'who's who', the composition of the government and statutory boards, organizations and clubs, and seventy-two listed religious denominations. The commercial directory also shows various differences from the contemporary situation, as do the various industries of the early 1960s. Differences in diplomatic representation and the island's newspapers are also quite notable.

923   Barbados Industrial Development Corporation Annual Report.
Bridgetown: Industrial Development Corporation, 1973- . annual.

Contains the chairman's annual report together with details of new industrial enterprises, expansions, closures, awards, and the financial statement of the corporation.

924   The 1985 South American Handbook.
Edited by John Brooks.   Bath, England: Trade and Travel Publications, 1985. 61st ed. 1,438p.

Barbados is dealt with on p. 1,338-43, and although the account is strongly tourist-oriented, there are general sections covering the people, economy and Bridgetown.

925   The Caribbean Handbook 1986.
Edited by Jeremy Taylor.   St. John's, Antigua: F.T. Caribbean, 1986. 244p. maps.

After an editorial introduction focusing on West Indian history, banking, telecommunications, CARICOM, currencies, tourism, etc., country-by-country summaries are provided. The Barbados section appears on p. 41-52 and includes key facts, location and physical features, travel, hotels, telecommunications, the media, business environment, the economy and history.

926 **A guide to records in Barbados.**
M. J. Chandler. Oxford: Blackwell, 1965. 203p. map. bibliog.

A work which originated in work undertaken surveying the records of Barbados from 1960-61 while the author was archivist in the Department of History, University of the West Indies. A real *vade mecum* for those pursuing research on Barbados, this guide covers all major departments of central and local government, and the records of churches, organizations and individuals. There are useful appendixes relating to legislation, newspapers and microfilms.

927 **The Cambridge encyclopedia of Latin America and the Caribbean.**
Edited by Simon Collier, Harold Blakemore, Thomas Skidmore. Cambridge, England: Cambridge University Press, 1985. 456p. maps. bibliog.

Seeks to provide a one-volume account of all aspects of Latin America and the Caribbean. The treatment is entirely thematic and there are six major parts dealing respectively with: the physical environment, the economy, the peoples, history, politics and society, culture (languages, literature, music, the visual arts, theatre and cinema, the media, science). Barbados is considered in a number of places, with sections referring to its history, independence, oil, tourism and sugar industries, for example. Each major section of the book is accompanied by suggestions for further reading. The volume is lavishly illustrated with full-colour photographs and maps.

928 **A Year Book of the Commonwealth 1985.**
Commonwealth Secretariat. London: HM Stationery Office, 1985. 538p. map.

Contains information on geography, climate, transportation, the economy, history, constitution and constitutional development, and a list of government ministers and ministries. The Barbados section is on p. 113-16.

929 **Directory of associations in Barbados.**
Compiled by Hazelyn Devonish, assisted by Angela Skeete. Bridgetown: Reference Department of the Public Library, 1983. 106p.

A total of 166 local associations are classified alphabetically under the headings of health, education, industry and commerce, industrial relations, science and technology, agriculture, horticulture, community development, women, social welfare, youth, environment, creative arts and culture, religion and sport. There is also a miscellaneous section. For each organization, the objects, membership, qualifications and publications are detailed. Additionally, there is a list of twelve regional and ten international organizations with bases in Barbados.

284

930 **Latin America and Caribbean Review 1986.**
Managing Editor, Richard Green. Saffron Walden, Essex,
England: World of Information, 1985. 216p. maps.

Intended primarily for businessmen. The account of Barbados (p. 155-57), written
by Canute James, a freelance journalist based in Jamaica, covers the sudden
death of Prime Minister Tom Adams in March 1985, marginal improvements in
the economy, and the future outlook, together with a business guide.

931 **Barbados export directory.**
Information Research Division, Barbados Export Promotion
Corporation. Bridgetown: Barbados Export Promotion
Corporation, 1985. 172p.

After a statement of the aims of the Barbados Export Promotion Corporation, a
brief synopsis of the island is provided. Thereafter exporters are classified
according to related product groupings, international standard industrial classifi-
cations, and services. The latter includes services to exporters, general services
(transport, marine, construction, advertising, data processing, photography,
printing), professional and consultancy services (architects, surveyors, engineers,
accountants, agricultural consultants, management training, research), and
banking services. The publication concludes with an alphabetical listing of goods
produced in Barbados.

932 **South America, Central America and the Caribbean, 1986.**
London: Europa Publications, 1986. 582p.

The latest volume of an annual publication designed to provide a survey of the
political and economic life both of the region as a whole and of the forty-six
countries within it. After a series of short essays surveying the region, and
providing details of regional organizations, the individual countries are described.
The section on Barbados (p. 138) is restricted to a 'facts-in-brief' format, covering
statistics, government, diplomatic representation, banking, trade, industry,
transport and tourism.

Caribbean and Central American databook.
See item no. 10.

The Commonwealth Caribbean: the integration experience . . .
See item no. 600.

Caribbean economic handbook.
See item no. 613.

Directory of artists in Barbados.
See item no. 865.

Bibliographies

933 **The catalogue of the West India Reference Library.**
Introduced by John Aarons. Millwood, New York: Kraus
International Publications, 1980. 6 vols.

This catalogue of the Institute of Jamaica's West India Reference Library is in
two parts: authors and titles (volumes one to three), and subjects (volumes four
to six). Covering the period 1547 to 1975, the collection emphasizes regional
works dealing with history, travel and description, government, economic and
social conditions, literature, sugar, slavery and African culture. Books and
pamphlets are classified according to the Dewey system (with the exception of the
fiction category), and periodicals are categorized by means of a modified Cutter
system.

934 **West Indian literature: an index to criticism 1930-1975.**
Jeanette Allis. Boston, Massachusetts: G. K. Hall, 1981. 353p.
bibliog.

A modified version of an M.Phil. thesis presented to the University of the West
Indies. The index is prefaced by an introductory essay which highlights the
problems of the novelist in exile and the distinction between internal and external
criticism. Part one comprises an index of authors with general evaluations and
appraisals of specific works, while part two provides an index of critics and
reviewers and references to their essays. There is also a chronological listing of
articles and books on West Indian literature. Featured Barbadian authors include
William Arthur, Leo Austin, Edward Brathwaite, Austin Clarke, Frank
Collymore, Geoffrey Drayton, James Emtage, A. N. Forde, Michael Foster,
Lionel Hutchinson, Oliver Jackman, George Lamming, Bruce St. John, Karl
Sealey, G. C. Thomas, H. A. Vaughan and John Wickham.

935 **Bibliotheca Barbadiensis: a catalog of materials relating to Barbados 1650-1860 in the Boston Public Libary.**
Staff of the Boston Public Library. Boston, Massachusetts: Public Library, 1968. 27p.

A chronological listing of printed books, pamphlets and manuscripts related to Barbados, a few of which are only to be found in this collection. The booklet concludes with a name and title index, together with a list of donors who made the Boston acquisitions possible.

936 **Our ancestral heritage: a bibliography of the roots of culture in the English-speaking Caribbean.**
Compiled by Edward Brathwaite. Kingston: Savacou Publications, 1977. 194p.

A partially annotated bibliography prepared for Carifesta in 1976. Subject areas include: bibliographical references and studies, Caribbean background, the Amerindians, Europe, European settlement and settlements, plantations and planters, slavery, the European alter-renaissance in the Caribbean, the European church and missions in the Caribbean, Africa, Africa in the New World, and Africa in the Caribbean. Specifically grouped works on Barbados occur in the sections on the Amerindians, European settlement and settlements, and slavery. The compiler stresses that this bibliography is very much a first draft.

937 **The complete Caribbeana 1900-1975: a bibliographic guide to the scholarly literature.**
Lambros Comitas. New York: KTO Press, 1977. 4 vols.

The most comprehensive bibliography of the region. Volume one, under the broad title of 'The people', deals with such topics as travel, history, demography and ethnic groups. Volume two covers cultural institutions and includes religion, language, health, education, housing and politics. Volume three encompasses resources and comprises economics, main industries, the environment, human geography, soils, crops and livestock. The final volume contains an author index and a geographical index listing entries by Caribbean territory.

938 **Bibliography of the West Indies (excluding Jamaica).**
Frank Cundall. Kingston: Institute of Jamaica; London: H. Sotheran, 1909. Reprinted, New York, London: Johnson Reprint, 1971, 1972. 179p.

A country-by-country listing in chronological order of books, pamphlets and magazine articles, some of which are held by the prestigious Institute of Jamaica to which Cundall was attached as secretary. Barbados, referred to by the compiler as the 'sentinel of the Caribbean', appears first, and contains about 100 entries. Unfortunately only a few of these unannotated items are readily available today.

939 **A study on the historiography of the British West Indies to the end of the nineteenth century.**
Elsa Goveia. Mexico City: Instituto Panamericana de Geografia e Historia, 1956. 183p. bibliog.

A century-by-century evaluation of the printed histories of the region to be found at the University College of the West Indies and the Institute of Jamaica. Works available only in manuscript, biographies, and publications dealing exclusively with the slave trade are excluded from the analysis. There is a subsection containing four 18th-century studies of Barbados (p. 41-49). Three other publications specifically treating the island occur elsewhere in the text.

940 **A guide to source materials for the study of Barbados history 1627-1834.**
Jerome S. Handler. Carbondale, Edwardsville, Illinois: Southern Illinois University Press; London; Amsterdam: Feffer & Simons, 1971. 205p. map. bibliog.

An extremely useful bibliography of the period from settlement to the abolition of slavery in Barbados by a leading Caribbean scholar stationed in the United States. This annotated work stems from Handler's own research into slavery in the island. It comprises printed books, pamphlets and broadsheets, parliamentary papers, newspapers, prints and manuscripts. In most cases the location of sources in a variety of repositories is also supplied.

941 **Caribbean writers: a bio-bibliographical-critical encyclopedia.**
Edited by Donald Herdeck. Washington, DC: Three Continents Press, 1979. 943p. map. bibliog.

A massive collection of approximately 2,000 authors and 15,000 works covering the English-, French-, Dutch- and Spanish-speaking territories. The West Indian section, co-edited by John and Dorothy Figueroa, presents a country-by-country list of writers, together with an alphabetical listing of their lives and major works. Also featured are bibliographies, critical studies, general anthologies, background books and selected journals. Forty-one writers from Barbados are cited. Some are young authors who rarely appear in comparable international texts (e.g. Margaret Gill – 'Canecutter', Elizabeth Clarke – 'Mudda Africa', and Anthony Hinkson – 'Tradition'). Others, e.g. Rudolph Kizerman – 'Stand up in the world' and J. Ashton Brathwaite – 'Niggers . . . This is Canada', are now living overseas.

942 **Current Caribbean bibliography. Vol. 1, nos. 1-2**
Edited by Harold Holdsworth. Port of Spain: Caribbean Commission Central Secretariat, 1951. 18p.

Subtitled 'an alphabetical list of publications issued in the Caribbean territories of France, Great Britain, the Netherlands and the United States during 1951'. The titles are alphabetically listed by author and most are official serial publications. There are only a few entries on Barbados.

943   **The English-speaking Caribbean – a bibliography of bibliographies.**
Alma Jordan, Barbara Comissiong.   Boston, Massachusetts:
G. K. Hall, 1984. 411p.

Compiled by the chief and deputy librarians of the St. Augustine campus of the University of the West Indies in response to the call by researchers for a systematic listing of regional works. There are over 1,400 annotated entries arranged by subject matter and located in the appropriate repository. Items are mostly Caribbean-oriented rather than specifically Barbadian.

944   **Dictionary of Caribbean biography.**
Edited by Ernest Kay.   London: Melrose Press, 1969. 335p.

The first publication of its kind. The volume includes information based on questionnaires sent to notable biographees of the region, which is extended to include all countries of the Caribbean basin. There are approximately 3,000 entries.

945   **An annotated bibliography of research on contemporary fossil reefs in Barbados, West Indies.**
John B. Lewis.   Montreal: McGill University, 1978. 63p. (Marine Sciences Manuscript Report. no. 30).

Containing a little over 200 annotated entries, this bibliography covers work on the ecology and geology of Barbadian reefs, the plants and animals found on them, organisms of the water flowing over reefs, and the chemistry and physics of inshore reef water. Some early descriptive general volumes have also been included where these have had some historical bearing on the line taken in subsequent research. The author served as Director of the Bellairs Research Institute of McGill University (located on the west coast of Barbados) from 1954 to 1970.

946   **Women in the Caribbean: an annotated bibliography.**
Joycelin Massiah with Audine Wilkinson, Norma
Shorey.   Cave Hill, St. Michael, Barbados: Institute of Social and
Economic Research, University of the West Indies, 1979. 133p.

Contains 408 entries on material available in various Barbadian repositories. The Barbados items are arranged alongside those of other Caribbean territories in eleven sections: general, role and status, law and politics, family and fertility, economics and employment, education, literature and the arts, religion, women's organizations, biography and autobiography, and general reference works. The last mentioned is subdivided into bibliographies, periodicals, special issues of journals and newspapers, and population census reports.

947   **West Indian collection.**
National Library Service.   Bridgetown: Barbados Public Library,
1967- .

A series of periodic updates providing bibliographical details of additions to the West Indian collection of the Barbados Central Library. (Latest listing, no. 73, January-March 1986.)

289

948 **National bibliography of Barbados, January-December, 1983.**
National Library Service. Bridgetown: Government Printery,
1985. 84p.

A subject listing of books received by the Public Library and those published by
nationals living abroad. The titles are grouped under the Dewey decimal system
of classification. Most of the entries stem from government agencies and other
national organizations, and include addresses and official reports. The volume
includes references to the *Official Gazette*, comprising parliamentary debates,
bills, acts and statutory instruments. A list of publishers and printers in Barbados
is also provided.

949 **A bibliographical guide to law in the Commonwealth Caribbean.**
Compiled by Keith Patchett, Valerie Jenkins. Mona, Jamaica:
Institute of Social and Economic Research and the Faculty of Law,
University of the West Indies, 1973. 80p. (Law and Society in the
Caribbean, no. 2).

Intended for researchers, and also compiled in the hope that the law library of
the University of the West Indies may complete its collection with the addition of
the featured entries. Primary sources (law reports, legislation, official sources and
periodicals) are listed for the region in general and for each of the participating
territories in particular. A similar pattern is followed for secondary sources,
comprising bibliographies, general works, legal history, public law and private
law. There are 39 items on Barbados out of a total of 847 titles. Unfortunately the
names of publishers are omitted.

950 **Barbadiana: a list of works pertaining to the history of the island of
Barbados prepared in the Public Library to mark the attainment of
independence.**
Prepared by the staff of the Public Library. Bridgetown:
Government Printing Office, 1966. 44p.

A select unannotated bibliography of over 500 titles, all of which are available at
the Barbados Public Library. The entries are divided into four major themes:
historical and descriptive; government and politics; social and economic; and
education. Several government publications and other official documents are
included.

951 **Publications and theses from the Bellairs Research Institute and the
Brace Research Institute of McGill University in Barbados, 1956-
1984.**
Holetown, Barbados: Bellairs Research Institute, 1984-85. 52p.

As the introduction to this listing explains, the Bellairs Research Institute of
McGill University was founded in 1954 on land donated by the late Commander
Carlyon W. Bellairs, in memory of his wife. It is located just to the north of
Holetown on the west coast and research there has concentrated on marine
biology and oceanography with a smattering of geography, geology and sociology.
From 1960 to 1970, the Brace Research Institute, associated with the Faculty of
Engineering at McGill and concerned with weather and climate, was also located

290

at Bellairs, although this has now moved to Quebec. The bibliography lists articles, reports and theses derived, at least in part, from work based at the Bellairs and Brace Institutes. It is intended that periodic updating of the lists will be undertaken. Enquiries are invited via the present director, Dr. Wayne Hunte, Bellairs Research Institute, St. James, Barbados.

952 **A guide for the study of British Caribbean history 1763-1834.**
L. J. Ragatz. Washington, DC: United States Government Printing Office, 1932. 725p.

An eleven year work which preceded the compiler's well known *Fall of the planter class in the British Caribbean 1763-1833*. This annotated bibliography contains material found in sixty-nine public and private collections in North America, Europe and Jamaica, all but the last of which were visited by the author. Specific entries for Barbados cover the laws of the island and historical writings (several being anonymous broadsheets and tracts).

953 **Bibliografía actual del Caribe.** (Current Caribbean bibliography.)
Staff of the Regional Caribbean Library. Hato Rey, Puerto Rico: Biblioteca Regional del Caribe y Norte-Sur, 1972. 170p.

A computer-arranged Dewey classification of almost one thousand titles, followed by an alphabetical index. The Barbados entries are limited and some are repeated two or three times.

954 **Women in the Caribbean: a bibliography.**
Bertie Cohen Stuart. Leiden, the Netherlands: Department of Caribbean Studies, Royal Institute of Linguistics & Anthropology, 1979. 163p.

Contains 651 entries with their original Caribbean-language title, plus a few works in German and Portuguese. Partial annotations are in English. General bibliographies and those of individual women are followed by some introductory material and details of women's organizations, and then the main part of the bibliography features family and household, cultural factors, education, economics, and politics and law. There are about twenty titles relating specifically to women in Barbados.

955 **Women in the Caribbean: a bibliography. Part two.**
Bertie Cohen Stuart. Leiden, The Netherlands: Department of Caribbean Studies, Royal Institute of Linguistics & Anthropology, 1985. 246p.

Intended as a supplement to the earlier bibliography (see previous item), this contains titles from 1979 to 1985 along with earlier works omitted from the previous volume. The arrangement is the same, with the exception of a new subsection on creative arts and the deletion of women's organizations. This time names of publishers are included. Some references are to unpublished student work. Once again, not all entries are annotated, but where this is done the language used is English. The compiler indicates her intention to add to the collection with further bibliographies.

956 **Caribbean: a collection of dissertation titles 1861-1983 searched.**
University Microfilms International. Ann Arbor, Michigan:
University Microfilms, 1984. 84p.

Masters and doctoral theses are grouped by country and theme. The themes comprise: accounting, agriculture, agronomy, American studies, anthropology, archaeology, biological oceanography, biology, botany, chemistry, demography, ecology, economics, education, energy, engineering, entomology, fine arts, folklore, geochemistry, geography, geological survey, geology, geophysics, health sciences, history, home economics, hydrology, instruction, journalism, language and literature, law, linguistics, library science, literature, management, marine sciences, marketing, mass communications, music, oceanography, paleontology, physical oceanography, philosophy, physics, physiology, political science, psychology, recreation, religion, social geography, social work, sociology, speech, theatre, theology, urban and regional planning, and zoology. The Barbados section contains forty-one entries.

957 **Education in the Eastern Caribbean: a select bibliography.**
Audine Wilkinson. *Bulletin of Eastern Caribbean Affairs*, vol. 7, no. 4 (Sept.-Oct. 1981), p. 36-44.

Comprises books, journal and newspaper articles, documents, papers, pamphlets, conference proceedings, official reports and theses. While most of the material deals with education in the West Indies, there are a number of items which refer specifically to Barbados. These include references to: Codrington College, the University of the West Indies, the Mitchinson Report, education of girls and women, Harrison College, the first island scholarships, the common entrance examination, external examinations, secondary education, vocational training, the Samuel Jackman Prescod Polytechnic, performance in mathematics, teacher education and team teaching.

958 **Select bibliography on the economy of Barbados.**
Maxine Williams, Aldeen Payne. In: *The economy of Barbados 1946-1980*. Edited by De Lisle Worrell. Bridgetown: Central Bank of Barbados, 1982, p. 167-95.

This bibliography comprises several government and private sector reports in addition to doctoral theses, articles and monographs. The entries are listed alphabetically under seven separate headings: agriculture, bibliography, economics, history, industry (including tourism), public sector and trade.

Index

The index is a single alphabetical sequence of authors (personal and corporate), titles of publications and subjects. Index entries refer both to the main items and to other works mentioned in the notes to each item. Title entries are in italics. Numeration refers to the items as numbered.

306

Danforth, S. T. 232
Daniel, J. 865
Daniel, S. 198
Dann, G. M. S. 11-12, 203-205, 210, 400, 501
Darnell Davis, N. 314, 335, 455
Dash, J. M. 845
Dash, J. S. 780
Data processing 931
Dathorne, O. 834
Davis, C. G. 671
Davis family 443
Davis, Karen 423
Davis, Kingsley 764
Davis, Kortright 453
Davis, N. D. 314, 335, 455
Davis, P. 32
Davis, W. M. 74, 114
Davison, R. B. 430
Davy, J. 149
Day, C. W. 148
Day, M. 75
de Chabaneix, G. 797
de Lisser, Herbert 840
Deane Commission 561
Dear, J. S. B. 555
Death 461
    causes 63
    of a slave 374
    premature 146
    rate 396-397
    registers 314
    slaves 381
Debt
    external 599, 654
    public 654
Decentralization 666, 743, 747-748, 769
Decoration 776
Deep Water Harbour Committee 716
Deep-water harbour 48, 165, 716, 720
Defence 40
Defence counsel 547
Deficit financing 643
Dellimore, J. 566, 658, 816
Delson, R. M. 303
Demas, W. G. 31, 602-603
Demerara 447
Democracy 326, 355, 481, 564, 598, 734
Democratic Labour Party 543, 552, 562, 729
Democratic revolution in the West Indies 491

Demographic change 67-68
Demographic Yearbook 737
Demography 30, 54, 395, 732
    and agricultural structure 690
    bibliography 937
    dissertation 956
    historical 34
        slave registration 381
    statistics 737, 738
Denham, W. W. 233-234
Denmark
    Caribbean possessions 327, 461
        legislation 374
Denominations 922
Department of Agriculture 281
Department of Statistics 212
Department of Women's Affairs 520, 524
Dependency 37-38, 594, 603, 614, 618, 668
    on US economy 623
Dependency under challenge: the political economy of the Commonwealth Caribbean 580, 589-590, 596, 665, 668
Dependent territories 40
Deportation 531
Dermochelys coriacea 248
Desalinification 819
Deserts 50
Desserts 877-883
Desultory sketches and tales of Barbados 151
Devas, E. 217
Development 51, 61, 197, 490, 529, 570, 589, 599, 624, 694, 742
    agricultural 80, 570, 573, 616
    dependence on foreign capital 595
    economic 22, 34, 52, 58, 571, 583, 597, 600, 608, 616, 744, 753, 765
    fisheries 699
    government programmes 726
    industrial 3, 621, 656, 659, 661-663, 665-666, 726
    policy 27, 628
    political 389, 537, 552, 591
    regional 760
    role of women 518
    rural 615
    social 2, 22, 738, 765
    statistics 741
    substained 808

310

zones 214
Development administration: field research in Barbados 570
Development of the British West Indies 1700-1763 318, 390
Development of higher education in the West Indies with special emphasis on Barbados 818
Development planning 20, 570, 605-606, 609
  for tourism 196, 202, 214, 216, 219, 730
  Industrial Development Corporation 656
Development Plans 728
  (1973-77) 607
  (1983-88) 616
Development of the plantations to 1750: an era of West Indian prosperity 1750-1775 391
Development policy in small countries 628
Devon 447
Devonish, H. 929
Dewey classification system 933, 948, 953
Diabetes 63, 504, 508
Dialect 164, 178, 192, 444-448, 831, 837, 853, 856
Dialog Information Retrieval Service 884
Diatoms 116
Díaz, A. Maldonado 835
Dickson, W. 370-371
Dicotyledons 242
Dictionary of Caribbean biography 944
Dictionary of Caribbean English usage: selected entries 444
Diet 163, 310, 502, 512, 669
  18th century 313
  Rastafarian 421
  Westernization 649
Diksic, M. 290
Diplomatic representatives 183, 922, 932
Directories
  artists 865
  associations 929
  commercial 922
  exports 931
Directorships 475
Directory of artists in Barbados 865

Directory of associations in Barbados 929
Discovery 1, 305, 452
  by English (1605) 304
Discrimination 455
  racial 491
Diseases 333, 499, 504
  and remedies 250
  herbal 333, 500
  communicable 504
  malaria 59
  smallpox 353
  tropical 163
  venereal 490
Disestablishment 453
Dishonesty 144, 499
Disraeli, Benjamin 394
Dissolution of the West Indies Federation, a study in political geography 583
Distinction, death and disgrace: governorship of the Leeward Islands in the early eighteenth century 311
Districts 12
Dividends 4
Divorce houses 172
Divorce laws 521
Doctors 504-505
Documents of West Indian history. Vol. 1: 1492-1655 326
Documents on international relations in the Caribbean 40
Dollars
  spent by tourists 198
Dolphins 267
Domestic slaves 144
Domestic work 724
Dominica 159, 174
Dominican Republic 539, 584
Dommen, E. 604
Doncaster 330
Donkeys 13
Donn, W. L. 86
Donoghue, J. 672
Doran, E., Jr 781
Down the islands: a voyage to the Caribbees 156
Downes, A. S. 659, 726
Doxey, G., and associates 206
Drama groups 864
Drax family 338

311

312

316

FAO 699
Food and drink 17, 163, 181, 184-185,
    193, 333, 499, 516, 877-883
  compared with English 351
  Crop Over 392
  expenditure 630
  imports 658, 679
Food poisoning 322
Food production 544, 658, 816
  and tourism 206
  falls short of potential 704
  for slaves 387
  home 605, 705
  self-sufficiency 618
Forbes, R. 167
Forde, A. N. 838, 842, 859-860, 934
Forde, Henry 522
Forde, N. 519-521, 557, 566
Foreign exchange
  earnings 202
  rationing 650
Foreign investment 10, 589, 612
Foreign policy 40, 43, 579, 587, 611
Foreign Sales Corporations – FSCs 647
Forestry 84
Forests 58, 240
  as discovered 243
  clearance 78, 220, 802, 810-811
    (1627-55) 82
Forte, A. 395
Fortifications 145, 150, 313, 568
  architecture 777
Fossils 139, 250, 356, 956
  algae 116
  birds 112
  vertebrates 135
Foster, A. 49
Foster, M. 934
Foster, N. 335, 338
Fountains 330
Four years residence in the West Indies
    144
Fourteen islands in the sun 168
Fox, George 162, 454, 471
Foyo, M. 246
France 587
  attack feared 379
  Caribbean possessions 327, 539, 542,
    585, 859
    publications 941-942
  threatened invasion (1782) 367
  wars 311, 315, 340

Franchise
  limited 321, 561
Francis, A. 198
Franck, H. 152
Frank Worrell 870, 873
Frankfurt 714
Franklin, Benjamin 894
Franklin, C. 541
Franks, G. F. 115
Fraser, H. 504
Fraser, H. S. 784-787
Fraser, P. D. 613
Free trade 625
Freedmen 69, 377-378
  legal status 377
  lifestyle 155
Freedmen in Barbados 303
Freedom 307, 484
  individual 544
  loss 12
Freedom of speech 364
Frere, H. 339
Friendliness 28
Friendly societies 152, 355, 476
Fringe reefs 128
Frogs
  whistling 221, 225
*From Columbus to Castro: the history
    of the Caribbean 1492-1969* 327
Froudacity 160
Froude, J. A. 153, 160, 176, 321
Fruit 333
  figs 334
  trees 704
FSCs – Foreign Sales Corporations 647
Fuge, D. P. 116
Fundamental Baptists 449
Funerals 146
  negro 157
Fungi 254, 264
Furnivall, J. S. 497
*Future of tourism in the Eastern
    Caribbean* 219

G

Gaile, G. L. 718
Gale, Louis 176
Gale, Trevor 903
Gale, Valence 903
Galinier, J. L. 290

International Business Machines –
    IBM 813
International Computers Ltd – ICL
    813
International Confederation of Free
    Trade Unions 734
International crisis in the Caribbean 587
International organizations 929
International relations 564, 570,
    576-591
    see also Regional integration;
West Indies Federation
    economic 31, 40
    with Brazil 580, 587
        Canada 4
        Colombia 587
        Cuba 584
        France 587
        Great Britain 37, 582, 584-585,
        587
        Mexico 578, 580, 587
        Netherlands 587
        USA 4, 37, 42-43, 296, 582, 584,
        587, 589
        Venezuela 578, 580, 587
International Systems Associates 813
*Interstitial fauna of selected beaches in
    Barbados* 284
Intertidal zone 259, 284
Inter-tropical Convergence Zone 99
Intimate glimpses of the West Indies 164
*Introduction to the study of West Indian
    literature* 853
Investment 4, 216, 650
    American 10, 589, 624
    fixed capital 634
    foreign 612, 659
    industrial 723
    public sector 616
Iowa 7
Ireland 447
*Islands in between: essays on West
    Indian literature* 843
Islands in the sun 167
Isolationism 311, 327
*Issues in Caribbean international
    relations* 556, 577, 579

J

Jack-in-the-Box Gully 272

Jackman, E. 11
Jackman, Mr 463
Jackman, O. 934
Jackson, Capt. William 309
Jackson, Jean 523
Jackson, John 162
Jackson, R. M. 569
Jacobins 150
Jamaica 33, 42-43, 109, 159, 299, 309,
    319, 366, 370, 391, 443, 485, 518,
    544, 574, 596, 768, 829
    architecture 774, 777
    conquest 316, 322
    demography 411
    dread talk 448
    Jewish communities 460
    library service 887
    Ministry of Education 45
    primary education 828
    problems of tourism 215
    runaway slaves 360
    shells 251
    slave trade 368
    sugar 327
    urbanization 761, 765
    withdrawal from Federation 585
Jamaicans 29
James, Canute 930
James, C. L. R. 160, 840
James, J. 619
James, L. 843
James, N. P. 121-122
Jazz 846, 850
Jenkins, V. 949
Jet set 168
Jew Street, Bridgetown 455
Jewish cemetery 455
Jewish Historical Society of England
    467
Jewish inscriptions 465, 468
*Jewish monumental inscriptions in
    Barbados* 468
Jews 418, 467
    communities 460
    Portuguese 455
Jill Walker's cooking in Barbados 880
Job creation 730
Job motivation 206
Job satisfaction 206
Joe's River 125, 136, 802, 810-811
Johns Hopkins University 377
Johnson, D. 485

internal 397-398, 760
overseas 601
return 431
  contribution to society 433
  problems 432
  rural-urban 58, 65
  to Europe 65
    N. America 65
  see also Emigration; Immigration
Military assistance 625
Military barracks
  Bridgetown
    19th century 144
Military hosptials 149
Militia 150, 336, 379, 568
Militia Act 332
Millbourn, P. E. 720
Miller, E. 821
Miller, K. 193
Miller, S. 193
Millipedes 281
Millwalls
  see Windmills
Minas Gerais 682
Minerals 70, 111, 119, 250, 356
Mings, R. C. 213
Ministry of Agriculture 804
Ministry of Education 821, 827
Ministry of Finance and Planning 744
Ministry of Health and National
    Insurance 506
Ministry of Housing and Lands
  Housing Planning Unit 789
Ministry of Tourism and the
    Environment 803, 808
Minorities 421-426
  Rastafarians 408, 421-422
  redlegs 25, 149, 152, 166, 168, 170,
    172, 175, 423-426
Miocene period 139
Mission halls 477
Missionaries 458
  educational role 312
  Jacobin 150
  Methodist 373
  Morarian 162, 373, 463
    records 517
  Wesleyan 452
Mitchell, D. 462, 472
Mitchell, H. 539, 585
Mitchinson Commission (1875) 815
  Report 957

Mitigation of slavery 371
Mittelholzer, E. 171, 840
*Modern Caribbean geography: for
    certificate examinations* 53
Modern plantation in the Third World
    678
*Modern secondary geography of the
    West Indies* 45
Modernization
  and fertility reduction 404
  of agricultural systems 687
Modyford, Thomas 309, 316, 319
Moisture 694
  soil analysis 79, 696
  sugar yield 696, 702-703, 708
Molasses 171, 324
  production 313
  recipes 881
Molluscs 251, 356
  Puerto Rican 285
Momsen, J. D. 65, 700
Monetary base 642
Money demand 651
Mongoose 281
Monmouth Rebellion 418
Monocotyledons 242
Monopolies 485
Monroe Doctrine 584
Montastrea annularis 133, 263
Montreal 819
Montserrat 159, 316, 658
Montserratians 29
*Monumental inscriptions in the
    churches and churchyards of the
    island of Barbados, British West
    Indies* 465
Moore, R. 830
Moral decay 12, 458
Moral Rearmament 873
Morals
  criticized 146, 158, 163
  role of education 823
Moravian Church 159, 302, 337, 373,
    449
  archives 461
  missionaries 162, 461
Mordecai, J. 540
Mordecai, P. 848
More Developed Countries – MDCs
    31, 829
More than a word 484
Morgan, Henry 294, 319-320

Morgan, V. 645
Morris, M. 843
Morris, R. 541
Morrison, C. J. 701
Morrissey, M. 66
Mortality rate 63-64, 398
  cancer 507-508
  diabetes 508
  infant 336, 414, 513
  ischaemia 508
  malnutrition 510
  slaves 327, 365
    during transatlantic crossings 388
  vehicle accidents 508
Mortgages 350, 788
Mosquito bush 500
Mosquitoes 281
Moss, R. 39
Moss, S. 566
Mosses, 264, 272
Motherhood 409, 411, 413
Motor vehicles
  accidents 63
    mortality 508
  density 64
Mottley, E. 541, 866
Mount Hillaby 18
Mountjoy, E. 121
Moxley, J. H. S. 499
Moyne Commission (1939) 170, 502,
    514, 567, 729, 815
Muds 810
Mulattos 155, 158, 370
Mule trams 13, 152
Multilateralism 580
*Multinational corporations and black
    power* 664
Multinationals
  domination by 197, 207, 593
  racial implications 664
Multiracial communities 41
Munro, I. 845
Murder 553
Murray, R. N. 312
Murray, W. 734
Museums 185
Mushrooms 254
Music 182, 188, 358, 855, 927
  calypso
    political 541
    Crop Over 392
    dissertation 956

folk songs 473, 862
jazz 846, 850
negro 157
reggae 421
myths
  about madness 503

N

Nag, M. 406
Naipaul, V. S. 836, 840
Nair, N. K. 407
*Narrative of a visit to the West Indies in
    1840 and 1841* 162
NASA – National Aeronautics and
    Space Administration 884
Nation 484, 896, 898, 901, 905
  food column 882
  10th anniversary special 895
Nation Company Ltd 889, 893
National Aeronautics and Space
    Administration – NASA 884
National assistance 525
*National bibliography of Barbados,
    January-December, 1983* 948
National Commercial Bank 632
National Commission on the Status of
    Women in Barbados 405, 524, 733
National Cultural Foundation 866
National Health and Nutrition Survey
    (1951) 515
National Health Service 505, 513
National identity 42, 537
National Insurance Scheme – NIS 513,
    648
National library service 947-948
National Petroleum Corporation 655
Nationalism 37, 295, 829
Natives of my person 844
Natural gas 539
Natural history of Barbados 231, 250
Nazi persecution 468
*Near-surface subaerial diagenesis of
    Pleistocene carbonates, Barbados,
    West Indies* 120
*Need for and the possibilities of
    agricultural diversification in
    Barbados* 707
Negro in the Caribbean 393-394
Negroes
  disparaged 152, 177

342

344

345

349

352

Map of Barbados

This map shows the more important towns and other features.

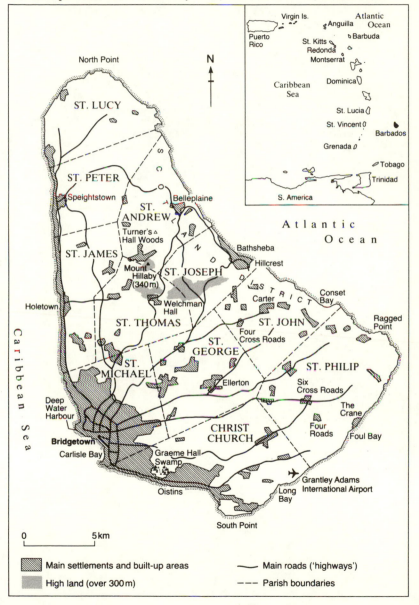